Outdoor Education

Outdoor

EDITED BY

DONALD R. HAMMERMAN
NORTHERN ILLINOIS UNIVERSITY
DEKALB, ILLINOIS

AND

WILLIAM M. HAMMERMAN
CALIFORNIA STATE UNIVERSITY
SAN FRANCISCO, CALIFORNIA

Education

A Book of Readings

82364

SECOND EDITION

BURGESS PUBLISHING COMPANY
MINNEAPOLIS, MINNESOTA

1   2   3   4   5   6   7   8   9   0

Dedication

To the teachers, administrators, leaders,
parents and students who have contributed
to the growing body of outdoor education
literature.

Foreword

The philosophy and practice of outdoor education have evolved through the years from experiences in outdoor centers and laboratories, the involvement of community agencies, and the influence of outstanding individuals. It is important that the writings of these individuals, expressing their points of views at particular times, should be made available to those now concerned in outdoor education. The selections in this book clearly express the authors' points of view at the time of writing in a form readily available to the reader. By perusing the collection, one may not only gain a perspective of the history and changing emphases in outdoor education but may realize more clearly how to meet present and future needs.

The rapid developments in outdoor education and in education in general make essential the continuing reevaluation of programs and practices. Changes in teacher education, evaluation, and research continually bring new insights and knowledge. Finding up-to-date materials to interpret these changes has been one of the tasks of the editors. This they have well accomplished.

Outdoor education was first conceived as a means of acquainting children with the natural environment, enriching the school curricula, and teaching more effectively those outdoor-related subjects that were already part of the curricula. The movement was ahead of its time in its stress on those things best taught outdoors—the interrelationships of living things to each other and to the environment. Only recently have people in general been alerted to the importance of this principle and made ecology a household word. Educators have taken up the challenge and have increasingly explored the rich possibilities of the outdoor setting for education. Programs today are generally broader in scope than the pioneering efforts. They include studies of the man-made as well as the natural environment in their attempt to halt the destructive practices that have led to our present environmental predicament. Moreover, they include greater age ranges than programs of the past; and attempts are made to reach children and adults of all ages, not only through schools, but through all agencies, public, private, and voluntary.

The editors of this book are eminently fitted to bring together these writings. They have had first-hand experience with outstandingly successful outdoor educational enterprises and have acquaintance with programs and leaders throughout the world. Their selection of pertinent materials for inclusion in this book is based on sound judgment.

—Reynold E. Carlson, Professor and
former Chairman of the Department
of Recreation & Park Administration
Indiana University

Preface

Ever since outdoor education sparked the imagination of educators as a curriculum innovation over forty years ago, there has been a gradual increase in the amount of periodic literature published in this field. During the past two decades, several excellent films and books have dealt with this topic. In addition, increased interest on the part of researchers and institutions of higher learning has been witnessed through the number of new courses, programs of study, and graduate degrees pertaining to outdoor education.

This volume has been compiled in order to capture the flavor of the experimental and developmental years of the outdoor education movement as expressed in periodicals. The greatest number of articles have dealt with the meaning, scope, rationale, and philosophy of education in the out-of-doors. The best of these expressions of thought have been assembled in Chapter 1. No new development takes place in the curriculum of our schools without leaving its mark upon the history of education. Chapter 2 traces outdoor education's early development as an outgrowth of the camping movement to its current status as an integral part of education.

The utilization of the out-of-doors as a laboratory for learning can take many directions. The selection of articles in Chapter 4 describes a variety of programs conducted in the United States, while Chapter 5 covers international programs. Chapter 3 complements the fourth chapter with articles dealing with "what" can be taught beyond the classroom and "how" to approach teaching and learning in this "extended classroom" in the most efficient and effective manner. Environmental education is treated separately in Chapter 6 and Chapter 7 is devoted to teacher education in the out-of-doors. The final section reports ways in which outdoor education has been evaluated and its implication for the outdoor educator.

In spite of the diverse types of programs sponsored in the name of outdoor education; the increased push for programs stressing environmental awareness; splinter groups searching for new patterns of education in the form of alternative schools during the past decade, one basic principle seems to emerge "loud and clear"—the utilization of the out-of-doors as a learning laboratory is a very effective approach toward creating a healthy learning climate for both pupils and teachers.

The information and thoughts contained in this volume will, we trust, adequately represent the scope of the outdoor education movement, to date, and serve as a supplementary reader for the serious student of outdoor education.

January 1973

Donald R. Hammerman
William M. Hammerman

Contents

Chapter one
Outdoor Education:
An Emerging Educational
Philosophy

INTRODUCTION

As the curriculum innovation labeled outdoor education emerged on the American School scene, educational literature soon began to reflect statements of aims, objectives, and values. Philosophical points of view expressed by early leaders in outdoor education revealed a complexity of cultural and social forces at work influencing the development of a growing movement in education.

The educational program of the Civilian Conservation Corps, for example, created a psychological readiness for subsequent acceptance of learning in the out-of-doors as a legitimate school function. Other influencing factors included: (1) a general move toward increased outdoor recreational activity, (2) a general reaction against traditionalism in education, (3) the effect of pragmatism upon the aims of education, (4) the need for conservation education, (5) the need to preserve and promote the democratic ideology, (6) the community school concept, and (7) the prevailing influence of experimentalism in education.

The writings of this period reveal a general recognition of the inherent educational values of camping. These values were expounded by renowned educators such as: William H. Kilpatrick, Boyd Bode, Jay B. Nash, and Fritz Redl. Outdoor education pioneers who lent their voices to developing a philosophical rationale were: L. B. Sharp, William Vinal, E. DeAlton Partridge, Hugh B. Masters, George W. Donaldson, and Julian W. Smith.

WHAT IS OUTDOOR EDUCATION? *

L. B. SHARP

Educators have learned more and more through the years the importance of teaching from natural situations. Most of the things children learn about are brought to school, to be touched and handled and studied. The school, of course, keeps getting bigger, in order to house the collections from which the children study. We know we are on the right track, for we know the best way to learn is to come in contact with the things we seek to know.

Outdoor education, in its simplest aspect, merely says: Don't try to bring the whole world into the school. Rather, take the children out to where the world is. Outdoor education begins just a step outside the door of the school. On the way to and from school, our youth pass by or·through the very things that they go into the classroom to study about.

Authors of textbooks pass on second-hand information they have found by observation and discovery. It is always the person who sees, discovers, or explores a situation who gets the most out of it. This, in short, is the whole thesis of outdoor education. Such learning is faster, is more deeply appreciated, and is retained longer.

The first step out of the school building takes you far enough to find some of the things in nature that are pictured and described in the schoolbooks. First, there is the earth, then, even in the poorest neighborhoods, some plant growth, a great deal of weather; and always some animal or insect life. Beyond the school yard lies the community: a fit subject for study, surely. Government, public

*Reprinted by permission of American School and University magazine from The School Executive 71:19-22, August, 1952.

health, safety, law and order, business, society, industry—all these should be seen firsthand if any useful knowledge of them is to be gathered. And out beyond the community, usually, are the woods and open spaces. This is the outermost circle in which outdoor education operates, and it has a good many values of its own.

In a unit of geography, a teacher spent three lessons trying to teach her class about contours, and succeeded only in making them think that contour lines may somewhere be found on the earth, where they would appear to be wavy, as they appeared in the geography books and on the blackboard. But at the rear of the school, there was an eight-foot hill. With encouragement from the teacher, the members of that class could have made their own contour map of their own school grounds. They could have made a level, and with this and a ruler, could have figured the height of that small hill and the percent of grade. This could all have been done in one forty-minute class period, and a fuller grasp of the significance of contours would have been acquired. The unit of learning would have cost the school district less money. Outdoor education is a method of teaching, as well as a principle of using the out-of-doors wherever possible.

In a unit in civics, the high school group learned about the water supply when the city fathers shut down the water in order to clear the corrosion out of the pipes. The school was closed for lack of water. Education, it would appear, had to stop. And when the added pressure on the pipes caused some of them to burst, the school holiday was prolonged. No one thought to take the civics class out to study the municipal water supply, to make tests of the water, to figure the per capita consumption, to study the water table maps to see if it were possible to drill wells, to learn what is meant by watershed, and to learn why restrictions are necessary in the watershed area to insure water supply. Also, it would have been a good public service if some of these youngsters had volunteered to help during the water emergency. Education need not have stopped. It could have gone on at an even more exciting and valuable pace. The school, perhaps, had to close down. But that should not put an end to learning. The school is not education; we must learn to think of it as merely the headquarters from which learning activities are directed.

In another school the teacher and youngsters were studying geology, using a textbook with pictures showing formations to be found in some remote area. While they were studying, within a quarter of a mile of their school, the Highway Department had made a forty-foot cut through a section of a big hill. There, exposed to the eye, were formations of the rock strata of that area representing two-and-a-half million years of geology. There was exposed an eighteen-inch vein of coal. Many excellent fossils were uncovered, as well as leaf prints which told an important story of the formation of the rocks and of the coal. A trip to this cut in the hill would have been worth more than all the lessons in the book. It would have cost less.

Good textbook material and references are valuable in helping students and teachers understand about conservation of our natural resources; but reading alone will not insure genuine understanding. In many schools throughout the country, groups are learning through actual experience about protection of the soil, filling in ditches to keep the soil from washing away, planting trees, making shrubbery piles for game birds, protecting feeding stations for song birds, studying planting and harvesting of crops and what is meant by contour farming. At the same time they are having a chance to see the wild flowers and animals in their natural habitat, to experience the hills, valleys and streams, and to gain a respect for the land. Surely this is essential education for everybody.

There are some things, however, that can be learned better in the classroom. It is merely a matter of selection. For often, we find that the three essentials—teacher, learner, and the presence of the thing to be learned—operate very effectively under the open sky. It is out-of-doors that the greatest integration occurs in the process of learning: Sooner or later everything relates itself to everything else. Learning out-of-doors is a natural process. In a classroom, subjects tend to become artificially separated from the rest of the world. One cannot explore housing conditions in the community without touching history, sociology, health, science and other fields. A group of students cannot undertake field work in science without concern for personal health. And everything in nature leads out, sooner or later, to related subjects of interest. Outdoor education forces the issue of integration in the curriculum, to study and experience things in their total relationships—one thing to the other. It puts greater emphasis upon the facts and ideas that are most important—a natural selection of important things to know and appreciate.

Some teachers take to outdoor teaching quite naturally. Others learn the new techniques gradually. Some resist completely. It is largely a matter of training. In the main, teachers are trained to do their work in classrooms and other controlled places. They cannot be expected to discover immediately how to handle groups of children in the classroom of the out-of-doors. A teacher using the out-of-doors has to overcome the fear of not knowing something when she is asked. There is that deep-seated feeling, a part of the teacher, that she is paid to know things. With the growth of outdoor education it is coming to be accepted that the teacher will have quite a different outlook. The spirit of learning together is now more characteristic than the attempt to play the oracle who knows all.

But with the spirit of observing together and learning together, comes a better relationship between student and teacher. Many of the worst abuses of teaching tend to disappear. If the student may ask a question without raising his hand—and thus, perhaps, stumble upon something the teacher doesn't know—he may also express his own views in his own natural voice; and that is certainly good. In the outdoor classroom the student stands beside the teacher; they are facing in the same direction, looking toward the object that is under observation;

they are partners in learning. Teachers who have given outdoor education a trial are quite emphatic in saying that it improves the chances for mutual trust and confidence. And they say, further, that when they go back into the indoor classroom with those same students, much of the stiffness has gone out of the educational process, to be replaced by a new kind of eagerness never before seen within those walls.

The greatest benefits of outdoor education only come, however, when students and teacher take to the woods together. This is recommended as an occasional departure in school life, not as a substitute for school. There is great benefit in a single day of it if that day has been well planned as an adventure in learning. The benefit multiplies if the adventure stretches over several days or longer—if it becomes a camping experience. Camping stands at the very peak of outdoor eduction; and school camping, in many school systems, has come to play a very important part in the learning process. School camping is not something to do when school is over; but something to do in order not to miss the benefits that are so easy to gain when a group goes into the open to live and study together.

The experience of living in the out-of-doors together as a regular part of the school program is not a fad, frill or an extra. Indeed, it is a must for the modern school. Here students meet the more subtle problems involved in group living, the problems connected with the unselfish and unbiased consideration of others, the problems involved in fears and prejudices. Thrown together in a single group with others who have different backgrounds—social, racial, economic, religious— the student learns good and valuable lessons very quickly and by very natural means. Lessons in democracy do not have to be instigated and assigned by the teacher.

A few years ago, the New York City Board of Education sent out some classes—fifth and seventh graders—to live in a favorable camping environment during regular school time, in order to test the effectiveness of learning out-of-doors. These classes were not "excused from school"; they were sent to school at camp. When the experiment was over, these pupils had to take the same tests and examinations that were given to corresponding classes that stayed in New York City, in school. The camping group had to solve all their own problems as they went along; and the test was to see whether they learned as much along specific subject-matter lines, as did those who studied the subjects in the orthodox manner. What else the camping group learned was extra. At camp the youngsters took exploration trips to the lake bog, to the hills, and to the marsh lands. They worked with their hands in the soil. At the camp farm, they gathered eggs, milked cows, fed pigs. They saw how potatoes were grown. They lived in small groups, planned most of their own menus, and cooked their meals over the open fire. They operated their own bank and used check books; they ran their own post office. They modeled out of native clay, cut wood for the fire, built and repaired shelters, went on overnight trips and slept under the open sky. The wide range of new experiences and the problems of living and working together added up to an impact upon their lives that the usual school experience was not able to make; but did these children lose out in their regular lessons? Two control groups were used, of corresponding grades. These groups stayed in school and followed the regular lesson plans. Tests were given in both groups before and after the three weeks' camp. *On the majority of tests, the camp group was superior.* The fifth grade's arithmetic score was far superior to that of the grade that stayed in school and studied arithmetic!

School camping is no longer a novelty. Far and wide in many states, some experience of camp life has been added to the curriculum. Many school systems have tracts of land that can be put to use as campsites. Other school systems have kept this problem in mind when acquiring new land for school construction, and have provided suitable tracts for this purpose. Often the problem can be solved by making use of state properties, of the vast areas managed by departments of parks and conservation. Still other schools have arranged to use city-owned or county-owned parks for the school camping experiences.

In almost every case, where there has been a will to add the benefits of camping to the curriculum of the schools, places have been found where, with woods and open fields, the children could gain the experience of natural living as a means of sharpening and deepening all of their learning. If all of the units of learning that can best be handled out-of-doors were organized around certain fixed periods of school camping, the mounting costs of education could be materially reduced. If a fraction of the money being used in big-school construction could be used to buy idle wood lots for camping sites, something very rich, wholesome and valuable to the community could be instilled into youngsters' lives.

It is estimated that 50 percent of our youth drop out of school before the end of the twelve-year period and that 35 percent drop out during the last four years. Studies of this problem reveal that these young people, for the most part, have failed to make adjustment to the traditional ways of learning: they grow restless, and launch out seeking new adventures. Experiments that are now going on, in taking some of the learning out-of-doors, give us good reason to hope that at least a partial solution to this problem may be found. Outdoor education may restore to the whole school program enough of the natural and the reasonable, so as to give that program a wider appeal to the restless spirit of the adolescent.

Outdoor education is a commonsense method of learning. It is normal; it is plain, direct, and simple. The school youth who have experienced it respond actively and with sound learning results.

OUTDOOR EDUCATION—A DEFINITION *

GEORGE W. DONALDSON AND LOUISE E. DONALDSON

Outdoor education is education *in, about* and *for* the outdoors. Its guiding principle is that famous statement of L. B. Sharp's: "Those things which can best be taught outdoors should there be taught." Its *raison d'être* is that twentieth century people have removed themselves from the land—and both they and the land are worse off for it! Its methodology is as old as mankind—learning by using the senses out where the subject matter exists. Its motivation is fundamental to practically all youngsters and most grown-ups. It's fun to work and play and learn outdoors!

IN THE OUTDOORS

It may appear redundant to state that outdoor education is education *in* the outdoors. But there was once a school superintendent who claimed that his schools could not operate a school forest because there wasn't a *textbook* on the subject! And a teacher was heard to ask if the new high school would include a *room* for teaching casting! It is important that "in the outdoors" be given an important place in the definition.

ABOUT THE OUTDOORS

Outdoor educators have no quarrel with the idea that much subject matter *about* the outdoors can best be learned indoors. They would simply demur that learnings having to do with the outdoors are sometimes incomplete and often insipid if the whole learning experience is limited to the indoors.

The typical biology unit on amphibians offers an excellent example of the relationship of indoor and outdoor teaching. Students can read about and discuss both structure and function of a bullfrog. And this is best done indoors. In a good biology laboratory, the students can go the next step—manipulation of an actual frog. Dissection of the frog is an excellent device in teaching structure. But the frog doesn't function as a frog in the book, the discussion, or the laboratory.

*Reprinted by permission of the publisher, the American Association of Health, Physical Education, and Recreation, from the *Journal of Health, Physical Education, Recreation* 29:17, 63, May, 1958.

The teacher who wants students really *to know about* frogs will take his students to a frog pond, where structure and function are so subtly yet firmly interrelated. The bulging eyes, the put-in-wrong tongue, and the powerful leg muscles make sense when the frog uses them in his own environment.

FOR THE OUTDOORS

The word *for* in this definition is the key word. *For* is central not only because it limits the field, but because it implies a positive and a moral approach. It strongly suggests that both the learner and the outdoors are better because of the experience. *For* implies both a mental attitude toward the outdoors and a set of skills and abilities which will enable the learner to do something about his attitudes. Skills are not enough; neither are good attitudes without implementation.

Words, especially definitive words, sometimes confuse a simple concept. Outdoor education is simple. It is as simple as a leisurely walk around the school grounds by a kindergarten teacher and her children. They might look for signs of fall, or of spring. They might investigate a simple plant community. The teacher need not know all about seasonal changes in living things. Nor need she be an ecologist. She just needs curiosity and a bit of good old American ingenuity.

OUTDOOR EDUCATION RESOURCES

There are many fine outdoor education resources on or near most schools. Without too much additional effort, the creative teacher can take his children to nearby city parks, nature museums, and the like. Short excursions within walking distance of the school can add much to a child's understanding of the outdoors.

But the very fact that schools exist in population centers means that much outdoor education must take place at some distance. Day-long trips may be necessary in many instances. Such trips should constitute no great problem for schools which readily transport athletic teams, bands, student councils and various other student groups. Some schools will use their own buses for such transportation; some will organize parent committees to furnish automobiles, and an increasing number have purchased one or more buses for educational excusions. A few school systems have gone the next step and furnish a professionally educated guide to assist the teacher in using outdoor education resources.

OUTDOOR SKILLS INSTRUCTION

Instruction in a number of outdoor skills, like shooting, casting, boating, archery, and nature photography is making its appearance all over the country.

Impetus has been given by the AAHPER Outdoor Education Project, especially to courses in shooting and casting. Offerings are integrated into physical education courses or into the school recreation program. Those few states which have moved in the direction of the extended school year are welcoming such activities as "naturals" for the summer programs. Local recreation authorities have also indicated a vital interest.

FAMILY CAMPING

Family camping is probably the growing-est thing in the field of recreation today. Because of its independent nature, it is well-nigh impossible to document its growth. But in its independence lies its strength. Family groups, traveling with gear ranging from adapted household items (maybe with a tent, maybe not) to carefully assembled outfits reminiscent of African safaris, have flooded public camp sites since World War II. Their numbers increase apace.

A few colleges and recreation agencies have offered "Family Camping Clinics"; magazine articles have appeared; one book has been written. Family campers are adventuresome people. They don't ask for even the help they need. They don't join associations and they'd rather go camping than attend a convention! May their tribe increase. It is quite possible that educators can best facilitate this increase by leaving them alone until they ask for help!

SCHOOL CAMPING

School camping has been called the apex of outdoor education programs. Its growth in the postwar years has been phenomenal. Because it offers many opportunities to teach about the outdoors, plus teachable moments in other fields such as social living, health, and work, it has caught the imagination of educators from coast to coast. Thousands of youngsters, mainly in upper elementary grades, now spend a week in an outdoor environment specifically tailored to child nature.

From its feeble beginnings a few years ago, school camping has boomed to the point at which it is estimated that some 300 school districts in the United States offer some sort of camping experience at one or more grade levels.

CENTURY'S MAJOR CONTRIBUTION

Outdoor education has already been termed the major contribution of the twentieth century to education. To the present its documentation has been poor, its research skimpy and most often shallow. Its proponents have been doers rather than writers. Let us hope that such an enormously challenging field will attract doers *and* writers, workers *and* thinkers.

WHAT IS THE EDUCATION POTENTIAL IN THE OUTDOOR SETTING? *

WALLACE WHEELER AND DONALD HAMMERMAN

The concept of extending the classroom to a natural environment setting is perceived as an instrumentality of significant potential for developing behaviors in consonance with widely accepted educational value ends and means. The ends referred to in this context are those of individual self-realization and social peace. This is interpreted as the peaceful, and successful solution of persisting problems of health, occupation, recreation, physical environment, scientific technology, etc. The primary means for moving toward these ends is fundamentally a *manner of thinking* whereby resulting behavior gives evidence of strong regard for verifiable knowledge, democratic meanings and understandings, and for good human relations. The importance of the outdoor educational setting in developing desired human behaviors lies mainly in its broad array of natural instructional materials, and in its potential for a diversity of human arrangements not ordinarily available or possible in the usual classroom environment.

The outdoor learning environment may be found immediately beyond the schoolroom door, in the schoolyard, in a nearby park or vacant lot, or farther afield in a situation requiring resident facilities for groups of teachers and pupils to live and study together for extended periods of time. Effective use of the outdoor instructional environment requires careful consideration of the goals to be pursued. Final selection of these goals will depend, in large measure, upon the current behavior inadequacies or learning needs of a particular group of pupils.

Consideration of our value means suggests several general areas for the development of objectives and the employment of various outdoor teaching procedures. Thinking is perceived here as the potential ability of a normal human being to envision or clarify a problem or objective, to deliberately select or create a behavior or plan of action to meet it, to activate the selected behavior, and to evaluate its consequences. The outdoor learning environment furnishes innumerable opportunities for the involvement of these basic characteristics of thought. These include the initial development of general objectives, procedures, and evaluative measures suggested by our value means and value ends. From such general planning, specific problems and objectives will be

*Reprinted by permission of Ray Page, Superintendent of Public Instruction and editor of the *Illinois Journal of Education*, the *Illinois Journal of Education*, and the authors from *Illinois Journal of Education* 55:2-4, December, 1965.

derived, providing opportunities for their thoughtful attack, involving desired learnings, knowledge, skills and attitudes.

The development of an appreciation for verifiable knowledge suggests the need for the educational enterprise to provide the student with skills and abilities that will enable him to select from and add to the growing accumulation of facts through his lifetime. This means effective mastery of the four symbols that man has invented for acquiring, storing, and communicating knowledge—the word, the number, the musical note, and the artist's symbolism. The extended classroom provides a unique instructional climate to enhance the probability of enriched learning experiences designed to accomplish growth in using the four symbols.

Democratic understandings suggest not only a strong respect for political democracy, but also for social and economic democracy. Teachers and pupils who establish general and specific objectives, and plan procedures and evaluate measures associated with utilizing the outdoor setting for instruction, find that this experience affords a rich assortment of opportunities for arriving at decisions through group deliberation and consensus which is the backbone process of political democracy.

The resident outdoor education experience also lends itself to the optimum development of appreciation for social democracy. Each individual may enjoy similar privileges and is subjected equally to similar restraints regardless of race, creed, color, station, or any other artificial designation of class which tends to negate the importance of the individual.

School groups frequently engage in various money raising endeavors to help defray expenses for the resident outdoor experience. These fund raising projects often take the form of candy and popcorn sales, stunt nights and variety shows, selling school pencils and sweatshirts, sponsoring card parties for the parents and the community. These activities provide an opportunity for the practice of economic democracy since each individual is able to participate and contribute to the joint effort of the group.

The outdoor school environment provides countless opportunities for learning experiences designed to help elicit a strong appreciation for good human relations. Good human relations involve the development of understandings of one's self and consideration of other human beings. Ample opportunities to develop good manners and other considerate behaviors are evident in the many socially interactive occasions immanent in the total living situation of the resident outdoor experience.

Most youngsters have an overwhelming curiosity which drives them to seek for the what, the why, and the how of things. They need to explore and discover not only to satisfy this natural curiosity, but in order to achieve what psychologists have called "self-realization." The outdoor learning experience where pupils and teachers explore and discover together provides the environment necessary for acquiring knowledge and experience pertinent to finding solutions to the persisting problems of self-realization.

For example, the resident outdoor school (or school camp) is essentially a community of children. They not only constitute the membership of this community but are largely responsible for the development of program and upkeep of the facility. Children, away from home for the first time in their lives, are literally forced to stand upon their own feet. In this community of their own, children are exposed to the kinds of challenging experiences which enable them to spread their wings and proceed along the path toward becoming self-reliant human beings.

Concomitant learnings to be realized in the outdoor instructional setting include:

— appreciations and insights relating to a better understanding of one's physical environment.
— acquiring outdoor recreational skills which lead to the more fruitful use of one's leisure.
— pursuing healthful, physical activity in natural surroundings.
— coming to grips firsthand with some of the basic concepts underlying the biological and physical sciences.

Extending the classroom to the natural environment, from time to time, can provide a methodological pipeline for enriching "in-school" curriculum contents with "outdoor school" concrete experience.

SOME PSYCHOLOGICAL BACKGROUNDS OF CAMPING *

E. DeALTON PARTRIDGE

From the very beginning of the camping movement there have been leading educators who hailed it as a great advance in educational method. President Eliot of Harvard described organized camping as "the most significant contribution to education that America has given the world." Plans for the future of American education as set forth by important policy-making groups such as the American Council on Education and the American Youth Commission call for camping as an integral part of public education.

What is the basis for this belief in camping as an educational method? Is there any evidence to indicate that children learn better or faster in a camp situation than in the traditional school room? How do modern psychologists appraise

*Reprinted by permission from Camping Magazine 15:6-8, March, 1943.

camping in light of their growing knowledge of human behavior? These are questions that every person interested in camping should consider seriously.

John Dewey, who is responsible for many of the theories underlying modern education, has long advocated learning through actual experience. Writing at a time when there was little scientific evidence to bolster his views, Dewey pleaded for an educational program that would bring youngsters into contact with reality. It has only been within recent years that psychologists through painstaking and careful research have been able to examine the validity of Dewey's claims and it is in this area of psychological findings that camp leaders can find much to bolster their faith in the camping method properly used.

Those who have worked with youth in camps are usually impressed with the alacrity and eagerness with which they attack problems in the outdoors and the never-ending stream of learning situations that camp life uncovers. However, the fact that those who believe in camping have *felt* that it was a superior method of teaching the younger generation has not proved the matter beyond a reasonable doubt. Furthermore, there has been no systematic attempt to assemble the findings of modern psychology and interpret them in light of camping methods. Such a survey would take many months and cover more ground than can be encompassed in this brief report. It will be profitable, however, to review some of the more important trends in modern educational psychology and apply them to the camping method.

LEARNING THE MEANING OF THINGS

A surprising amount of time in the educational life of the child is devoted to the process of learning the meaning of words or concepts. For much of this process the schools have and still continue to rely upon the written or spoken word. In order to learn the meaning of a word like "conservation" a child reads about it in a book and listens to the teacher describe it, then tries to answer questions in words to the satisfaction of the teacher. If he can repeat the right phrases he gets a good mark on his test and is considered an apt pupil . . . but does he know what "conservation" really means? The psychologists who have made extensive studies of how children learn say *no*.

It is now known on the basis of countless experiments and the study of child concepts at various age levels that it is practically impossible to convey to a child exact or adequate meanings in many areas *except by actual experience.* Indeed, the psychologists who have studied the matter say that even if you talk yourself blue in the face it is quite impossible to carry meaning to a child, but rather the child must develop it himself out of his own experience. Of course, he can be aided in his learning process by skillful adults who can help him to see relationships or who can at the right moment instruct him in points he otherwise would miss.

However, right here is where the real rub comes in the teaching process. In many cases teachers themselves have concepts that are either entirely wrong or on a purely verbal level. Far too many teachers try to pass on concepts to their pupils which they themselves have failed to substantiate by anything besides vague book-learning. An example will help to make this point clear.

Last spring a group of 32 undergraduates from five different teachers colleges were taking a ten-day course in camping education. Some of them had never before slept outdoors and were doing so for the first time. Every day they were having some new experience about which they had read or heard by word-of-mouth, but now they were seeing, feeling and tasting reality.

On one field trip they came upon a large ant hill. The leader stopped to make some observations about ants, then pointing to a nearby twig he asked if anyone knew what he saw there. Ants were crawling up and down the twig stopping occasionally to "feel" small white spots that looked like miniature sea shells stuck upside down on the twig. Everyone of the 32 saw the twig and not one knew what it was. Yet when asked if they ever studied about how ants cultivated aphids as cows for the secretions they gave off, every student there held up his hand. They all could have answered correctly a question such as "Do ants cultivate other insects for their own use such as humans use cows?" . . . but not one of them would have recognized the real thing if an eager pupil had brought a twig full of aphids and placed it right under his nose.

Thus in the classroom there are apt to be several hurdles to real, precise learning. Teachers with shallow verbal concepts trying to convey word meanings to youngsters can never take the place of firsthand experience. This implies, of course, that besides being good for youngsters camping experience would help make better teachers. On the basis of recent surveys there is reason to suspect that many teachers are woefully lacking in firsthand experience as a background for their teaching. Nearly one-third of 300 teachers in training answered on a recent questionaire that they thought the average chicken laid ten eggs or more a week; more than one-half of them had never preserved or helped preserve food and two-thirds said they had never walked more than ten miles at one time in their lives.

There are no data to support this assumption but it is reasonable to suppose that those who are in positions of leadership in a typical camp are likely to have a richer experience background than the average teacher simply because the camp director must look for these things in hiring a staff. If this is true, then youngsters should get better educational experiences in camp than in school if the camp is administered in such a way as to utilize these opportunities.

Educators have recognized the need for first-hand experience in the learning processes of pupils. In the lower grades, for example, teachers who know their psychology make certain that as they teach they bring to the child actual experience as a background for the words he uses. Field trips, demonstrations, activities are the vehicles employed to do this. But the teacher faces all kinds of obstacles in the process because the school building and regulations concerning it are so often designed to shut the child away from life in order to make it easy for the teacher to pursue book-learning and the use of words without being interrupted by things outside. In camp, however, the child can be and usually is in contact with the very things about which he reads and talks. The camp program *can be* run in such a way as to make every hour meaningful to the child by actual experiences. Furthermore these experiences can be utilized by skillful adults to further enrich the life of the child so that future reading and discussion will have a background of real meaning.

Notice that we said the camp *can be* the source of real experiences. Those who are interested in giving camping its just place as an educational institution must not fall into the error of believing that there is something mystical and magical about camp surroundings that cause children to learn more and better and faster regardless of the type of administration. There has been a tendency in the past on the part of camping enthusiasts to assume that fresh air, exercise, and sunshine were natural forces that simply lifted the child into a state of sweetness and light and that all a camp needed to do was to bring these two—the child and the natural forces—together.

Let us make no mistake about it, camping has tremendous educational *possibilities*, but these possibilities must be carefully cultivated by intelligent leadership before they bear fruit. The most careful students of modern psychology do not agree with those who believe that good education requires that we turn the child loose to follow his own inclinations and desires without any adult help. In fact, their studies show that in this kind of a situation children never learn the best or most economical way possible and are quite apt to learn the wrong things as well as the right. Guidance and leadership are just as necessary in camp, and perhaps more necessary than in the classroom because of the tremendous number of possibilities that will go unused unless they are carefully exploited.

Those who study educational psychology in college these days read passages like the following in their texts:

> Throughout our entire discussion on the nature of meaning and the development of understanding, we have constantly emphasized the importance of extending, enriching, and deepening the individual's experience. How can the school accomplish this purpose?
>
> One of the first steps should be to exploit the local environment, to the fullest possible extent. Nature study, general science, biology, and physical science are usually too bookish as they are now taught. The woods, streams, rocks, farm lands, and natural phenomena of all kinds are laboratories as essential as the formal laboratory and classroom . . . [1]

---

[1]Gates, Arthur I., Jersild, Arthur T., McConnell, T. R. and Challman, Robert C., *Educational Psychology*. New York: The Macmillan Company, 1942, p. 443.

Thus there is a distinct trend, based upon careful experiment and study, toward more realism in the teaching of American youth. There is now ample psychological evidence to justify the faith in a properly administered camping program as a place to teach real meanings to children.

THE ROLE OF CAMPING IN EDUCATION TODAY *

W. H. KILPATRICK

How does education today see camping? What part does camping play in any inclusive educational program as this is conceived by the modern educator?

The problem seems to divide itself naturally into two subordinate questions: (1) How does modern thought see and understand education? (2) What is the role of camping in such an educational outlook? The treatment of these two questions will of necessity overlap; life, when seen adequately, seldom presents clear-cut separations or isolations.

I

How does modern education see itself? What is there *modern* about it? How does education at the best see its aims?

What aims shall guide education? It seems possible to state three main specific aims which education is to keep in mind: (1) helping the young to grow into more adequate selfhood or personality, (2) helping to enrich life, (3) helping the young to grow into more adequate social relationships. And here again do we find overlapping and interaction. There can, for instance, be no growing into more adequate personality which does not at the same time both enrich life and bring better social relationships. However, naming the three aims as if separate will help to guide efforts.

Before taking up any one of these aims, it will be necessary to consider learning. There are different ways of conceiving the learning process and these different ways will affect personality very differently. An older notion, now largely rejected, held that children are naturally bad. If one believed this, he would put a stop to everything naturally interesting to children and be quite willing to have all dealings with them put simply on a basis of unending coercion. Another past notion was that children's minds are naturally empty and

*Reprinted by permission from *Camping Magazine* 14:14-17, February, 1942.

have to be filled from the outside. On this view education became a pouring-in process, a pouring-in and a storing-up until childhood was over. Still another notion, held by some moderns but not here, is that all suppression is wrong, that care must be taken not to suppress the natural impulses of the child lest personality maladjustment be induced. There is a problem here, but we do not simply turn children loose to do as they please.

II

On what basis are we to choose the view of the learning process to follow? First, we must go to science to see how learning actually does go on and what effect it has on personality. If we treat the child one way, we find that certain learning and personality results will follow. If we treat the child in a different way, we see that other learning and personality effects are properly to be expected. It is the business of education to find out by scientific study what these different possibilities are. Second, we must study how some kinds of life are good to live and others less good or bad, and from such study to set up aims as to the kind of life and the kind of personality to encourage. Then how to get together effectively the accepted aims and the correlative learning possibilities— that is the practical problem of education.

The kind of life here considered good is that represented by democracy and the highest ethical conceptions we can get. We wish to build up each person, on the one hand, to be ever more adequately self-directing and, on the other hand, ever more strongly in justice and the equal treatment for all together. The self-direction then is the kind that acts on thinking, that thinks before it acts and as it acts to the ends that the resulting conduct may be both wise and just. On this basis all the personalities are to be so developed, without discrimination, that they may live as best possible together. Freedom is limited to what fits with this kind of equality of opportunity; and as to governing, all should share democratically in making the decisions that concern them.

With this kind of life in mind we now seek such a theory of the learning process as will help to make for the desired kind of life and personality. Fortunately, it seems to be true that the long-run most efficient way of managing the learning process is at the same time the best way to build the desired kind of personalities.

III

Learning is going on all the time while one is actively awake. The connection between learning and living is, if possible, even closer and more intimate than this.

First, what do we mean by learning? A friend proposes to take me driving over a certain new crosscountry route, explaining that he *learned* it just a week ago; and goes on to tell how he made various mistakes then but now he knows it. And sure enough, as we drive along, I can see that what he learned a week ago comes back into his mind to direct the turns that he is to take. This then is what we mean by the verb to *learn*, that certain past experiences stay with one, after they have been lived, so as to come back into present experience to help carry it on. I live and what I live stays with me, after I have lived it, to come back again appropriately into my life. Before a thing can be *learned*, it has first to be *lived*. If it is a feeling, I can't learn it until I have first felt it. If it is a thought, I can't learn it until I first think it. If it is a skilled movement, I cannot learn it until I first make that movement. I learn only and exactly what I live.

That the camp is a place where children can and do live is at once obvious. We begin now to see why a camp is so good a place for children. It provides real living, and so brings learning far and away better than does the older type school. Hour for hour, a camp is often more educative than school because in it the children can better live what they are to learn.

But there is more yet about learning. We have seen that we have to live a thing if we are to learn it, but do we learn all we live? Do all who are present together in any experience live and learn the same thing? The answer is no. Suppose an accident happens. If all the bystanders are questioned as to what took place, they may tell—and honestly so—very different stories. Each one learned what he thought he saw. Did he learn what he lived? Yes, each one learned what he lived as he *accepted* it.

This notion of *acceptance* calls for further study. I am driving to Town A and miss a turn so that I reach not Town A, but Town B. What do I learn? I learn each of the several things that I accept in connection with the experience: that I have gone astray, certainly; that this is one way to reach Town B if I ever wish to go there, certainly; that I was careless and must hereafter look more closely, possibly; that it was a certain particular turn just after the bridge which misled me, yes, if that is the way I think about it, if I so accept it.

How about degrees of learning in connection, for clearly we learn some things more strongly than others? The answer to degree of learning seems to turn partly on degree of thought connections, partly on degree of feeling. Here I seem greatly annoyed to find myself in Town B, annoyed partly because I hate to fail, but more annoyed this time because I, being late, was keeping a dinner party waiting. The more, then, I thought about any separate item of the experience and the stronger I felt about it in connection, the better or the stronger I learned that item.

Space forbids further discussion here, but we can sum up the discussion on learning as follows:

We learn what we live, only what we live, and everything we live. We learn each thing we live as we accept it to act on and we learn it in the degree that we count it important and also in the degree that it fits in with what we already know.

IV

Some of us who remember the difficulty we had with arithmetic or grammar can now understand better how children learn better at camp. Take swimming. Do the boys live their swimming? They certainly do, for the most part they live it tremendously. How about the school arithmetic in comparison? Did they live the arithmetic as fully as they live the swimming? No, swimming enters into a boy's life with a fullness that is seldom true of arithmetic. In fact, for most boys, if it had been left to them, they would have omitted a good deal of the arithmetic. What parts would they have left out? Counting? No; they need that in living. Making change out of a dollar? No, not when they are old enough, for they need that in living. Long division? Yes; most of them would gladly omit it or at least postpone it, for they seldom need it in their living.

In other words, camping is on the whole much more successful at teaching its lessons than is the ordinary school of the older type, because the children live the camp life much more fully than they live the most that goes on in the more formal school. Moreover, in the well-run camp the boys and counselors are on the same side, not opposed to each other as are boys and teachers in the formal school. This greatly helps the learning. When all the other boys put stress on any given thing, any one boy is almost sure to count it important. He will try to live that thing and will accordingly count it important to him personally. In this way he learns that thing better.

With the new principles of learning before us, we are then prepared to ask more explicitly, what is the role of camping in modern education?

V

We are now ready to take up the three main specific aims for education set out earlier: (1) to help each boy or girl to grow into more adequate selfhood or personality; (2) to help each one to enrich his own life by upbuilding himself; (3) to help each one to grow into more adequate social relationships. It is at once obvious that these three so overlap and interact that treating any one almost treats the other two. But let us begin as if we were treating them separately. The different emphasis will give better color to the combined picture.

1. How can the camp help youth to grow into more adequate selfhood or personality? The answer to this we are now prepared to base on the discussion of learning as given above. These young people will build personality only and exactly as they live the traits to be built.

Consider "emotional maturity," the sense of being an effectively self-directing person accepted by others as a worthy member of the group. Young people need to grow up into this "emotional maturity"; they need then to achieve a dependable self-direction and a sense of respect from others as it is exercised.

The home is, for most, a difficult place in which to achieve these necessary attitudes. The young begin life highly dependent on their parents and necessarily so. The parents, on their part, have to exercise control and they learn it so strongly that they find difficulty in turning loose the control they thus early build; they accordingly find difficulty in weaning their children emotionally and morally. The young have to learn—by so living—to stand on their own feet and to make decisions in their own right. This does not mean learn to live selfishly, learn to make decisions that disregard others—exactly contrary. The young people have to learn themselves to make—not simply accept from parents—decisions that properly take others into account. Until the young have abundant opportunity—under wise guidance—to practice making such decisions, they have small chance to grow into "emotional security."

It is just here that the camp can render invaluable service. While preserving proper restraints, the camp can and does, almost inevitably, give young people the chance to live together on terms that normally make for the desired emotional security and maturity. In camp each youth has the chance to live as a personality among his peers, with a minimum of adult domination. What suggestion he needs in order to make him consider others will come largely from the others of his own group. The wise counselor watches what is going on, but leaves as much of the education as possible to the inherent group living. And this inherent living, if it can work wisely, works best. In comparison with most schools especially most secondary schools, the camp, hour for hour, can be far and away the more successfully educative. The conventionally minded school still hands down most decisions from teacher to pupil; the good camp builds up decisions from within the group. Insofar the conventional school is emotionally and morally miseducative, while the well-run camp can be truly educative.

Space forbids further detailed discussion of building personality. Other aspects will come out in the further discussion.

2. How can the camp help youth to enrich life? With urbanization on the decided increase in our country, the average city child lacks the chance to swim, boat, roam the woods, learn trees, learn birds, build campfires, cook over the fire. Some or all of these things and more the camp can offer. It is an entrancing life to youth. True enough, most of what is learned cannot be carried back directly to the city. But life is forever different because of having lived these enrichments. Books have richer content and life has different hopes.

3. How can the camp help fit the individual better into group life?

As long as schools were run as hitherto, with the children sitting at separate desks and the teacher making all the decisions, there was little opportunity for the young to learn, except by themselves on street or playground, how to live with others. Much of such boy-with-boy kind of learning is good, but—with no older heads present to help guide—some of it can be hard. Slum conditions breed juvenile delinquency, while supervised playgrounds reduce it; it is the kindly supervision that makes the difference. It is here that the camp is strong, as we shall in a moment further say. The new type school is of course here much better than the older type, but as intimated above this kind of education has not yet sufficiently remade the secondary school. Under such circumstances the camp offers better opportunities at group living and in many ways. If the camp is wise, there is much opportunity for discussion and shared decisions. It is this sort of living democracy that best teaches democracy. In fact, it is impossible for our young people to learn democracy except as they live democracy. And the camp offers marvelous opportunity at living democratically.

In contrast with the school, which still suffers under traditional handicaps, the camp need have no fixed program of content activities and no fixed-in-advance learnings to be achieved. The camp is free to be a place of real living and therefore a real educational institution as most schools are not. The camp can sincerely build itself on living, on honest worthy living, and nothing else. Go back a moment to the conception of learning: our children will learn what they truly live. It is the business of adults, in home, in school, and in camp, to seek to build up a good quality living among the young—the kind of living that is fit to be learned and so fit to be built into character. From hurtful tradition, most homes and schools don't understand this. The camps can. Nothing stands in the way.

The camp can thus spread a more adequate ideal of education. They must work in season and out that the young committed to them shall live, live well, live nobly, finely—in one word, that they live in their hearts the kind of traits worthy to be fixed in habit and character. This is the role of camping in education today.

VALUES OF SCHOOL CAMPING *
HUGH B. MASTERS

From the pioneer life of this country comes a basic concept for redirecting secondary-school education. The notion that people learn through working together in small community groups on common problems is a heritage from our forefathers, as fundamental to democratic living today as it was yesterday. With

*Reprinted by permission of the publisher, the American Association of Health, Physical Education, and Recreation, from the *Journal of Health, Physical Education, Recreation* 22:14-15, January, 1951.

this concept as its core, camping education as an extension of the regular secondary-school program is a new development for vitalizing learning experience.

Traditionally, camping has not been a part of the public-school program. Many activities of today's camping programs were merely the necessary ones for daily living in early America. Living in a simple community setting with the necessity for using its resources to provide needs was not a unique experience then. In 1950 it is.

For city children, camping affords an opportunity for understanding the sources and processes of securing those necessities upon which their lives depend. Rural youngsters have a chance to gain insight into the cooperative and competitive social aspects of community life. The camping experience can evoke an appreciation of the development of civilization that might never come from reading history books.

If we did not believe that it is imperative to recognize change and adapt education accordingly, schools would have remained static, rigidly disciplined training centers limited to the basic tool subjects. Instead experimentation and evaluation are constant processes for the purpose of meeting ever-changing needs. This peculiar strength of our educational system derives from the fact that it is free, universal, and controlled by local people.

Across the country the values of school camping programs are being studied. Much attention has been focused on the pioneering work in Michigan where the State Departments of Education and Conservation have developed year-round camping experiences as an integral part of regular school.

Camping education is a new direction. It represents an experiment in learning that takes place outside of the classroom. Ideally, the setting is an actual school camp which may be established using already existing state and federally owned lands. Here, students with their regular classroom teachers spend at least a two week period.

Although most of the school camp programs have been conducted as part of the elementary school, such programs can be even more potent educational experiences on the secondary level. Granted that the administrative problems are greater for the secondary school, the results in terms of real-life learning can outweigh the difficulties involved.

ADVANTAGES OF SCHOOL CAMPING

School camping is based on sound educational concepts.

It provides direct learning. There is an opportunity for active participation in planning, executing and evaluating activities.

It is based on the interests of children. The camping idea in itself is so appealing to the normal school child and so charged with opportunities for educational and social growth, that our schools cannot fail to capitalize on this significant fact.

It provides for individual differences of children. Often a difficult schoolroom task where children are required to master the same academic material in the same amount of time with the same solution to the problem, camping provides a wide range of opportunities. Everyone has a chance to express initiative, show ability, and achieve status in the group.

It is planned for all children. More than ever before in our history, we believe that education must include everyone. This gives a responsibility for providing schooling that meets common basic needs, at the same time providing for the wide span of individual differences. A camping program is one of the best ways of providing for individual interests, abilities, and needs.

It represents a return to the realities of the simple life. Education must be concerned with such basic things as food, shelter, and clothing. Verbalism alone cannot satisfy the need or deepen the understanding.

It provides a range of socially successful and satisfying experiences. In the attempt to meet this need, schools have offered an ever-increasing number of subjects to an ever-increasingly diversified student body. Camping experience uniting all in the practice of democracy can aid in the development of a more lasting bond in the culture.

It includes the elements of risk and adventure that are essential to the proper growth and development of the child. The change from school and home living opens a new and different experience with a degree of surprise that demands the corresponding degree of responsibility to make the needed adjustments. These simple, yet very subtle, differences from the established routine of school and family living constitute a most effective teaching element in the camping situation.

It uses existing facilities. Many schools have neglected to carry plans into action because of the false notion that the camping program has to wait until the school can purchase a site, build buildings, and secure necessary facilities. The school should encourage the maximum use of its present staff in the planning and developing program before bringing in additional personnel.

State and federally owned lands and facilities should be used. Some communities have worked out contracts with many different private and public agencies for the partial use of their facilities. What is most needed is the use of the creative imagination of students, teachers, and parents in a careful study of all available resources.

OPPORTUNITIES IN CAMPING

What are the unique opportunities of the camping program? Let's take a look at the program. It starts long before the school bus discharges its load at the camp site. Effective results cannot be achieved if camping is operated as an isolated activity. Long before the day arrives, school activities are centered on the anticipated camp experience. This is similar to the preparation made for a trip, providing real motivation for poring over road maps, studying climate and customs. The precamp experience is motivated by the same force and filled with the same learning opportunities.

All areas of the curriculum have a contribution. Reading lists can include books that will add to the enjoyment of camp life, reserving classical requirements for another time. Knowledge of camp cooking, animal life, and folk lore add immeasurably to a rich camp life. What a good opportunity is afforded the science class to learn about poison ivy—not from a page of reading and a photograph to be forgotten—in order to avoid the painful consequences of an encounter with it at camp.

Ability to read weather maps will have real meaning for students in their outdoor school. How to perform folk dances for fun nights at camp is a contribution that can be made through the physical-education class. Music, both vocal and instrumental, is a natural for camp. So are games and sports. And a study of the history and development of the region should have real meaning.

At camp, there are many rich opportunities for learning. Most important, there is a chance to use that learning. Facts are not stored for future use alone. Day by day camp living demands action and stimulates new learning in a very real situation.

Think of the knowledge and skill involved in building a camp shelter. It takes the classroom theory plus a lot of practical know-how. One boy, having constructed a shelter and found it leaky, made this observation, "Grownups must have a terrible time building houses!" That kind of understanding might never follow a classroom unit of study on housing.

CONTRIBUTIONS OF CAMPING EXPERIENCE

When teachers and students return to school buildings at the end of the camping period, new relationships have been established. There is a far greater understanding of interests and abilities and aspirations. The learnings motivated by camp experiences are continued in the regular school program.

In its brief history, the school camping experience has demonstrated major educational contributions in four areas: social living, work experience, recreational living, and healthful living.

In the area of social living, the school camp offers unexcelled opportunities for the camper to assume some responsibility for the operation and control of the camp. Without realizing it, he acquires desirable attitudes toward public and private property. The community problems that arise in a normal and natural way in a school camp promote constructive attitudes toward cooperative action.

Work has dignity in the American culture. Affording a work experience for boys and girls is another significant contribution of camping. Most present-day homes do not provide enough work experience for young people. A camper engages in the kind of jobs necessary for his own safety and well-being as well as that of the entire group.

In good camping situations, campers take care of the mail, the commissary, conservation, and banking necessary for the continuing program. Here, too, subjects learned in the classroom are put to use. Mathematics, reading, and writing become important in relation to improved living.

Camp recreational experiences are different than the common spectator variety. Activities are simple and in keeping with the physical environment. The recreational program builds upon and supplements those activities normally carried on in the school, drawing heavily upon the learning that the student has acquired in literature, music, art, science, physical education and other subjects. The camp is the ideal place for using these experiences.

All education has good health as a major goal. Health education in camp is a direct 24-hour-a-day living experience. This makes it possible to work on problems of eating, resting, and exercise. Youngsters can be understood in terms of physical, mental, social, and spiritual health. In a new environment, habits of healthful living are easier to develop.

THE SCOPE OF OUTDOOR EDUCATION *
JULIAN W. SMITH

Outdoor education is becoming an increasingly significant development in the curriculums of schools and colleges throughout the country. The change from a rural society to an age of mechanization and urban living, which has deprived most youth of close contact with the land, and the search for direct learning opportunities, has focused attention on the need and value of using outdoor resources in the educational process.

The increased amount of time available for people to engage in activities of their own choice has resulted in a surge of interest in outdoor pursuits. These developments are making an impact on education, both on the methods of teaching and in the enrichment of educational experiences.

In recent years, outdoor education has come to mean an emphasis in education, encompassing the use of the outdoors as a laboratory to supplement

*Reprinted by permission of the publisher and the National Association of Secondary School Principals from *The Bulletin of the National Association of Secondary School Principals* 44:156-58, May, 1960.

classroom learnings, and the acquisition of knowledge, attitudes, and skills for a wiser use of the outdoors and natural resources. The term, "outdoor education," is currently described as education *in* and *for* the outdoors, and includes those learning activities which can be conducted more effectively in an outdoor setting and the teaching of skills necessary for wholesome outdoor pursuits.

In secondary schools, outdoor education has important implications for the use of natural settings in teaching the physical sciences, conservation, social science, and other subject matter areas and activities. Many schools are providing field experiences in camps, school forests, school farms, school gardens, parks, and other outdoor areas to supplement and enrich the curriculum. Health education, physical education, recreation, and club programs are being broadened to include outdoor activities, such as shooting, firearms safety, casting, camping and outing, archery, boating and water activities, winter sports, and others. Such enriched programs offer opportunities for wider participation in individual and lifelong interests and include important learnings in conservation, safety, and a wise use of leisure time.

Outdoor education, as herein conceived, is not another subject of discipline to be included in an early crowded curriculum, but represents a practical and sound approach in the achievement of the accepted objectives of education. It represents a better utilization of resources available in the learning process and is a functional application in meeting the needs of today's living.

SCHOOL CAMPING

One of the most sensational patterns in outdoor education that has developed in recent years is the use of camp settings for the extension and enrichment of classroom experiences, often called "school camping" or "outdoor classrooms." This type of outdoor education has grown rapidly over the last two decades. It is estimated that there are more than 500 school districts in the United States that use camps for laboratory experiences. While this has largely been a development in the later elementary-school curriculum, there have been a number of secondary schools involved—particularly in Michigan and California.

The common procedure is for classroom groups and their teachers to use available camp facilities for a period of a school week to achieve the objectives which can be obtained best in an outdoor environment. The school district provides the instruction and transportation, and the home pays the cost of food and lodging, which normally amounts to approximately $10 a week. Resource leadership is largely from the community and helps supplement the effort of the regular teachers in exploring the unique learning opportunities that are available in the camp setting and outdoor areas.

In secondary schools, the instructional units selected for this type of outdoor education may be science, physical education, unified studies or core studies, or special activities. Students, teachers, and parents in schools that have thus utilized their outdoor resources have been enthusiastic about the effectiveness of learning that has occurred. The camp setting provides unique opportunities for a better understanding and practice of good human relationship, social living, citizenship and health; and, in addition, it contributes to many subject matter areas. Some specific examples of how the outdoors can be used effectively in the secondary-school curriculum are described in the following pages.

THE OUTDOORS AS A LABORATORY

The effectiveness of direct learning and the solution of practical community problems has been adequately documented, but there is great need for this kind of realism in secondary education. A few brief examples of how the curriculum can be enriched through the use of an outdoor environment will serve as illustrations:

Science. While biology teachers have probably used the outdoors more than others, much more can be done in interpreting biologic principles and facts when living things are viewed in their environmental context. Environmental studies, collection trips, and field work help in understanding the physical world and man's relationship to it. In chemistry and physics, teachers dealing in soil elements, water supply, sanitation, and astronomy find the outdoor laboratory extremely useful. In agriculture and conservation, school farms, gardens, and forests all constitute practical laboratories for developing better concepts.

Social Science. Field experiences have long been used and found effective in social science. Trips to abandoned farms, for example, give vivid illustrations of the changes of modern living, and the inspection of modern farm areas portrays the importance of land management and conservation. Secondary schools that use camps as outdoor classrooms find additional opportunities through "learning by living" in a camp community. Understanding of democratic living and the responsibilities involved in operation become much clearer in this kind of setting.

Other Curriculum Areas. Many creative experiences in the oral and written language can be enhanced through the use of the outdoors. In arts and crafts, the use of native materials helps interpret the beauty of nature. In homemaking and shop, opportunities are offered for teaching skills relating to outdoor living, such as outdoor cooking, outdoor clothing, constructive skills, planning for family camping trips, and many others.

Clubs. Supplementing the various curriculum areas, clubs serve to open many new avenues in the interest of the outdoors. Such clubs might include: outing activities, hiking, bird study, telescope, gardening, boating and water activities, lapidary activities, archery, and a variety of other specific interests.

Outdoor Skills and Sports. The areas of health, physical education, and safety have great potential in offering rich opportunities in outdoor education. These not only include the teaching of outdoor skills and sports, but also open new avenues of interest that lead into the other curriculum areas. An example would be the relationship of teaching casting to the study of fish life, habitat, and management. A comparable illustration could be made for shooting. Outdoor skills may be included as units of instruction in regular scheduled classes and may be conducted through clubs, intramural sports, or special activities.

THE SCHOOL CAMP LINE-UP FOR NATURE EDUCATION *

WILLIAM GOULD VINAL

A nature teacher may point with pride to the number of microscopes, the size of the aquarium, and the variety of stuffed birds. Unfortunately, the apparatus that looks well does not always contribute to the welfare of the individuals who sit in the room. It is astonishing to see how many teachers are so busy equipping laboratories, purchasing textbooks, testing children, and instructing children to use materials that they have no time left to deal with nature. Armchair nature study plus lip service where one grinds out facts and credits, such as is typical in many high schools, is the lowest stage of nature leadership. Laboratory equipment is not impressive as such materials are static. Nature education must be dynamic.

If there is a camera in the room, that is one thing. If there is a camera plus a teacher who knows photography, that is an additional advantage. If the leader's interest includes a liberal sprinkling of field photography plus a goodly number of children, that characteristic excites attention. To get the right spark of enthusiasm, the kind that will launch a camera club let us say, there must be the right mixture of materials, participants, and leadership. That is dynamic photography. Dynamic field photography is good nature education.

Teachers of elementary science are getting uneasy. They sense that changes are going on. It may be significant that more changes are going on outside of the scholastic walls than within the walls. Schools, and perhaps rightly so, are conservative when it comes to new ideas, and yet science teachers have been ingrained with the principle that change is a natural law. What are some of the recent new slants that are significant to teachers of elementary science? The population is changing its location to the country. The technical science day is getting shorter. The leisure science day is getting longer. We are machine

*The Clearing House, April, 1936, reproduced by permission.

technocrats for fewer and fewer hours and then tramps, gardeners, and campers for longer and longer hours. First we must be conscious of this shift of emphasis. Second, we must adapt ourselves to progress. The mastodon did not adapt himself to a new environment, and where is he today? He exists in museums. Teachers who do not adapt themselves can take a place alongside the mastodon. They will then exist as examples of historic methods, as good as dead.

It is evident that science teachers must do some rethinking. The Pilgrims were rethinking when they wrote the Mayflower Compact. The colonists were rethinking when they drew up the Declaration of Independence. The abolishing of slavery was the result of rethinking. All of these movements not only took rethinking; they took time. To emancipate children from schoolroom poison, to search for truth in the sunlight, and to declare independence of textbooks will require rethinking. To reshape our objectives so that the book will develop the individual instead of the subject of science, so that no one is "failed" but each has the opportunity to advance according to his own capabilities would seem drastic to some pedagogues. And yet for the past fifty years such a liberal policy has been used in camps.

The ideal situation for nature education involves certain requirements. For convenience in rethinking it is proposed to present these requirements one at a time. Such a scheme will not only make it simpler to analyze the situation but will give certain pegs which we may use in checking up on our present program. At first thought it would appear that the first three items have no relation to nature education. On the contrary, they are an integral part of it.

1. *There must be correct food habits.* Such a statement seems commonplace. We have been teaching that for years. And with what results? Breakfast has become the great American relay race. We stoke the furnace as though it were something to have over with. Some even concede that there can be no pleasure in eating spinach. We no longer linger, Lettie, over the tea cups as we have to get to something more interesting. Dinner in camp is interesting. We may even gaze across the lake at a sunset. We talk over the canoe trip. We plan to climb Mt. Washington next week. We reminisce about the last stop at the Tip Top House. We may burst out in song. We eat our spinach with relish. Meal time at camp is a happy time. It is a mixture of folk lore, folk tales, and folk music.

2. *There must be sound sleep.* What science teacher does not emphasize that? Religiously and fervently, too. What availeth this doctrine if the constituency begrudges sleep? Everything belies such a principle. Every evening there are motion pictures, piano lessons, parties, dancing, club meetings, and they are all-important. In camp one is glad to sleep. After a day in the open air, following the long, long trail, one welcomes the roost. There is no competition. Sound sleep is both a philosophy and a habit.

3. *There must be sound sex attitudes.* Sex is the theme of the stage and of the motion-picture house. It is not always presented in a wholesome setting. Sex

is not overemphasized in camp, and in nature it occurs under normal conditions. It is not something to be avoided, but also it is not to be unduly stressed.

4. *Nature education best takes place where nature is.* This would seem trite if it were not true that most so-called nature study is compartmental or monastic. The young animal must have materials, space freedom, responsibility, play, rest, security, and guidance. If this is true of the kitten and the wolf cub how much more true it is of the child who is also a biological animal. All should be educated in outdoor life and not for it. As in Cooper's *Leatherstocking* novels, attitudes and skills are of greater significance than are bald facts. Schools cannot compete with camps as locations for the presenting of nature.

5. *There is no nature education without action.* A schoolroom can be full of a number of things and still be a vacuum. Unfortunately, many schoolrooms are vacuums when it comes to nature. There should be a stream of child activities where the child works and does not just listen. There should be children caring for growing flowers, building observation beehives, breeding guppies, raising a pair of ring-necked doves, and making geranium cuttings. The schoolroom is a clubhouse. Such a program means a path of daily activities. It is subject matter out of experience rather than experience out of subject matter. Such experiences could take place either in school or in camp. Similar discoveries could be made in one's back yard. Self-achievement, in whatever place it is attained, must come through everyday experimenting, observing, and reasoning. Citizenship must come through participation in citizenship in school, home, street, park, or camp. Nature recreation must come through reading, travel, and camping. There are bound to be richer nature activities in seven twenty-four-hour days at camp than in five five-hour days in school.

6. *Children should be given the opportunity to work in the laboratory of life* rather than be given entrenched studies about the activities of life. The first is camp and the second is school. In camp everything is in the terms of living. Camp is a school of realism where human and natural values count instead of subject values. Food, sleep, chores, play, gardening, cooperation, teamwork, all count. Creative art as with the Indian is the self-expression of the environment. The creative songs in camp are about nature, the exploits of camp, the love of camp, its valleys and lakes. Whether a child is in the garden, or on a canoe trip, or in the group singing at the campfire probably has nothing to do with his I.Q. The leaders are looking toward the socialization of the individual and not just toward educating him. The materials of camp are the materials of life.

7. *There must be challenging new experiences involving play, work, and study groups.* As living fish may be a common means of nature education in both school and camp let us analyze the situation with that medium as the center of the stage. Merely having a fish at hand is no guarantee of a satisfying experience. One anemic goldfish in a glass jar will result in mere *gazing* on the part of the bystander. We have passed the gazing stage in our parks, games, and

biological education. Several goldfish chasing each other through castles and grotesque grottoes may be *amusing*. We are not running amusement parlors. The care of a pair of guppies, the breeding of which is a real experience, brings up problems to be solved. It is a *basic experience*. A field trip to catch sticklebacks in order to raise more sticklebacks is a *challenging experience*.

In camp there may be a series of fishing experiences over a long period of time. To be successful one must study the habits of trout and bass so as to outwit them. To be within the law one must know the law and have an appreciation of conservation. To reach remote places one must use the map, trails, and compass. To cook a fish on the trip one must know how to pan it, bake it in clay, or perhaps how to dry it. And then there are a thousand and one unexpected experiences. Fishing experiences that involve work, study, and play are the most enriching. There is nothing to certify that a child in camp will get more than a goldfish experience and there is no reason why a school cannot make the richest offering. Since many camps are nearer the best fishing grounds and since camps do not have a traditional curriculum it would appear that the most enriching experiences in fishing will more often be found at camp.

8. *There must be a variety of nature offerings.* When one boy builds a birdhouse it may be work. For another child the same activity may be play. Thomas Edison said that he never had done a day's work in his life. His teacher sent him home as a dunce, and explained that she could not do anything with him. Who was the dunce? A good leader will run a three-ring circus so that every child will have an opportunity to discover play in work. There are many routes to the North Pole. The real test is in how many experiences we will offer rather than how many courses or hours the journey will take. One way to check up on our camp activities is to find out whether they are the ones in which the villagers have inherent interest. Is the school or camp such that any villager could join in and feel at home? Are the nature offerings a back-to-the-country awakening? Do the children have an opportunity to choose?

9. *Nature recreation is nature education.* The best nature education is nature recreation. That is the theme that has been running through this bit of philosophy. This may send some readers back over the numbered items with a fine-tooth comb. Try them out with the seven objectives of education as put down by the National Education Association.

10. *Vital nature education requires good leadership.* This is another thread that must be evident in the discourse whether in school or in camp. At the present time leadership is the weakest link in the chain of nature education. It would be absurd to claim that sending a child to camp ensures good nature education. It does put the child in an excellent environment, but he must have guidance. A nature guide is a person who has been over the ground or in a similar situation before. He has had experience. The person selects his guide because of this experience, ability, and sympathy. He asks for guidance in solving a problem

or in meeting a situation. It is individual attention that he wants and not class advice. It is an any-time-of-the-day need rather than from 9:00 a.m. to 12 noon or between 1:30 p.m. and 3:30 p.m. It may come at a recreation period.

11. *The time is near at hand when all people will experience nature education in camp.* In any case all nature education will not take place in school. For some children, all their nature education will take place outside of school. This will be through parents, chores, newspapers, neighborhood, and camp. The bookworm variety of most schools is not going to be enough. There are 52 so-called extracurricular activities in the public schools of Cleveland. One of the most recent activities to knock at the school door is camping. East Technical High School has its camp in the Bedford Metropolitan Park. The classes in woodworking and in electricity and shopwork, etc., had a hand in constructing the cabin. The School of Education has a course in outdoor leadership. The Social Welfare Department has also put the city in the camp business, and it has built Camp Cleveland at the city farm. The City of Los Angeles has family camps. The number of nature trails built in recent years is most encouraging. Cleveland, Buffalo, Springfield, Pittsburgh, Wheeling, Cincinnati, and other communities have municipal nature trails. *Nature education is a public utility.*

12. *What is ahead of us in nature education?* It was my privilege to attend the Twenty-First National Recreation Congress recently held in Chicago. Keeping in mind that the camp movement was American born, there were two very significant German-born movements presented at the congress. One of these movements has already gained considerable momentum in America. I refer to the Youth Hostels.

Richard Schirrman, founder of the Youth Hostel movement, presented a most convincing story. He was a teacher in Westfalen, Germany. He liked to hike with his pupils but found a lack of suitable quarters where boys and girls could stay nights with safety and at a low cost. There are now 4,000 youth hostels in 18 countries. In our country there are 33 shelters which occur every 15 miles on a 500-mile loop extending through three states. The loop begins at Northfield, Massachusetts, and extends through the Green and White Mountains back to Northfield. The movement was introduced into this country by Isabel and Monroe Smith who also spoke at the Chicago meeting. The significance of this movement in the realm of international good will and understanding cannot be overestimated. Someone suggested that if Ramsay MacDonald, Mussolini, Hitler, and Herriot, could have gone on a three weeks' hostel trip together when they were young they might have avoided their present difficulties.

The second sphere of outdoor activity was presented to the congress by a German delegation who came to extend an invitation to hold the next International Congress in Germany. They represented the organization *Kraft durch Freude* (strength through joy), which aims to solve the social question. It is designed to do away with the materialistic conception of life and to restore the idealistic conception which grows from the natural phenomena of life. A part of the program to elevate work to the plane of a culture is the holiday program. The Office for Travel, Hiking, and Holidays in the organization *Kraft durch Freude* provided more holiday sea trips last year than all the English and German shipping companies combined. These trips have included the English Channel, Norwegian fjords, the Azores, and Madeira. In a large way the *Kraft durch Freude* is restoring the love of nature and fatherland as well as of the family. Here again are the seeds of international knowledge and mutual understanding.

What can we expect as a result of this back-to-nature movement? My whole life has been given to selling the values of nature education. Perhaps I am too enthusiastic about its possibilities. However, if I have stirred new thoughts as to the goals of nature education, if I have moved you to take account of stock in your own program, my effort will have achieved its purpose. Perhaps the story of the "Lost Sister of Wyoming" will best illustrate what I hope. In 1778 three Delaware Indians captured Frances Slocum, who was only five years old. Her home was in the Valley of Wyoming, Pennsylvania. She learned to love the free life. She was discovered in 1835 but would never return to live with her white relatives. If our children can be given a nature education in early life we can guarantee for the future the public support of parks, playgrounds, camps, and travel, for all. Never again will we return to slavery.

A CAMP IS A CHILDREN'S COMMUNITY *

LOU AND GEORGE DONALDSON

Even the best of today's adult communities fit children poorly. They are grown-up in size and operate at grown-up tempo. More important, for educational purposes, they are operated *for* and *by* grown-ups. This means that children cannot participate; theirs is the role of submission to the mandates of adult society.

While our towns and cities grow larger and more complicated by the day, sociologists are expressing concern over the difficulty even grown-ups have in identifying themselves with their communities. Thoughtful educators are even more concerned because it follows that children, whose citizenship-learning experiences depend almost entirely on what is done in the home town, and it is even more difficult to feel "This is *my* community; I have a part in making it what it is."

*Reprinted by permission from *Camping Magazine* 27:13-14, April, 1955.

Granted that a good home is a kind of community, even the best of modern homes lacks many features of the true community. Its greatest handicap is its lack of numbers of people. Modern schools, aware of the problem, have made much progress through such innovations as student government and teacher-pupil planning but they, too, labor under real difficulties. Schools are part-time institutions—part day, part week, and part year. As such, they lack the totality which characterizes camps.

And because camps have these problems they have the unique opportunity to teach children about the problems—and some of the answers. Here children can, if camp directors will let them, face some of the puzzles which will be theirs for the rest of their lives. Here, in the controlled environment of a children's camp, communities can operate at near-ideal levels. The young citizens can come to identify themselves with a *good community*. They can participate in making it good. As only craftsmen can, they'll learn to respect their own handiwork. And, in the process campers can but become better citizens.

Too many camps have not conceived themselves as children's communities. Few, indeed, go the next step and think of themselves as citizenship laboratories. Camp people must square up to these problems. We think the first step is that of determining the characteristics this children's community should have.

Here, in all humility, are offered the nine characteristics toward which we are striving in our camp:

I. THE CAMP COMMUNITY IS SMALL

Camps, like cities, can become so large as to be incomprehensible. When a camp director finds himself resorting to various mechanical devices because people are getting in other people's way, he has already reached that point. Problems are solved in the director's office because that is the most expedient way; children are not thinking participators, they are automatons.

Camps should be small, too, because for many children they provide the first "home-leaving" experience. This experience will be made easier for the child and he will feel more secure if he can find in camp a somewhat homelike atmosphere.

Just how big is too big will be determined by many factors. Each director will have to decide for himself. For our own purposes we have assumed that our pattern simply will not operate efficiently with more than 80 campers.

II. THE CAMP COMMUNITY IS PERMISSIVE

It lets children have experiences. It encourages them to face problems. It may even leave some organizational problems unsolved in the pre-camp conference!

Permissiveness as here used does not imply anarchy or *Laissez-faire*. Rather, it implies a responsible attitude toward problem solving.

But, there's another side to the coin. The camp which truly believes in allowing children to face community problems will consciously refrain from doing anything *for* children which they can reasonably do for themselves. All those community services in which children can participate will be so organized.

III. THE CAMP COMMUNITY IS ACTIVE

Activity is probably the outstanding characteristic of child nature. Whatever else he is doing, you may be sure he'll be active! It follows, then, that the community planned for children will be one in which a great premium is placed on activity—not activity for activity's sake but thoughtful, rational, purposeful activity toward the end of better living in a better community.

IV. THE CAMP COMMUNITY IS REAL

Children are realists. They want and need no "busy work" or fake motives. Any camp which accepts its community responsibilities has plenty of real problems. All it needs to do is decide to let the campers face reality.

The camp will let children plan, work, and solve the real problems which abound in this simple community.

V. THE CAMP COMMUNITY IS IDEALISTIC

Because of its relative smallness and because it is a controlled environment, the camp should, while being real, be idealistic, too. No one would suggest that, in an attempt at reality, we duplicate in camps the conditions which breed delinquent behavior. Yet few of us envision how far we may go in the opposite direction.

Here, in a place specifically designed for children, we can apply everything we know about what is good for children. We can create a well-nigh perfect physical environment. Even more important, we can, through careful selection of personnel and good staff training, create a warmly human social environment.

VI. THE CAMP COMMUNITY IS A PLACE OF WORK

Many campers evaluate their work experience as "more fun" than anything else they do. Under wise leadership, the adult distinction between work and play simply doesn't exist for them.

The camp which, for instance, has ready-cut firewood for the campers is missing a real educational opportunity. These campers not only miss learning a valuable skill but, more important, they lose the sense of accomplishing something for the community. Woodpiles grow in camps where children begin to feel the social implication of the old woodsman's maxim: "Always leave some firewood for the next fellow."

VII. THE CAMP COMMUNITY IS A BENEVOLENT PLACE

Kindness and regard for human dignity should characterize the social climate of the camp. Here, where the child is both king and subject is the ideal opportunity to demonstrate that goodness is both good and possible.

Too many camps, almost military in philosophy, go far to the other extreme. The individual is subjugated, meekness becomes the desirable social trait, and initiative is squelched. Little wonder that these camps become "every-man-for-himself" communities. The "devil" of undiluted self-interest can easily take more than the "hindmost" in such an environment.

VIII. THE CAMP COMMUNITY IS A SPIRITUAL COMMUNITY

Here, amid the wonders and mysteries of the out-of-doors, exists an unparalleled opportunity to share with young citizens the "why" of it all. A sense of reverence, of humility, of worship comes easily because here the master plan can be seen, unobscured by the complexities of civilization. Mature leadership can make the camp a richly rewarding spiritual experience.

IX. THE CAMP COMMUNITY IS FUN

The dead serious tone of the foregoing does not imply that children's motives are the same as those of the adults who plan camping experiences for them. Children have always gone to camp for fun. We suspect they always will. And there's nothing wrong with it.

Adults go wrong in planning for children when they assume that fun is purpose rather than method. Wise camp leaders will exploit the fun impulses of children for all they're worth. And, if they're truly good leaders, they'll have fun too!

ADVENTURE IN OUTDOOR EDUCATION *

JULIAN W. SMITH

It is natural for children to seek the outdoors! Filled with energy, curiosity, and adventure, most boys and girls take to outdoor activities like ducks to water. They are not too unlike adults in this respect, for untold millions of Americans are thronging into the open spaces. Some of them are merely trying to escape from the fast tempo of modern urban living, and others are searching for recreation and adventure. The relationship of man to his physical world is a fundamental factor in human living, and an understanding and appreciation of the outdoors should be the heritage of every human being.

WHAT IT IS

Outdoor education is becoming a familiar term these days. Like other educational terminology, "outdoor education" has different shades of meaning to different people. Applied to school and college programs, outdoor education includes those direct learning experiences that involve enjoying, interpreting, and wisely using the natural environment in achieving, at least in part, the purposes of education. With this concept, the outdoors constitutes a laboratory—a learning climate for the things which can be learned best outside of classrooms.

Outdoor education is a logical development of the emerging community school and the college and is designed to serve all the people. The outdoors is one of the rich community resources that should be used in a broad educational program where a great variety of learning experiences related to the physical environment and natural resources can take place.

An analysis of school and college curriculums would indicate that many of the learnings considered essential could be achieved through outdoor education. The general goals of education, such as self-realization, human relationships, and civic responsibility are readily discernible in outdoor education, with specific implications for a command of the fundamental processes—health, citizenship, worthy use of leisure time, vocations, and ethical character.

No single department, subject matter, field, or individual interest has a corner on the outdoors. In reach of nearly every school and college in the United States

*Reprinted by permission of the publisher, the American Association of Health, Physical Education, and Recreation, from the *Journal of Health, Physical Education, Recreation* 26:8-9, 18, May-June, 1955.

will be found open spaces, parks, camps, recreation areas, sanctuaries, museums, zoos, vacant lots, and other types of public and private lands and facilities which can be used in the process of education. Many schools and colleges now have, or could acquire, larger field campuses, camps, and special land areas to use for nature laboratories, in addition to the community resources already available. The park-school and extensive school sites are good examples of planning for outdoor education. The new designs of elementary and secondary school buildings which make it easier to use adjacent lands are significant developments.

ILLUSTRATIONS

Outdoor education in schools and colleges, in its simplest form, occurs when a teacher or leader and a group of "would-be" learners take off to the outdoors for purposes related to accepted objectives. It may be an elementary class that goes outside the classroom to see the first heralds of spring; a class off for a week of school camping; a physical education lesson in archery, casting, or shooting; or a college class in zoology that wishes to delve deeply into the scientific aspects of nature. Some common avenues of outdoor education are described briefly as illustrations:

1. *Classroom-related field experiences,* where the trip into the outdoors becomes a "lab" period related to planned activities in curriculum. They may be short trips on the school grounds or extended experiences in connection with a special field, such as science, physical education, conservation, recreation.

2. *School farm, forest, and garden programs,* where the school or college has access to lands that will serve as laboratories. School farms can offer general instructional opportunities as well as a place for agricultural practices. In some areas, the school farm program may include the camping idea where children have opportunities to live together, observe and care for farm animals, participate in gardening, and roam over the wooded "back forty." As well as being a laboratory for science, gardening may be one of the most practical activities in outdoor education because of its recreational values.

3. *School camping*—one of the newest and most sensational developments in outdoor education—is the use of camps for an extended educational program by schools and colleges, whereby democratic social living is combined with learning about the natural environment and adventures in outdoor living. In school camping, children and teachers, together, have direct learning experiences related to many areas of the curriculum. Nearly one-half of the states now report programs ranging from pilot efforts to year-round operation. An increasing number of colleges have acquired camps whereby students have camping opportunities combined with teacher and leadership training.

4. *Day activities in outdoor areas,* sometimes called day camping, is another pattern used by schools, colleges, recreation agencies, and youth-serving groups.

Classes and organized groups have opportunities for field study combined with outdoor recreational skills.

5. *Outing and club activities,* usually considered a part of the curricular offerings, provide for organized special-interest groups. While usually conducted on an informal basis, such activities may be related to areas such as physical education, recreation, science, and others. Activities often include camping, hiking, and other interests of students, such as archery, shooting, fishing, arts and crafts, and bird study.

6. *Casting and fishing* are becoming more popular activities in schools and colleges. Fishing and allied activities, such as skish, spinning, bait and fly casting, which more nearly may be called universal sports, are particularly significant in view of increased leisure time and the desire to seek the lakes and streams so prevalent in many parts of the country. Adaptable to all age groups, casting and fishing are closely related to camping, conservation, and outdoor living skills. These activities fit well in the physical education, recreation, and adult education programs and have implications for science and other fields. Like other parts of an outdoor education program, training (including actual participation) is needed in order that those interested can derive the maximum benefits from the outdoor living that accompanies them. One needs only to observe the number of fishing licenses sold to realize the importance of this sport in American life today.

7. *Shooting and hunting,* like casting and fishing, are extensive and wholesome leisure-time activities in the American culture. More than 13 million hunting licenses are sold in the United States. More maximum satisfactions and values accrue in shooting and hunting when there is training in gun handling and safety, marksmanship, conservation, outdoor skills and woodsmanship, care and use of public property, etc. Such activities as riflery, pistol shooting, skeet, trap shooting, and archery, appropriately designed for the various age groups, fit well into physical education, clubs, recreation, adult education, and conservation activities in schools, colleges, and community organizations. In Michigan and New Hampshire, for example, state-wide institutes and clinics are conducted for school and college staff members in an effort to help develop sound educational activities centered around the natural interest of students in hunting and shooting. Assisting in these training ventures are such organizations and departments as the National Rifle Association, the Sporting Arms and Ammunition Manufacturers' Institute, state departments of conservation and education, colleges, sportsmen's clubs, and police.

8. *Boating, sailing, canoeing, and other water activities* are becoming increasingly popular in some sections of the country and provide wholesome recreational pursuits for many people. These sports are also related to other interests such as fishing, hunting, and traveling, and should be related to safety, conservation, and outdoor skills.

9. *Winter sports,* including skating, skiing, tobogganing, snowshoeing, and others are gaining in popularity in states where the climate permits. Schools and colleges located in winter sports areas should consider offering appropriate training for participation in such activities. Like others mentioned, they are related to other outdoor skills and often can be included in programs.

10. *Community adult education and recreation* are offering a wide variety of activities in keeping pace with the public's great surge of interest in many outdoor activities. Many of the ones mentioned elsewhere in this article apply to adults, but others can be added that center about hobbies, such as making outdoor equipment and the training for advanced skills in outdoor sports.

NEED FOR IT

Outdoor education, broadly conceived, includes voluntary group and individual activities, with or without professional leadership, as would be provided by schools, colleges, and other agencies. Camping, hiking, traveling, hunting, fishing, mountain climbing, orienteering, hosteling, exploring, collecting, and nature study, are only a few activities that attract great numbers of people. Millions use national, state, and local parks and other public areas; others visit museums, zoos, sanctuaries, and botanical gardens, or just drive in the open country to observe natural beauty and seek other satisfactions in the outdoors.

Many of this generation do not have the skills and appreciations necessary to get the greatest satisfactions from these pursuits. This is a challenge to education in a day when greater numbers of citizens who have longer weekends and paid vacations are turning to the outdoors for recreation and adventure.

LEADERSHIP

To provide outdoor education as envisioned here, colleges and universities will need to intensify their efforts in pre-service and in-service training. More actual and direct experiences in the outdoors will be needed, along with methods and techniques adapted to teaching in informal situations. It is fortunate that there is already a sizable pool of source leadership available in agencies concerned with the management of natural resources, schools and colleges, and in many national, state, and local organizations. Much technical service can be supplied by business and industry that make and distribute sports equipment. Good teachers and leaders find the guiding of the learning process not unlike that employed in modern classrooms.

The essential features of training for outdoor education seem, therefore, to include: (1) an understanding of human beings and how they learn; (2) the ability to interpret the outdoors as a climate for learning; and (3) the necessary skills and techniques to teach and guide in an informal setting.

Much can be done, and is being done, to modify and expand present curricular offerings to accomplish these things. An all-campus and multi-disciplinary approach is needed, involving all appropriate fields and departments, to provide adequate training. In-service and pre-service preparation must include realistic outdoor field experiences with children and teachers in communities. There should be much less separation of theory, methods, and practice than is usually the case. New developments are already under way in several colleges and universities that will provide teacher and leadership training in outdoor education as an important part of general education.

ROLE OF AAHPER

While outdoor education is the responsibility of many educational fields, it becomes evident that there are unique implications for health, physical education and recreation. In many instances, teachers and leaders in these related fields will be asked to assume leadership along with colleagues in science, elementary education, and other special areas in initiating and developing school and college programs of outdoor education. The American Association for Health, Physical Education, and Recreation, for example, has recognized this responsibility for many years through its divisions and sections, through publications, audio-visual aids, and by providing consultant services to schools and colleges. One of the newest and most promising developments is the recently constituted Council on Equipment and Supplies. Following the business, industry, and education cooperative pattern, programs are under way which will intensify the Association's efforts in outdoor education. Other departments of the NEA and several professional organizations concerned with camping, recreation, and conservation also are giving leadership.

FUTURE

Outdoor education appears to be one of the significant educational developments of the mid-century. It grows out of the needs of the people and contributes to better living. While it has specialized aspects, it must remain in the context of general education and thereby make its unique contribution to the accepted objectives of education. Only in this manner can the outdoors have its full effect in sane living and make it possible for man to find his true relationship to the universe and the eternal verities.

WHAT ARE THE ISSUES IN CAMPING AND OUTDOOR EDUCATION? CAMP-CENTERED? SCHOOL-CENTERED? *

R. P. BRIMM

Camping and outdoor education are not new in American schools. According to National Education Association Research Bulletin No. 4, one of the earliest camps operated as a part of a school program was in a private school in Washington, Connecticut, in 1861. The earliest public school camping venture was in Dubuque, Iowa, in 1912. But school camping's growth has been relatively slow and is still in its developmental stages in most sections of the United States.

In school camping, as in other areas of educational practice, there are disagreements which should be considered by schools now operating camps and by schools which are planning such programs. Outdoor education has not yet been hampered by long-established tradition. Schools are free to develop the type of program they feel is the best and most adaptable to their own situation. However, just as there should be a basic philosophy to direct the growth of any program, so there should be one to direct the growth of outdoor education. Existing school camping programs seem to lean toward one or the other of two extremes: "Camp Centered" or "School Centered." The two might be described as shown in the accompanying box.

Examination of the characteristics of these two approaches to school camping brings out basic differences in philosophy. For the educator the major problem is designing a program which will do the job best and provide the most valuable learning situations.

At present, a high percentage of school camping programs lean toward the "camp-centered" point of view. This is understandable because leadership in these programs has come largely from persons whose experiences have been with summer camping programs sponsored by agencies and organizations other than public schools.

The fact that the camp-centered program is the prevailing pattern does not necessarily mean that it is the better plan for school camps. If a school camp is to become an integral part of a school program, it must be tied closely to classroom work and serve as a supplement to learning situations developed by teachers.

*Reprinted by permission from *Camping Magazine* 31:14-15, January, 1959.

SCHOOL-CENTERED

1. Camping experiences are evaluated on their contribution to the work of the classroom.
2. Experiences are planned in the classroom. Practical applications are possible in the camp so the experiences are more meaningful.
3. The program is centered around "classes" in mathematics, science, English, art, and other classroom subjects of the school. Time is given to recreational activities but this is not stressed.
4. The classroom teacher operates the program with the help of resource persons in much the same manner as a resource person is brought into the classroom.
5. Pupils are housed in comfortable cabins and their food is prepared by hired personnel. Occasional "cook-outs" give limited experiences in living in the open but this aspect of the camp is not considered highly important.

CAMP-CENTERED

1. Camping experiences supplement the school curriculum with new and different experiences which are not directly connected with the classroom work.
2. Experiences are not planned to bring out specific learnings but valuable concepts are gained by incidental experiences.
3. Recreational type activities dominate the program with "nature study" groups, "crafts" groups and other activities which contribute to academic learnings but are not named to parallel the courses offered in school.
4. A trained staff in outdoor education operates the program with the pupils and teachers participating.
5. Much time is devoted to living. Primitive living, including out-of-door cooking and building shelters, take a large portion of the time. One of the major objectives of the camping experiences is recapturing some of the aspects of our pioneer ancestry.

The classroom organization of our public schools is at the heart of the instructional program. This does not imply that all learning must take place within classroom walls, but it does mean that a systematic approach to learning experiences must be organized in an atmosphere with some degree of formality. Without systematic planning there may be many duplications of experiences and, worse, omissions of valuable learning situations. School camps must be evaluated upon their contribution to the classroom program. "Nature study," "crafts" and similar terms label the groups in the traditional camp program.

There is no reason why the activity groups of a school camp cannot be "classes" in science, art and mathematics. Experiences can be made just as attractive under school names as under other names. The classroom learnings become more meaningful if directly identified with the experiences of the camp both in name and content.

In reality a school camping program is an extensive field trip designed to supplement the learnings of the many subject matter areas of the school. Camp programs offer many excellent learning experiences which may supplement any school subject, and teachers should take full advantage of the opportunities available.

A field trip emanating from a class in science is much more valuable to classroom work if it is well planned to fit into the material being covered in class. Background information covered in the classroom makes the excursion experiences much more understandable and complete. Likewise, thorough examination of specimens brought back to the classroom and a discussion of the experiences make the excusion more valuable in terms of understandings and retention of learnings. In any situation, unplanned experiences occur and contribute to learning. But, in the classroom, on excursions, or in camp most worthwhile learning situations will come from a planned sequence of events.

If school camp is to contribute to classroom instruction, camp experiences must supplement work carried on in classroom. Prior to camp a body of subject matter should be introduced into the classroom, with plans to use the camp period for actual problems which supplement the materials studied. After camp, the experiences will be carried back to the classroom and the unit of instruction continued in a meaningful manner.

Under this concept of school camping, the teacher must direct the program. Out-of-door specialists can be of great value in helping organize programs and acting as resource persons in much the same manner as a resource person is used in a classroom. However, the major responsibility for school camp program must be in the hands of the teacher. He cannot turn the class over to a camp staff and expect to take back to school a group of experiences which will adequately supplement his classroom work.

School camps can make maximum contributions to school work if organized with the instructional program of the school in view. The "pioneering" type of camp often requires so much time in living that other organized objectives of the program are lost. Excessive time spent in building shelters and preparing food over open fires may detract from other aspects of the program. Duplication of, for example, the Boy Scout or other agency program in a school camp is hardly justifiable. The various agencies which operate camping programs have specific objectives, and school camps should have a different set to prevent duplication.

Every effort should be made to build a camp program which will be broad enough to cover the instructional areas of the school. However, it is better to delete a subject matter area in the camp program than to set up artificial experiences which will contribute little. It is also wise to omit areas which cannot be tied into the school program. For example, if the art teacher is not available for the camp program it would be better not to have art in the camp. An art program, based on the use of native materials, can be very valuable to the classroom program in art, but if it cannot be used by the teacher of art then its value to the total school program is limited.

It is true that some teachers cannot adapt themselves or their programs to the out-of-door situations. But a good teacher can take her program into any situation where learning experiences are available, and camp offers unlimited opportunities for valuable experiences in all areas of instruction.

Schools do have textbook teachers who cannot go beyond the materials of a book, and plans for camp programs must recognize this fact. It would be just as foolish to set up a camp program for this teacher as it would be to furnish supplementary books for her use. If she cannot go beyond the textbook, then the reference books would never be used and camp experiences would contribute nothing to her instructional program. On the other hand, teachers who can see the applications of their instructional program, and who can use resource persons effectively, can do a good job in school camp.

Many school camp programs fail to continue and many fail to start because patrons of the school will not support a program based on narrow, specialized interests. Programs based entirely on recreation, music or nature study, for instance, would probably appeal to a limited number of persons. If a school camping program is to be sold to the public it must be based on the value of its contribution to the instructional program of the school and must be as broad and all-inclusive as possible.

A CASE FOR OUTDOOR EDUCATION *

DONALD R. HAMMERMAN

That outdoor education has come of age is demonstrated by the fact that an increasing number of institutions of higher education have incorporated outdoor learning experiences into their professional education sequence. School camping, or *resident outdoor education*, has made a significant impact upon public education across the nation, with the number of "outdoor school" programs continuing to develop at a rapid rate.

Since 1947, outdoor education has developed from an experiment in camping

* *The Clearing House*, September, 1963, reproduced by permission.

education[1] to the place where over 800 school districts in practically all of the United States participate annually in a resident outdoor education experience.[2] Outdoor education has obviously permeated American public school education to a far greater degree than is commonly recognized. In such school systems as Battle Creek (Michigan), Cleveland Heights (Ohio), and Los Angeles and San Diego (California), outdoor education is, and for a number of years has been, firmly entrenched as an integral part of the total educational program. The number of school systems utilizing the concept of the extended classroom as another avenue through which curricular goals may be realized continues to grow each year. Outdoor education as a curriculum experience has been influenced by the same changing cultural conditions, social forces, and educational concepts that were instrumental in determining the role to be played by the contemporary public school.

THE FUNDAMENTAL TASK

The only rationale upon which justification for outdoor education can be maintained is the fact that it helps to fulfill, in a way that "indoor instruction" cannot, the aims of education. The educational systems of this nation would be hard put to justify operating camplike programs in direct conflict with the services presently performed by other agencies and institutions. The outdoor school, on the other hand, can be justified as an extension of the ordinary school facility, whose purposes and aims are in keeping with the aims of education.

What fundamental purpose, then, should resident outdoor education serve? It should provide the setting for curricular experiences that cannot be offered, or achieved as readily, within the confines of the school building. School studies are very often far removed from reality. The outdoor school setting provides the natural environment where pupils have the opportunity to come to grips with reality—where close, first-hand observation, independent investigation, analysis of data, and problem solving are the order of the day.

The American public school ought to provide an opportunity to learn the ways of democracy by living it. Very little living actually takes place in our classrooms today. The socialization values which our educative institutions purport to foster should be implemented through realistic practice in the total-living situation that is provided by the resident outdoor school experience.

Another fundamental task of outdoor education is to provide purposeful work experience for youngsters. The transition from an agrarian society to a

[1] For a full report on this pilot project see New York City Board of Education, *Extending Education Through Camping,* Outdoor Education Association, Inc., 1948.

[2] Julian W. Smith, Director of the Outdoor Education Project for the American Association for Health, Physical Education, and Recreation, in conference materials distributed May, 1962.

highly industrialized nation, along with accompanying urbanization, has placed the modern-day pupil in a situation where there is minimum opportunity for purposeful work experience. The modern home has long ceased to fill this need. Nor can the school, under ordinary circumstances, fulfill such a need. The unique setting of the resident outdoor school, however, with its emphasis on self-responsibility, helps to satisfy the basic need that man feels to perform useful work.

POSSIBLE APPROACHES

During the past decade there has been a strong tendency for some outdoor education programs to acquire a high degree of organization and standardization. This is a move in the wrong direction. Granted, outdoor education should be an integral part of the curriculum. Likewise, outdoor learning activities should be closely related to the ongoing, indoor instructional program of the schools. In fact there should be no significant distinction between education and outdoor education. The distinction, if in fact it exists at all, is merely one of setting, wherein certain facets of education may be more readily facilitated. This distinction, no matter how slight it may appear to be, is nevertheless of fundamental importance.

Outdoor education should complement the ongoing instructional program of the school. It should not become school-like, however. When the structure and content of the outdoor school curriculum become too much like those of the indoor school curriculum, so there is virtually no difference, outdoor education will have expired. Only by retaining its individuality can it continue to enrich school curriculums. Educators should resist the tendency to standardize and regiment outdoor school curricular experiences. There should, in fact, be a concerted effort to preserve the sphere of experimentation within which early school camping ventures operated. Solving the problems of daily outdoor living, for example, is one of many possibilities that may constitute the core of the outdoor school curriculum. Various learning activities grow out of the problems faced in living and working together in a miniature community. Furthermore, these experiences of living and learning in the outdoor school relate to the overall goals of education. The general objectives of education, as defined by the Mid-Century Committee on Outcomes in Elementary Education, fall in the areas of (1) physical development, health, body care; (2) individual social and emotional development; (3) the social world; (4) social relations; (5) ethical behavior, standards, values; (6) the physical world; (7) communication; (8) quantitative relationships; and (9) esthetic development.[3]

---

[3]Chester W. Harris (ed.) *Encyclopedia of Educational Research* (New York: The Macmillan Company, 1960), p. 431.

Outdoor education is simply one of an infinite number of approaches through which the achievement of these goals may be facilitated. As a teaching-learning medium it cuts across subject matter areas and is interdisciplinary in nature. School camping, or resident outdoor education, is one means which may be employed to help carry out the curricular aims of the school. No modern educational system can afford to ignore this frontier of curriculum development. Outdoor education provides an avenue for facilitating, complementing, and enriching instruction without which no system of education can truly be said to be complete.

WHERE WE HAVE BEEN—WHAT WE ARE— WHAT WE WILL BECOME *
The Taft Campus Outdoor Education Award Lecture, 1970

JULIAN W. SMITH

WHERE WE HAVE BEEN

To trace the history of outdoor education from its beginnings would be an impossibility. For significant developments in education usually are results of many events rooted in the past. In the case of outdoor education, one cannot determine its origin in terms of a single event—even a series of happenings. Some writers have gone as far back as Socrates and Plato; others have suggested private school programs in the late 1800s which conducted "outing trips." Still others would say that summer recreation programs in California or out-of-classroom activities in the Atlanta Public Schools in the 1920s were forerunners of one pattern of outdoor education, namely, resident outdoor schools.

It seems more likely that many influences—educational philosophers, innovative educators and special programs and events—contributed to outdoor education as we know it now. In Michigan, for example, the Tappan Junior High School of Ann Arbor, sponsored excursions which terminated in a two- or three-day tent camping experience on school-owned property in the northern part of Michigan. The Cadillac (Michigan) Public Schools acquired a large acreage of forest lands and a camp. Both of these programs occurred in the 1930s during a period when L. B. Sharp was pioneering "camping education" in connection

*Reprinted with permission from *Journal of Outdoor Education* Vol. 2, Winter, 1968, pp. 3-6.

with Life Camps, Inc. In this same period, however, the W. K. Kellogg Foundation in Battle Creek, Michigan, was experimenting with resident camp experiences for what were then called disadvantaged children in socio-economic status and in health.

With these influences and countless others, it took a single event—circumstantial if not accidental—to set in motion the first resident outdoor school conducted on a year-round basis and as an integral part of the school curriculum, to open the era of outdoor education which has developed rapidly in the last 35 years. The event that served as the benchmark for the resident outdoor school as a pattern of outdoor education was a program at the Clear Lake Camp near Battle Creek, Michigan, which through the cooperation of the W. K. Kellogg Foundation involved three Michigan Schools—Lakeview of Battle Creek, Decatur, and Otsego—using the facility during the school year 1940-41. Students of grades 4 through 12 were involved and each group was at the Clear Lake Camp for a two-week period. From this time on, what has been called school camping, and is now generally known as the resident outdoor school, spread in Michigan and extended to other parts of the country.

The purpose of this account, however, is not to trace the history of the many individual programs that have developed throughout the United States, but to look at the periods of growth and their characteristics that have made outdoor education one of the significant developments in education during this century. For these purposes, the account will be in brief chapters with only approximate dates to indicate the time.

Chapter I

The period prior to 1940, which has been briefly described, would span a long period, even if limited to the United States. This development in education has had several labels, such as field and camping trips, outings, recreation, camping education. It is certain that organized camping had an important influence on the beginnings of outdoor education, coupled with the educational philosophies of Dewey, Kilpatrick, and others whose writings and leadership gave rise to "progressive" education.

Chapter II

The period 1940-1950 witnessed the growth of resident outdoor schools, including such well-known programs as in the Battle Creek, Michigan, area, conducted at the Clear Lake Camp; San Diego (California) City-County Camp Commission with a program at Cuyamaca; Tyler, Texas; Cleveland Heights,

Ohio; and others in Michigan, California, New York, Washington, and elsewhere. During this period, particularly in the late forties, the term "outdoor education" was used more frequently, largely, however, with reference to resident outdoor schools. A number of significant events occurred between 1940 and 1950 which influenced the nature and scope of outdoor education, such as the first state legislation in Michigan which permitted school districts to acquire and operate camps as a part of a school program; grants of funds to several state departments of education to encourage the development of outdoor education; the cooperative project in Michigan with the State Department of Education, the State Department of Conservation and the W. K. Kellogg Foundation, which had a great impact on resident outdoor schools; experimental programs for secondary and older youth; and a National Conference on Community School Camping in Michigan in 1949, which gave initial impetus for a number of well-known programs such as occurred at Northern Illinois University and Southern Illinois University.

The nature and growth of outdoor education was still influenced somewhat by organized camping, but developments in curriculum, National Camp, and programs in Michigan made possible by the Kellogg Foundation were strong forces. Near the end of this period the surge of interest in all forms of outdoor pursuits began to add a broader dimension to the concept of outdoor education.

Chapter III

The decade of the fifties was a period of rapid growth of resident outdoor schools and a greater emphasis on other forms of outdoor learning such as the use of school sites and other outdoor areas for out-of-classroom experiences. In 1954, the Outdoor Education Project of the American Association for Health, Physical Education, and Recreation was initiated and gave added thrust to outdoor education and broadened the concept of the term to include the teaching of skills, attitudes and appreciations necessary for satisfying outdoor pursuits. The Outdoor Education Project was a significant development in outdoor education since it helped keep pace with the growing interest in outdoor education and encompassed more aspects of the school curriculum, particularly in physical education and recreation. Education in and for the outdoors came to be a more common interpretation of the term. Another important development in the 1950s was the expansion of efforts in teacher and leadership preparation, both in-service and pre-service. A National Conference on Teacher Education for Outdoor Education, held at the Clear Lake Camp in Michigan in 1953, had considerable impact on teacher education as did the Outdoor Education Project which emphasized the interdisciplinary approach to outdoor education.

It was during this period of growth in outdoor teacher education that the Taft Field Campus was established by Northern Illinois University under the leadership of President Leslie Holmes. He had attended the National Conference on Community School Camping in Michigan and soon thereafter began to develop Lorado Taft's art colony which was named the Taft Field Campus. Mr. Paul Harrison was the first director of the Taft program and was instrumental in securing a large and experienced staff, several members of which had been associated with other well-known programs throughout the United States. Don Hammerman was employed as program director and later became head of the Department of Outdoor Teacher Education. George Donaldson, formerly director of the Clear Lake Camp in Michigan and later at Tyler, Texas, joined the staff, as did Morris Wiener who was formerly a member of the staff at Tyler. Douglas Wade, once associated with the New Jersey State School of Conservation; Oswald Goering, currently chairman of the AAHPER Council on Outdoor Education; John Hug, formerly of the Clear Lake Camp staff, are among other well-known leaders in outdoor education who became members of the Taft staff in more recent years.

Chapter IV

This period (1960-68) showed growth in a wide variety of outdoor education activities, particularly the use of outdoor settings by elementary schools, teaching of outdoor skills, and the increase in the in-service and pre-service preparation of teachers and leaders. A large number of summer workshops were established by colleges and universities and several institutions developed programs of graduate study. Examples include Indiana University, Pennsylvania State University, State University of New York Colleges, Northern Colorado University at Greeley, and New York University. The climate for the expansion of outdoor education programs and the development of facilities became much more favorable nationally due to a number of influences such as the Outdoor Recreation Resources Review Commission report, the Bureau of Outdoor Recreation, federal legislation dealing with conservation and outdoor recreation, and a number of federal programs in education such as the Elementary and Secondary Education Act (Title III of this act was responsible for the development of more than 50 outdoor education programs of varying types, many of which continued after the end of federal funding). This period would be characterized as one in which outdoor education had wide acceptance as a development in education—with many new patterns unfolding, gains in the number of land areas and facilities, and the emergence of many new leaders. An example of national leadership was the creation of the Council on Outdoor Education and Camping by the AAHPER which already has a membership of over 300 leaders throughout the United States. Three national conferences on outdoor education have been sponsored by the Association.

Chapter V

A fifth chapter, beginning in the late 1960s, opens wide avenues for outdoor education because of the increasing concern and attention now being given to environmental quality. In the context of the school, grades K-12, outdoor education is becoming the approach for the development of attitudes and behavior through direct learning experiences with the natural environment. While there is a rash of new terminology and some "name changing," the simple yet sound concept of outdoor education outreaches any one emphasis or goal, for its strength lies in diversity and its reach cuts across the entire curriculum. Outdoor education centers on human growth and learning as well as helping individuals to improve the physical world.

What We Are

Outdoor education has become a development in curriculum—an emphasis in education—designed to both enrich and extend the program of the school. Aptly described as education *in* and education *for* the outdoors, outdoor education now takes many forms which can only be briefly described here.

1. *Outdoor-related classroom activities* and units of study using available outdoor materials and resources to enrich and extend learning opportunities. Weather study, bird and animal life, erosion and pollution, art from outdoor scenes, aquariums, rock collections are examples of the use of outdoor life and resources in the regular elementary and secondary school programs.

2. *The use of the school site and other outdoor areas as laboratories* to extend the classroom. Field trips and outdoor projects are used to help achieve classroom objectives and effect learnings often impossible in the bounds of four walls. The use of nature trails, study of animal and plant life near the school, observation and study of aquatic life in nearby ponds and streams, creative outdoor play areas are examples of the use of outdoor laboratories.

3. *Resident outdoor schools,* in which students and their teachers use camp settings for learning opportunities achieved best in a camp community and outdoor laboratory. This is one of the most sensational and effective forms of outdoor education and offers extensive opportunities for learnings centering around social living, healthful living, work experiences, outdoor skills and interests, and the application of many of the school's educational objectives and

purposes. On school time and as a regular part of the curriculum, the outdoor school serves to motivate and vitalize learning and contributes greatly to the development of good human relationships, better understanding between students and teachers, and opportunities for democratic living. The outdoor school thus achieves a greater dimension by combining outdoor learning with active participation in problem-solving in a "child's community." The potentials for learning, aptly termed "teachable moments," in such settings are rich and almost limitless.

4. *The teaching of outdoor skills,* usually in physical education, recreation and club programs, and the development of attitudes and appreciations through many activities in the curriculum are important aspects of outdoor education. This aspect of outdoor education is paramount in educating a citizenry for obtaining maximum satisfactions from outdoor interests and pursuits, and in becoming responsible citizens in the protection of and improvement of our outdoor resources.

5. *Work-learn experiences in outdoor areas* for secondary school youth, such as the improvement of the land, forest and game management, construction of facilities, conservation projects to improve the natural environment, and learning outdoor skills and interests are challenging and effective forms of outdoor education. Somewhat reminiscent of the CCC of the 1930s a number of school-sponsored programs of this type are proving effective, particularly for potential dropouts who do not thrive on the academic diet of the traditional secondary school.

Outdoor education thus is anchored in the basic principles of learning and the best curriculum practices. The reaches of outdoor education are encompassed in the basic objectives of education and are made possible through direct and concrete experiences which fall in the cognitive, affective and motor performance domains of education. Outdoor education may well make its unique contribution to the affective domain—behavior changes.

Some of the current outcomes of outdoor education as enumerated by many experienced teachers and administrators involved in outdoor-related learning include:

— better self-concept (self-realization)
— awareness of and respect for the natural environment
— adventure in learning
— communications
— behavioral changes (social; teacher-student and student to student; care and protection and improvement of the physical environment)
— lifelong interests and skills for the constructive use of time
— creativity
— development of the inner man (spiritual)

What We Will Be

Outdoor education as it is developing is an integral part of the educative process contributing to learning and to teaching—extending the curriculum to encompass all of the outdoor learning environments in the community. There will be less concern about the label—for outdoor education at its best is good education. To circumscribe outdoor education—to separate its many teachable moments from the learning areas which characterize its diversity would render this new and fresh approach to learning less effective and would place it in the category of other "special" kinds of education. Wrapping the rich learning opportunities in and for the outdoors in a package, whatever the label, will blight what has become a force to make education more relevant for today. Outdoor education in the future must make its major contributions to the growth and development of the human organism so that people and nations can live together in peace and help man live in harmony with his physical universe. As for man's relationship to nature, R. Thomas Tanner has said, "We must understand, even more profoundly than did Bacon, that 'nature is only to be commanded by obeying her.' If we insist upon making a fight of it, we must expect to lose."[1]

A guide for living from the Christian ethic and paraphrased from a verse of scripture from the Bible might well be: "For what shall it profit a man if he gain a quality environment and lose the quality of his own life."

---

[1] R. Thomas Tanner, "The Science Curriculum: Unfinished Business for an Unfinished Country," *Phi Delta Kappan*, LI:7 (March 1970), p. 355.

Chapter two
Historical Perspective

INTRODUCTION

Outdoor education is part and parcel of the contemporary history of education. Most of the early ventures in camping education were geared to a philosophy of "roughing it." Little attempt was made to relate the "camping out" experience to the school curriculum. Later, as forward-looking educators began to recognize the educational potential of outdoor education, greater effort was made to tie in the outdoor learning activities with classroom studies. The enactment of special legislation in some states was instrumental in giving a boost to the development of outdoor education facilities.

During the developmental years of outdoor education three programs emerged as dominant influences. These were L. B. Sharp's National Camp and Life Camp operations; the Battle Creek program at Clear Lake, Michigan; and the Tyler Texas Outdoor Laboratory.

Three basic developmental periods characterized the growth of outdoor education in the United States. These were the Period of Inception (1930—1939), the Period of Experimentation (1940—1952), and the Period of Standardization (1953—   ).

The Period of Inception occurred at a time when the public schools were broadening their objectives to educate the "whole child." Thus the total-living experience of camping education was viewed as an ideal laboratory for expanding the functions of the school.

The experimental school camp ventures that characterized the second stage of development were indicative of the growing concern among educators to seek new means for enriching curriculum in the broadest sense. By the middle fifties outdoor education was well entrenched in a number of school systems across the country and, in fact, to a certain extent, had become quite standardized.

During the three stages of development, resident outdoor education underwent a fundamental change. This was a transition from extracurricular, summertime activity, to a fully accepted function of the ongoing instructional program of the schools. In the process, resident outdoor education became less camplike and more closely patterned to the school program. The outdoor school curriculum shifted in focus from the necessary routines of camp living to a closer alliance with the subject matter areas of the school curriculum. Pre-camp preparation in the classroom and post-camp follow-up activities were considered as a unified continuum. Thus school camping, or resident outdoor education, became an integral part of the school curriculum.

A concomitant of most maturing movements is the tendency toward higher and more complex levels of organization. The general trend to standardization was brought about, in part, by the move to organize outdoor education at both the state and national level. California, Minnesota, New Jersey, and New York, for example, have formed their own state associations for outdoor education. Other states, while they do not have a formal state organization, have established advisory councils for outdoor education.

Two national organizations have exerted prime influence on the continuing development of outdoor education. The late L. B. Sharp founded the Outdoor Education Association, Inc., in 1951. The American Association for Health, Physical Education, and Recreation established the Outdoor Education Project under the direction of Julian Smith in 1955. The Outdoor Education and Camping Council of AAHPER was formed in 1965. In the West, the Association for Environmental and Outdoor Education was incorporated in 1954.

These developments are indicative of the expanding role of the school in contemporary society. Outdoor education has found a place in general education; its history should be chronicled.

SOME HISTORICAL BACKGROUNDS OF CAMPING*

L. B. SHARP AND E. DeALTON PARTRIDGE

The idea of learning in the out-of-doors is not new. Indeed, learning by direct experience accompanied by personal instruction was the customary method of passing on human culture long before there were classrooms, libraries, texts, or professional teachers. And this early type of education must have been effective, because it worked. The culture it carried was passed on from one generation to another, and the priceless gems of human knowledge that grew into our science, art, and industry remained sufficiently intact to be passed on and added to through the centuries.

Even after the educational process grew to such magnitude as to require the development of specialists who earned their livelihood as teachers it was by no means necessary to confine all teaching inside the four walls. Many of the great teachers of history never thought of retreating inside a building. Christ, Aristotle, Socrates, and others managed to make a profound impression upon their followers without the advantage of rows of seats, blackboards, or a lectern behind which to preserve professorial dignity.

Perhaps every generation has had its vocal advocates of more realism in education. It is almost as if it were following the lines of least resistance to become more verbose. The study of books, the delivering of lectures, the assignment of rote learning all take less imagination and effort on the part of the teacher than to organize experiences around actual life situations. All through human history, education without constant vigilance has fallen into this pattern. Pestalozzi rebelled against it and set up his own unique method of learning by living. Rousseau rebelled against it, too, on a philosophical level. Others saw in

*Reprinted by permission of the publisher and the National Association of Secondary School Principals from *The Bulletin of the National Association of Secondary School Principals* 31:15-20, May, 1947.

his writings a battle cry to carry youngsters away from artificial, meaningless routines into the fresh air of realism.

In America the protest against shallow verbalism and rote learning has been more than an individual matter. It has taken the form of an organized movement which grew out of our natural heritage of outdoor living into a basic philosophy of education that has assumed extensive proportions.

It is only natural, perhaps, that organized camping as a method of youth education should have been conceived, born and grown into maturity in America. The underlying reasons for this are to be found in the American frontier tradition, the natural outdoor resources on the one hand and the degree of rapid industrialization on the other.

The romance of the out-of-doors, the challenge of hewing a home and livelihood out of the wilderness, the frontier tradition of "roughing it" are a recent part of our national life. When the Pilgrims landed in New England they went forth as campers to conquer a hostile and uninviting wilderness. As subsequent waves of settlers came, the frontier was pushed ever back. Young men went forth to carve their destinies in the yawning unknown to the west.

Cities grew up, of course, and many people lived their entire lives in these urban areas. But the wilderness and the frontier were always beyond the horizon, beckoning the young and adventuresome. The lore of the frontier wafted through the cities and helped to wash them clean of pretense and artificiality. Self-reliance and ability to stand on one's own feet were part and parcel of the American way of life.

But along with the active and expanding frontier there was growing up another phase of our western civilization that was to have a profound effect upon all modes of life. This great change in American life was coming in the wake of the industrial revolution. Out of the great wealth of this continent, combined with the inventive and organization genius of its people, was coming an industrial age that had no precedent in human history. Transportation and production methods were making it possible for more people to live in a smaller space than ever before. Centralization of population and goods was the inevitable result of this trend. While the frontier was moving westward, the East was becoming urbanized with all of the attendant ills of proverty, squalor and artificiality.

Education, which had been established as a responsibility and necessity of a democratic society, was moving away from the home to the one-room school and then away from the one-room to the multi-room school.

Along with the mass production of industry and the high specialization of production there came a mass organization of education—larger classes—more subjects. The family, which had assumed certain responsibilities in the moral and religious training of youth, began to lose its grip on them, and there grew up supplementary public and semi-public agencies to aid youth in their leisure hours.

It was, then, only natural that the outdoor tradition and the wake of industrialization should produce a rebellion that would take youth away from the city and give them a chance to see and smell—even for a short time—the splendor of nature. Parents who had grown up during their youth in the out-of-doors wanted the benefits of these experiences for their own children and were willing to pay for it.

That this movement toward realism and naturalism met a latent need in our society is obvious since it gained steadily in support. As far back as the 1870s organized camps were established. Beginning slowly at first, the movement began to take hold and had grown to considerable proportions by the turn of the century. Since 1910 the number of private and organizational camps has increased steadily.

A movement as extensive as camping in America today could never have developed the support it has unless it met some kind of definite need. The fact that such organizations as the Boy Scouts, the Girl Scouts, the Y.M.C.A., the Y.W.C.A., to mention only a few, have the wide support they do today is ample evidence that the American people believe in and are willing to support camping and outdoor experiences for youngsters.

Organized camping in America has followed two general lines of development—private camps and organization camps. For the most part, private camps have catered to those upon the upper end of the economic scale. Organization camps have tended—but not entirely—to provide outdoor experiences for those in the lower economic brackets. As a result, camping for the great mass of American youngsters in the middle class has not been a reality or at least only at considerable sacrifice on the part of the parents.

It is not surprising, then, for a movement as important and widely supported as camping is to be considered as a regular and integral part of school experience. In recent years, camping as an educational method has been recognized and encouraged by the important policy-making groups in American education, and school camping programs are springing up across the country.

CAMPING HAS CHANGED TOO

Camping has undergone some interesting and important changes, too, since the first organized camp was established late in the last century.

According to the dictionary *to camp* means: "to pitch or prepare a camp to sleep out-of-doors," and this is precisely what the first camps attempted to provide for youngsters. But as time went on and camps grew in size it seemed to become more and more necessary to *organize* the camping experience and to *schedule* activities. In other words, instead of taking care of greater numbers by setting up more small camps with all of the inherent values therein, expansion came by developing larger and larger camps with centralized programs.

This centralization of program and organization meant the need for more and more specialists to head up the various "departments" of the camp. There were the water-front specialist, the craft specialist, the nature specialist, the sports specialist, the evening program specialist, and even the hiking and camping specialists.

Along with the specialists in many camps have come the "gadgeteers" and the assembly-line gadgets where the child is simply the last step in a prefabricated construction experience.

Camping has grown up, too, with other notable movements in American life, some of which have had considerable effect upon camp programs. With the increase in leisure, for example, there has come the organized recreation movement with many attendant benefits to city youngsters. But along with organized recreation has come both a specialization of equipment and personnel, and in too many cases the camp is simply an organized playground with all of the equipment and devices that are used in the city simply moved out into the woods. Where this has happened there has been a tendency for the camp program to revolve around the equipment and facilities, and the youngsters have not had a chance to participate in the experience of living and planning their lives in small groups.

All of these tendencies have moved camping away from the original meaning of the term and, at worst, have robbed the youngster of the very experience for which he should be going to camp. Now as the schools move toward an active camping program it is imperative that this program be carefully planned to provide the real educational experiences that are inherent in it. If camping has a unique offering to make to American youth—and there is every reason to believe that it has—then great care should be exercised to make certain that the camp program is conducted in such a way as to make that contribution possible. Where a camp is supplied with all of the paraphernalia of organized and scheduled recreation—slides, swings, teeter-totters, giant-strides, and even smoothed surface areas for play with attending regulations and supervision, then it is difficult to conduct a true *camping* program where youngsters are placed in a situation that requires of them a disposition to solve their own problems, cooperate with others, and come to know the ways of nature.

In other words, the history of camping and the peculiar needs that this movement should fulfill in modern American life call for a careful evaluation of any local program if it is to accomplish fully its aim. It is not sufficient simply to get youngsters out-of-doors. It is not sufficient to organize their recreational life—no matter how well or in how much fresh air.

If education in its fullest and truest sense is learning to live at its best, the school with all its facilities and programs should accomplish insofar as possible that aim. Basic skills are essential, but, unrelated to the larger purpose, they will not bring about the desired results. Good living is made up of a flow of experience including personal behavior, work, study, appreciation of the finer things in life, happy and constructive use of leisure time. Beyond and above this, an appreciation of, and respect for, one's land and country and an enrichment of spiritual life are needed.

In order to make appreciable progress toward this ideal, youth must have practice in living together in an environment and in a manner that will bring about their greatest and best total personality growth and development and result in better understanding between all groups, creeds and races. The school-community camp not only furnishes the best opportunity for development of these qualities, but if the camp is properly organized and conducted, it will be necessary for these qualities to emerge in order for happiness and a good way of living to be realized. This phase of education can best be gained in a school-community camping program.

In camp, especially in a small group procedure, it is not possible to shirk individual responsibility, sharing, and cooperative planning. It is not possible for a youth to hide behind a curtain of make-believe and keep his real self from emerging. He cannot dodge or fake for long. The necessities of living in the camp environment force his hand. This comes quickly in camp, and when it does, there can be real tolerance, understanding and happiness, the essentials of good citizenship.

It is an accepted thesis in education that learning takes place faster and is more effective through direct experience. An analysis of the subject matter content set forth in the course of study shows that much of the material exists in the immediate community and the surrounding country. The school camp program will see to it that campers have opportunity to explore, discover, and solve on their own questions posed in their school books. This kind of education is fun and more effective in the long run.

In these days of evolving a program for effective peace, there is a high premium placed upon tolerance and understanding among peoples. An effective program must begin with each individual if it is to spread in neighborhoods, communities, the country and the world. The place to begin is with the practice of individuals of different creeds, races, and colors living, sharing, and learning together. Our schools are made up of such groups; the school-community camp provides a place for the practice of living together.

There is some opportunity in the unusual school program for this democratic process to take place, but it does not approach the intensity and degree necessary to live happily in a camp situation. In school, youth are together approximately six hours a day and five days a week. Camp living is made up of a continuous flow of experience twenty-four hours a day, seven days a week for as long as they are in camp, making it possible and even necessary to adapt themselves to a cooperative pattern of living and learning.

This steady flow of experience over a long, unbroken period of time with adequate leadership and guidance makes camping education perhaps the most promising new development in education today. The evidence thus far is so clear and promising that it seems safe to predict that the future direction of education will be toward the out-of-doors.

Perhaps it is true that human events move in cycles. Man has built himself a great technology and great cities to go with it where human beings can revel in a myriad of artificial gadgets and close themselves away from the basic and all-pervading rules of nature. And now he has harnessed a force that in one single flash can destroy a whole city and most of the inhabitants in it. But the great question is not whether man can control this force, but rather whether he can control himself and whether he has the knowledge and skill to raise a generation of people who can live peaceably together.

Perhaps after all, it is not knowledge and power that count so much as the ability and disposition to live peaceably with man and nature. The greatest responsibility facing educators today is to find where this type of life philosophy can best be taught.

THE HISTORY OF ORGANIZED CAMPING:
THE EARLY DAYS*

H. W. GIBSON

FOREWORD

To assemble the scattered information concerning the genesis of the organized camp movement and present it in one volume is the purpose of this thesis. The accomplishment of this has required considerable research in order that the information secured may be accurate. Much credit is due Eugene H. Lehman and Porter Sargent for their faithful recording of important events in the early history of the movement. Their patient persistence in following leads resulted in uncovering information which otherwise would have been lost. To David S. Keiser is given the credit of securing the story of Dr. Rothrock and his unique camp. Acknowledgment is also given to those who have furnished historical items and verified many incidents and happenings of the early camping days. This is a history rather than an analysis or interpretation of the movement

*Reprinted by permission from, *Camping Magazine* 8:13-15; 26-27, January, 1936.

and it is compiled with the hope that it will be of assistance to students and others seeking information about the organized camping movement.

Chapter I
THE EARLY DAYS

Biography is the only true history. Great movements in history have always revolved around some outstanding figure. History is best understood through biography. People are the makers of history. —Gamaliel Bradford.

The history of the organized camping movement is largely the history of persons, men and women, possessing the pioneer spirit and the vision of bringing back into our highly civilized and, in many respects, artificial method of living, those values of life which come from living in the great out-of-doors. Since the time of Moses people have camped out along the banks of streams, by the shore of lakes and in the mountains, but camping as an organized, cooperative way of living, is a comparatively recent movement and is distinctly American in its origin.

"Our race began its career in the open," writes George W. Hinckley, in one of his delightful little books. "After a time it began to build houses. The houses were made closer and closer, tighter and tighter, until air was shut out. If a man were feeble, it was understood that the most dangerous thing he could do was to breathe air out-of-doors after sunset until the sun was well into the heavens again; night air was believed to be deadly though it was all that was available. The race was dying; dying of its own stupidity; dying from in-doorness.

"Then there arose apostles of fresh air; they preached the doctrine of out-doorness; the race was getting its breath again, and coming into its own."[1]

A rather unique analysis of this in-doorness tendency is expressed in the following quaint quatrain:

When ye houses were made of straw
Ye men were made of oak
But when ye houses were made of oak
Ye men were made of straw.

Previous to the birth of the organized camping movement, a group of "men of oak," because of their understanding of the out-of-doors and wealth of outdoor experience, and through the contagious enthusiasm of their writings, inspired and stimulated a new interest in the joy of outdoorness. Daniel Boone, Davy Crockett, Kit Carson, Thoreau, Isaac Walton, "Adirondack" Murray, "Nesmuck" Sears, W. Hamilton Gibson, Col. Buzzacott, and later Daniel Beard, Ernest Thompson Seton, Edward Breck, Horace Kephart, and a host of others,

[1]G.W. Hinckley, *Roughing It With Boys,* p. 1.

represent the real, woodsy type of outdoor life—a noble roster of rugged personalities, whose discipleship to "nature in the raw" wins our admiration and as we read their books, there wells up within us a feeling of regret that so much of the real love for the out-of-doors which they had, is being supplanted in our modern camps by the conventions of modern life, thus exposing our boys and girls to a camping experience somewhat formal and complex. It is said that history repeats itself, and it may be that the spirit, if not the practice, of the pioneers may again return and save our present-day camps from the danger of ultra-efficiency and super-scientific management.

LAYING FOUNDATIONS IN 1861

History is being made more rapidly than it is being accurately recorded. Although the organized camping idea is only a half century old, considerable difficulty has been experienced in securing data concerning its origin. It was Eugene H. Lehman who, in his search for material and data for an article on "Camping Out" for the Encyclopedia Britannica, discovered that camping, as an organized, educational project, was undertaken as early as 1861 by Frederick Williams Gunn, the founder of the Gunnery School for Boys in Washington, Connecticut. Mr. Lehman writes in Spalding's *Camps and Camping* for 1929,[2] as follows:

On May 26, 1928, I wrote a letter to Mr. Hamilton Gibson, the present headmaster of the Gunnery School, requesting information relative to Gunnery Camp. He replied as follows under date of June 23, 1928.

"My dear Mr. Lehmann:

"I am responding to your letter of May 26th and giving you as best I may the information regarding Gunnery Camp requested in that letter.

"As very few of those who remembered the camp are now living, I referred the matter to Mrs. John C. Brinsmade, daughter of Mr. Gunn, and I inclose with this note her statement. I know that Mrs. Brinsmade has consulted and verified all dates and facts as reported by her. Insofar as I know, this is the most complete and reliable statement of the Gunnery Camp that can possibly be procured. I trust that it may be of interest to you and may be also what you wish in the way of information.

"Very sincerely yours,
"Hamilton Gibson."

Here is the statement referred to and signed by Mary Gunn Brinsmade (Mrs. John C. Brinsmade):

"The Gunnery Camp—The First School Camp

"The Gunnery, a home school for boys, was founded in the fall of 1849 by Frederick William Gunn and his wife, Abigail Brinsmade, in Washington, Connecticut. They began with ten boys, the number gradually increasing to seventy boarders, with a large number of day pupils.

[2] E.H. Lehman, *Camps and Camping*, 1929. p. 38.

"The school year was divided into two parts—the summer term from the middle of May to the end of September, and the winter term from the middle of November to the end of March.

"When the Civil War began, the boys were eager to be soldiers, to march, and especially to sleep out in tents. They were given opportunity to roll up in blankets and sleep outdoors on the ground, and sometimes the whole school would camp for a night or two in this way at a lovely lake nearby. In the summer of 1861, Mr. and Mrs. Gunn took the whole school on a hike, or gypsy trip, as it was called, about four miles to Milford, on the Sound, near New Haven. This trip took two days. The tents, baggage, supplies, etc., were carried in a large market wagon. There were also a few comfortable carriages and two donkeys, but many walked much, and some of the boys all of the way. Camp was established on the beach at Welch's Point and named Camp Comfort. Here two happy weeks were spent boating, sailing, fishing and tramping. This proved such a helpful and delightful experience that Mr. Gunn repeated it in the years of 1863 and 1865. Old boys came back to join the merry troop, and with friends of the school, some of them ladies, made up a party of sixty or more in the following trips.

"At a later period this seaside jaunt gave place to a Gunnery Camp at Point Beautiful on Lake Waramaug, seven miles from the school, and for twelve years the school spent two weeks in August, camping in this picturesque and delightful spot. The Gunnery was one of the latest schools to adopt the long summer vacation and this change eliminated the summer camp.

"In your letter of May 26, you mention Camp Chocorua, founded in 1881 by Mr. Ernest Balch, as the *first* camp.

"Frederick William Gunn carried on a series of successful camps for boys from the summer of 1861 to that of 1879. The number of campers increased from sixty the first year to one hundred or more in the last years. This camping was part of the school regime, and not an organized camp for the purpose of money-making. And the Gunnery School encamped fifteen times in the twenty years before the date of 1881 as the founding of Camp Chocorua.

"This camping is so far back in the past that only a few persons are left to whom I could refer you. You may find in 'The Master of Gunnery,' published in 1887, and to be found in some public libraries, a brief confirmation of these statements; also Dr. J. G. Holland in his story of 'Arthur Bonnicastle'[3] gives a very good picture of Gunner Camp. His son and his grandson are alumni of the school. I was fortunate enough to be a member of every one of these camps. My father was Frederick William Gunn. He died in 1881 and John C. Brinsmade, my husband, succeeded him as Headmaster and was there forty years until he retired in 1922 when the present Headmaster, Hamilton Gibson, became Head of the school.

"It may also interest you to know that baseball was introduced into the Gunnery School in 1860. The game was brought to the school by three brothers, sons of Judge William H. Van Cott of New York City, the first President of the Mutual Baseball Association of that city. For years

[3]See J.G. Holland, *Arthur Bonnicastle*, pp. 288-292.

the boys played the game three afternoons a week and on Saturday, and in the long summers the nines through this constant practice grew very proficient.

"Sincerely yours,
"Mary Gunn Brinsmade (Mrs. John C.)"

The above statement clearly ascribes the honor of being "Father of The Organized Camp" to Frederick William Gunn, who in 1861, seventy-four years ago, established Camp Gunnery.

THE DR. ROTHROCK CAMP—1876—THE FIRST PRIVATE CAMP

The published statement of Mr. Lehmann regarding Camp Gunnery, stimulated others in doing research work, among whom was David S. Keiser. He discovered the "North Mountain School of Physical Culture" conducted in 1876 by Joseph Trimble Rothrock, a practicing physician of Wilkes-Barre, Pennsylvania.[4] Mr. Keiser quotes from a biological sketch which Dr. Rothrock wrote for "Some American Medical Botanists," edited by Dr. Howard A. Kelly, the eminent gynecologist, and who is still actively engaged in his profession as a member of the staff of Johns Hopkins Medical School, Baltimore, Maryland. This book was published by the Southwark Company, Troy, N.Y. Dr. Rothrock states:

In 1876 I had the happy idea of taking weakly boys in summer out into camp life in the woods and under competent instruction, mingling exercises and study, so that pursuit of health could be combined with acquisition of practical knowledge outside the usual academic lines. I founded the school on North Mountain, Luzerne County, Pennsylvania, and designated it a School of Physical Culture. There had been, I think, but a single attempt to do this work at an earlier period. . . . The multitude of such camps now (about 1913) shows that the seed fell into good ground.

The camp was located on property adjacent to a hotel, the North Mountain House, located about thirty-three miles northeast of Wilkes-Barre, and was 200 yards from Lake Ganago. The campers were twelve years of age or older and came mostly from Philadelphia and Wilkes-Barre. The camp opened on June 15 and closed on October 15th. The tuition was probably $200.00 for the four months. There were twenty campers and five "teachers" at this first camp.

Dr. Rothrock believed in advertising, at least he was not averse to others broadcasting the story of his cultural enterprise, for, on July 18, 1876, there appeared in the *Wilkes-Barre Times*, an editorial on the inauguration of the camp; also a long letter from a correspondent was given prominence.

The 1876 enterprise not having paid expenses, Dr. Rothrock decided to spend

[4]Davis S. Keiser, *Camper and Hiker*, April 1929, p. 4.

the next year in Alaskan exploration. Mr. Lewis H. Taylor, then a teacher in the Wilkes-Barre High School and who later became a distinguished physician, carried on the camp in a small way in 1877 with a few boys and several teachers. In 1878 a Mr. Kelly, (who today is the famous physician on the staff of Johns Hopkins Medical School, Baltimore, Maryland), joined Mr. Taylor and conducted the camp. They advertised in the *Philadelphia Bulletin* and in the *Wilkes-Barre Times* and had a camp of about twenty boys. At the end of the season the camp was closed. "The bills and counselors were paid—and as to profit, there wasn't any."

Dr. Rothrock was greatly interested in forestry and in the Capitol building at Harrisburg, Pennsylvania, is a memorial tablet erected in his memory by his friends. The inscription on the tablet reads as follows:

The Father of Forestry in Pennsylvania
Joseph Trimble Rothrock, 1839-1922
Patriot, Soldier, Pioneer, Forester, Botanist, Sportsman, Physician, Educator, Author, Public Servant, Distinguished Citizen and Loving Husband and Father, Leader in the Conservation of Our Forests and Streams.

THE FIRST CHURCH CAMP - 1880

Rev. George W. Hinckley in 1880, when pastor of a church in West Hartford, Connecticut, conceived the idea of taking the boys of his parish on a camping trip. He established his camp on Gardner's Island, Wakefield, Rhode Island. In his party were seven boys including three Chinese high school boys who were being educated in America.[5]

In a letter received from Mr. Hinckley on February 12, 1934, he recalls the following incident in connection with the 1880 camp which is worth recording:

At this distant day I cannot recall much about that camp except two or three incidents which I used to offer in addresses to illustrate some point. Frank Fenn was a fatherless, motherless boy whom I was befriending in the parsonage—giving home and school privileges. A few days before we were to leave West Hartford for Wakefield, he told me that he heard that I was going to take three Chinese boys with the party and he wanted to know if it were true. When I replied that it was so, he exclaimed, "That is all I want to know. If I can't camp out without taking along a lot of heathen Chinese, I don't want to go."

I explained to him that he need not go but I was going, and if no one else went, I would take the three Chinese boys anyway. Frank changed his mind in a day or two and went with us.

One of the first days in camp we were sitting at the long table under the trees, when a boy from one of my "best families" said to one of the Chinese students: "Woo, chuck me a biscuit will you," to which Woo

[5]Porter Sargent, *Handbook of Summer Camps*, 1929, p. 19.

replied, "I will pass you a biscuit; we needn't act like heathen even if we are in the woods," and the "heathen Chinee" to whom Frank Fenn had objected had formulated an under-lying principle of camp life.

Mr. Hinckley later founded the Good Will Farm for boys which has become a famous institution located at Hinckley, Maine, and where the Good Will Camp was held for many years. It took the form of an Assembly with a daily program consisting of "sane and sensible" religious periods; an educational program; swimming, baseball, tennis in the afternoon, and sings, talks and entertainment in the evening.

"Adirondack" Murray (Rev. W. H. H. Murray) was Mr. Hinckley's great example of physical manhood and so great was his admiration for this man, that he erected on one of the trails in the Good Will Woods, a massive structure of stone work bearing three tablets in his honor. The tablets read as follows:

To Adirondack Murray

Rev. W. H. H. Murray is buried on the Murray Homestead in Guilford, Conn., where he was born April 26, 1840. He died March 3, 1904. A splendid type of physical manhood, magnetic personality, preacher, writer, unique character. He was the father of the modern outdoor movement, and by his writings inspired multitudes with love of mountains and lake, camp and bivouac, woods and trails. This is erected by G. W. Hinckley in recognition of a great service to humanity 1920.

The second inscription is taken from the preface of one of Murray's books and reads:

To all that camp on shores of lakes, on breezy points, on banks of rivers, by shady beaches, on slopes of mountains, and under green trees anywhere, I, an old camper, a wood lover, an aboriginal veneered with civilization, send greeting. I thank God for the multitude of you; for the strength and the beauty of you; for the healthfulness of your tastes and the naturalness of your natures. I eat and drink with you; I hunt and fish with you; I boat and bathe with you; and with you day and night enjoy the gifts of the good world.

The inscription on the third tablet reads as follows:

The End of the Trail

Mr. Hinkley writes that it was the custom to go to this monument once a year, usually on the last evening of May and hold a brief ceremony. "Just at dusk we would sing America; then we would repeat the Lord's Prayer; then there would be a short address and the singing of Good Will's 'Trail Song.' After the singing was ended, fagot of birch was lighted, and laid on a part of the stonework, and this was called 'lighting the symbolic camp-fire.' "

Frederick William Gunn, Dr. Joseph Trimble Rothrock, Rev. George W. Hinckley—educator, physician, clergyman—recognized the need of bettering boy life, through rational, healthful living out of doors. By this simple life, rugged virtues which were characteristic of the early pioneers, could be practiced, and without precedents to follow, conferences to inspire, or organizations to promote, they proceed to make real their ideal. These three men made a contribution to the organized camping movement of greater significance than is recognized at the present.

Unselfish motives, sympathetic understanding, tactful leadership, and sound principles of work, play and study, were applied to the administration of their camps and many of the boys, who camped with these leaders of contagious personalities, became men of influence and importance in the business and professional life.

THE HISTORY OF ORGANIZED CAMPING : ESTABLISHMENT OF INSTITUTIONAL CAMPS*

H. W. GIBSON

Chapter III
ESTABLISHMENT OF INSTITUTIONAL CAMPS

"Our boys and girls take to camp life as naturally as ducks take to water, and in the opinion of many, this kind of life, for a part of the year, has become almost a biological necessity. For untold generations sunlight and fresh air, woods, fields, lakes and mountains, have served as nature's background for development to make man, through contact with these natural agents, all that he is today."

Dr. Dudley Sargent[1]

YOUNG MEN'S CHRISTIAN ASSOCIATION CAMPS

Ever on the alert to take advantage of an opportunity for development of the mind, body, and spirit, the Young Men's Christian Association saw in this adaptation of life in the open to that of organized community outdoor living a new way of approach to character building, alive with great possibilities.

Early in the summer of 1885, Sumner F. Dudley, a young business man, associated with his father and brother in the manufacture of surgical instruments, in Brooklyn, and a summer resident of East Orange, N.J., borrowed a tent, hired a boat, and gathered seven congenial Newburgh, N.Y., boys who belonged to the Y.M.C.A., for a camping trip to Pine Point on Orange Lake, about six miles from Newburgh. To this meagre equipment, however, were

---

*Reprinted by permission from *Camping Magazine* 8:18, 19, 26-29, March, 1936.

[1]Summer Camps, *Red Book Magazine*, Introduction, 1923.

added his genial personality, unbounded enthusiasm, ardent love for out-of-door life, and the keen receptivity and impressionability of the boys—the essential elements for a successful camping trip.

In *The Watchman* of August 1st, 1885, at that time the official journal of the Association, Mr. Dudley describes this first camping trip as follows: "I have just returned from an eight days in camp conscious of having one of the most profitable times of my life; with me have been seven of the leading members of the Boys' Branch of Newburgh.

"Location, Orange Lake; name of camp, Camp Bald Head; because all but one member of the party had temporarily lost nearly all their hair from their heads; weather, delightful, just enough rain to add variety; fishing, very moderate; swimming, called for three times a day; health, good; accidents, none; appetite, ravenous; hearty, manly fun, any quantity; good nature, largely developed."

George A. Sanford, when General Secretary of the Newburgh Association in 1885, and who passed away January 13, 1934, at the age of 76, was the man who suggested to Mr. Dudley, the idea of taking a group of boys on a one-week camping trip. Mr. Sanford writes in *American Youth*, April, 1920, that the camp was called "Bald Head" for "reasons more hygienic than esthetic, as most of the boys had their hair closely cropped before starting for camp."

The second summer, Mr. Dudley's camping party numbered twenty-three boys and was located on Lake Wawayanda, N.J. In 1891 the campers increased to eighty-three and a new location was found near Westport, N.Y., on Lake Champlain. J. H. Worman, editor of *Outing*, a warm friend of Mr. Dudley, offered the use of part of his land. This offer was gladly accepted and the camp was permanently established. Mr. Dudley's camping experience evidently influenced him to give up business and enter the work of the Y.M.C.A. In 1887-88 he served the Orange, N.J., Association as General Secretary and then became a member of the Board of Directors, serving until his death, March 14th, 1897, at the age of 43. Mr. Dudley is buried in Roseville, N.J., and a pilgrimage to his grave is taken each year by representatives of the Y.M.C.A. Camps of New Jersey.

Mr. Dudley never married. Summer after summer he gave his energy unsparingly to his camp. At his death he left the entire camp equipment to the New York State Y.M.C.A. Committee. As a memorial to a life of unselfish devotion, the camp was named Camp Dudley. In 1934, the Golden Jubilee of the camp was celebrated, having been in continuous operation for fifty years, and is, therefore, the first and oldest existing organized camp.

From the seed sown by this young man in 1885 has grown a worldwide camping movement, reaching many thousand boys through Y.M.C.A. camps located in all parts of the world. The Associations in the United States and Canada conduct today, 1,234 camps with an enrollment of 134,593 campers and owning camp property valued at $5,092,596, with an annual operating budget of $1,012,200.

SPREAD OF THE MOVEMENT AMONG OTHER ORGANIZATIONS

It was not until 1890 that the organized camp idea caught the imagination of leaders of boy life. There were a few Associations that conducted short-term camps or more strictly speaking, nomadic camps or camping trips. One such camping trip was managed by the Knoxville, Tennessee, Association, under the leadership of Dr. J. W. Stewart, July 11-22, 1887, but the record is very meagre and no doubt it was a hiking trip rather than an organized camp.

In 1894, the writer was elected a delegate from the Lancaster (Pennsylvania) Association, to the Golden Jubilee of the founding of the Young Men's Christian Association, held in London, England. Upon his return in June, from this memorable trip, he took a party of fifteen boys, members of the Lancaster Association, on a camping trip to Schiebley's Grove, along the Conestoga Creek, near Lancaster, and spent two weeks in carrying out a regular camp schedule. Later the camp was moved to Mt. Gretna, Pennsylvania, and the name changed to Camp Shand in honor of the president of the Association. The camp has been maintained without a break in its existence since 1894, and is, next to Dudley and Wawayanda, the third oldest Association camp.

BOYS' CLUB CAMPS

The first Boys' Club to conduct an organized camp was the Salem (Massachusetts) Fraternity. This was in 1900. During July and August of that year, seventy-six boys were members of a seven-week camp, held at Rowley, Mass., and Hampton Falls, N.H. Mr. Herbert L. Farwell, who is still the superintendent of the Fraternity, was the leader of the camp. Mr. R. K. Atkinson, Director of Education of the Boys' Clubs of America, Inc., writes that the total number of camps conducted by Boys' Clubs, as reported in 1935, is 60, and the number of different campers attending these camps was 26,088. The property owned by the clubs and used for camping purposes is valued at $1,508,377.

"FRESH-AIR" CAMPS

Dr. Lloyd B. Sharp, in his book *Education and the Summer Camp, an Experiment*, traces the development of camping as a part of the social service work in New York City. He states that the first fresh-air home for New York City children was established in 1872 by the Children's Aid Society of New York on Staten Island. The word "camp" was not used in explaining these activities of the Society. Newspapers such as the *New York Times* and *New York Tribune* daily told the story of the venture, and money was given in sums which made it possible to turn the experiment into an achievement. Life's Fresh Air Fund was established August 11, 1887, and the Tribune Fresh Air Fund in 1888. In 1925 Dr. Sharp was appointed Executive Director of the Activities of Life's Fresh Air Fund, and directed the reorganization of the camps. "In the reorganization the word 'camp' replaced the term 'Fresh Air Farm.' Many policies were changed. The whole program was placed upon an educational basis and a broad program of camping activities was inaugurated."[2]

BOY SCOUT CAMPS

On September 23, 1910, a dinner was tendered to Lt. General Sir Robert S.S. Baden-Powell, K. C. B., by the Boy Scouts of America, at the Waldorf-Astoria, New York City. The writer was a guest at this dinner and heard General Baden-Powell, when he was introduced by Ernest Thompson Seton as "Father of the Boy Scout Movement," say "You have made a mistake, Mr. Seton, in your remarks to the effect that I am father of this idea of Scouting for boys. I may say that you are the father of it or that Dan Beard is the father. There are many fathers! I am only one of the uncles, I might say. The scheme became known at home, then I looked about to see what was being done in the United States, and I cribbed right and left, putting things into a book just as I found them."

At this dinner a beautiful red leather-bound volume entitled *Boy Scouts of America* was distributed. It was a handbook written by Ernest Thompson Seton, incorporating much of the material appearing in his Birch Bark Roll, and contained a chapter on "Camping" dealing more exclusively with camping trips rather than organized camping.

Scouting was looked upon as a program activity. In 1908 the writer wrote to General Baden-Powell in London for his book *Scouting for Boys*, and received from him not only a copy of the book but also official badges and other material. Under the inspiration of this, "Scout-craft" was introduced as an activity in Camp Becket in the summer of 1909,[3] one year before the Boy Scouts were organized in America.

In 1911 the National Council of the Boy Scouts appointed an Editorial Board, consisting of William D. Murray, George D. Pratt, and A. A. Jameson, who prepared an official *Handbook* which included a chapter on Campcraft, which the writer had the honor of contributing.

At that time scouting was a craft rather than an organization, and in the first official *Handbook* it states that "the aim of the Boy Scouts is to supplement the various existing educational agencies, and to promote the ability in boys to do things for themselves and others. It is not the aim to set up a new organization to parallel in its purpose others already established. The opportunity is afforded

[2]Lloyd B. Sharp, "Education and the Summer Camp," p. 11.

[3]*Association Boys,* December, 1909, p. 314.

these organizations, however, to introduce into their program unique features appealing to interests which are universal among boys. This method is summed up in the term 'Scoutcraft.' "[4]

Scoutcraft, true to the American habit of organizing, soon became a tremendous organized force with centralized control, and today has one of the most thoroughly organized camping departments in existence, under the capable leadership of L. L. McDonald, the National Director of Camping, with offices at 2 Park Avenue, New York City. Much attention is given to a definite camp leadership-training program for Scoutmasters and assistants.

Mr. McDonald writes that "the Chicago Camp, Owasippi, at Whitehall, Michigan, is the oldest of the permanent Council Camps operating under Council supervision on its own permanent camp-site. This camp was established in 1911, and D. W. Pollard was the Executive Director in charge. During the same year the Philadelphia Council, Boston, New York, Columbus, and other Councils were operating camps, and have carried on continuously an organized camping program since that time."

According to the figures given in Sargent's *Summer Camps*, up to March 30, 1935, the total number of 600 Boy Scout camps have a daily capacity of 60,000 boys; 55,526 acres in the total acreage for 292 camps reporting an equal total valuation of $4,447,473.[5] In addition to these permanent camps there are 2,000 to 3,000 Troops carrying on an independent organized camping program on a smaller scale, and upwards of 425,000 boys were actually enrolled as campers in some phase of the camping program for 1935.

The first Boy Scout camps with professional leadership on the cooperative plan could properly be recorded as of the year 1910, during which there were twenty odd Councils established.

GIRL SCOUT CAMPS

Camps have always been recognized as an essential part of the Girl Scout program ever since its organization in 1912. In 1922 it was decided to charter the camps throughout the country, rating them on first-year development, second-year development, and so on. Definite standards must be met in all camps. Small unit camping has been developed to a high degree of efficiency. Mass camping is discouraged. Day camping is encouraged. Trained leadership is required. A countrywide national training program is carried out each summer. In 1934, 78 courses were given with an enrollment of 1,625 students. An international encampment is held annually at "Our Chalet" at Edelboden, Switzerland, the gift of Mrs. James J. Storrow of Boston. Camp Edith Macy, at Briarcliff Manor, New York, conducted by the National Girl Scout organization

---

[4] *Boy Scouts of America Official Handbook* (1911), p. 3.
[5] Porter Sargent, *Handbook of Summer Camps* (1935), p. 157.

as a training center for leaders, is a model demonstration camp. A camp literature of exceptionally high quality has been developed, and a camp service department is maintained at the National Headquarters, 570 Lexington Ave., New York City. In Massachusetts, the former estate of the late Cornelia Warren, at Cedar Hill, Waltham, is used by the State Council as a camping area for unit camps; here scout activities, week-end trips, gypsy trips, and hiking are popular outdoor activities. The first camp was held in 1912 by the Savannah, Georgia, Girl Scouts. It was called Camp Lowland, and established by Juliette Low, founder of Girl Scouting. Total number of Girl Scout camps in 1935 was 984 and attended by 101,113 campers.

CAMP FIRE GIRLS

"The work and ideals of the Camp Fire Girls had its direct origin in the home, and later in the private camp, of Mrs. Luther Halsey Gulick on Lake Sebago, Maine. Here, meeting the needs of her own daughters, Mrs. Gulick worked out the beginnings of what was later, with some modification, accepted as the ritual and form of the Camp Fire Girls. The name of Mrs. Gulick's camp, Wohelo—which she had formed from the first two letters of each of the three words, Work, Health, and Love—became the watchword of the new organization. On March 17, 1912, the manual which had been prepared was given to the public, hence that date is our birthday."[6]

Janet L. McKellar of the National office, 41 Union Square, New York City, writes that the first camps of the Camp Fire Girls were conducted in 1914 by the Guardians' Associations of Chicago, Baltimore and Kansas City. These were attended by approximately 500. The number of camps in 1935 was 113 and 18,541 different campers were enrolled. The total value of property and equipment of the camps is $538,749.00.

Poetry, music, ceremony and ritual, color, and drama are used to express their ideas and ideals. Fire is the symbol of the organization, for around it the first homes were built. The Camp Fire Girls Camp program has in it the appeal of romance, beauty, and adventure in everyday life.

Y.W.C.A. CAMPS

The first Y.W.C.A. Camp was organized in 1874 by the Philadelphia Association. In a statement issued in 1934 by the National Board, is given the following information concerning this first camp or "vacation project" as it was called: "President Ulysses S. Grant officially opened the first summer vacation project for girls earning their own living just sixty years ago (August 4, 1874) when the Y.W.C.A. of Philadelphia opened 'Sea Rest' at Asbury Park, N.J.

[6]*Book of Camp Fire Girls* (1918), p. 9.

"This summer boarding and vacation house was for 'tired young women wearing out their lives in an almost endless drudgery for wages that admit no thought of rest or recreation.' Any young woman who was financially dependent on her own exertions and was of respectable character was eligible.

"The program of dedication was attended by many notables, including the President of the United States who gave the principal speech; the Honorable William S. Stokley, Mayor of Philadelphia, who presided; George H. Stuart and Bishop Simpson.

"Within the next ten years other vacation projects for young women were opened in Providence, R.I., Louisville, Ky., and Milwaukee, Wis., by the Y.W.C.A."

It is only recently that the Y.W.C.A. has given attention to girls of High School age through an organization known as the Girl Reserves. The total number of Y.W.C.A. camps, for girls and young women, is about 250 and attendance averages 100,000 each summer.

Under the leadership of Hazel K. Allen, progress is rapidly being made in administration and program-building. Miss Allen has written a book, *Camps and Their Modern Administration,* which will have a distinct influence on the development of both program and management of present and future camps of the Association. *Magic Casements* by Ruth Perkins is a chronicle of the development of a new kind of camp program, and *The Girls' Camp* by Abbie Graham, written from the point of view of a camp director, is a classic in camp literature.

A CAMP SCHOOL FOR BOYS

The earliest record we find of a camp school for boys is that of the Boston Young Men's Christian Association, who conducted such a school on Commonwealth Avenue Boulevard, Boston, July 7 to August 25, 1909. Tents were pitched in this attractive location and sessions were held from 9 a.m. to 12:30 p.m. daily, except Saturday and Sunday. The afternoons were spent in games, sports, and athletics, the boys returning to their homes for the night. William L. Phinney was Principal of the school and the camp features were under the supervision of Don S. Gates. Saturdays were devoted to hikes, trips to historical places, and field days.

"Camping as a function of the public school system had its beginning in 1912" says Dr. Marie M. Ready in a bulletin issued by the Office of Education of the Department of the Interior.[7] "At that time the Visiting Nurses' Association in Dubuque, Iowa, established a summer camp for malnourished school children, and the camp was conducted by that Association in cooperation with the Board of Education of that city. . . . Camping for normal children, as a part of the public school system, had its beginning about 1919. At that time

[7]Porter Sargent, *Summer Camps* (1935), p. 109.

Camp Roosevelt was established as a part of the public school system of Chicago, Ill."

In *Camping* for November, 1928, is an article by B. S. Graves of Highland Park (Michigan) High School, explaining the Highland Park plan. The city owns two camps—Camp Wallace for boys and Camp Wasaquam for girls—at Platte Lake, Honor, Michigan. The Recreation Commission pays 50% and the Board of Education 50% in financing the camp, in addition to a small fee paid by each camper. Full credit is given in the fall for work done at Camp.

Camps are maintained or directed by Boards of Education in six cities: Chicago, Dearborn, LaCrosse, Oshkosh, West Allis (Wisconsin), and in Jersey City.[8]

CAMPS BY OTHER ORGANIZATIONS

Adequate information concerning camps such as the 4-H Club Camps, Y.M.H.A. Camps, woodcraft Camps, and Church Camps is not available. Extravagant figures of camp enrollments, number of camps, and financial values have been published but are difficult to verify.

CONCLUSION

The institutional or organizational camps have for years been regarded as places where needy boys and girls could be cared for during the hot summer months at small expense, and while camps of such character have existed for more than five decades, there has been a decided change in the purpose and character of these camps in recent years. They are now recognized as great laboratories where life situations are studied, field work and research work carried on, and serious projects undertaken. Many of the organizational camps have developed camping to a fine art. Some educators have prophesied that municipalities and schools will include camping as a part of their educational program, and thus establish a year-round school project.

The greatest contribution that organizational camps have made to the camping movement is that of trained leadership and the establishment of standards. Through the holding of institutes, conferences, seminars and discussion groups, the old traditional type of camping is gradually being replaced by a new camp procedure, which calls for individual counseling and guidance in dealing with boys and girls, the abolishment of awards and honor systems, and the introduction of a system for self-improvement, personality enrichment, and individual achievement.

[8]Porter Sargent, *Summer Camps* (1935), p. 110.

THE SUMMER CAMP
REENFORCES EDUCATION *

PAUL S. MILLER

The first organized camp for boys was established on Lake Asquam, New Hampshire, about 1880 by Ernest Balch. This experiment proved so successful that other camps were established, and the movement began to spread rapidly. During the early stages of this development only camps for boys were established. It was not until 1900 that a similar movement for girls was launched by Mr. and Mrs. C. E. Cobb, who founded the first organized camp for girls at Bridgeton, Maine.

No one will dispute the fact that other camps were in existence before this period, but it is generally agreed that only during the past half century has organized camping in the modern sense become a related movement—one which is closely identified with the educational scheme for the youth of the land.

The values of the summer camps have become so well recognized that today throughout the United States, the provinces of Canada, and foreign countries more than two million boys and girls are enjoying the benefits of camping. It is estimated that in the United States alone more than 200,000 men and women devote their summers to staff work in the camps.

It was the purpose of the early pioneers of the organized camps to plan the summer vacation so as to bring the campers close to primitive life and nature. Here, out in the open, the boys were to learn standards of clean living, discover high ideals, match wits with the elements, and learn to take care of themselves. However, the ideals and objectives which these pioneers had set up for the camps were not always followed by their successors. In some instances, the routine activities were so intensive that camp life, from reveille to taps, became "institutional." In others, the "military type" of camp gained considerable favor. This period followed closely after the World War, which may have been a factor in creating it.

While these evolutionary changes were going on, it was evident that many parents had sufficient faith in the value of the summer camp to support it generously. They were conscious of the fact that our institutionalized education had made no provision for the long vacation periods of boys and girls during the summer months.

*The Clearing House, April, 1936, reproduced by permission.

It is not so many years ago that parents and teachers held to the common belief that the schoolroom was the only place for the education of children. In fact this belief is still prevalent in many communities today. The foremost educators of our time are, however, not willing to admit this. The school with its controlled environment is only one factor in the education and life of the youth. These educators recognize that the after-school and outdoor activities of boys and girls during the preadolescent and adolescent periods are frequently a greater influence, whether for good or evil, than the formal teaching in the classroom. As evidence of this fact, particularly on its negative side, we frequently hear the statements made by teachers at the beginning of the school year, that they must devote much of their time and energy to teaching their pupils proper habits of conduct and self-control. This condition may be the result, in some measure, of having spent an aimless vacation at home, on the street, or at the playground. It is unfortunate that many parents believe that they are providing an excellent vacation for their children by taking them to their summer homes or to resorts. Here adult activities are engaged in on a large scale. A planned program for children's activities is usually not found. Boys and girls are caught in the swirl of excitement and hectic amusement on the adult level and we have the pathetic sight of mere children aping the antics, dress, and language of pleasure-seeking adults whose chief aims appear to be nervous thrills and excitement. It is encouraging, however, to find that an increasing number of parents recognize the fact that education is a continuous process and that it concerns itself with the social, physical, and emotional development of the child.

One of the most significant movements in twentieth-century education is the development of the so-called progressive schools. These schools exemplify in actual practice the new type of education which emphasizes social values, substitutes freedom for formalism, and makes life experiences the center of teaching. In short, these schools hold to the belief that education is merely an unfolding process wherein child nature is its own best guide. In order therefore that these schools may function effectively and achieve their purposes, it is essential for a pupil to have a wide range of experiences, a good mental balance, and a strong, healthy body. A theory of education of this sort places a special obligation upon parents. It presupposes that the pupil lives in a wholesome environment throughout his entire developmental stage, not merely during the time that he attends school, but during his vacation periods.

In recent years there has also been a decided trend on the part of institutions of higher learning to turn to nature's classroom for the purpose of combining recreation and study.

As a result of this intensive interest, many schools and colleges are emphasizing summer education in natural laboratories. The travel-camp summer schools offer courses in geology, engineering, art, science, forestry, health, education, etc. Summer educational caravans are conducted on a large scale, as, for example, that of the Omnibus College of the University of Wichita, Kansas. Eleven hundred students were enrolled recently in such a tour. The Fresno State Teachers College conducts a course, Education for Enjoyment, in the Sierra Nevada Mountains; the University of California sends a group of students to the Yosemite; more than fifty colleges and universities subscribe to the research laboratories at Woods Hole, Massachusetts; Princeton University geology students camp in Yellowstone National Park; summer-school students at the University of Maine carry on their work in marine zoology in their Biological Station on the northeastern shore of Frenchman's Bay; New York University conducts a physical-education camp on Lake Sabago in Palisades Interstate Park; and Columbia University teaches engineering at Camp Columbia. This is only a partial list of the colleges and universities which offer a wide variety of courses in the school of the great outdoors.

There is evidence on every hand that the bookish education which we considered sufficient unto itself as late as a decade ago is hopelessly inadequate for the needs of our pupils today. Real life becomes the workshop of the classroom. It is the summer camp with its variety of activities which affords one of the greatest opportunities for a closer coordination between the work of the school and its purposes.

In recent years camp directors have made an earnest attempt to offer educational opportunities which parents have a right to expect. Many of the camps now employ counselors especially trained in the psychology of behavior. They are aware of the fact that living together over an eight-week period (which is equal to the total number of hours in school for the entire year) makes it possible for a counselor with technical knowledge to strengthen favorable character traits among his campers and to give such help as will change those which are unfavorable. Definite progress has also been made in the direction of a positive health program. Camp life, with its routine of play, study, recreation, leisure-time activities, long hours of sleep, and a balanced diet, offers an opportunity that is unsurpassed in teaching correct health habits. First aid and safety education also have a place.

In addition to the opportunities mentioned above, camp directors and counselors are taking advantage of the other educational aspects of camp life. Here the boys and girls are exposed to a whole world of knowledge not to be gained from textbooks, and not circumscribed by a fixed curriculum. They learn a new language—lore, of the woods, water, birds, flowers, wild animals, wonders of the mountains and the sky, campcraft, music, and the beauty of the wilderness. Intimate contact with experts in science, trained foresters, musicians, artists, and other interesting characters, even though these individuals may not have classroom teaching experience, helps boys and girls, for their sentimental conceptions of nature are gradually replaced by the facts.

The boy or girl who has participated wholeheartedly in the activities of a well-organized camp is prepared for the responsibilities of a larger world and has a greater number of group interests which will inspire and direct them. Such a child has taken the first steps on the road which leads to emotional self-dependence. This child's imagination has been awakened; and, in a true sense, he has been aided in thinking and planning for himself. If the educational program of our regular schools can be made flexible enough to adapt itself to the experiences which the boys and girls bring with them from their summer camps, we shall find an enriched curriculum and stimulating course of study. Then teaching will again become an adventure.

THE INTERESTS OF EDUCATION IN CAMPING *
ELMER D. MITCHELL

No educator, today, can escape realizing the import of camping as an educational process. This observation holds true whether or not the camping movement retains its present private and semi-private sponsorship or whether it grows more closely to the institution of education in this country and thereby allies itself more closely with the established curriculums in the schools.

It is not the purpose of this article to predict the future course of school-camp relationships from the standpoint of their support through public taxation. It is true, however, that there is a growing realization that camping has educational significance and that at present only a relatively few children enjoy the benefits of camping experience. An interesting study of the recreational interests of nine thousand school children of Saginaw, Michigan, recently revealed that, whereas approximately 87 per cent of the children expressed a desire to enjoy a summer camp, only 13 per cent actually attended. Seemingly, educators are aware of this discrepancy in the number of school children who go to camp during the summer months. Dr. Willis A. Sutton, Superintendent of Schools at Atlanta, Georgia, states that an objective of his school system is "a camping experience for every school child." The Board of Education of New York City has recently appointed a commission to study the problem of providing more camping opportunities for the school children of that city. In the Far Western states, particularly California, school camps have been in existence in certain communities for some time. More colleges and universities are initiating courses in camping; some are operating demonstration and experimental camps.

*Reprinted by permission of the publisher and Phi Delta Kappa from *The Phi Delta Kappan* 21:140-142, December, 1938.

These are the present-day trends; and it is the purpose of this article to review some of the developments in camping which have broadened the scope of its educational meaning and have brought it more closely to the attention of school authorities, in fact to the point, in some instances, where camping education has formed attachments and alliances with the public schools.

Camping started definitely as a recreational movement. The purpose was to supply an interesting vacation, one filled with the type of fun that boys like best. To be specific, back in 1881 Ernest Balch took a group of boys for a vacation into the woods. This was the first camp of which much has been written. There were certain chores for each one to do, but mainly the campers were free. The idea was to do as they chose—hike, fish, swim, or just "take it easy." In the evening, "cowboys and Indians," combat games, the camp fire, and ghost stories before bedtime comprised the usual order of events.

This type of camping experience was truly a recreative and health-building one, and camps based on this conception spread in numbers, although rather slowly at first. The Y.M.C.A. and other semi-public agencies grasped this unique opportunity to utilize vacations for purposes of health, wholesome fun, group cooperative effort, and moral training. So, too, did certain of the private schools as they came to realize that a separate summer program could be built up which would enroll many members of their regular school term.

Gradually a new emphasis came into camping and a new phase of camping education developed. If the first stage of camping can be called the "recreative stage" the second stage can just as truly be called the "skills stage." This education which first took the form of training in physical skills later grew to incorporate many carry-over interests and also appreciations. Expert instruction began to be offered in swimming, horseback riding, canoeing, sailing, tennis, nature, woodcraft, music, dramatics, arts and crafts, and other forms of hobbies. Camps vied with one another in obtaining counselors for these various pursuits and the mark of the successful camp was the ability to turn out finished campers in the sense of mastery of these camping skills. This stage, in its effort to promote skills in many activities, used the device of competition. It was a period that made an exaggerated use of honors and awards.

It took years, of course, to build up the camping curriculums to the point where they included such a wide variety of activities but during the 1920s an observer, looking back over camping history, can note that education was as much a part of the camping program as was recreation. Progressive educators, by this time, were aware of the educational aspects of camping. They saw that camping furnished an environment in which certain things could be taught better than in city schools. They saw in this environment something to broaden and supplement the yearly school program. Although educators were not yet ready to sponsor the camping idea they were ready to support it in principle.

Out of this second stage of camping development grew a third one, that of guidance. The teaching of skills was continued, it is true, but they were looked upon not as ends in themselves but as means to guidance in personality growth. It was realized that children, while mastering skills in an interesting environment in which their attention was absorbed, could be studied off-guard in a way not possible in a classroom situation. The camp was a veritable child laboratory, and this brought attention to the need for personnel experts. Case studies, clinical observations, test-and-measurement programs, and behavior records were all utilized in the careful study of the child. The cabin counselor thereby became more important than the skills counselor.

Out of this new interest in camping grew several offshoots. Education found in camping a help for the "problem," or maladjusted child. At camp he could live in a more or less controlled situation for twenty-four hours a day. Subsequently, philanthropic foundations began to set up camps for the help and support of underprivileged children. Municipal camps were established for children who could not otherwise afford to go to camp. Another unique development of this period was the CCC camp program, set up and operated by Federal support—thereby enlarging the conception of camping as an educational institution to include the training of older boys and young men. This training covered the objectives of health, character, reclamation, group adjustment, and vocational guidance. The Federal Government pointedly stated that it was most interested in the support of those progressive forms of education which would adapt youth to the changing social order. From that standpoint it gave its support to camps and to newer recreational programs as against the older traditional, more rigid system of schooling. Our country, however, while using the CCC camps to build up health, reliance, citizenship, and vocational independence, has not, as have the dictators of Europe, utilized them to build up an all-absorbing fervor for the state. It is significant to point out that dictatorships fully realize the influence of the camp in the training of their youth for the loyal support of nationalistic ideals.

Just at the present moment camping seems to be entering a fourth phase for which a name is not so easy to be found. Integration although possibly not the right word, comes close to conveying the meaning. Educational recognition is present. So far as the interests of educators are concerned camping has "come of age." Camps still furnish recreation, still teach skills, still guide in personality, but even more they are tying their influence to all other influences affecting child behavior during the year. In other words, camping sees its work as part of a year-round program, as part of a larger Gestalt.

There is a growing realization that camps cannot accomplish much in guidance in two weeks, or even two months. On the other hand, camp directors see their programs as important as any other phase of the educational program which the child encounters. They see their guidance programs enlarged to bring in parental education and parental cooperation, both before and after the children enroll in camp. They see themselves allied with formal schooling, with boys' and girls' clubs, with social welfare programs, with juvenile courts (in certain instances), with records of school progress, and with the newer guidance programs. In this manner the information possessed by the camp director becomes an asset to the club leader and school official in their guidance programs; and, conversely, these individuals have information to aid the camp director.

The new program means a reeducation of camp directors. They now count on the parents to be able to interpret the child's personality to them. No cry of theirs at the present is more urgent than that of the need for new methods and tools to work out cooperative arrangements with all agencies of the community that are concerned with the all-round development of each boy and girl as future citizens. The up-to-date camp director realizes that he is but one link of many in a chain of influences affecting youthful growth and behavior.

Camping today, therefore, must be thought of as an experience having all-year-round implications and as an education involving many educational and social agencies. The summer camping experience of the child is not an isolated one. It is tied up with all his other interests of the school year.

This new conception has bearing upon some very recent trends in camping. Because of the unique opportunity to study children in the camping environment many philanthropic foundations have established camps for underprivileged or unadjusted children. In such types of camps, arrangements are made so that these children may be followed throughout the remainder of the year through the medium of some social agency which furnishes trained leadership. As another trend, camp directors, and also agencies supporting camps, are looking to the universities for leadership in conducting the progressive types of programs that are now receiving experimentation. On the one hand, this means a demand for better trained counselors for the boys and girls who will be in camp; and on the other hand, it means a demand for a higher type of graduate study which will produce camp leaders who can interpret the camping movement in its broader relationships and who can devote research to the values of camping from the standpoint of educational and social psychology. The qualifications of camp counselors are being studied; researches are being conducted upon certain health problems of camp; and the newer implications of the mental hygiene aspects of camping are being perceived.

This tie-up of camping with higher education is definitely a trend of the day. The future camp leader will be trained not only in building camp programs and in the possibilities of camping experience for guidance and development, but also in the relationships of the summer camp program to those of other youth agencies that operate throughout the year. Moreover, the curriculums of many of the college and university departments will be altered so that students may acquire the necessary skills and information to become qualified counselors during the summer months. This much is safe to predict. Whether or not the camps will become a complement of the school system and be supported from public taxation is another matter. While there are certain developments in this direction, the trend seems destined to be a slow one in view of the heavy burden under which taxpayers are grumbling. What is possible is that more philanthropic and more federal aid to camping may be forthcoming. Then the schools can tie up with the camping programs without additional expense to themselves. This is a future not difficult to conceive. In all events, camping education is now receiving the sympathetic consideration of educators. In view of this interest and support many contributions from camping education to the formal school education are certain to be forthcoming.

THE MICHIGAN PROGRAM
IN ACTION *
EUGENE B. ELLIOTT AND JULIAN W. SMITH

Michigan's extensive outdoor resources have developed in the minds of its citizens an appreciation of the relation of these resources to the health and happiness of the people. The abundance of lakes and streams, hills and valleys, and vast wooded tracts of land give opportunity for great numbers of people to seek the out-of-doors for better living. A growing awareness that the out-of-doors should be used more extensively in the growing-up process of youth has led many to feel that there is need now for special effort in camping and outdoor education. The people recognize this, and, through the Legislature, are making available to public use great tracts of lands for recreation, group camping, and other kinds of educational ventures. This realization has also promoted the Departments of Public Instruction and Conservation to enter into a joint educational enterprise. The action, conceived by the State Educational Authority and the Director of Conservation, proposes to bring together the resources of both agencies. The plan is intended to enable the people of Michigan to enter more fully into the possession, enjoyment, and use of these natural resources and the more complete cultivation of their endowments. Such a plan is designed to lead at once to improved processes of education and the more complete development and wise utilization of the natural resources of the state.

In quest of ways to stimulate the growth and development of the complete person, many educators have, at length, perceived in the out-of-doors the

*Reprinted by permission of the publisher and the National Association of Secondary School Principals from *The Bulletin on the National Association of Secondary School Principals* 31:60-74, May, 1947.

existence of an environment of educational richness and promise. It is no longer controversial that the out-of-doors can supply a wealth of learning opportunities that surpass in a variety of ways, and implement in others, the academic materials with which the curricula of conventional schools are so often saturated.

In a state like Michigan, with its versatility of resources, an outdoor educational curriculum of almost infinite variety and opulence is available for the taking. How to proceed in the most sensible way in the educational and social utilization of Michigan's out-of-doors is a question still to be answered. There is much need for demonstration research and experimentation in this field. From the standpoint of both education and conservation, it seems desirable that a large-scale inquiry should be carried forward and that outdoor education, with special emphasis upon camping and conservation, should be subjected to scientific scrutiny with respect to state planning and to local operations in the way of program, personnel, plant, and finance.

With these thoughts in mind, the two state departments joined in an effort to attack the problems involved. In addition to use of the regular resources of the two departments, involving personnel and materials, additional emphasis is needed to stimulate experimentation upon the regular state functions of the departments. A proposal was made to the W. K. Kellogg Foundation whereby funds for experimental aspects of the program might be made available to supplement the resources already present. The W. K. Kellogg Foundation, having long had an interest in camping and having conducted several experiments in local communities, felt that there was sufficient promise and certain proved values in the proposed program. The Foundation decided to pass the responsibility on to the state agencies that would be largely responsible for state-wide study and application, and made a grant to carry forward such a project.

It was proposed to approach the camping, conservation, and outdoor education problem by enlarging the Experimental Division of Health, Physical Education, Recreation, School Camping, and Outdoor Education of the Department of Public Instruction to embrace the joint experimental project, and to associate it more directly with the continued effort of the department in the harmonization and coordination of those areas concerned with the health and better living of people. This fitted into the state pattern because the schools of the state were already cooperating with the department in carrying forward the division mentioned, and were sharing in its financing by making some funds available to the State Board of Education. This had been done through an appropriation by the Michigan High School Athletic Association representing all the secondary schools of the state and approved by the Michigan Secondary School Principals.

The general objectives first listed were:

1. Research in outdoor education and camping.

2. Development of more effective avenues of education in the wise use of natural resources.
3. Provision for consultant service to schools and other agencies interested in camping and outdoor education and conservation education.
4. Advice to boards of education in the acquisition and lease of properties as permitted by the Legislature under Act 170, P.A. 1945.
5. Consultative and stimulatory efforts in related teacher education through existing teacher education agencies.
6. Development, insofar as possible, of an appropriate program of adult education and recreation through existing facilities, whether school-owned or under the direction of the Conservation Department.
7. Stimulation of experimentation in the various types of school camping and outdoor education, especially the use schools can make of state lands in such programs.
8. Development of Departmental action with other agencies of state government that have a common interest in outdoor education and camping.

The work of the camping and outdoor education phase of the whole program got under way about September 1, 1946. An Advisory Committee was appointed to explore the many possibilities of action and to coordinate the efforts of many groups. Included on the Committee were school administrators, representatives of colleges, and other organizations, such as the Michigan United Conservation Clubs, the Department of Social Welfare, the Huron-Clinton Metropolitan Authority, the State Department of Health, the State High School Athletic Association, the State Y.M.C.A., the Michigan Recreation Association, the Michigan Press Association, the Michigan Tourist Council, and members of the Departments of Public Instruction and Conservation. For the development of administrative policies and operational methods, a small committee was made up of members of the Departments of Public Instruction and Conservation. The staff included the Chief of the Experimental Division of Health, Physical Education, Recreation, School Camping, and Outdoor Education, and a consultant in conservation furnished by the Department of Conservation, with many other members of both departments serving as technical staff whenever needed. A number of subcommittees were created to study special problems, the main ones being a camping committee, an outdoor education committee from the Michigan Secondary School Association, and a conservation education committee.

Early in the program a tentative list of long-time objectives was agreed upon to make more definite the general objectives listed above. They are as follows:

I. Better utilization of natural resources and the outdoors in providing real and direct learning experiences.
   A. Development of effective policies of interaction between the Departments of Public Instruction and Conservation.

B. Greater use of the state's natural resources by the schools in enriching the curriculum.
   1. State lands for exploration, camping, field trips, excursions.
   2. Parks, recreation areas, and other state lands for community recreation programs.
   3. Use by the schools of natural resources and the services of state agencies, especially the Department of Conservation.
   4. An expanded adult education program in the wise use of natural resources.

II. Experimentation and research.
  A. Extension of the curriculum through school camping.
    1. Demonstration and observation of programs in existing camps, such as St. Mary's Lake, Clear Lake, Indian Lake, and others.
    2. Stimulation of local community schools to use the out-of-doors more effectively in the learning process.
  B. Research.
    1. Desirable school camping facilities.
    2. Camping programs that are a part of the curriculum.
    3. Acquisition of sites and the administrative units to be involved.
    4. Camp administration costs.
    5. Legal aspects of financing by school districts.
    6. Training of teachers and counselors.
    7. Coordination of educational camping with existing camping programs.
  C. Pilot school camping programs.
    1. Use of state lands for school camping.
    2. School camps on land owned by school districts, especially in relation to adjoining or nearby state lands.
    3. More extended use of existing camps, such as CCC Camps, private and social agency camps, or others that may be made available by individuals or organizations.
    4. Day camping by schools and community recreation departments.
    5. Outpost and travel camping, using state resources. Study the possibilities of youth hostels.
    6. Summer camps for youth groups such as 4-H clubs, Junior Farm Bureaus, and others.
    7. More extended use of state group camping facilities by families, community groups, and organizations.

III. Training of teachers.
  A. The participation of teacher training institutions in a camping program, used as a laboratory for human growth and development and a training camp for counselors and teachers.
  B. Joint camping programs with schools, combining teacher education and school camping.

C. Short-time conferences and workshops for teachers and camp leaders.

D. On-campus conferences and workshops in camping and outdoor education.

IV. Appropriate publications and materials.

A. A stimulating bulletin on *The Schools Go Out-of-Doors.*

B. Outline of available state and local facilities for public and school use for camping and outdoor education.

C. School camping brochure.

D. Special materials on outdoor education for school use.

E. Bibliographies.

V. Determination of policies and possible legislation.

A. Procedures for using state lands for camping by school districts.

B. Financing camping by larger school units.

1. Desirable administration patterns for financing school camping.

2. Funds from local schools.

3. Other sources of revenue.

4. Authority of camp boards to make budgets and disburse funds.

5. Responsibility of county board of supervisors and other governmental units.

C. Coordination of state supervisory and regulatory functions with respect to camping.

1. Health Department.

2. State Education Authority.

3. Social Welfare Department.

4. Possibility of vesting the authority in one agency.

D. Liability with respect to teachers and students participating in camping and outdoor education programs.

VI. Service to schools and communities.

A. Consultant and technical service to community school systems with respect to the development of camping and the private groups and other agencies engaged in such programs.

B. Working relationship with the Michigan Secondary School Association through joint committees such as the Outdoor Education Committee.

C. Cooperation with the Michigan Recreation Association in developing camping programs.

D. Special services to the five communities with experimental agricultural and conservation programs in cooperation with the W. K. Kellogg Foundation.

E. Special service to the pilot programs of the Community School Service Project.

F. Cooperation with the Parks and Recreation Division of the Conservation Department in extending the use of state lands by schools.

VII. National influence.

A. Knowledge of, and information about, the operation of other similar programs throughout the nation.

B. Attendance and participation in national conferences involving the leaders in these fields.

C. Cooperation with the programs of National Camp, Life Camps, Inc.

LEGAL BACKGROUND OF SCHOOL CAMPING IN MICHIGAN

The advent of camping as a part of the educational program of the community school was recognized by the Michigan Legislature in 1945 when it enacted Act 170, enabling school districts to purchase, maintain, and equip camps to carry out an educational and recreational program. The Act took into account the fact that schools might wish to join in a camping program to serve a larger area than was usually covered by the individual schools and made provisions for such a joint endeavor. Local schools in the state may thus recognize camping as an essential part of the curriculum in expending school funds for this program.

Act 170, P.A. 1945 added the following sections to Chapter V, Part II of the School Code.

Sec. 33. The board of education of any school district except primary school districts may operate and maintain a camp or camps for resident and non-resident pupils for recreational and instructional purposes; or may cooperate with the board of another school district or the governing body of any other municipality of the state or with individuals in the operation and maintenance of such camps in any manner in which they may mutually agree.

Sec. 34. The board or boards shall determine the age and other entrance requirements for pupils attending the camp program. Fees may be charged both resident and non-resident pupils attending the camp or camps to cover all of the operation and maintenance costs of the program: Provided, That such programs shall be operated without profit. The costs of a camp program shall not be included in the determination of the per capita costs of the regular school program of any school district.

Sec. 35. The board or boards may acquire, equip and maintain the necessary persons for the operation of the camp program which may be conducted on property located either within or outside the territorial limits of the school district. The board or boards are hereby authorized to accept private contributions to be used exclusively for the operation of such camp or camps as may be established under this act. Camps may be conducted on property under the custody and management of the school district; on other public property under the custody of the state, the federal government, the state board of education, or any county, township, city or village with its consent; or on private property with the consent of the owner.

This recognition of school camping by the Michigan Legislature prompted the Superintendent of Public Instruction to give leadership and assistance to schools interested. Camping became one of the activities in a new Experimental Division established in the Department of Public Instruction in 1945, known as the Health, Physical Education, Recreation, School Camping, and Outdoor Education Project. So much interest developed in the first year that it led to an enlargement of the Division to include the Camping and Outdoor Education Study described previously in this article.

Camping has been prominent in Michigan for many years because of the large number of private and public camps. The great increase in the number and kinds of camps, and the attendant large groups of children and adults, necessitated state policies and regulations to protect the health and welfare of those involved. In 1944, the Michigan Legislature enacted the law, Act 47, which vested in the Social Welfare Department the responsibility for licensing child welfare agencies and for regulating and supervising the care and placement of minor children. The law was interpreted to include the licensing of camps in the state. The Department of Social Welfare has authority at any time to investigate and examine the conditions of any home or other licensed place, as well as to examine the books. The acceptance for board and care of five or more children under 17 years of age and living apart from their parents, relatives, or legal guardians, primarily during the summer months, constitutes a camp as far as the licensing function is concerned.

The Department of Health may visit any licensee to advise on matters affecting the health of children and to inspect the sanitation of the building. As school camps develop, it will mean that three state departments will have legal responsibilities—that is Social Welfare, Health, and Education. As time goes on, there will be need for much coordination and possibly a simplification of this program.

TEACHER TRAINING FOR OUTDOOR EDUCATION

Michigan's interest in camping and outdoor education has centered much attention on the problems of pre-service and in-service training of teachers. There have been significant beginnings in the training of a few leaders, and plans are under way for including many others. Camping administration and counselor courses have been offered for some time in several Michigan colleges and universities, but actual on-the-job training is more recent. Michigan has been fortunate in having several leaders and teachers attend National Camp of Life Camps, Inc., over a period of years. The W. K. Kellogg Foundation scholarships have stimulated some of this excellent training at National Camp, and several of these leaders now have made significant contributions to camping in Michigan. Some of the specific efforts in training by camps and institutions are described briefly.

Clear Lake Camp, under the direction of Western Michigan College of Education, Kalamazoo. In February, 1945, Western Michigan College of

Education and the W. K. Kellogg Foundation entered into a jointly sponsored five-year experiment for seeking more effective ways of training teachers, particularly in camping and outdoor education, as well as for better understanding of child growth and development. The experiment was set up to provide opportunity for teachers, pre-service and in-service, to live with children in a school camping setting. Fifth-, sixth-, and seventh-grade pupils from neighboring communities lived together in camp for two-week periods, and the program is a part of the elementary curriculum of the cooperating schools. The pupils come as classes and are accompanied by their teachers. The objectives of the experiment are:

1. To study the feasibility and worthwhileness of school camping and outdoor education as an extension of the public school curriculum.
2. To seek to determine whether teachers, and particularly beginning teachers, are better because they have spent a week or two with pupils in a camping environment.

The opportunities of the camping experience take place as a part of the course of human growth and development, coming during the latter portion of the sophomore and junior years. A few days are spent at camp as participant observers, the college students living with the campers and participating with them in the program. The camp staff then has a number of meetings with the student teachers. Another opportunity is furnished when a student, while doing his directed teaching during his senior year, may live at the camp one or two weeks. There is also offered a two-week credit course in camping and outdoor education, which is often elected by physical educational majors and minors. In the past, there have been summer workshops in camping and outdoor education; in 1947 there will be one of six weeks duration, carrying six hours of graduate or undergraduate credit. Throughout the year, there are many conferences and workshops for teachers and administrators as well as some sponsored by outside agencies.

St. Mary's Lake, Battle Creek. The St. Mary's Lake Camp is under the direction of a camp board made up of representatives of schools and other groups in Calhoun County. The schools of the county participate in a year-round camping program, the groups of pupils and their teachers coming for a two-week period. The fourth-, fifth-, and sixth-grade groups were chosen first, but other grades and groups have been included from time to time. Some of the opportunities for teacher-training are as follows:

1. Visiting fellowships at the camp for periods of a month or more.
2. Students from a field course in community relations, Michigan State College, spend a month at camp.
3. Summer workshops for Michigan State College.

4. Short-period training sessions for teachers or administrators, as well as for local schools that may be contemplating a camping program.
5. In-service training of teachers of the schools of the county participating in the camping program. This probably is a most significant feature of teacher training at St. Mary's Lake Camp because it involves throughout the year, for two-week periods, many teachers who, in reality, serve as members of the camp staff.
6. There are many conferences and short-time workshops throughout the year for teachers and administrators and other groups.

OTHER TEACHER TRAINING OPPORTUNITIES

Central Michigan College and Northern Michigan College provide opportunities for teacher training at the Apple Blossom Camp and Indian Lake Camp, respectively. Northern Michigan College also plans a workshop at the Bay Cliff Camp during the summer of 1947, and Central Michigan College will conduct a month's workshop at a camp. The University of Michigan Fresh Air Camp provides unique opportunities for special social study. Wayne University also has carried on summer camp sessions for special groups. Michigan State College has extended its recreation curriculum to include courses in camping and the University of Michigan, Wayne University, Albion College, and others have camping courses.

Teacher training institutions have cooperated with the Conservation Department in providing a two-week credit course each year at the Higgins Lake Training School, involving conservation and outdoor education. The Camping and Outdoor Education Study is planning for several short-term workshops and training conferences for the summer of 1947 to be held throughout the state. A good beginning in teacher training has been made, but much more will be done as time goes on. Clear Lake Camp, St. Mary's Lake Camp, Indian Lake Camp, and others are serving as pilot and laboratory programs in demonstration research on camp curricula and teacher training.

LOCAL PROGRAMS OF OUTDOOR EDUCATION AND CAMPING

In Michigan the whole emphasis on outdoor education and camping has been on the extension of the curriculum of the school and its enrichment through use of the out-of-doors. There is no prescribed pattern of camping or any other form of outdoor education that is being urged or recommended for all schools. Rather, the approach has been to suggest that each school use the out-of-doors to meet its local needs, building upon the program already in operation and adding to the school plant the natural laboratory which lies outside the walls of the building. Consequently, many patterns and avenues for enrichment of the curriculum are taking form.

Schools having an unusual interest and desiring to move forward in experimentation in outdoor education and camping were chosen as pilot communities by the Camping and Outdoor Education Study. The local programs can best be described by outlining some of the patterns and schools and by brief descriptions of some programs already under way.

OUTDOOR EDUCATION AND SCHOOL CAMPING PATTERNS IN MICHIGAN

1. *Camp property owned by a school or group of schools.* A board of education in Michigan, under Act 170, P.A. 1945, may purchase property and build a camp in the same manner as it would the regular school plant. The same thing might be done by a group of schools in a united effort. An illustration of this situation is Cadillac, Michigan. Some years ago the board of education purchased suitable property for a school camp. Some buildings have been erected and there has been a summer camping program for the schools and other youth groups for some time. The program is now being extended to include more youth and to identify it more closely with the school program. Some of the buildings may be winterized so that at least a limited amount of camping may be done during the regular school year. A number of other school districts in Michigan already own tracts of land that may be developed for extended camping programs.

2. *Camp property owned by a governmental unit.* There are a number of camps owned or under the direction of a local governmental agency, such as the board of supervisors of the county park board. In some instances, the agency acquired a CCC Camp from the Federal Government. In this kind of a situation, the facilities can be made available to the whole county; in some instances, they will accommodate all youth agencies interested in camping, in addition to the school programs. A new and unique situation of this kind was found at the Indian Lake Camp, Iron County, Michigan. This camp is located on a beautiful lake in a virgin maple forest, has splendid facilities constructed by the CCC, and is now owned by the county under the direction of a park board. The camp was about to be sold a few months ago, but a few farsighted community leaders saw the possibilities of keeping it for the youth of the county. It was turned over to a committee which planned and developed a complete camping program during the summer of 1946 for the schools of Iron County and other youth agencies. Northern State Teachers College cooperated in the plan and combined the program of camping with counselor training. The schools, under authority of the new camping law, paid for instructional costs for each person, while a cost fee was paid by parents for food. A much more elaborate program is being planned for 1947, and it is expected that some of the buildings will be winterized for year-round camping. Nearly 500 youth of Iron County last year had the privilege of educational camping because the public saw the need and because some

leaders saw the possibilities for using the resources already available without any appreciable outlay of cash. Such a situation could be possible in many sections throughout the country.

3. *Camps owned by private or community agencies which are made available for school camps.* There are several instances where private foundations, such as the W. K. Kellogg Foundation, the Mott Foundation, and others have made a camp available for the use of schools. Many of the schools in southwestern Michigan have had experience by using the W. K. Kellogg Foundation Camps at Pine Lake, Clear Lake, and St. Mary's Lake. At the present time, St. Mary's Lake Camp is leased to a camp board in Calhoun County, and an extensive year-round camping program has been carried on for the schools. The Mott Foundation has provided a camp for Flint for a number of years. In the past, camping has been a summer activity, but plans are now under way for extending the program over a longer period and making it more largely a part of the regular school program.

Another variation in this category of camping is a camp which was purchased and developed by the Parent-Teacher Association and other community clubs connected with the Tappan Junior High School, Ann Arbor. The deed to the camp is held by the board of education, but interested community groups are still participating in further development and expansion of its use. A most successful program has been conducted for a number of summers, and the school is now attempting to expand its program to include more youth and a broader range of educational activities.

One of the newest projects in an active stage of development is a camp for Saginaw County. A piece of land has been given by interested citizens of St. Charles, Michigan, and the plan is being carried forward through the cooperation of the Lions Club of that city, the County School Commissioner, and other interested groups. The site has already been approved by the Michigan Department of Health, and plans for development of a camp that will serve large numbers of youth, especially rural groups, are now under way.

4. *A camp under the direction of a college.* There are a number of situations where a college or university owns or operates a camp, combining teacher training in a camp situation. In some cases, groups of schools in the region served by the college have the opportunity of participating in camping. A situation of this kind is found at Clear Lake Camp, where the W. K. Kellogg Foundation has leased the camp to Western Michigan College of Education. Other teacher training institutions having camps are Northern Michigan College of Education with the Bay Cliff Camp, Central Michigan College of Education with the Apple Blossom Camp, the University of Michigan with its Fresh Air Camp, and others. In all of these cases, plans are now under way for extending the use of the camp to include more youth and identify it more closely with the educational program of the school and the teacher training program of the institution involved.

5. *Camps used cooperatively with youth agencies, social agencies, and*

schools. In some communities, camps built by groups such as the 4-H clubs, Y.M.C.A., Y.W.C.A., Camp Fire Girls, Boy Scouts, Girl Scouts, and others can be made available part of the time for school use. This will make better use of facilities and will, in some cases, coordinate the efforts of many agencies. A number of such situations are already possible in Michigan, and steps are being taken toward extending the camping program in this manner.

6. *The use of state lands for camping.* The greatest possible opportunity for extending camping to large numbers of youth will be the use of state-owned facilities which, in Michigan, are under the direction of the Conservation Department. These will include recreation areas, game areas, group camps, and other state lands. Consideration is being given now to the development of policies so that such lands may be available to schools. It is possible, in some cases, that schools may be able to erect temporary buildings; in other instances, camps already maintained and operated by the Conservation Department can be made available for the use of schools. Two or three significant developments will illustrate this pattern. The schools of Huron County, Michigan, the 4-H Clubs, and other agencies are developing a camping program for the county. A group camp is being developed by the Conservation Department at Sleeper State Park, and plans are now under way for the use of the camp by the schools for some periods. This program will become a part of the regular program of the schools.

Another illustration is at Allegan, Michigan, where the schools are working with the Conservation Department in the use of state lands for school camping for a number of the schools in that county. A group camp already there may possibly be used by both the schools and the Michigan United Sportsmen Clubs.

The schools of Menominee County are making plans for using the facilities of the group camp at Wells State Park. This park is a beautiful site and well located for camping, and can be used for periods in the summer, early fall, and late spring.

The board of education of Kalamazoo, Michigan, is at the present time considering ways whereby school groups may use some of the facilities of the group camps in the Yankee Springs area. These facilities are extensive enough so that school groups can use them in addition to the general public. This is an excellent illustration of how facilities already in existence can be more widely enjoyed.

7. *Day camping.* Day camping is possible and will then reach nearly every school program, as well as recreation departments, social agencies, and other organizations. It is a simple way of utilizing the out-of-doors to supplement classroom instruction, in addition to providing for the development of outdoor skills and to making possible many direct learning experiences. There have been a number of day camp programs in operation, but special effort is now being made to extend them for greater use by schools and other agencies.

The schools of Van Buren County, Michigan, are planning to use the Van

Buren State Park for day camping and outdoor study. Plans are under way by which schools will transport student groups and their teachers to the park for the day. The park executive will work with the schools in making the best use of all the facilities in learning situations.

The Recreation Department of Pontiac and several other local agencies are planning to make use of some of the excellent facilities of the state recreation areas nearby for an extended day camping program in connection with summer recreation. This is a significant development in community recreation. It should point the way for greater use of Michigan's outdoor attractions.

The schools at Dowagiac have operated a successful day camp for a number of years and are planning to extend the program to a more inclusive type of school camping.

Many other communities will begin with day camping as a simple, yet effective, means for extending the curriculum.

8. *School forests.* There are many tracts of land in Michigan under the direction of schools, known as school forests. Such lands are made available to schools for reforestation. They constitute a valuable resource for outdoor education, serving as a laboratory of the school. In some cases, simple camping facilities are constructed for use of school groups. Science classes have made excellent use of school forests. Several schools are searching for additional ways to provide direct learning experiences.

Muskegon, Michigan, has a school farm which includes a forest. The school conservation club has made frequent use of it and ways are being worked out to include a broader educational program.

The Spalding Township School, Powers, Michigan, plans to build camp facilities in its school forests. School groups, as well as Boy Scouts and other youth groups, then can use it for short or more extended periods.

Big Rapids, Sault Ste. Marie, and others are experimenting in extending the use of their school forests. There are several hundred such school forests in the state which offer great possibilities for real outdoor experiences.

9. *The school site as an outdoor laboratory.* Some boards of education, in acquiring new school sites, are selecting those that include woodlots or land suitable for the development of a natural setting. Such a combination of facilities will provide for outdoor education and camping as a part of the community school program.

Waterford Township, near Pontiac, has a thirty-acre tract where a new school will be built. Twenty acres of the land are wooded, with a stream flowing through the area. The school staff and a community group are planning for the use of this site to include many forms of outdoor education, camping, and recreation.

10. *Travel camps and excursions.* A very possible type of outdoor education and camping for schools, recreation departments, and other youth agencies, is

the excursion. Some schools now provide buses or station-wagons which transport students to places of unusual interest. One pattern is to provide a staff, perhaps a fine teacher or recreation leader, making the program a part of the offering of the school. Usually such trips are taken in the summer and combine both education and wholesome recreation. Dowagiac sponsored a summer excursion covering a large portion of Northern Michigan and giving the participants an opportunity to camp in many of the state parks. The whole trip, made for a nominal sum, included boys thirteen to seventeen years of age.

A group of boys from Midland, with competent instructors, took an extensive canoe trip. Central Michigan College sponsored an excursion covering several Western states. There are many other schools that are conducting similar types of activities.

11. *Clubs and special activities.* Many secondary schools have organized clubs according to the special interests of students. Among them are:

Hunting and fishing	Arts and crafts
Bird study	Riding clubs
Nature study	Hiking clubs
Fly tying	Junior sportsmen clubs
Bait casting	Hobby clubs
Rifle clubs	Guide clubs
Archery clubs	Science clubs
Camera clubs	Taxidermy

One of the most interesting new developments is the organization of guide clubs. Some clubs are already under way in Baldwin, Roscommon, Mio, Newago, Gaylord and Kingsford. The following general outline will describe the nature of the club:

I. Purpose.
   A. Development of skills—woodcraft, building a fire, finding directions, use of a canoe, preparation of food, and other skills.
   B. Obtain knowledge of the territory in which the community is located.
      1. Historical background and lore.
      2. Knowledge of woods and streams.
      3. Study of game habitat.
   C. Being of assistance to the local community in providing for tourists, hunters, and fishermen.
   D. Provide income during the vacations, weekends, and summer months.
II. Activities.
   A. Exploration and study of hunting and fishing territory.
   B. Development of skills, cleaning game, deer drives, fly casting, etc.
   C. Study of the nature and habitat of game animals and fish.

III. Administration.
  A. Establishment of cooperative working relationship with resorts, hotels, etc., in the use of guides.
  B. Cooperate with other local services, such as restaurants, garages, hotels, etc., that would be desired by tourists.
IV. Qualifications for membership and procedures.
  A. It might be a club of boys.
  B. It might include both boys and girls of high school age.
  C. A plan might be worked out with the Department of Public Instruction and the Conservation Department for giving recognition or certificates for attainment.
V. Resources.
  A. Printed materials from the Conservation Department and other agencies concerned with wild life.
  B. Visual aids.
  C. Consultant services from state departments.

There have been other successful clubs and special activities. Among the most popular are fly tying, rifle clubs, Audubon clubs, taxidermy clubs, and junior conservation groups. Schools are assisted by the Camping and Outdoor Education Study in the organization and development of such activities.

12. *Extended use of field work and other forms of out-of-classroom activities.* Several schools are developing better techniques and teacher skills in conducting out-of-classroom learning. One of the most interesting series of experiments is in agriculture and soil conservation. Through funds made available by the W. K. Kellogg Foundation, five schools—Wayland, Olivet, W. K. Kellogg School (Augusta), Nashville, and Middleville—are developing a community program. A staff member is employed to work with students and adult groups in developing good agricultural and soil conservation practices as a part of the community school program.

13. *Other plans.* There are a number of other schools in Michigan engaging in outdoor education and camping activities that combine some of these patterns. Some have not yet located a site and other resources, others are working with the staff of the Camping and Outdoor Education Project to determine ways of action. Many others have occasional activities, such as weekend camps, excursions and field trips.

It seems evident to educators that activities, similar to those outlined must result in wiser and wider use of Michigan's natural resources, and must bring keener enjoyment to her citizens.

THE SAN DIEGO, CALIFORNIA COMMUNITY SCHOOL CAMP *

EDWIN E. PUMALA

Should camping be an integral part of the educational program offered by urban and rural schools? Educators and interested lay citizens of San Diego City and County, California, have been drawing toward this belief for several years, and in the spring of 1946, they conducted an experimental community school camp at Cuyamaca State Park, California, to test their theories. Results from a considerable investment of time and effort and a relatively modest outlay of money have been very satisfying to all concerned.

The twin aims of the project were ambitious ones: to make democracy real and understandable to boys and girls through experience in out-of-doors living; and to give every child of appropriate ages in San Diego City and County a camp experience. Although only one week encampments were possible in the beginning stage of the project, the first aim has been realized to a remarkable extent, an achievement largely due to the sound planning of the camp director, William N. Goodall. Only a beginning, but an encouraging one, has been made toward the second goal. The sixth grade level was selected for the experimental program, and from March 17 to June 14, 1946, 1201 campers plus some 300 parents, teachers, volunteers, and visitors received a camp experience. During the summer, playground groups, a Boys' Club, the 4-H Club, and various church groups reserved the camp, which made its facilities available to approximately 125 persons weekly.

Elementary-school principals of San Diego, meeting to evaluate the project, voted unanimously to continue and expand the program for the school year 1946-47. Thus Community School Camping in San Diego, long a dream, has become a reality.

HISTORY OF THE PROJECT

The idea of a public year-round camp in San Diego County was conceived seven years ago by a group of nature-loving citizens who saw the possibilities for healthful development of youth for civic betterment inherent in a community

*Reprinted by permission of the publisher and the National Association of Secondary School Principals from *The Bulletin of the National Association of Secondary School Principals* 31:100-5, May, 1947.

camp program open to all school children. Parent-teacher groups, the county and city superintendents of schools, a member of the County Board of Supervisors, and various individuals championed the idea. A committee was formed, the outgrowth of which is the present San Diego City-County Camp Commission, a five-member board representing city and county governments, city and county schools, and parent-teacher organizations. The committee negotiated for land and buildings and various federal departments and with the State Park Commission, obtaining a former CCC campsite in a state park area fifty miles east of San Diego. As soon as military regulations would permit, they began a program of rehabilitation and development of the camp property.

In 1944, plans were laid for a summer camping program, but not until the summer of 1945 could a full-scale season of camping be organized. A San Diego educator well-seasoned in camping was chosen executive secretary of the Camp Commission, and extensive improvements of buildings and grounds began. A June-to-August season of two-week camping periods was set up for children eight to fifteen years old who were not eligible for agency camps. Nine hundred youngsters took advantage of this camping opportunity, which provided horseback riding, an arts and crafts program, archery, and other sports in a mountain setting. A local school principal acted as camp director, the executive secretary of the Camp Commission assisted, and various teachers, specialists, and juniors acted as counselors.

In September and in December of 1945, church groups held special encampments on the Camp Commission's property, which was named Camp Cuyamaca for the state park in which it is located. These groups furnished their own leadership and supplies.

In November, 1945, after consultation with the W. K. Kellogg Foundation, who had operated a community school camp program in Michigan prior to the war, a full-time, year-round camping director was chosen to head the various camping activities projected under the sponsorship of the Camp Commission. These embraced, briefly, the setting up of a year-round community school camp program which would provide a camp experience for all children in San Diego City and County schools enrolled in grades five to twelve, the eventual establishment of five or six camps to include mountain, desert, and beach environments, and the provision of facilities for family and adult camping. At this time, the only member of the staff besides the director was a caretaker retained from the summer, 1945, program.

In January, 1946, the hiring of a secretary made possible the acceleration of planning activities. A camp staff was assembled; city and county school administrators prepared to enter the program; and information regarding the plan was made public. On March 5, the staff began preparations at camp; curriculum specialists from the schools met with them to plan the program of activities and pre-camp and post-camp integrated instruction in the schools. On March 17, the first group of campers, seventy-one pupils of the John Adams School in San Diego, arrived, accompanied by two teachers and three parent volunteers.

March in the mountains of San Diego County is reasonably mild. There was, however, occasional snow during the first three encampments, and there was more than occasional rain. All this dampened the campers' spirits not at all; in fact, the snow was a major thrill to city-dwellers from San Diego's mild climate. The versatile camp staff planned a satisfying program of wet-weather activities, and the safety-type oil heaters in each dormitory took care of the cloths-drying problem. Enthusiastic reports from campers, parents, and teachers began to reach the camping director.

A teacher accompanying the first group of campers told of the considerable gain in citizenship made by her camper-pupils as contrasted with the non-campers. In one brief week, the youngsters had assimilated important principles of group cooperation. They had learned enough to be able to make suggestions for the control of unsocialized individuals. They had enjoyed the camp experience so much that long-faced, they complained the following Monday morning of being "campsick." They were eager to share with their classmates the songs and stories learned at camp.

School administrators visiting the camp were struck by the happy demeanor of the campers, with the precautions of their health and safety, with the orderly freedom of activity which prevailed. Here was democracy in action, and it was education of a most important sort.

The staff, after some experimentation, came to include the following individuals: a director, in charge of overall planning; an assistant director charged with in-service training of staff and the leadership of women counselors; a nurse, four senior counselors, to plan and direct activities in the field of arts and crafts, nature lore and science, music and dramatics, campcraft, and recreation; six cabin counselors, to supervise the children in dormitories and mess hall, teach grooming, cleanliness, health habits, manners, by example and leadership (one of these workers is in charge of the dining room and assists with office and trading post routine; the others rotate dormitory supervision and assist with such camp activities as trail hikes, cook-outs, arts and crafts program, council-fire ceremonies). There are also two maintenance men, one of whom procures camp supplies from town; a chef; an assistant cook; and a kitchen helper. Various volunteer leaders assist this permanent staff nucleus, teachers accompanying their classes to camp; parents and other community leaders interested in particular encampments; adult volunteers, junior volunteers (for summer program), and apprentice counselors working toward cabin counselor or senior counselor positions.

PROGRAM OF ACTIVITIES

The program of activities is geared to the sixth-grade level and to the environment. So far as possible, choice of activities is encouraged. Every precaution is taken to insure the safety of the children.

The trail hike with nature lore painlessly introduced is a favorite activity. The camp is located along a small stream at an elevation of four thousand feet. Wooded slopes ascend to east and west, and farther up the valley are higher peaks. Chaparral growth, pine, and deciduous trees present a fascinating variety of plant forms. Wild flowers and flowering shrubs succeed each other in delicate bloom throughout the spring and summer. In the autumn, leaf coloration presents an interesting experience for California coast-dwellers. The Cuyamaca region has produced a series of Indian legends dealing with geological upheavals, mountains, trees, and streams; these are worked into both nature hike and story-telling activities. Tree-naming games, star-study, animal stalking, a nature trail (the children participating in its lay-out), murals of animals on the walls of the dining hall (these were painted by the assistant cook, who also fiddles for square dances and tells yarns at camp fires), plaster casts made of animal tracks, a science museum, a miniature zoo, a fish pool, and an aquarium are some of the means used to bring to the campers realization of the riches of the natural environment in which they are living.

Arts and crafts work stresses the use of nature materials—shrubs, pine cones, wood. Plaster casts of leaves are made into attractive plaques. A native clay bed, yielding brown clay nearly as pure as strained clay, was discovered by the craft counselor on a hiking trip with the children. This is used for modeling figurines of the animal life observed in the park.

Camp fire programs stress group singing and story telling. School groups are encouraged to share music and dramatic programs, previously prepared, with the group at camp. Often folk dancing or a costume party will form the evening's entertainment.

Handling of knives and axes, building the camp fire, cooking out-of-doors, use of woodworking tools are among the skills taught by the campcraft counselor. Archery, tumbling, and wrestling are free-time activities supervised by the recreation counselor.

Arithmetic skills are made functional through the Trade Winds Bank and the Camp Trading Post. Each child deposits his spending money in the bank on arrival. He makes out a check for each purchase at the store and must keep his bank balance accurately. The remainder is refunded as he leaves camp. A library, drawing on both city and county library loan collections, provides the needs of both campers and staff. An attractive reading room is open daily at free periods, and books may also be taken to dormitories for the week.

To reach the main goal of the program, development of skill in a democratic way of life, many means are used. Almost immediately after arrival, children go to dormitories with their cabin counselors. At once the opportunity for choice presents itself: a bunk and bunkmate. After preliminary instructions and a tour of the grounds, the children go to the mess hall for supper. The democratic process begins. Someone volunteers as waiter at each table. Two more offer their services as dishwashers. The fact that others have rights enters each child's consciousness as he waits for the rest to be served before beginning the meal himself. There is plenty of food, so no one needs to be afraid he will not get his share.

After learning to make up his own bunk, the camper goes to an inspiring council-fire service, where he takes the Camp Cuyamaca Pledge, modeled on the State Park Commission's "Golden Rule of Out-of-Door Manners."

Results of this method have been apparent in comments of children, teachers, and parents. The community is becoming increasingly aware of the program and its benefits, and is becoming proud of the project as a community enterprise. School authorities in city and county have been convinced of the project's value and are seeking ways to strengthen and extend the program. It is now, in fact, a community school camp.

With the Cuyamaca project well under way, plans for expansion of the program are being laid for the second camp: Palomar, a beautiful mountain site in a small and exquisite valley and the home of the famous Palomar Observatory. Here is big pine country with a small lake nestled between the peaks. Boating, swimming, and fishing can be part of the activities program. Requests to use this beautiful playground are already being received by the Camp Commission. The land has been leased to the county at no charge for a 20-year period, with renewal privileges. The county is furnishing the cost of improving buildings and grounds. They have appropriated $40,000 this fiscal year for the project.

An important part of the planning in the development of Camp Palomar concerns the use of high school youth in a work experience camp project, with skilled supervision by school vocational leaders and counselors. Tentative plans call for a four-hour paid work day and a four-hour supervised study and recreation period. Each encampment will be for at least a ten-day period.

A third mountain site in a national forest area has been offered to the Commission, and desert and beach areas for future use are under consideration.

The successful completion of the experimental phase of the school camp in the spring of 1946 and the inauguration of the plans for expansion were not accomplished without the surmounting of numerous obstacles. To obtain the first camp-site seven departments in Washington had to be consulted and the State Park Commission permission secured. The fact that so many groups have cooperated to bring about the program's success has in itself made problems in reaching decisions and pursuing a single-minded course of action. The backing of able, enthusiastic, and tireless champions of the idea has, however, brought fruition to the dream. Legislation now pending in the California State Legislature may simplify financing for the future.

Lessons learned from the surmounting of these various problems have been many. To succeed, a community school camp must have a nucleus of civic-minded backers, adequate financing, sound and sufficient leadership. Many people must be informed of the new plan and must become converts through the contagion of leadership, because of the standards of camping upheld and by virtue of the value of the camp program offered. Coeducational camping meets children's needs and the campers themselves will become ardent advocates of the community school camp. Not a child has returned from Camp Cuyamaca who was not glowing with happiness from his experience.

To other communities, San Diego has this word of advice: take your time, gather funds, plan well, work hard. You'll find the dividends well worth the effort.

CAMPING EDUCATION—A PHILOSOPHY *

R. T. DeWITT

Camping, as a learning environment, is slowly but surely making inroads on the educational scene. Until recent years camping has been considered a vacation activity for boys and girls of the upper socioeconomic level with the educational possibilities used as a selling point to parents. Through the years there have been a few clear-thinking, sincere men and women teachers who were employed in camps during the summer. They began to realize that the potential educational experiences for the developing child were virtually unlimited and the surface of the possibilities only scratched. These people began to ask themselves why, if camping has educational possibilities and such an environment could be made available to the school child, would not such an arrangement be an asset to the child's total education? Before administrators would allow such addition to the curriculum, it had to be proved beyond any doubt that a day, a week, or three weeks in a camping environment could be of equal or greater educational value as the same period of time spent in the classroom.

Notable among the early experiments conducted to prove the educational possibilities of camping were the Kellogg Foundation experiment in cooperation with the Battle Creek schools under the direction of George Donaldson, the Life

*Reprinted with permission from *The National Elementary Principal* 28:3-5, February, 1949. Copyright, 1949, Department of Elementary School Principals, National Education Association. All rights reserved.

Camps experiment under the direction of L. B. Sharp, the San Diego City-County experiment, and the George Peabody College experiment. These trials at educational camping were evaluated either subjectively or objectively and all of them lived up to the preliminary hypothesis. They were proved so educationally sound that all of them are being continued in some form. Reports of these projects have so stimulated other camping people, teachers—principally those in the elementary field—and school administrators, that in widely scattered sections of the nation city and county boards of education are buying camp sites and installing camping facilities or they are making arrangements for the use of existing private or agency owned camps.

What is it about the camping environment that makes it an educational situation as good as, or better than, the traditional classroom? What phases of a child's life are more significantly developed in camp than in the classroom?

It must be assumed, first of all, that the camp experience will be guided by people well grounded in sound elementary education principles and method. They should proceed on the assumption that education is the chief aim of camp, with enjoyment on the part of the camper a means toward this end. The basic philosophy back of all activities should be clearly defined long before the first day of camp—yes, even before preliminary planning has begun.

A sound basic aim might be to provide the essential real life experiences for the child in the camp environment which could not be provided so well in any other learning environment.

It may or may not be an inherent trait in children, both boys and girls, to dream of the day when they will spend time outdoors fishing, hunting, cooking over an open fire, or sleeping in a tent. In order that these activities may be more orderly and enjoyable there should be group planning for the experience, meal planning, and the learning of such skills as are needed for shelter building, fire making, hunting and fishing. Here in this same environment, with guidance, a child may be stimulated to wonder about the trees, birds, rock formations, and stars to such an extent that he will investigate them.

In such an environment, with so many interesting activities, the project method has been found to be a highly successful means of bringing about essential learning. The children decide on a project. They set before themselves one chief aim. Before this can be realized certain hurdles must be overcome, each of which is a phase of total education. Three examples are in order.

The children desire good food at a reasonable price while in camp. In order to have good food it is necessary to plan meals on the basis of likes, dislikes, nutritional value and cost. It is necessary to buy the food, to prepare it, place it on the table, and then to clean up afterwards. With the one chief aim of placing good food on the table, a child has learned cooperation with others, food value nutritionally and economically, arithmetic, how to make a fire, cook, reasons for refrigeration and sanitation.

A child desires to make a letter opener. He goes into the woods, selects a tree that he knows to be of no benefit to the woods or as future commercial lumber, but the wood of which will make a useful object. He chops down the tree, splits it up, carves his letter opener and puts a fine finish on a beautiful, useful object. In this project he has learned the value of trees to the woods and to mankind, he has learned the use of saw, axe, and knife, and he has made an object for his desk at home to which he can proudly point and say, "I saw this growing in the woods."

In order to have a fish the child catches it, cleans and cooks it. He has pitted his wiles against those of the fish and won, and the process has given him a deeper understanding of what is involved in placing food on the table at home. He has also the deep satisfaction of knowing that he did it himself.

Through experience in camping the child has an opportunity of learning at first hand many facts of nature and the correlated relationship of animals and plants and their individual and combined contributions to humankind. He learns something of cooking, how to care for his living quarters and clothes. He learns the hazards of the out-of-doors and how to remain safe in such environment.

In addition to the skills mentioned it is possible in group living, through interdependence on each other, for the child to develop a sense of cooperation and independence and to make social adjustments.

In an experiment conducted last spring by the writer and others of the staff of the George Peabody College for Teachers, in which the seventh grade of the Demonstration School was placed in a camp environment for a week, an effort was made to determine what was actually achieved. The pupils, parents, and staff were asked to make a statement as to what they wanted the camp experience to do for the child. When camp was over they were asked to make a statement as to what they felt the camp actually had done for the child. The second report was somewhat different from the first for several reasons but chiefly because of some educational emphasis during camp of which the parents and children were not aware when writing the first statement. Generally all the aims were achieved in some degree.

When the results of the experience were summed up they were placed in two categories titled "tangible" and "intangible." In the former there were: knowledge of nature, how to prepare food, safety, camp crafts, and how to plan programs. Under intangible were grouped cooperation, knowing each other better, knowing other people, independence, good time, and better social adjustment.

The counselors, children and parents were convinced that these phases of education could not have been accomplished so well in the classroom as they were in camp.

The Peabody experiment ran for a week. More could have been accomplished had it gone on for two or three weeks. However, it is possible to have worthwhile educational experiences during a weekend in the open or even during an afternoon nature walk or an evening cookout. Through the planning together of teacher and pupils worthwhile educational objectives may be set up and followed through to conclusion whether the time allowed is an afternoon or three weeks.

These things being true, it is hard to understand how alert educators can ignore the camping environment in the future elementary education.

A DECADE OF PROGRESS IN OUTDOOR EDUCATION *

JULIAN W. SMITH

The decade (1955-1965) was a significant period in the growth of outdoor education. New programs of varying types were initiated in hundreds of schools and colleges; existing programs were improved and expanded; and additional resources, including lands and facilities, became available. The greatest single achievement during the ten-year period, however, is the broadened concept of outdoor education which includes the use of the outdoors as a laboratory for learning and the acquisition of knowledge and skills necessary for wise and satisfying outdoor interests and pursuits. In helping to establish this broad concept of outdoor education and create a greater awareness of the need and potential for this development in education, the Outdoor Education Project of the American Association for Health, Physical Education, and Recreation has made a major contribution.

AIMS AND PURPOSES OF THE PROJECT

Recognizing the great increase of public interest in all kinds of outdoor pursuits creating an urgent need for education for the wise and satisfying use of the outdoors and natural resources, the American Association for Health, Physical Education, and Recreation (a department of the National Education Association) established the Outdoor Education Project in 1955. Cooperating in the venture were business and industry groups concerned with outdoor education, member departments of the NEA, and other organizations involved in outdoor-related educational programs. It was decided from the beginning that the Project should devote its full efforts to all aspects of outdoor education

*Reprinted by permission of the author and publisher from *Journal of Outdoor Education* 1:3-5, Fall 1966.

through the preparation of leadership, the improvement of educational programs through the use of the outdoors, and the preparation of needed materials. Like other educational ventures of this type, the Outdoor Education Project serves as a spearhead to accelerate the growth of outdoor education. The AAHPER as a member of the NEA family represents the complete spectrum of education and is the first and only professional education organization to give national leadership to outdoor education in its broadest sense. There has been full cooperation with other professional associations and organizations in the achievement of common purposes.

A TIMELY VENTURE

The educational decade in which the Project emerged is characterized by contrasts. On the one hand, there were strong forces in support of the highly academic aspects of education. Gains made in outdoor education against this backdrop are remarkable. On the other hand, the climate for the emphasis on outdoor education has been good, particularly in view of the great surge of public interest in all forms of outdoor pursuits and the current national developments in support of resources and programs. In this sense, the Project was a forerunner to many significant events, such as the report of the Outdoor Recreation Resources Review Commission, the creation of the Bureau of Outdoor Recreation, the Land and Water Conservation Fund Act, and other important developments in federal and state governments.

The Project's efforts consequently were on two fronts: Interpreting the value of outdoor education in the learning process and in academic achievement; and in helping educate for a more "literate" outdoor public. Thus the Project's concern for the teaching of skills, attitudes, and appreciations necessary for outdoor pursuits was extremely timely. Likewise, new programs using the outdoors to enrich the curriculum and improve learning were developing. Many of these were stimulated by federal and state legislation and agency services. These developments called for strong leadership by the Project and kept the efforts and funds committed to outdoor education in its totality.

COMMITMENTS OF THE OUTDOOR EDUCATION PROJECT

The Project, from the beginning, was dedicated to the development of strong leadership in outdoor education. The funds provided by business and industry, added to the resources of the AAHPER and the cooperation of Michigan State University, made it possible for thousands of school and college administrators and teachers, camp, recreation and community leaders, conservationists, and others interested in outdoor education to participate in a wide variety of in-service education and planning activities. Consultant services are provided to schools, colleges and communities. The financial contributions from business and industry have been administered similarly to foundation grants to educational institutions and organizations. The AAHPER submits carefully planned proposals with a budget each year to the cooperating organizations of business and industry. It is significant that at the school and college levels the Project's efforts have cut across all segments of education since the AAHPER is a member of the NEA family. It is interesting to note that of the more than 18,000 people participating in the Project-sponsored workshops the number has been about equally divided among school and college administrators, elementary and secondary teachers, and leaders in physical education, recreation, and conservation. The Project has been guided by a National Advisory Committee of outstanding leaders and assisted by many special committees with special assignments.

A BRIEF RESUME OF ACTIVITIES, 1955-1965 [1]

1. Teacher and leadership preparation:
   Outdoor education workshops:
   > 180 state and regional workshops in 40 states (75 of these sponsored by the Outdoor Education Project and 105 in which the Project cooperated).
   > 18,500 teachers and leaders have participated in these three-day workshops.

   Graduate outdoor education workshops and courses:
   > 10,000 selected teachers and leaders have attended the 25 workshops and seminars conducted each summer by colleges and universities in cooperation with the Outdoor Education Project. The graduate workshop held in Michigan each summer has attracted leaders from many states. Here over 500 people have had two weeks of study in outdoor education.

   College and University physical education and recreation programs:
   > 30,000 prospective physical education teachers and recreation leaders have received instruction in outdoor skills.

2. Outdoor schools:
   Entire classrooms spend one week of school in camp and have instruction in outdoor education:
   > 1955: 300 school districts in the United States
   > 1965: 1,000 school districts
   > 500,000 children now have learning experiences in outdoor schools each year.

3. Interpretation and promotion:

---

[1] Obviously, the Project lays no claim to being the single force behind all of the activities cited herein.

Outdoor education programs, exhibits and demonstrations conducted in state and national workshops, conventions, and conferences:

AAHPER national, district and state associations	attended by	200,000
School administrators and teachers		250,000
Camping and recreation personnel		150,000

4. Publications:

Outdoor Education

Outdoor Education for American Youth

Casting & Angling

Shooting & Hunting

Marksmanship for Young Shooters

Education in and for the Outdoors

Teaching Casting and Angling

A Manual for Archery Instructors Workshops

Outdoor Education Newsletter

5. Growth in the number of children and youth in outdoor skills programs:

1955: 360,000 enrolled in schools and colleges offering outdoor skills.

1965: 2,500,000 received instruction and participated in outdoor skill activities through schools, colleges, camps, and recreation departments.

6. National conferences on outdoor education:

May 1958: Washington, D.C.

May 1962: Kellogg Gull Lake Biological Station, Hickory Corners, Michigan

Each conference attended by approximately 100 leaders in outdoor education, conservation, recreation, and industry.

Next National Conference: October 1966, Washington, D.C.

An important recent development is the creation of the Council on Outdoor Education and Camping in the AAHPER. The Council, with approximately 200 members, represents many disciplines and constitutes a professional base of operation for those who have an interest in outdoor education. The strength of any professional association lies in its potential to develop leadership and the best evidence of success of the AAHPER's Outdoor Education Project is the large number of those who can be counted among the leaders in outdoor education.

The Outdoor Education Project's responsibility is greater now than ever before as a "cutting edge" and in playing a supporting role to states and local educational systems in the development of leadership, programs, and facilities. There is a special challenge and opportunity to assist in the planning and development of new programs that are being initiated with federal encouragement.

Many factors influence change and are responsible for developments in education to meet modern needs. The Outdoor Education Project is one important source of leadership and influence in this era in which it serves and contributes to the ultimate objective of improving the quality of living in our times.

Chapter three
The Outdoor Laboratory:
What and How

INTRODUCTION

The purposes for which the out-of-doors is utilized as a laboratory for learning may take many directions. No one goal or single set of objectives has governed the way in which outdoor education has developed. The conservationist, the recreation leader, the scientist, and the classroom teacher have a variety of reasons for working with youth in the outdoors. The reason for a "lesson" might be the development of certain appreciations, self-realization, techniques of discovery and investigation, democratic understanding, or re-creative experiences.

Outdoor education has been defined as the utilization of the out-of-doors to facilitate and enrich learning related to the school curriculum. This interpretation implies that outdoor education in the schools is an integral part of the curriculum that involves an extension of the classroom to an outdoor laboratory beyond the school building. This laboratory can be right outside the classroom door on the school yard; it could be a nearby vacant lot or park. It might be the city zoo, bird sanctuary, or something more distant such as a state or national park. Outdoor education involves a series of direct experiences in any or all phases of the curriculum dealing with natural phenomena and living situations which increase perception and understanding of our own lives and environment. The total range of subject matter areas can be taught: art, geography, history, language, arts, music, mathematics, science, and physical education. These "lessons" may last from five minutes to one hour, to an entire day or one week. All grade levels, from kindergarten to college can benefit from a program of complementary learning experiences in the out-of-doors.

Most educators believe that outdoor education is basically a method or an approach to learning. Certainly, the outdoor laboratory lends itself ideally to a wide range of teaching strategies and techniques that are useful not only in the outdoor classroom, but can be transferred back to the indoor classroom with considerable effectiveness. The articles found in this chapter reflect the "variety" that developed in the name of outdoor education.

OUTDOOR EDUCATION AND THE DISCOVERY APPROACH TO LEARNING*

PAUL E. BLACKWOOD

The entire physical universe is the realm of study which interests scientists. Some are engaged in the careful study of the motions of bodies in the universe of stars and planets, others the motions of electrons and protons in the innermost structure of atoms. From the largest aspects of the universe to the most minute are drawn areas of study that interest scientists. What can be known about the structure of matter be it in large or small packages? What can be said about energy in molecules, in galaxies, in plants, in animals, in man? What can be learned about the interrelationships between matter and energy? Are there some unifying ideas that can be verified which will help us understand the apparent variety and haphazardness of events in nature? What are the over-arching and all-inclusive descriptions of things and events in our universe

*Reprinted by permission of the author and publisher from *Journal of Outdoor Education* 1:6-8, Fall, 1966.

which will help us understand and explain particular events and phenomena and will give us an increasingly broader and sounder basis for making predictions? To find such answers to such questions is the hope and the challenge of scientists.

Today there are numerous developments in science education to help pupils understand the role of science and scientists in seeking such answers. The new science curriculums for young children, for high school, or for higher education, almost without exception place a high value on helping pupils come to understand the nature of science. The learners are introduced early to opportunities to discover the fundamental concepts through direct experiences with objects and forces in their environment and with a variety of learning resources to help them understand and interpret their observations. Pupils are encouraged to use whatever inherent tendencies they have to investigate, to inquire and to explore, and are given systematic help in refining their ways of making investigations. As pupils move through the school science program, it is hoped they will become more and more mature in their knowledge of basic concepts of science and better equipped with the tools of learning that characterize scientists at work.

"Science is no more a collection of facts than a house is a collection of bricks," said Poincare, the famous French mathematician. This sentiment runs consistently through the new science curriculums. But the *discovery of facts* is another matter. For discovering facts is one of the basic and perhaps most important activities of scientists. Someone has even proposed the definition that *science is the discovery of new facts.* It is rather needless to be limited by a single definition of science, for there are several ways of characterizing or defining science. But thinking of science as the discovery of new facts does give us a tremendous running start toward the goal of excellence in science teaching. It is this way of looking at science that is responsible for the renewed emphasis on the role of the laboratory in teaching science.

In outdoor education the laboratory is often a pond or a field or a star-filled sky. Or, it may be a rocky hillside, or a mucky swamp, or a dead tree trunk. As often as not, the problem being studied may require intense activity in a library or in a building equipped with microscopes or chemical apparatus. Outdoor education surely does not stop when one goes indoors to explore a question. Nor, does it automatically begin when one goes out-of-doors.

Let us consider how the emphasis on building science programs rich in opportunities to investigate, to inquire, to explore, to discover new facts, is useful when applied to programs of outdoor education.

To assess outdoor programs from this point of view would mean, as a minimum, that we ask from time to time, "Do participants have an opportunity to discover new facts?" If they do, then we know we are on the right track. If they don't, then perhaps a reassessment is in order.

In this "discovery approach" there is an assumption that pupils should actually have experiences that are science-like, that are similar to what scientists do. What then are some of the things scientists do? Two examples will serve.

First, scientists describe things. They make descriptions of things in our universe. These may be descriptions of objects, events, processes, inter-relationships, or changes in the environment. Scientists are making descriptions when they answer such questions as: What are things like? What happens when? How do things take place? When do events occur and recur?

Secondly, scientists attempt to explain things. They make explanations of events, processes, and changes that take place. They try to collect evidence that will answer why things happen the way they do. In answering "why," scientists attempt to identify the cause and effect of relationships between events.

In making descriptions and explanations of phenomena in nature scientists are continuously engaged in using techniques of discovery. They use instruments of measurements: rulers, scales, thermometers, clocks, meters. They use microscopes and telescopes. They use the ideas of others from books and from conversations. They experiment. They keep careful records of their observations. Above all, scientists think and reason. These should all be prominent ingredients of what pupils do when they are engaged in the science-oriented aspects of their outdoor education program.

Notice that both *describing* and *explaining* are processes involving action. Simply memorizing facts and information discovered by others does not fill the bill.

Without implying that all activities or studies in science or in outdoor education be related to making investigations in which new facts are to be discovered, let us consider further what genuine commitment to that approach might mean.

It would mean a careful identification of problems and questions which pupils can investigate with the hope of some success in getting new facts. It would mean that in a well-planned outdoor education program, "research questions" with pay-off value would be identified for potential use with participants of different ages or different experience backgrounds in connection with the various phases of the program. The clue to identifying such questions is that no one knows the specific answers to the questions. The specific data from which a broader learning might be derived will be available only after the participants collect it. It is not in a book; it is not in a scientist's, or a teacher's, or leader's head. The facts discovered through active exploration by participants are new facts in the sense that they are not known to anyone, not available in reference books, or in the science books used by the learners.

In outdoor education, it is possible to identify a large number of "small researches" that will lead to the discovery of new facts. Here are some examples:

1. How many hours does it take moist bean (radish, corn, tomato) seeds to

germinate at room temperature? In good soil in a shaded area? In good soil saturated with water? In very dry soil?

2. What is the average height of 10 bean seedlings under favorable growing conditions after a 5-day growing period?

3. What is the average height of bean seedlings after a 10-day growing period in good loam soil? In sand? In poor soil?

4. How many corn pollen grains fall on a sticky microscope slide placed 10 feet from a blooming corn plant?

5. How many different kinds of plants can be found in a one-block area near our school? In a 10 square foot area in a forest? In a 10 square foot desert area?

6. How long does it take for one quart of water to evaporate from a bird bath? From a quart jar?

7. How many grams of minerals are in one gallon of sea water?

8. How many and what kinds of birds appear at a bird-feeding station on April 23 (or any selected day)?

9. How many and what kinds of worms are in a selected sample of rich soil?

10. What is the length of the shadow of a 3 foot stick placed upright in a sunny spot 10 feet south of our school building at 10, 12, and 2 o'clock?

11. What is the length of the shadow of a 3 foot stick placed upright in a sunny spot 10 feet south of our school building at 10 a.m., on November 15, 20, and 25 (or other selected days)?

12. What is the average temperature of the air at the southeast corner of the school building at noon during the week of December 6th?

13. What is the temperature of the soil 2 inches below the surface each hour on the hour from 9 to 3 on a school day? At noon on the 15th of each month?

It can be seen that these sample questions suggest "researches" which pupils can plan and carry out. Each research will yield some data, some facts. It should be understood that the "new facts" have no great value in themselves but are useful in stimulating pupils to take the next step, interpreting and explaining the facts. Sometimes the pupils will be able to arrive at a generalization or statement of a scientific principle based on their collection of data or facts. For example, as a result of analyzing the facts about germinating radish or tomato seeds, they may decide that *seeds sprout faster in a warm temperature than in a cold temperature.* Or they *may discover* that *seedlings grow better in rich loam than in sand.* It is true that such general statements may not be new to all pupils or to scientists. Rather, such scientific principles or concepts may have been known for centuries. This is not the point. The point is that pupils will have had the experience of deriving scientific generalizations from observed facts which they themselves have collected.

The great value of the discovery approach, then, is that pupils have real experience in using the methods of scientists. The ideas gained about their environment will have more meaning when pupils have learned them through direct observation based on investigations of their own. But equally important, the ability to use the methods of discovery will remain as a powerful tool for further learning long after specific facts have been forgotten.

COGNITIVE LEARNING AND OUTDOOR EDUCATION *

JAMES WARD

Education generally seems to be seeking to give increased attention to the skills that have to do with the construction of meaning of thought. Such skills might be referred to as the intellectual operations, perception-cognition; in short, the operation of the knowing process achieving the product of knowledge.

The increased attention to the skills of perception-cognition carries fundamental assumptions. Every physiologically normal individual is capable of learning to operate at an advanced intellectual level; all have vast potential for expanded sensibility and powers of mind. We cannot assume, however, that such powers will naturally and inevitably develop to a high level. Education must directly, explicitly, and continuously seek their further development.

It is commonly believed by enthusiasts of outdoor education that the outdoor setting especially lends itself to helping the individual expand and appreciate the commingling of his sensory powers, his intellectual powers, his aesthetic powers. How might this belief be justified? What are some avenues by which it might be realized?

The outdoors has a strong *being quality,* a quality of being real, alive, and in the process of happening. Things can be seen in actual context, relationships and process. One is actually involved in and learning about what *is.* The tangible quality appeals. It pulls the senses. In other words the natural setting and content is an empirical setting, one that can make strong use of inductive teaching and learning. Here observation is central and offers limitless sensory data to the individual. Learning is individualized.

Yet the actual and tangible quality can be a limitation to cognitive learning, i.e., learning that uses and treats, reasons with the data it receives. One can remain at the level of perceiving, be merely a collector of facts, of sensory information. Clearly one should go on to reason, to infer, to treat and make use

*Reprinted with permission from *Journal of Outdoor Education* 2:3-6, Winter, 1968.

of that which is perceived. Further meaning must be abstracted and constructed. The outdoor environment, then, can capture the attention strongly, but it can hold it to the level of the immediate, the specific and concrete. There is, of course, no real dichotomy between the powers of perception and cognition. Inextricably related and mutually dependent, they produce one's world of meaning.

What is thought of as subject matter and the approach to it will strongly influence how the student will perceive and then reason with what he gets. Consider the examples of subject matter concepts in the following two categories:

I	II
trees	process
rocks	form and perspective
birds	cyclic relationships
mammals	cause and effect

Category I is made up of concepts that can remain at the "fact collecting" level. "There are oaks and maples here." "That oak is taller than that one." "The bird is black. It is feeding on the weed seed." "There is water in the gully." Thought is directly limited to a chronicling of the facts. Yet abstraction is involved in the perceiving (gathering) of the information, for perception must make use of the mind's concepts to order and schematize what is perceived. Such abstraction is a "first order" abstraction, i.e., directly tied to facts of the specific instance. A higher order of abstraction is necessary if the individual is to infer meaning from the facts. He must collect items of fact and then make meaning constructs from what his senses have told him. He must reason.

Category II is made up of concepts that are highly abstract. The generalization that an effect may have multiple causes contains no specific elements of the concrete. It can be inferred only if the individual can observe what is happening to things and has an awareness of relationships. One must learn that things do not exist removed from their context of process and relationships. The world is not just a noun world; it is also a verb world.

To develop facility with abstraction would involve the ability to perceive and to reason from various orientations, to have flexibility of mind. It may be assumed that there is available a limitless quantity of sensory data and that they can be put together in an infinite number of ways or mind constructs. An infinite number of "facts" are available and thoughts may be constructed from such facts. What are some principles that pertain to the improvement of the powers of abstraction?

The knowledge and thought framework that one brings to bear on the act of observation helps to determine how much and how precisely one "sees." Facts are important. The more one knows, the more one tends to see—but what one sees is cast in terms of what one knows.

Picture yourself walking over a bed of gravel. The crunching sound and feel of the rocks has drawn your attention. As you look down at what is under your feet what you see will be determined by what you know about rocks. If the only appropriate concept that you have available in your mind is *rock* then your perception would be limited to just an awareness of rocks. You might be aware of rather vague and inchoate differences of color and texture, but you're still seeing nothing more than rocks. If, on the other hand, you know (have available) more specific concepts such as agate, jaspar, flint, etc., your powers of perception will be able to move in and discriminate that much more precisely. Perception moves in on and is arrested at a level of precision that is predetermined by the concepts we bring to bear, concepts cast mainly in language. What do we abstract when we observe the sensory field? We "see" the cognitive framework that the sensory experience calls up in our mind. We *see* the framework and we see *with* it.

Numberless examples of the principle could be described. It is highly important that children discover—and explicitly so—that it takes knowledge in order to perceive. Perception cannot even exist without the organizing and schematizing power of some kind of cognitive framework. A person can walk through a forest and be limited to seeing nothing more specific than trees or perhaps just a smear of *things.*

A strong relationship exists between language power and the power to know. The mind's concepts are primarily cast in the contentive words. Such words serve as nodes of coherence that attract meaning for the individual as he observes and experiences his surroundings. A given contentive abstracts various elements from out of the sensory field and brings the elements together to form or to expand a concept. Meaning precipitates out of the totality of the event. Elements may, for example, merge and be synthesized as *beauty, instinct,* or any "appropriate" concept. Sensation is transformed via symbolism into meaning. Abstraction occurs. All meaning may be thought of as inferential, implicit—in the sense that it is made, synthesized, constructed, "read" by the mind. Vague ideas and feelings can be made manifest by language. When such feelings or ideas are explicitly rendered into language then they can be said to exist at a useful level. "Boys and girls, what can you read from the trees?"

Any given phenomenon or event system (itself a synthetic construct of the observer) offers limitless meaning possibilities to be read; and the meaning can be cast at various levels of specificity or, if you will, generality. First, the event must be attended, must be noticed. (How much escapes notice?) At the first level of abstraction, that of perception, the observer is seeing the *specific instance.* He sees water running down the gully, let us say. His attention might be drawn to dirt and sticks being taken loose and carried away by the water. So what? Maybe he will wonder why. The curiosity about cause may lead him to a simple generalization: rainwater, as it flows, moves dirt. Facility with abstraction and his power of reasoning by analogy can lead him to higher order abstraction, e.g., water is a source of power or material objects can be moved by a force.

It takes sophisticated powers of abstraction to be able to get from the observed event system of *"The* water is moving *the* stick" to "Water moves sticks" and on to "Water is a potential source of power." Notice again that one could easily remain at the level of seeing only the specific instance—and not be able to see it as representative. Reasoning can lead to the discovery and explicit construction of a principle.

One can move up the ladder of abstraction from the more concrete to the more abstract by first noticing and then cohering the elements of the specific instance. The elements are classified and ordered and at some point are perceived as evidence of a simple generalization. More and more abstract generalizations may be formed, each one linked to the previous and lower level of abstraction by a common factor. Perception of the common or linking element is central to the ability to reason by analogy.

Events, things, and occurrences are ordinarily thought of as existing at the concrete level and the specific instance. This level is the manifestation level. Natural phenomena (the explicit) can be thought of as standing for or representing natural principles, generalizations (the implicit). An infinite number of principles wait to be inferred from the world of natural events. "Boys and girls, isn't it exciting to realize that there is no end to the knowledge that the mind can gather and construct?"

In sum it may be said that the cognitive framework that the individual uses in the act of perception serves as a standard of comparison for abstracting objective characteristics. Theoretically, everything has limitless objective attributes. The number and kind of attributes that the individual pulls out from his field of perception will entirely depend on the knowledge framework against which he mirrors the object of perception. Further, the cognitive framework is itself flexible and can be organized and reorganized *ad infinitum* for observing any thing or event. All of which is to say that we *can* look at the world from various orientations—thus flexibility of mind. Certainly it is practical to understand that there is no end to the knowledge that can be gathered and constructed and expressed. It is also exciting and zestful. The world is filled with wonder, and it is good to be alive.

What do such ideas say to the teacher? Use the outdoor setting to foster sensibility. Try looking out at the world in different ways. Strive to get children to discover and deal with such concepts as *relevancy, context, relationships, function, process*—for unless the individual is able to get beyond the immediate and concrete his thinking will remain limited and superficial.

Further, it is to be remembered that emotions and feelings become involved in the natural environment. It is not the place to be aloof and detached, for one is in on happening. The personalized and subjective involvement can heighten

the sensory awareness. Certainly the related power of imagination can foster flexibility of outlook and the ability to reason by analogy. The oldtime object lesson and nature study approach to science was accused of fostering an animistic and anthropomorphic outlook toward nature. Hence it was bad science, for it tended to defeat the objective and scientific approach. Perhaps. However, the old approach may have distinctively helped one to identify and have a personalized relationship with nature, promoted a feeling of deep appreciation and interest for nature. Along with the personalized and subjective approach, an objective and scientific outlook could be developed. The two together could be powerful for individual sensibility and rationality.

ENRICHING THE SCHOOL CURRICULUM BY USING THE IMMEDIATE ENVIRONMENT *

REYNOLD E. CARLSON

Psychologists for many years have insisted that learning takes place only where it can connect with experience. Yet often we go confidently ahead teaching mere words in a textbook without regard to the child's real life associations. An English teacher asked for an essay on a sunset; and the school librarian was puzzled by the number of students asking for descriptions of sunsets. Probably few of the class had really seen a sunset or been led to an appreciation of its beauty if they had seen one. Descriptions by others about sunsets have value; but in this case should not an original essay be written from observation of a sunset itself?

Firsthand experiences in the out-of-doors can do much to vitalize and enrich the present school program. Too few youth in America today have opportunities to grow plants, care for pets and farm animals, prepare food and shelter, do home chores, tramp through and learn to know the fields and woods, or make things with knives and carpenter's tools . . . to mention but a few of the things which were a part of the normal process of "growing up" of boys and girls a few generations ago. These experiences have value not only because of satisfactions they bring in themselves but also because they can serve as the basis for an understanding and appreciation of what is taught in school. There is hardly a spot in the school curriculum, be it social studies, science, art, mathematics, English, or other subjects, that cannot be enriched by a well-planned outdoor program.

*Reprinted by permission of the publisher and the National Association of Secondary School Principals from *The Bulletin of the National Association of Secondary School Principals* 31:83-86, May, 1947.

The provision for outdoor experiences takes many forms in many places. Some schools have children's gardens; some maintain school forests; some make use by classes of the varied resources of the community parks, greenhouses, dairies, industries, outlying farms, wildlife sanctuaries, zoos, and nature trails.

One midwest community has found it desirable to propagate in the school greenhouses all the plants that go into the city's parks. Some communities maintain school camps, either on a year-round basis or on a summer basis. A southern state is now considering a high school travel program in which days would be spent in visits to outdoor areas and industries and nights would be spent in state park camp areas. One school has developed trails and outdoor camp activity centers in a wooded area adjacent to the school building.

SCHOOL GARDENS

In order to explain these experiences further let us take a few examples in detail.

Many schools carry on garden projects during the spring and summer. Generally in such projects each child cares independently for a small plot. Here is an activity which may be related to many aspects of the school program. The whole problem of soils, seeds, fertilizer, germination, and how plants grow and reproduce must be considered. Here is a firsthand experience which illuminates science instruction. To the many youth who go through life without such contact with growing plants, the words of the science textbook may remain little more than words.

The garden can also give reality to economics, geography, and social relations. The problems of the world's food and how it is raised, how money is made from farm crops, and how farmers live and work begin to take on new meaning. If the garden is a truck garden, in which great numbers of youth work at the same time, it involves learning how to get along with others, to respect the property of neighbors, to give assistance when needed, and other aspects of community living and working. For many youth a meaningful work experience within their capabilities is desirable; and here is one place where the child, in cooperation with the forces of nature, works and generally reaps a harvest in proportion to intelligent effort.

The garden activity also has a relation to numbers and measurement. The child comes to know the meaning of length and area from actual practice. Some projects provide a record-keeping system whereby each records the monetary value of what is produced and the hours of labor necessary for that production.

The writing of compositions can be based upon the garden experience. In short, there are few places in the school curriculum which cannot be enriched by a garden program. Elementary and high school ages both can benefit, the program being adaptable to various age levels.

Cleveland, Dearborn, Atlanta, and other cities have through many years found gardening a desirable educational activity in the school program. But it is more than an educational activity in the traditional sense of the word; it is related directly to the leisure-time and self-occupation problems of youth. It can become a recreational experience for the vacation months, and it can establish a recreational interest of lifetime duration.

EXPLORING THE IMMEDIATE

Outdoor explorations are another way of linking the textbooks to the realities they describe. Knowledge of the world begins at home, and from the simple things in our environment we can open up the world. Every community has at hand resources for outdoor education. Our problem is to recognize their potentialities.

At a teachers college many years ago, I met with a biology class made up of rural elementary teachers taking summer work. The course was concerned with technical biology, and the students were learning how to dissect a shark. Yet not even the instructor of the course was acquainted with the Chinaberry tree that grew in front of the science building, a species that probably grew in the yards of most of the schools from which the student teachers came. The student teachers were learning highly technical details of a thing far removed from everyday experience when they badly needed an acquaintance with the common things in their own school environment. It would be natural to expect that to the youth under these teachers the common plants, birds, mammals, and insects remained mere names in books or diagrams or pictures. How often I have heard teachers or students say something like this, after their first experience on a field trip. "So that's a lichen! I've seen the word in textbooks ever since I can remember, but this is the first time I knew what it was." Why should this natural environment of ours not be, at least in its common aspects, well-known to us all? Should we not be able to lead every pupil to a friendly familiarity with the plants and animals he sees daily?

A trip to an old abandoned farm can be the basis for an understanding of the life of people of a past generation as well as a comprehension of problems of plant succession, conservation, and land use. It can throw light upon the factors that make for the happiness and success of people. It can moreover be an experience of exploration wherein students work out for themselves some of the problems of existence and evaluate them.

An excursion to a quarry may arouse interest in nature's storehouse and how man puts it to his own use in building stones, cement, brick, decorative stones, and precious minerals. Such a trip may also be an experience in examining the evidences of geology, in seeing how the processes of earth formation have operated and are continuing to operate. A geologist once said "There are symphonies in stone for those who can understand them. . . . The story of creation is writ in the rocks." Lucky the child whose teacher leads him to such a realization!

Even the overgrown vacant city lot may provide a stimulus to the school curriculum. A study of such a lot through the seasons will reveal a variety of plants and animals adapted to the struggles of city life—ragweed with its multitude of flowers; grasses and weeds from across the sea; and animals, be they merely the lowly English sparrows, starlings, mice, and insects.

I have for over two years watched a neglected fifty-foot lot in a metropolitan area. Here I have observed twenty-eight species of birds, including one ring-necked pheasant; five trees; eight shrubs; and herbaceous plants, not all yet identified, running into the scores. Two snakes, mice, cottontail rabbits, and hundreds of species of insects have been seen there. Through a magnifying glass, I have watched the young aphids being born alive and the pupae of the ladybird beetles feeding on the aphids. The drama of life goes on in intensity even in this unsightly, weed-filled, "vacant" lot.

Near many of our schools are spots of historical significance where we may re-live in retrospect the stirring events of American history. Visits to homes of the first settlers or others who have made distinctive contributions to American life, to Indian village sites, to early forts, to scenes of battles, to old trails associated with the expansion of our land all can give reality to the study.

The variety of possible explorations is tremendous. Every community, be it city, farm, desert, or mountain, can find and use the resources indigenous to itself. Every youth ought to find what is interesting and significant in his own environment.

GUIDANCE IS NEEDED

It must not be assumed that because a group has been taken out of doors that *per se* something desirable has happened. Preparations for outdoor experiences must be as carefully, if not more carefully, made than for class work indoors. What is done must be meaningful to the student and should be selected in terms of his age and interests. The members of the group should understand the objectives of the trip; what to look for; and how the trip is to be conducted. Careful advance plans relative to transportation, grouping, and equipment will help insure success. Distribution of mimeographed materials relative to the trip may be appropriate.

We all enjoy the thrill of discovering things for ourselves. It is better for the teacher to encourage discoveries by the students themselves than to give them too much information. To aid them in their discoveries on a trip, a list of things to look for may be prepared in advance and given to each student; or a list of problems to be solved or questions to be answered may be assigned to individuals or small groups. A quest game, using "station to station" technique, may be played. Or the teacher may direct questions to the group, answers to which can be secured by observation. Each teacher will need to experiment with techniques of stimulating interest, collecting data, and handling the group out-of-doors.

After the field excursion is over there ought to be opportunities for the students to evaluate and discuss what was found. Data gathered afield may be the basis for much that is done indoors.

It has been said that the teacher's job is one of opening windows and pulling up shades that people may see. After asking a group of young people to draw a picture of a bird, an art teacher received many complaints of their inability. Her reply: "It isn't that you don't know how to draw," she said. "It's that you don't know what a bird looks like." The face of bird and animal and field and tree and stream and cloud and flower ought to be a familiar face.

OUTDOOR EDUCATION: ITS PROMISING FUTURE *

GEORGE W. DONALDSON
AND ALAN D. DONALDSON

Outdoor education has moved into a decade bright with promise. Prophecy and prediction are as dangerous in this field as in others. Indeed, outdoor education enthusiasts—as the writers surely are—have great difficulty distinguishing between prophecy and hope. In fairness, then, it should be stated at the outset that this paper is a mix of fond hopes and prophecy; only time will tell which is which.

After steady but unspectacular growth through the 1940s and 1950s, outdoor education experienced a surge of quantitative and qualitative growth in the 1960s. Powerfully urged on by an increasing ecological awareness as well as by a variety of federal activities, it gained a whole new thrust. Especially, impetus was given by Titles I and III of the Elementary and Secondary Education Act of 1965. Other new ventures were doubtless spin-offs of federal activities, but it is apparent that substantial numbers of the new ventures began for the simple reason that outdoor education is an "idea whose time had come."

An important breakthrough of the 1960s was the beginning of outdoor education for inner-city children and youth. Title I of ESEA provided the new

*Reprinted by permission of the publisher, the American Association of Health, Physical Education, and Recreation, from *Journal of Health, Physical Education, Recreation* 43:23-28, April, 1972.

money which funded a dozen or more of these programs. In terms of the pupil personnel served, this move into urban centers where, in the view of many educators, outdoor education is most needed, is probably the most significant gain of the last decade.

But outdoor education was on the move in other important ways. A healthy diversity of programs came into being as the movement fanned out over the country. Indeed, variety may be said to be the watchword of outdoor education activities in the United States over the last 25 years. Every section of the country has become involved; no state is without some kind of program. It is this variety and geographical spread which bolster the promise of outdoor education in the seventies. This promise, this hope, is spelled out in the following pages.

The rapid geographical spread of outdoor education practices would, taken alone, guarantee more participants. More important, however, is the fact that educators over the country are rapidly coming to the conclusion that outdoor learning experiences have contributions to make to all age groups and to groups with diverse economic backgrounds.

Outdoor education, as a self-conscious movement in American education, began as school camping—and school camping was originally pegged at fifth or sixth grade level. These grades were originally selected for administrative reasons, chief of which was that these were the oldest children in self-contained classrooms. Unfortunately, the early practice threatened to become traditional; many schools accepted as dogma, "Outdoor education is for upper elementary children."

In recent years, innovative educators have moved away from this early practice. Today, we see and read about outdoor education across the board. Preschool children and kindergartners have joined with middle schoolers, high school pupils, and collegians in partaking of the instructional richness the outdoors offers. The trend away from specific grade placement is well established; the decade of the seventies should witness the end of this restrictive custom.

College programs of great variety have come upon the scene. While details of these programs are properly discussed elsewhere, their existence is noted here to illustrate the increased availability of outdoor learning.

Adult education organizations are increasingly providing outdoor courses, workshops, conferences, seminars, and the like. Most of these offerings focus upon teaching people to use the outdoors wisely and well as a recreational resource. Recreation agencies, public and private, are increasing their emphasis upon outdoor educational recreational activities.

Outdoor education, heretofore an exclusively middle class phenomenon, will experience a great class spread as more and more inner-city schools move their pupils outdoors for living and learning experiences. It may safely be predicted that the rapid geographical spread of the 1950s and 1960s will be paralleled by a client spread in the 1970s. "More people in more places," may well be the distinguishing characteristic of outdoor education in this decade.

Too often in the past, outdoor education was conceived as school camping only. The excuse was heard, "We'd have an outdoor education program but we don't have a camp." While school camping programs have grown apace, recent years have witnessed an even more rapid growth in nonresident activities.

Increased attention is being given to the use of the school site, proper, as a place where exciting teaching and learning can take place. Many teachers who have conducted "school site surveys" have been amazed to learn of the outdoor education potential of, literally, their own backyards.

Although still far from standard practice, school administrators and architects are giving increased attention to the educational possibilities of the entire school plant, not just the school building. In some instances, site selection is influenced by the relative richness of the outdoor environment. Sometimes the size of the site is subjected to the same criterion. Schools are being located in the erstwhile exotic environments of swamps, lakes, woodlands, and hillsides. Buildings are located and construction carried on in ways which preserve the biophysical and aesthetic environments. Teachers consult with landscape architects in view of, "How can we landscape this school site for optimum educational use?" A few fortunate teachers have even been allowed to modify existing school sites toward the end of educational efficiency. Some, with their pupils, have actually created microcosms of several environments right on the school yard.

This decade should see a veritable explosion of school-site learning activities, for these are readily available to all teachers. Teachers will find almost none of the oft-cited difficulties (permission, red-tape, transportation, liability) in school-site teaching. They will also find many, if not all, of the plus factors. As school sites come increasingly to be viewed as integral parts of the educational plant, opportunities for teaching on those sites will expand greatly.

Sites near schools, within easy walking distance, are coming into much more general use. Schools have found both public land-holding agencies and private organizations as well as individuals to be willing to share their holdings. When teachers come to see their *communities* as media for teaching and learning, many more of these easy sites will be identified and exploited. This is a major challenge for the seventies.

School farms, forests, and gardens will increasingly come to be seen as places for children to see and actually to participate in the raising of food and fiber. In our ever-urbanizing society, down-to-mother-earth experiences will become vital elements in the good education and the good life. American schools will move toward that end in this decade.

Transportation, once seen as a major problem in getting pupils and rich learning environments together, has become more readily available. More important, school boards and administrators are proving more willing to budget and expend funds for it. The net result is a greatly increased mobility of students and teachers.

Regional centers like the Tennessee Valley Authority's Youth Station in Kentucky and the Cispus Center in Washington will probably increase in number and influence. Fine facilities, beyond the capabilities of all but the richest school districts, will be made available to schools on a regional basis. These centers will be staffed with small but expert corps of specialists whose function is to interpret the environment to teachers, who will in turn carry on their own instructional programs. In addition to conducting on-site activities, staff members of such regional centers will serve as valuable in-service education resources to regional schools, thus greatly expanding the influence of the centers.

The 1970s should witness groups of students moving freely and frequently about their communities in search of the best educational environments. Or they may be involved in programs like travel-camping, where geographical limits are greatly expanded. City children will learn about rural environments; children of the mountains and the plains will visit the seashore; and vice versa.

Summer educational travel will likely stretch the limits farther, even to foreign shores. Certain colleges and universities have already begun foreign study with emphasis upon outdoor activities; schools will surely follow their lead.

Relative ease of transportation should have a profound effect on resident programs, too. Students of outdoor education have noted that distance from school is no longer the all-important criterion in selecting an outdoor center as it once was. Many schools purposely transport their children some distance to camp sites in order to achieve—again—the best educational environment, not simply the nearest one. It is not too hard to imagine that there may even be "camp exchange" programs being carried on before the decade has run its course in which, say, a coastal community will trade its camp for a time with that of a mountain school.

School will, in the seventies, move closer and closer, in their search for the very best educational environments, to meeting the L. B. Sharp dictum, "Those things which can best be taught in the outdoors should be taught there." And alert, aggressive school people should not be satisfied with anything less than the best outdoor environments.

Outdoor education, which because of its special needs for "lands for learning" has already contrived remarkable devices for using the lands of others, may well be in the forefront as education generally becomes more community-oriented. Schools over the country have found that the physical resources they need are, indeed, available. Even New York City has, within easy distance, enough children's camps to begin a resident outdoor education program.[1] Other communities, notably several in southern California, have learned the same thing. The excuse, "We didn't have a camp," will simply not suffice any longer. While there are probably not enough year-around camps to service all the nation's schools, there are almost certainly enough to meet the demands of the seventies.

In the meantime, a challenge is to research exactly what is needed in the way of optimum facilities for resident programs. The day of readily available, other-owned camps will surely pass. Outdoor educators will be wise to know precisely what they want when they confront the problems of locating, designing, and constructing their own. Using facilities owned by others can make a rich contribution to this kind of research; living with another's mistakes is instructive, besides being a great deal more economical!

The current environmental push has already resulted in community awareness of the unique roles of outdoor education. Community environmental/conservation agencies came rapidly to the view that here is an on-going educational method precisely tailored for many of their objectives. Typically, their response is to seek or permit some sort of alliance. They may share lands for learning, expert personnel, instructional materials, or funds. In turn, outdoor education shares important ways of teaching and learning. Surely, two current movements which have so much in common will join forces more effectively in this decade. Outdoor educators and environmentalists will do well to form many kinds of mutual aid alliances in the seventies. Both groups, and more importantly, the communities they serve, will benefit.

As outdoor education and the various governmental agencies, local, state, regional, and federal, come to know each other better, it seems inevitable that they should mount a rich variety of shared enterprises. Many of the vital concerns of governmental agencies are educational in nature. And many of these educational concerns relate in one way or another to the outdoors. At this point of mutual converging concerns, governments and outdoor education will increase their cooperative activities in the 70s. There is little doubt that a major focus of these converging concerns will be environmental in nature.

Government agencies will make the same kinds of contributions as community agencies. Schools will, in response, share a quarter century of educational know-how.

Fortunately for the purposes of land-poor schools, many governmental agencies are anything but land-poor. In point of fact, a significant number of these agencies own camps and other properties immediately available for

---

[1] Eugene M. Ezersky, *City to Country* (New York: Educational Facilities Laboratory, Inc., 1969).

educational uses. There are already across the country models of federal, state, municipal, and county properties in use by schools. The seventies should see more governmental agencies following the lead of Michigan and Wisconsin, whose newer state-owned camps are specifically designed for school use in addition to their traditional summer use. While there are fewer and less exotic examples, one can also see the beginnings of a trend which may far exceed the shared use of camp facilities. Government agencies, notably the National Parks and the U.S. Forest Service, are urging schools to use their vast land resources on a day-use basis. Acceleration of this highly desirable trend is predictable.

Implementation of the Environmental Education Act (P.L. 91-516), delegated to state governments, will doubtless spin off appropriate outdoor education activities over the nation. A challenge of the decade for outdoor educators will be that of maintaining their own integrity in the face of an emotion-laden movement such as has already begun to confuse terminology; "environmental education," "outdoor education," and "conservation education" are all too often used interchangeably.

Obviously, the entry of state governments into environmental education will create a bandwagon effect. Outdoor educators will do well to hold firm to the essential notion of the field; outdoor education is method, peculiarly useful in learning about the environment, but nonetheless *method*.

The curriculum changes only as changes come about in the people who teach. A corollary is: Methods of instruction change when teachers want to change them. These simple principles, honored too often in the breach, account for the term "staff development" in the above key statement instead of "curriculum development." Curriculum development, then, is in reality "people development." Outdoor education poses no exception to this fundamental principle. Schools which are interested in building solid, defensible programs of outdoor instruction will not violate the time-honored principle of local curriculum development. The seventies will witness countless teachers, principals, and supervisors, as well as a rich variety of specialists and consultants, busily seeking their own local answers to questions like:

What, in our curriculum, is best taught outdoors?
What, not presently in our curriculum, can we do now that we have the
    freedom to teach outdoors?
How shall we teach outdoors?
Where shall we teach outdoors?
Who can help us teach outdoors?

Outdoor education will do well to forswear the apparently easier method of simply adopting a curriculum from someone, or somewhere else. Currently available are attractively produced "packages" of materials for which extravagant claims are made. They will, in the introductory words of one of the packages, work "wherever there is a piece of land, a teacher, and a child." One firm offers "tailormade programs for your district . . ." in outdoor education as well as other areas. Paper programs are easily procured from these packages. Programs which intimately and deeply affect teachers and children are harder to come by but they are well worth the effort. This effort is one of the great challenges of the seventies.

In meeting this challenge, schools will have rich and varied assistance. Departments of state governments, especially education agencies, offer varying degrees of help; all offer some. Colleges and universities are rapidly assuming a leadership role in staff development. Professional organizations, like the AAHPER's Outdoor Education Project, stand ready to help. Countless regional and local agencies have significant contributions. Quality as well as quantity of assistance to schools will improve dramatically in this decade.

But local effort is still the key to action. Typically, an outdoor education program begins because one or more local people want it. Its quality is largely determined by the qualitative factors of energy, imagination, and determination of people on the scene. There is no substitute for these factors, energized "where the action is."

There is heartening, though still spotty, evidence that outdoor education is recovering from the academic panic it, like education in general, suffered in the 1950s and which spilled over into the 1960s. Until Sputnik, outdoor education was developing in a healthy, balanced fashion. Then, in a turnabout which will surely amaze scholars of the future, it began to justify itself almost solely in terms of cognitive learning. It began to "divide itself up" into the academic disciplines. And, in the opinion of the authors, it began to lose much of its early vigor and virtue.

The great attraction which outdoor education held for many restive educators in its early day was its holistic, problem-centered style. Children and teachers went outdoors when the outdoors offered a better way of solving an educational problem or a place to have wholesome, invigorating living experiences. Never did they go outdoors to "study science" or to "learn mathematics." But all this changed. Even some school camps began to build their daily programs around the academic disciplines.

The recent advent of more adventurous programs like back-packing and canoe tripping and a renewed emphasis on outdoor skills appear as symptoms of a returning balance. The new emphasis on "open schools" and "schools without walls" will reinforce the movement of outdoor education back to a balance among cognitive affective, and psychomotor learning. Outdoor education will once again be "education *in* and *for* the outdoors."

Since its beginnings in this country, outdoor education has applied its methodology to increased understanding of and positive action on environmental problems. Accounts of early programs invariably tell of conservation studies and, more important for changing attitudes, actual work on the problems studied. Conservation areas, child-planted forests, and the like marked practically every outdoor education site. Indeed, it is entirely possible that a share of the nation's awakened ecological awareness is traceable to the influence of these early outdoor education ventures. Pupils involved in them have been full-fledged citizens and voters for a decade or more.

Now that schools as well as other institutions and agencies are generally accepting responsibilitiy for developing the information, the attitudes, and the skills needed to solve environmental problems, outdoor education's role is even more clear. It will freely share the methodological know-how developed over a quarter century. No small part of this methodology bears on the "will-to-do."

If outdoor education has a secret, it must be the demonstrated fact that active learners who experience real problems in context are impelled to do something about the problems. Most students of environmental problems know that current knowledge in the area far exceeds our will to solve the problems. It follows, then, that environmental learnings in the affective domain will be a major contribution of outdoor education.

Current emphasis on environmental education and on outdoor education may well have a synergistic effect. But professionals in both fields will be wise to guard against an opposite effect. If either field is narrowly conceived or viewed as bureaucratically competitive, both will suffer. Worse yet, the real losers will be the young.

The decade of the seventies will witness a shake-down in the present tenuous and sometimes controversial relations between the two groups of educators. Cooperation and accommodation are greatly to be desired, and the sooner the better.

Research studies in outdoor education have concentrated primarily upon resident programs and administration. While these studies were obviously of value, it cannot be fairly stated that they offer a balanced program of research. Furthermore, they fail to yield what many educators want to know.

Briefly, studies are needed in the following areas.[2]

---

[2]For a more detailed statement of research priorities, the reader should see George W. Donaldson, *A Position Paper: Research Utilization in Outdoor Education* (Las Cruces, N.M.: ERIC/CRESS, 1970). Also the 1970-71 Report of the Committee on Research and Evaluation, Council on Outdoor Education and Camping, American Association for Health, Physical Education, and Recreation (mimeo).

In-depth research into the various historical roots of the field.

Philosophical studies.

Empirical studies in the area of curriculum and learning.

Broadened administrative studies.

Studies focusing on the education of teachers for outdoor instruction.

Practically all outdoor education research to date has been done in graduate schools as master's and doctoral theses. Much of it appears to have been done on subjects easy to study rather than in terms of what is needed to be known. This situation will continue until some prestigious agency begins to lead in the establishment of priorities.

Outdoor education has, since its beginnings in America, been long on action and relatively short on scholarship. Innovation is exciting; scholarship, especially to action-oriented people, is less so. For this reason, a prediction of a decade of meaningful research must be predicated upon an "if." If leadership emerges, in the form of an institution or a professional committee, research will increasingly focus upon what educators want and need to know about outdoor education. Lacking such leadership, it is doubtful that much relevant research will come about.

The last few years have seen proliferation of college programs in outdoor education. While not all of them are specifically designated as "teacher education," their net effect may well manifest itself in many teachers who use the outdoors for instructional purposes. At least two studies [3] that probed the experiences which incline teachers toward educational use of the outdoors strongly suggest that it is satisfying, enriching *personal* outdoor experiences which do so. Considerably fewer teachers credited professional experiences as their impelling force.

In fairness, it should be stressed that the teachers studied in both pieces of research came largely from an era in which little attention was given to professional preparation for outdoor instruction. Later studies may provide contradictory findings.

But, at this point in time, it may reasonably be assumed that the teachers most likely to make use of outdoor resources in their teaching are those who have had fulfilling outdoor experiences. Exactly how these experiences are best provided remains to be discovered. In an increasingly urbanized society (in which fewer *personal* outdoor experiences are almost automatically a part of

[3]Vincent A. Cyphers, "A Study to Determine the Significant Outdoor Experiences for Elementary Teachers." Unpublished doctoral dissertation, Colorado State College, Greeley, Colorado, 1961.

John W. Hug, "Analysis of the Factors Which Influence Elementary Teachers in the Utilization of Outdoor Instructional Activities." Unpublished doctoral dissertation, Indiana University, Bloomington, Indiana, 1964.

growing up) it is only reasonable that organized education assume the task of providing these impelling experiences. Just as schools have filled a culture gap by instituting outdoor education programs, collegiate institutions will increasingly provide college level programs.

Evidence now available suggests college programs will be of these types:

Specifically designated departmental approaches in colleges of education.
Inter-departmental efforts within colleges of education.
Ventures by departments other than education, such as recreation, sociology, etc.

Such diversity will continue through the decade and, while the debate as to the "best way" will doubtless go on apace, it is consistent with the American tradition of local decision making and probably a healthy symptom. Colleges and universities will continue to develop new programs, many of them not even using the terminology of outdoor education. Professional outdoor educators, viewing themselves as methodologists, will encourage a rich diversity, caring little who does the job.

The end result of college-level activities will be seen as a populace committed to a wise and ennobling care for and use of the outdoors. A necessary condition for such care and use must be teachers who care and who understand educational use. This may well be the overriding challenge of the decade of the seventies.

SCHOOLGROUNDS FOR TEACHING MAN'S RELATIONSHIP TO NATURE *

JOHN W. BRAINERD

Children tend to grow up faster than they can learn. Teach them as fast as one may, one day they are grown citizens less well informed than one might wish. One meets students only briefly as they beanstalk from kindergarten to twelfth! Even the brightest learn slowly when one measures their progress against the amount to be learned these days as human knowledge increases each minute. One struggles to spoon a few golden grains into our pupils' minds while looking apprehensively over our shoulders at the towering granaries of scientific information being gleaned from many fields of research. Even as we master space, time seems to be defeating us.

*Reprinted by permission of the Editor of *School Science and Mathematics* from *School Science and Mathematics* 64:428-34, May, 1964.

The critical shortage of time does not just involve children who grow faster than they can learn, of knowledge which increases faster than it can be communicated, or even of national survival in a political race with non-democratic ideologies. The greatest problem of modern times is the rate at which the human species is altering its natural environment relative to the speed at which individual humans are learning about that natural environment.

Despite the enormity of human numbers on the planet today, *individuals are important* in determining the destiny of the race. This concept is basic to democracy, in which one tries to provide equal opportunity for individuals to show their worth and give leadership. Any teachers may now have in our class a student who may someday be a national or international leader. Yet there is little time adequately to teach this (unrecognized) child the mathematics of population growth, the chemistry of polluted water, the biology of germ plasm, and the physics of a radioactive atmosphere.

It is necessary to teach basic principles of mathematics and science during these magic years in the formation of individuals. One tries in the process to develop their *inherited aptitudes*. But in the limited time available, one is apt to slight the environment-stimulated attitudes which help the maturing students gain better understanding of the applications of science to human welfare. If school doesn't thus excite pupils about nature, when they get to college they are not apt to elect courses which make them struggle perceptively with humanity's problem of trying to share peaceably the natural resources of an overcrowded planet.

One should make better use of the school environment to stimulate pupils to pursue science and mathematics. Practical schoolgrounds problems will incite some to take a career-interest in the complicated problems of environmental modification by Man, an animal too often considering himself master of nature. While there are enough researchers developing new colors for detergents, too few evaluate effects of detergents on aquatic populations in the streams. School experiences as well as economics influence attitudes of researchers. How many students will give in to pressure to enter hush-hush research on biological warfare rather than insist on constructive research helping Mankind adapt sanely to an over-populated environment? If schools don't excite more students who will give such leadership, *Homo sapiens* may soon be the first species to commit conscious suicide by defilement of its natural environment.

Use of schoolgrounds for environmental studies also can help many more students become wise followers. Non-career citizens with an understanding of natural resources are needed to vote wisely and to act intelligently in the little ways that can count so heavily, as in disposal of a cigarette.

Agreed that a scientific approach to Man's place in Nature is imperative for our rabbiting race, how can teaching in these areas be improved? Unfortunately one finds several limiting factors existing at the same time! Complaints include:

"Our text has very little on this subject, and we must follow the text"; "Conservation is in the last chapter, and we often don't get to it"; "Our principal (superintendent) is interested only in rockets"; "My class is too large"; "A religious group would object"; "We are not allowed to take the class outdoors more than once a year"; "I do not know enough about it." These restraints are more real than imagined, but they may be minimized by increased effort, by taking a positive approach. Here are a few suggestions, all based on the thesis that more attention must be given to introducing children to nature. (See Brainerd, J. W., "Taking the School Out-of-Doors," *School Science and Mathematics,* January, 1960.)

1. Emphasize repeatedly that Man is a part of Nature, miraculously special but not wholly distinct, not independent, not best at everything, not necessarily destined to rule the rest of Nature. The concept of fusion with one's environment can be approached in many ways, such as by studying the continuous extension of the atmosphere into one's bronchi and lungs, with a fraction of the oxygen even extending into the living cells throughout the body. There should be a healthy blur to the definition resulting from the study of the wonderful question, "Who am I?" One can open doors from which students can explore their own philosophies, helping by giving facts and raising questions.

2. Leading from the pupils' own chemistry, mechanics, numbers, and so on, bring out their relationships to the classroom environment. For instance, consider the room's atmosphere in terms of oxygen, humidity, heat, carbon dioxide; smell of garlic, perfume, and sweat; room to move about; and rates of change of the various factors. Use the language of numbers to express the observed and measured facts.

3. Discuss scientific methods of studying classroom environments by making measurements and conducting experiments. Create and solve the related mathematical problems. Be sure to bring out the broad overlap of the natural and social sciences. College freshmen are often excited over the behavioral sciences which they are meeting for the first time, when they should have already had them as a stimulating part of their earlier science training. Study the difficulties of experimental work with the human animal; then try experiments with students divided into experimental and control groups. Have half the class face their desks toward the windows and half the class away from them for a day; have each pupil write down brief, subjective comments about the results (if any) of his orientation in relation to radiant energy in the classroom environment; then have an objective statistical study made of the collected comments.

4. Invite a social-science class to sit in with the science or mathematics class (share-a-chair session), studying the classroom before and after this overcrowding. While the social-science class is visiting, have a joint discussion of science and mathematics as disciplines helpful for studying problems of sharing resources of the classroom environment.

5. Discuss what is "natural" in the classroom environment, and the degree to which Man has made things "artificial." Is a molecule of water exhaled by a student a natural object, different from a molecule over the Pacific? What about hot air over the teacher's head? A board making the top of a desk? The radiation from a light bulb? The light coming from the sun in through the window glass, and from an open window? Show relativeness rather than absoluteness of "natural" and "artificial." Pose mathematics problems of suitable level related to the above, and show how physics and chemistry are needed to study most if not all biological problems.

Next take the pupils outdoors to study the environment of the school with its inevitable Nature: atmosphere; geological substrate of rock, soil, or paving; water (intermittent if not permanent); vegetation (even if only weeds in the cracks or pollen in the air); wildlife (only pigeons? . . . no parasites on the pigeons?); and of course the human animal, who is also a part of Nature. Take a research approach with the class; don't take them out to show them! Try:

1. *Observation.* Help the pupils to see as well as to look. Challenge them to take another look, to perceive more closely, to watch for change. Make them conscious of designs, both man-made and natural. Astronomical patterns of solar radiation and planetary winds are observable in every school yard. Watching and recording the physics of the atmosphere with the aid of a weather station can lead to a lifetime interest in human geography as well as in basic physics. Microclimatic studies of the school yard can lead to watching the patterns of human behavior as children seek the shade of a tree in hot weather or the lee of a wall on a cold, windy day.

2. *Identification.* Teach recognition of natural objects such as plants, animals, rocks, minerals, topographic forms, phases of the water cycle (such as insoak and runoff), cloud formations, and wind velocities. Have students learn accepted names useful in communicating with other scientists, including some of the technical names (though not too many or too fast). Often it will be necessary to learn identifications along with the students; sometimes they can learn first and teach the teacher.

3. *Collection.* Teach considerate collecting, acquiring for a worthy purpose. Show that indiscriminate collecting provides a vacuum-cleaner-bag type of accumulation which does not further the orderly processes of scientific investigation. Emphasize that a carefully thought-out plan clearly stated enables a student to make an orderly collection which is much more likely to be meaningful. Differentiate between temporary collections useful while studying the school pond, school woods, or school lawn, and permanent collections carefully prepared, labeled with India ink on high quality paper, and systematically stored in protecting cabinets suited to the type of collection. Such permanent collections for reference are woefully lacking in modern schools. Many excellent ones were discarded when nature study went out of fashion.

Now that the importance of ecology has come to the fore, one must promote reference collections, convincing both school administrators and school architects of their necessity.

4. *Measurement.* Mapping exercises on schoolgrounds have been used for years to further interest in geometry and to give practice in units of linear and areal measurement. Instead of resurveying the ball field or parking lot each year, one may use these exercises to provide a variety of maps for ecological studies, showing school woodlands, shrublands, flowerbeds, watersheds, shaded areas, and even animal territories. Today there are available excellent directions for measuring physical factors in the school environment such as radiation and humidity, and the biological factors provide countless counting and mathematical problems! Many children can become fascinated by censusing animal populations, one of the most beneficial educational exercises that a school can offer.

5. *Recording.* Accuracy and orderliness of records should be stressed, as with laboratory work. Special techniques such as mapping and photography often intrigue pupils at first far more than does the scientific interest of the problem; then some of them catch the excitement of being on the edge of the unknown and they grow from technicians into scientists.

6. *Experimentation.* On the schoolgrounds a wonderful teaching environment awaits the imaginative teacher who dares move beyond the controlled laboratory environment where (he hopes!) he experiments with only one variable at a time. An endless variety of possibilities sit on his window sill and lie in the flowerbed by the door. For instance, if your school has a lawn, have the students fence off a meter quadrat in an odd corner; note what happens in this enclosure when the lawnmower and foot traffic are kept out. Record changes in temperature, insect fauna, and the varying reactions of the human animals. (You had better get prior reactions from the principal!)

Or if the school yard has only packed soil, dig an experimental ditch 10 centimeters wide and 10 deep and a meter long *just* inside the fence. Note what this does to air currents, how gravity affects soil and surface water, the types of organic matter which accumulate, what invertebrates or vertebrates become involved, and whether the soil becomes more or less productive of plants.

Or put a plastic covering over a manhole on a parking lot catchbasin during a heavy rain. Measure, estimate, or record photographically the amount of water thus retained—and don't leave the cover on too long! Yes, even the schoolground hardtop can make a fertile field for education.

Science and mathematics teachers should not be content with a few pet exercises outdoors each year on whatever grounds may be available. They should give leadership in helping schools create better teaching environments on school grounds. Many schoolgrounds these days are an educational farce. Stylish and expensive landscaping gives almost no thought to educational possibilities at many new school sites. Many a brook useful as a physics, chemistry, and biology laboratory gets buried in a culvert without a science or mathematics teacher being consulted. Many a little slope creating a variety of teaching situations for physics and biology is graded flat by a bulldozer operator who takes orders from some blockhead of an architect who thinks only in cubes because his science teachers never took him outdoors to study a hill when he was in school. If this educational trend continues, Man's privileged place in Nature will surely be forfeited. Students will go out into the world as insensitive to their environment as is the bulk of the populace today, building on flood plains, burning the watersheds, smogging the atmosphere, and filling in marshes without a thought for their ecological significance.

One must approach our school administrators with this problem at once, especially where new schools, or additions are being built but also at older schools where the inherited land-use pattern is not necessarily the best possible for all generations even though it has not changed since 1880. If possible science and mathematics teachers should approach school administrations with a rough plan for concerted action. In an existing school, one usually asks the principal to appoint a study group to consider more comprehensive use of the school grounds. When a new school is being built, it is most important to reach the school building committee and to help its subcommittee on school grounds. In any case, one must be polite, but firm: future generations of students must not be deprived of an outdoor laboratory in which to learn first hand and excitingly about the world in which they live. One must work for a land-use plan with a wide variety of environments, and put great importance on trying to include one or more "natural areas" to serve as control (check) areas for comparison with artificially and experimentally managed areas. The cost of such a plan may well be initially less than the common landscaping job, with lower upkeep, and with long-term community values such as decreased vandalism along with better education.

Science and mathematics teachers should work with teachers of other subjects. Science is not for future scientists alone. The arts need science as surely as sciences need the arts, lingual, graphic, and all the rest. Social and natural sciences especially must together increasingly attack the problem of Man in Nature. School lawn and sidewalk relationships are a fine site for starting such cooperation. Music teacher and mathematics teacher can find common ground while studying such natural phenomena as cricket populations in the school yard; and the physics teacher helping with sound recordings and the biology teacher aiding in identification, cricket physiology, and habitat studies should join the research team, bringing with them students infected by their teachers' contagious enthusiasm for exploring the mysteries of music, decibels, and sex as revealed in the world of crickets along the school fence. One should also keep in mind that for better education the schoolgrounds should not be thought of as just a science laboratory: they should just as much constitute an art studio.

The child at the desk must quickly grow into an adult who understands Man's role in Nature. He must see himself as a prisoner of Nature, hemmed in on every side by natural laws, yet a captive beloved, with many special privileges by which he can improve his lot and that of his fellow creatures. To be worthy, he must be both brave and humble; he must explore for knowledge and accept the facts. He must act quickly in the face of such new phenomena as lowered human death rates and rising birth rates on a world with a limited resource base. If he cannot handle numbers, if he doesn't understand population dynamics, he may turn out to be the person who some day in a moment of feeling overcrowded will push *The Button* which will extinguish the species. But with understanding and an eager attitude, he may become the scientist who will discover wise methods of population control which will make obsolete the insanity of war. . . . Or maybe it will be she, the little girl third back in the second row.

USING THE COMMUNITY *
RICHARD L. WEAVER

Most communities—small or large—are rich storehouses of resources available to the elementary school science teacher. The use of these resources will provide the spark for a dynamic and interesting program.

INVESTIGATING COMMUNITY LIFE

In the Williston School of Wilmington, North Carolina, the classroom teachers, principal, and students undertook an intensive study of Wilmington. Various classes volunteered to investigate different aspects of community life. One child, whose father worked on a merchant ship, brought in some coffee which was being shipped on her father's boat. This led to further inquiries about imported items, their origin, and their destination. It was discovered that many other fathers were employed on ships bringing in some of the ingredients of fertilizers, oil from the Gulf states, and numerous other things. Being a fourth grade, they relied largely on information provided by parents; but for older

*Reprinted by permission from *The National Elementary Principal* 33:171-179, September, 1953. Copyright 1953, Department of Elementary School Principals, National Education Association.

children a little added research would easily expand the study into many fields of interest. Certainly geography, science, mathematics, and history could all be woven into an integrated story.

Art, music, and crafts were used to tell their story to the other classes in a schoolwide open house and teachers' workshop. The principal, being an excellent photographer, took numerous kodachromes of the activities, which were used in the teachers' workshop.

Another class became interested in the fishing industry of the area. They visited the fish markets and fishing boats, again relying heavily on information from parents working on the boats. Over 20 species of fish were found to be of economic importance in the area and the children learned to identify them and the purposes for which they are used.

In the Forest Hills School of Wilmington, a second-grade group made a large mural of the school grounds and located all the trees on it in relation to the school building. The children learned the kinds of trees and discussed which ones they could add in order to improve the school grounds as an outdoor study area.

SCHOOL GARDEN PLOTS

At the Wrightsboro School in New Hanover County, near Wilmington, in the center of a thriving bulb industry, a school garden, in which various kinds of bulbs are grown, has been maintained for 12 years. Most of the bulbs are provided by parents who grow them commercially. A contest each spring among the 10 classes in the school keep up a lively interest in gardening, new fertilizers and insecticides, and cultivation methods. Experimental station employees nearby gladly serve as advisers when needed. I arrived one morning at 9 o'clock and three children were "breaking out" a new garden plot. I inquired about it and was told that the school had been allotted a new teacher, so they needed a new plot. You can't teach in Wrightsboro School and not have a garden.

BUILDING COLLECTIONS OF MINERALS

In a seventh grade at Garner School in Wake County, North Carolina, where students were encouraged to choose their own units of study, six selected rocks and minerals as their six-week unit. The teacher provided them with initial sets of rocks, samples of specimens she had collected. She suggested that they try to increase their own collections and to find cigar boxes to house their collections. Soon one boy asked if the class would like to visit his father's stone-cutting establishment. Of course, they wanted to go, and the trip was arranged. The father described the various marbles and granites, told them where he obtained the stone, and gave each of them chips of the different rocks. This experience aroused so much enthusiasm that many more students began collections and later selected the study of rocks as their next unit.

Most public buildings are trimmed with some form of rock. Tracking down the origin, the peculiar characteristics, and the reasons for using particular kinds would be a good group or individual project in any town or city.

PLANNING SCHOOL TRIPS

When a teacher and her eighth-grade class in Salisbury, North Carolina, were making preparations for a school camping experience, special committees were established to do certain things for the class on the way to and from the camp. The camp was located 60 miles from the school, and the trip was planned so as to include as many worthwhile observations enroute as possible.

A committee on agriculture made plans for observations of the kinds of crops being raised, the changes from one county to another, and so on. The committee on geography mapped out the route and was prepared to point out the rivers, mountains, and county seats and other towns they would see. The housing committee prepared to study the kinds of architecture, new building materials being used, and changes in styles from one town or county to another. Another committee planned to see how well farm machinery, barns, yards, and fences were cared for.

A wildlife committee prepared to observe the animals. The historical committee looked up the best places to stop to see churches, graveyards, and courthouses of special historic significance, and prepared to pass on important information to the others at these spots.

USING PUBLIC RECORDS

In cities, county seats, and many of the larger towns, the extent of information in courthouses and municipal buildings is unlimited, and in many cases hardly used by our schools.

In Fayetteville, North Carolina where I conducted a workshop on resource-use education, the 30 teachers and I visited the health center where we asked the staff members to answer some interesting questions. We wanted to know:

1. What diseases are found most frequently in the county?
2. What should children know about these diseases?
3. How can the schools help the health department reduce disease in the county?

The answer to our first question was: "Venereal diseases are two or three times as prevalent as any other, and the county incidence of venereal disease is higher than in any other county in the state." Intestinal parasites ranked second, and most of the information on this subject was entirely new to this group of teachers.

It soon occurred to us that if we were going to have students study health in Cumberland County, we would have to increase the emphasis on the diseases most prevalent and look for more specific information on the parasites responsible than we could find in our textbooks. In fact, the health department staff and local doctors seemed the logical and most important source of such data.

In another workshop we became interested in interpreting some of the early land-use patterns of the county from local deeds and wills. Such records are public property and are kept in courthouses. The earliest ones included much information on the kinds of trees of the area; the farm equipment used and passed on to the next generation, and even the crops raised; the kinds of materials used in the buildings; and amount of cleared and uncleared land; and the relative index of the level of living for the period.

Many boys and girls graduate from school without ever having examined a real deed or will. Very few know how such records are preserved and filed. Recorders and registrars are usually quite willing to spend time showing a group of school people how such things are handled, and helping them find specific information.

DEVELOPING A 20-ACRE SCHOOL SITE

In many cities and in some rural areas where consolidated schools are being built, school administrators are embarking on a somewhat revolutionary idea—that of having a school site large enough to provide numerous learning experiences in science nearby. Such sites of 20 or more acres can provide an outdoor laboratory with varied experiences, such as some of the following:

School Gardens. Some schools have suitable areas which can be devoted to garden plots for growing vegetables, bulbs, and flowers. Thus, each class can have an individual plot. Contests between classes often create interest. Produce can be used by the school, taken home by pupils, or sold. Flowers for decorating the school can be grown. By choosing vegetables which will mature early, most of the value of the garden can be achieved before school closes. In some cases children near the school can take care of later maturing varieties after school closes. It is worthwhile for children to learn how to prepare soil for planting, how to select suitable varieties, and how to plant and care for their growth. Home economics classes can demonstrate proper preserving methods. Much about proper gardening, learned at school, can be valuable at home.

Starting Plants in the Classroom. Seeds and cuttings of many vegetables and house plants can be grown in the classroom during the winter and spring months and placed outside in appropriate places on the school ground during the summer, or sent home to be cared for by pupils during the vacation periods. The closer the school gardens are to the classrooms the better, as more attention can be given to them.

Growing Shrubs and Trees. A rooting bed can be made by enclosing an area with brick, stone, or tile block, filling it with clean, washed sand, and covering it with strips of wood to cut down the amount of light. Cuttings of most shrubs can be rooted in this bed by placing pieces of the stems in the sand during the late summer and keeping the sand well watered. The shrubs can be removed when rooted and planted in appropriate places, or hardened in other beds where some fertilizer can be added to stimulate growth before finally locating them in permanent positions. Some schools have grown enough shrubs to landscape the entire school site.

Tree seeds can also be germinated and seedlings can be transferred to beds for later use in landscaping. Such trees as poplars and willows will also grow from pieces of the stems placed in the rooting bed. The rooting beds should be as near the agriculture department or school building as possible. A convenient water supply is obviously essential.

Wildflower and Rock Gardens. The more rugged areas of the school site can often be set aside for planting wildflowers and the development of rock gardens. Plants can be transferred from the region around the school and cared for in such gardens. These can be labeled and their relative abundance observed.

Tree-Growth Demonstration. Tree growth can be studied by obtaining the ages of various trees with an increment borer used by foresters. The age can be included in the name labels. Posts and logs often used around parking areas and playgrounds will also show annual rings, in which case comparative studies are possible. Sections of older trees can be obtained and preserved when such trees have to be removed on or near the school grounds. Occasionally stumps can be preserved in place. The date of cutting should be recorded on them so that historical events in the community can be related to the growth of the trees.

Campus Arboretum. The campus should have as many species of local trees and shrubs on it as can be integrated with the plans for playground space. These should be labeled so that children and teachers can identify them and make comparisons with nonlabeled trees elsewhere. Various classes can add needed trees as class projects and as a culmination activity for tree study.

School Forests. Since many school sites are not large enough for some of the above projects, other areas can be secured for the development of projects not possible on the school property. These areas should be as near to the school as possible to facilitate use. They can be developed as school forests where many valuable teaching demonstrations and work experiences are possible. Planting, thinning, and selective cutting of trees are easily taught on these areas, along with erosion control, fire prevention and control, values of various species of trees, succession of forest types, natural planting, and production of forest by-products like Christmas trees, posts, and firewood.

Such school forests should include as many of the features suggested above for school grounds as cannot be conveniently located at the school itself. Help can be obtained from the state division of forestry, the U. S. Forest Service, and the forest experiment stations.

Legislation has been passed in some states making it possible for boards of education to purchase or accept ownership and control of areas for school forests. The information on a particular state can be secured from the state department of public instruction or the state department of conservation.

Wildlife Sanctuary. The whole school ground can be designated as a wildlife sanctuary and certain things done to increase the number of birds and mammals which will visit or make their homes on it. Planting Lespedeza bicolor and Multiflora rose, obtainable from the state conservation departments, will supply food and shelter for many species of birds. Developing thickets, brushy fence-rows, and allowing certain areas to "go wild" will supply additional food and shelter. Weeds permitted to grow in the garden during late summer months will produce food in the fall months for sparrows, goldfinches, and other seed eaters.

Birdhouses, especially for bluebirds, can be built and placed about the grounds. These need to be single-holed houses placed in open areas, as bluebirds usually will not nest under trees. Plans for suitable houses for all hole-nesting species can be obtained for 25 cents from the National Audubon Society, 1000 Fifth Avenue, New York City.

Feeding shelves and trays and drinking fountains for birds can be placed at or near classroom windows where birds can be studied closely by all pupils. Such things as sunflower seed, millet, stale bread and doughnuts, and suet will be eaten by 15 to 20 species of birds. Feeding devices do not need to be elaborate and, if kept well stocked with food, birds will usually find them and continue to use them. Some shelter in the way of trees or shrubs near these feeders will increase their use.

Many berry-producing, bird-food shrubs can also be used in school land-scaping, such as pyrocantha, mountain ash, dogwood, eleagnis, sumac, and viburnum.

Bog Garden. If the school is located in a suitable place, a small stream or spring can be dammed so as to provide a bog garden where aquatic plants and animals can be placed for observation and study.

Fish Pond. If water is available for a fish pond, fish can be raised and made available for study. The use of fish as fertilizer, the effect of predatory fish, and many other valuable lessons can be illustrated. If a natural water supply is not available for a bog garden or fish pond, it might be feasible to use the school's water supply and pipe it into such areas.

Turtle Pit. In a few instances a school may want to develop an area for temporary housing of reptiles such as turtles, snakes, and lizards. This area, of course, should have a water supply and fencing adequate to keep the animals from escaping and the children from falling into it.

Erosion Control and Soil Study. Most school grounds and surrounding areas are susceptible to erosion because of the intensive use of small, crowded areas. Certain soil-holding plants like lespedeza, kudzu, and honeysuckle can be used to help improve this condition in areas where their excessive growth can be controlled. Various devices, too, can be installed to assist in checking the flow of water, such as terraces, diversion ditches, runways, and the like. Such work can be done by the children and kept as a permanent exhibit for teaching purposes. Small run-off demonstrations can be set up to show the relative effectiveness of different kinds of ground cover. Banks can be exposed in such a way as to demonstrate topsoil and subsoil. A soil auger can be used for such demonstrations in other areas.

Nature Trails. A nature trail can be developed on many school grounds or in school forests. The trail should take in most of the kinds of habitats available. Signs can be used to identify the various plants and animals and to tell interesting facts and stories about them. The research required to secure the needed data, the making of signs, the art work, and the correct grammar and spelling make the development of such a project a unique method for obtaining cooperative action of staff and pupils. Advice on planning such trails can be secured from the National Audubon Society.

Weather Stations. The erection and maintenance of a weather station on the school grounds will be of great interest to many pupils. Regular rainfall and other data can be recorded and posted on the school bulletin board by various committees and classes. Directions for developing a weather station can be secured from the nearest U.S. Weather Bureau office. Since the equipment of a weather station must be protected, it can be erected in the patio or a courtyard which can be fenced off and locked. The same precaution would apply to the turtle pit, small fish pond, bird bath, and bird feeders.

Outdoor Classrooms. Placing some logs or stones in a circular position in a suitable spot on a hillside will make it possible to have a classroom outdoors for use in warm weather. These areas can be screened off with cedars and other evergreens so that considerable privacy can be secured.

Picnic Area. A fireplace with appropriate seats of stones or of logs can be erected in an area for outdoor meals and class get togethers. These can also be screened from other areas by evergreens.

Outdoor Theater. If suitable ground is available, an outdoor theater for plays, singing, and commencements can be developed. Sloping ground facilitates such plans. Streams or ponds can be utilized for scenic effect.

School Camps. Some schools are finding it desirable to have children camp outdoors for a week or more to study nature, conservation, forestry, soil and wildlife management, geology, and related topics. Schools can use public and private camp sites already available, but some will want eventually to own their own sites for such instruction outdoors.

Fields for Crops and Horticulture. The demonstration fields for agriculture and horticulture need to be as near the classroom and shop as possible. Pasture plots, seed-testing areas, tree nurseries, and vegetable and tobacco plots can be developed for study and practice.

PLANNING

These suggestions, of course, are incomplete. They do offer, however, infinite possibilities for the alert administrator and faculty. Education, we must remember, cannot be confined to classrooms.

A Master Plan. Before too many of these suggestions are initiated, it would be desirable to develop a master plan for the school grounds which would cover short-time objectives and also the long-range planning for the property. Locations of future additions to the building and to athletic grounds need to be considered in order to avoid costly changes later.

The total plan for the school property should include the trees and shrubs needed for improving the appearance of the building and for helping to define the various play areas, walks, outdoor demonstration areas, and parking space. Each piece of property, of course, requires special treatment to capitalize on the contour of the land and the peculiar features of the buildings or particular requirements of instruction. Many times shrub screens and attractive hedges can be used to separate various areas or to hide unsightly spots adjacent to the school grounds. Trees take a long time to grow and their planting and removal need to be studied very carefully and fitted in with the long-range development of the property; therefore, the combined thinking of administrators, maintenance personnel, and instructional staff, plus as much professional help from landscape architects as possible, is needed to perfect a satisfactory over-all plan.

Help on landscaping can be secured from such sources as local nurserymen, the state highway commission, the state department of public instruction, and the state extension service.

Community Cooperation. Even though one teacher can do some of these things alone, it is well to use all the resources of the professional staff and to invite cooperation from all sources available. Such sources would include maintenance men, the custodial staff, parents, local nurserymen, and representatives of such agencies as the Soil Conservation Service, the state conservation department, and the state extension service. Full and effective development demands community-wide thinking, planning, and action.

THE CONCEPTUAL FIELD TRIP *

MATTHEW J. BRENNAN

"I have a leaf just like hers, but mine is an example of change in living things, and hers is an example of dependence among living things. Somehow they seem to be related." Indeed they were. For the rhododendron leaves the children collected both showed change. One of the children simply looked a little more closely and had noted that the change in the color and appearance of the leaf had been caused by an insect—a leaf miner dependent on the leaf for food and a home during its larval stage. These sixth graders from the Seth Lewelling School in Milwaukie, Oregon, spending a week at Camp Westwind on the beautiful Oregon coastal dunes, were developing concepts of science, concepts of environment, and concepts of conservation.

Since educators first directed their attention to the idea of helping children develop concepts rather than filling their minds with facts, the "concepts" approach has found general acceptance. Textbooks, elementary science projects, and more recently, a series of teachers' curriculum guides for conservation education have been developed under the South Carolina Curriculum Improvement Project using the same concepts.[1] Even so, in the field, teachers still stuff their pupils with facts. So, too, do some interpretive naturalists in the park and forest programs, for the public go in for the "whole load approach." A teacher, forester, or park naturalist may take a group out into the field and proceed to tell the children numerous facts he has learned during his formal education and in his work experience since, in a period of one hour or less.

At some resident outdoor education programs, the children get the "whole load" on a different area of science every day (sometimes two a day). On a trip through a National Park or National Forest, the child or visitor may be exposed to all about the geology, soils, plants, animals, and the type of conservation which the managing agency practices on the area. The result is that children in school and summer tourists are environmentally illiterate—they have no concepts of environment and particularly their own interdependence with the environment.

If the conceptual approach is acceptable for textbooks, teachers' guides, and media materials, why not try it for teaching and learning in the field—in the natural science laboratory? A "conceptual field trip," can be used effectively,

*Reprinted with permission from *Science and Children*, March, 1970. Copyright 1970 by the National Science Teachers Association, 1201 Sixteenth Street, N.W., Washington, D.C. 20036.
    [1] Brennan, Matthew J., Editor. *People and Their Environment*, Teachers Curriculum Guide to Conservation Education. J. G. Ferguson Company, Chicago, Illinois. 1969.

lasting 5 to 10 minutes, offering a child acquaintance with a single concept of environment. In this way, rather than the "whole load" the teacher can present to the class a sequentially planned series of field experiences which will lead to development of several concepts of environment.

In an analysis of the "whole load" presentation of several foresters, explaining the reasons for block cutting of Douglas fir, black walnut, or cherry, why not prepare a list of the concepts they briefly mention: germination on mineral soil, response to sunlight, tolerance to shade, effects of crowding, thinning. These concepts can be better developed in a planned elementary science sequence, rather than through a unit taught a day or longer.

For example, at The Pinchot Institute, many interesting field trips are taken with children at all levels. With kindergartners, the Institute has had great success with a ten-minute trip to see three trees. One is big and tall and straight, the forester's dream tree. The second is a hemlock that blew down in a storm several years ago. Its roots are still intact and the tip has turned up toward the sun. (Or is it away from the pull of gravity?) The third tree was bent over when another fell on it in a storm. Three of its side branches are now growing upright.

At the kindergarten level, we are told that children cannot develop a concept of plant response to sunlight. That is generally done in third grade (or is it fourth?) by putting a box over a geranium plant in the classroom window. Nevertheless, when the five-year-olds are asked what they have learned from seeing these trees, several in the class will invariably say, "All of the trees are trying to get up to the sun."

The other concepts necessary to an understanding of forestry can be developed just as easily as the child progresses through elementary school science.

Back to the quotation at the opening of the article from the sixth grader at Camp Westwind in Oregon. Last May, a different kind of "conceptual field trip" was tried with these students from Seth Lewelling School. As the field trip began, the children were asked to look for two things:

(1) evidence of change (concept: living things and the environment are in constant change); and (2) evidence that one living thing is dependent on another living thing—that living things are dependent on one another, or interdependent. (Concept: living things are interdependent with their environment and each other.)

The directions for the ten-minute field trip were simple: "In the next ten minutes, find as many examples as you can of change and dependence."

The children regrouped after ten minutes. They were loaded down with dead leaves, flowers, and seeds. The students saw all kinds of changes, and discussed how these were caused. They decided that changes in living things were:

1. natural (species)—buds → flowers → seeds → dead remains;

2. natural (caused by other living things)—chewed, sucked, mined leaves;
3. physical—storm, erosion, flood, time;
4. chemical—pH, mineral deficiency, salt spray;
5. man-caused (In another hour the children might have decided that man-made changes are also natural. Is not man a natural animal?)

The children further decided that changes are going on all the time. Living things change, environments change, sixth graders change, constantly.

Concepts of dependence and interdependence are just as quickly developed through this type of experience. In the very short time spent on the field trip, the children are beginning to develop the third major concept of environment—*living things are the product of their heredity and their environment.* This concept also applies to populations of organisms. What would happen if an animal ate *all* the leaves of a tree? If man killed all grouse? Why are two Sitka spruce trees different? Two daisies? Two sixth-graders?

This type of field trip means a new role for the teacher—but it is an enjoyable one. All he has to do is direct his students to new experiences and help them explore unknown environments. Let them develop their own concepts of environment. Then every new experience they have in the environment in the future will reinforce their concept or cause it to be modified.

INTEGRATING CONSERVATION EDUCATION INTO THE EXISTING CURRICULUM OF THE ANN ARBOR PUBLIC SCHOOL SYSTEM (K-12) *

WILLIAM B. STAPP

INTRODUCTION

If we are to prepare the individuals of our society to make the kind of resource decisions that our nation will face in the future, our schools must embark on a comprehensive conservation program that will span the curriculum, kindergarten through the twelfth grade, and link the subject areas that relate most closely to conservation, especially science and social studies. This type of a program could stress the *characteristics, interrelationships,* and *uses* of our natural resources in the elementary grades, and emphasize the levels of

*Reprinted by permission of the publisher from *Science Education* 48:419-424, December, 1964.

management and *policy* at the secondary level. This approach to conservation could be made even more favorable to school systems if conservation could be integrated into a school system's existing curriculum.

Three years ago I was given the opportunity to help develop a conservation education program for the Ann Arbor Public School System. I accepted a newly created position, conservation consultant, in September of 1961 and started immediately to develop and integrate an outdoor and conservation education program into the Ann Arbor Public School System (K-12).

GUIDING PRINCIPLES OF THE PROGRAM

Very briefly, the guiding principles of the Ann Arbor Program are:

1. The program spans the curriculum, kindergarten through the twelfth grade, so that conservation understandings can be presented in a logical sequence and at the time that the learner is most receptive to the material presented. Isolating conservation as a single course limits the scope of the program and the number of students exposed to conservation understandings.

2. The program provides continuity and progression, so that the understandings developed in one grade grow and are expanded in subsequent grades.

3. The program links subject areas that relate most closely to conservation, especially science and social studies, so that both the social and scientific knowledge important in understanding and solving resource problems is properly developed.

4. The program is integrated and correlated with the existing curriculum in a manner that enhances the instructional goals of the school system.

5. The program gives the learner an opportunity to study some of our community's natural resources under natural conditions. This provides certain learning experiences that cannot be duplicated within the school building.

6. The program stresses attitudes and not vocational skills. I feel that the most important conservation impact that most of our urban children will have upon our natural resources will be through their action as community citizens.

7. The program emphasizes local resource problems so that our future community citizens will have the incentive and tools to cope effectively with our current and future resource problems. However, the conservation program should not neglect regional, national, or international resource problems.

8. The program is handled in such a manner that the learner plays an active

role in the learning process. The learner develops attitudes through personal experiences and thinking and not through the presentation of predigested conclusions.

9. The program provides a comprehensive inservice training program for teachers which operates throughout the school year and is directed at helping teachers increase their understandings, interest, awareness and teaching skills in conservation.

OPERATION OF THE ELEMENTARY PHASE OF THE PROGRAM

In operation, every elementary teacher in the Ann Arbor Public Schools has an opportunity to make an appointment to have her class guided through one of several resource sites in our community during the fall or spring months. The presentation of the program consists of three separate phases: orientation, field trip, and follow-up. Fourth, fifth, and sixth grade classes are scheduled for field trips Monday, Tuesday, and Wednesday mornings, and first, second, and third in the afternoons. Thursdays are used to give a 30-40 minute orientation to the six classes that are scheduled for field trips the following week. Fridays are left open for rescheduling field trips that have been cancelled due to inclement weather.

Prior to the classroom orientation, a "teachers' kit" is delivered to the teacher one week prior to the orientation. This kit contains written material on the grade level theme, several publications pertinent to the teacher's grade level, suggested follow-up activities, and a "grade level understanding check list." The check list is to be completed by the teacher and returned to the program coordinator two days prior to the orientation session. The purpose of the check list is to inform the program coordinator of the understandings pertaining to the field trip theme that have already been discussed with the students by the teacher, and understandings the teacher would like to have especially emphasized in the orientation and field trip. Each grade level presentation is patterned around the particular needs of each class.

On the day of the field trip the program coordinator returns to the school with one or more field trip assistants. The assistant field trip guides are volunteer citizens of the community that have been trained by the program coordinator. In most instances the assistant field trip guides volunteer their services for one field trip each week, and these are generally for the same grade level.

The field trip sites are both private and public lands in and around Ann Arbor. However, school sites and areas bordering schools are always used if the grade level theme can be carried out on the school site. Enroute to the field trip site, points of interest in the community environment are discussed that relate to the grade level theme. Upon arrival at the resource site the class is divided into smaller groups, each with its own trail leader. While in the field the resource site is interpreted in a manner that relates to the theme and understandings for the particular grade. In other words, each grade level, using its own site, has an entirely different field trip experience. On the return bus trip the field trip experiences are highlighted and the entire trip reviewed.

The kindergarten program is scheduled for a two-week period immediately following the termination of the fall program for the other elementary classes. The program consists of a 20-25 minute presentation by the program coordinator on "how plants and animals prepare for winter and live during this period of time." Charts and specimens are used in the presentation to help illustrate interdependence of plants, animals, soil, and water.

The program was established to accommodate two-thirds of all elementary classes in the school system, or approximately 230 of the 350 elementary classes. It was thought that this would meet the demand for field trips, since the program was entirely voluntary. However, this has not been the case. To accommodate more classes a waiting list is formed when all field trip appointments have been reserved. If no field trips are rescheduled during the week, due to inclement weather, classes on the waiting list are scheduled on Fridays. During the first three years of operation, approximately 75 per cent of all elementary classes, 7,000 students, were involved each year in an orientation, field trip, and follow-up experience. In addition to the regular elementary phase of the program, the program coordinator is requested to make many classroom and assembly presentations on a variety of conservation topics.

OPERATION OF THE SECONDARY PHASE OF THE PROGRAM

In the operation of the secondary phase of the program, the secondary science and social studies teachers request conservation topics they would like to have assistance in integrating into their courses. The program coordinator then prepares, mimeographs, and distributes to the classroom teacher subject material on the requested topic. Visual aids are also prepared to enhance the classroom presentation of the conservation topic.

The program coordinator is also available throughout the school year to assist the secondary science and social studies teachers by giving classroom presentations on any of the conservation topics they request, to prepare additional resource material for their usage, or to assist them in other related ways. Although the program coordinator is available to assist secondary teachers at any time during the school year, his time is primarily devoted to the secondary program during the winter months.

A few of the conservation topics that the program coordinator prepared, mimeographed, and distributed to secondary science and social studies teachers are: the effect of fire on the environment and its uses in resource management (general science); the impact of the Theodore Roosevelt administration on conservation (American history); the effect of pollution on stream biology

(biology); controlling water pollution (American government); the pesticide program (biology); population increase and its impact upon natural resources (economics); air pollution (senior science); demand for outdoor recreation (social problems). In addition to the written material circulated by the program coordinator, over 100 classroom presentations are made each year as well as several field trips, science club and assembly presentations.

INSERVICE TRAINING PROGRAM

One of the most important aspects of the program is inservice training for teachers. Due to the scope of the program the coordinator's personal contact with each class is limited. Therefore, it was vitally important in the establishment of the program and in its continuation to provide a comprehensive inservice training program for teachers. It was felt that the training program should be directed at helping the teacher to increase his understanding, interest, awareness, and teaching skills in conservation.

The inservice training program for teachers is multipronged, so that the teachers receive training in a variety of ways throughout the school year. The program consists of grade level, interschool, and school building presentations; a series of fall and spring field trips; and material prepared, mimeographed, and distributed to classroom teachers throughout the school year.

IMPLEMENTING PROGRAM INTO OTHER SCHOOL SYSTEMS

I feel that even though the program was developed for the Ann Arbor Public School System, it can be successfully integrated into other school systems in the country with slight modifications to meet the prevailing conditions unique to each school system and municipality.

Some of the ways that the Outdoor and Conservation Education Program of the Ann Arbor Public Schools might assist teachers and administrators interested in developing a similar program in their own cities are:

1. Consideration of the employment of a program coordinator to operate the program.
2. Consideration of the guiding principles formulated and incorporated into this program.
3. Consideration of the general operation of the elementary and secondary phase of this program.
4. Consideration of the nature and extent of the inservice training program for teachers.
5. Consideration of the use of community citizens in the operation of the program.

6. Consideration of the use of school, private, and public land in the operation of the program.

Perhaps one factor that could prevent a school system from developing an Outdoor and Conservation Education Program is the procurement of an adequately trained and motivated person to develop and operate the program. A school system interested in developing an Outdoor Conservation Education Program could send one of their present employees to an institution, such as the University of Michigan, to receive the proper academic training. Prospective conservation program coordinators receiving their training at the University of Michigan would have the opportunity of working in Ann Arbor's Outdoor and Conservation Education Program.

Some of the special qualifications that a program coordinator should possess in order to develop and operate an Outdoor and Conservation Education Program for a school system (K-12) are:

1. Broad educational background with specific training in education, conservation, and natural and social sciences.
2. Ability to operate at all three levels of the school curricula.
3. Ability to operate in both science and social studies.
4. Ability to teach both in the classroom and in the field.
5. Ability to design and operate an inservice training program for teachers.
6. A responsible individual who has both administrative and teaching skills.
7. Dedication to outdoor and conservation education.

A program of this nature can be instrumental in helping our future citizens to increase their awareness, interest, and understanding of the characteristics and interrelationship of our natural resources; and in helping them to understand man's dependence on the proper management and intelligent use of our natural resources. Through this greater knowledge and understanding of our natural resources, I strongly believe that as our students become adults and voting citizens, they will take a more active role in local, state, national and international resource issues.

SCHOOL CAMP: AN IDEAL
SCIENCE LABORATORY *

JOHN D. WILLIAMS

As part of the inservice training program, the faculty of Foxpark School decided to visit some other schools. Mr. Guy, the sixth-grade teacher, visited the neighboring county school, Mountain View. He wanted to pick up some ideas that would help make science more interesting to children.

His first impression upon arriving at Mountain View School was that the day would be wasted. As he looked around, he saw children identifying rocks and leaf designs in plaster molds, reading maps, recording bird calls, and pressing herbarium specimens. He saw nothing that to him resembled an elementary-school science laboratory.

A LABORATORY IN THE HILLS

"Don't they teach school any more?" he breathed to himself as he remembered that he had reported in a recent statewide survey that the handicap that most hampered his science program was inadequate laboratory facilities. "Do you have a laboratory?"

"Yes," said Mr. Johns, the principal of Mountain View. "Miss Topliff, our fifth-grade teacher, will show you her laboratory."

"This is our laboratory," said Miss Topliff as she pointed to her busy students. "We have just returned from school camp. Last week our laboratory was in the recreation camp in the foothills of the Snowy Range Mountains, 30 miles west of town. The boys and girls and I spent five days in this outdoor laboratory because many science phenomena are best taught in their natural setting. We tried for many years here at Mountain View to teach elementary-school science from a book or from model specimens. It was worth the effort, but we have discovered that children remember longer and with less distortion those things which they see and experience."

"But I don't know practical science. We follow a textbook very closely."

"I didn't know very much science either when we started teaching it a few

*Reprinted by permission from *The National Elementary Principal* 33:166-70, September, 1953. Copyright 1953, Department of Elementary School Principals, National Education Association. All rights reserved.

years ago. I learn with the children. I have acquired more insight into science since I have been going to school camp than in all the years of study in college and teaching from a textbook."

USING RESOURCE PEOPLE

"We use resource people from the community, too. Mr. Whittier, the science teacher from the local high school, came to conduct a field trip to study the geology of the outlying valley. He knows the history of the region and the valley formations very well. This was good follow-up on our unit, 'Our Changing Earth.' Sally invited her neighbor who has lived in the region for many years to visit the camp one night. He told exciting stories of early homesteaders and miners in the area."

LEARNING IS FUN

"This all sounds very interesting. Do you mean that I don't need a lot of expensive equipment and that a school camp makes an ideal science laboratory? I have always thought of camp as a place for a good time."

"Fun it is. We do not teach formal classes in science but science is discovered, pointed out, and studied as children prepare meals, take nature excursions, sit around the camp fire, and talk in formal groups. Learning is fun and some fun is learning."

"What are some science activities which help make your school camp fun for boys and girls?"

Miss Topliff said, "Let's move over to the corner and let the fifth-graders share their camping experiences with us."

JACK MADE WEATHER CHARTS

"Jack, you seem to be very much interested in weather charts. Did you make those at school camp?"

"Yes, Mr. Guy. My group set up a weather station. Before going to camp we visited the local weather bureau to study the various instruments used in predicting weather. Each day at camp we studied the weather and made the daily forecast in the camp newspaper. Now I am finding the average temperature for the week. The group will then compare it with the weather bureau reports for the same period and also with last year's camp report. Weather is important in our section of the country. We get lots of snow and we use our reports as one guide to selecting the week to go to camp. Miss Topliff, I think Mr. Guy would like to hear Bob's story about getting lost. He is working in the group across the room."

BOB GOT LOST

Bob told an interesting story of how he wandered by the wayside to observe ant hills and gopher holes while the children were on a late afternoon excursion to an abandoned silver mine. His interest in the social habits of the large red ants lasted for 15 to 20 minutes, for he wanted some of the ants for his anthouse. He suddenly realized the group had gone ahead. "I do not know my way back to camp." He remembered the fifth-grade unit on magnets before they came to camp. Luckily, Bob had a single compass in his pocket. "I need to go north. Which way is north?" His compass told him. The stars were shining brightly by now. Bob looked at the Big Dipper; he looked for the Little Dipper. The North Star was easy to find. This also gave him a clue as to direction. Bob was very thankful that around the campfire the night before the entire camp group had had a practical lesson on "What can one see in the night sky?"

When Bob had finished his story, Mr. Guy was convinced that children need practical applications of science generalizations and fewer memorized facts and scientific principles.

LEARNING ABOUT CONSERVATION

"I'm sure you have described a full week of science experiences, Miss Topliff."

"On the contrary," she said, "that is just the beginning. Would you like to hear about our conservation activities?"

"Indeed," replied Mr. Guy.

"Conservation of both human and natural resources is important. Before leaving school each of us had inoculations and a complete physical examination. Our school nurse stayed with us at camp as the camp nurse. She gave us lessons in first aid. Under her direction, we were allowed to treat fellow campers for simple cuts and insect bites. On our pack trips, we knew what to do in case of an accident."

"Nutrition is very important in camp. In our health classes, we planned wholesome menus for meals prepared in the camp kitchen and made weight charts. Many of us gained weight."

"Mr. Cartwright, the forest ranger, talked with us about the wise use of our forests. He showed us how to tell the ages of trees, how to select trees for cutting, and films on the prevention of forest fires. His crew gave us a demonstration on stopping a forest fire. Mr. Cartwright and Mr. Jenkins, the county agricultural agent, directed a reforestation project on a burned-over hillside. This is now our school forest. We wrote letters to the state university and state conservation department asking for seedlings which were promptly sent to us."

FIRST-HAND LEARNING

Mr. Guy interrupted apologetically with the idea that the afternoon had slipped away and it would be necessary for him to be on his way home. "I'm sure," he said, "there are many other science activities which enliven and enrich a school camping program. I would like very much to visit your camp next spring."

"Wonderful! We didn't have time to hear the children tell about their experiences in camp sanitation such as drainage, sewage disposal, water purification, dish washing, and preservation of food. But you will see that when you visit our camp next year."

"Before you go, Mr. Guy, I want to tell you about our first project," said Ned. "It was the most fun. We laid out and marked a mile-long nature trail. In this project we really learned the meaning of interdependence of plants and animals and balance in nature. Just reading about such things didn't mean much to most of us. We decided we wanted to participate in a conservation project. Some of us built check dams and planted an eroded hillside to hold the soil and make a home for animals.

"I remember another evening as we returned along the trail from a cook-out. Joe discovered a dragonfly flitting back and forth along the bank and among the rushes of a small stream. Listen! I hear Joe's group discussing this trip with Mr. Johns."

"Does the 'devil's darning needle' really sew up the mouths of liars, Mr. Johns?" asked Joe as he removed a dragonfly from the solution in which it was preserved.

Judy interrupted, "That is a snake feeder. My grandfather says they feed snakes."

"Neither is true!" exclaimed Tom. "Those are only superstitions. The dragonfly is really beneficial to man. If we opened the dragonfly's stomach, we would find it loaded with flies and mosquitoes."

"I'll see if that is true," Joe mumbled to himself.

By this time, Jim had almost stepped on a toad that had escaped from the terrarium, and the attention of the group was attracted.

Lucy cried, "Oh!" as Jim bent over to pick up the toad, "Toads make warts."

"I don't believe toads make warts," said Jim. "I have handled toads many times. They destroy insects."

As Jim carried the toad back to the terrarium, Joe was opening the stomach of the dragonfly. Sure enough, there were some flies and mosquitoes. Mr. Johns told of his many experiences with toads on the farm. After examining his hands, the children were convinced that toads do not cause warts.

VISIBLE RESULTS

The nature trail provided many opportunities for morning walks. Bill learned to imitate 10 bird calls and Mary collected 21 different flowering plants for her herbarium which was placed in the camp museum. Rosa learned to identify the various types of trout in the stream. Rock collections appealed to Rex and Ray. They took the responsibility of labeling the rocks on the trail and collected extra samples for the museum. Later, these will be taken home, for both boys are developing collecting hobbies.

"Camping is fun; I wish we could have stayed longer."
"I want to be an astronomer."
"School has been more interesting this year."
"I want to be a camp counselor."
"We know our teacher better."
"I want to be a forest ranger."
"Everyone has a place in this world."
"I want to be a geologist."

Such comments made by the Mountain View fifth-graders as they worked kept running through Mr. Guy's mind as he rode along in his car back to Foxpark. Science took on real meaning for him just as science has taken on real meaning for the boys and girls. After all, he thought, what happens to children as they scientifically work and think is more important than the number of pages they read each day.

"We may not be able to go camping for a whole week," he said to himself, "but next spring we are going to move our laboratory outside for some day camping."

EXTENDING SCIENCE EDUCATION
THROUGH ELEMENTARY SCHOOL CAMPING *

JERRY BEKER

"That which can best be learned in the classroom should be taught there, and that which can best be learned in the out-of-doors should there be taught." Dr. L. B. Sharp, known as the father of the Outdoor Education movement, has thus stated its basic guiding principle, maximal efficiency of school learning. School camping is an extension of the regular curriculum to the out-of-doors, but an integral part of that curriculum.

The school camping program enables regular classes, with their teachers, to spend a period of time living, working and playing together in a relatively natural camp environment. In effect, it represents an extended field trip into a natural laboratory situation with raw material for many, if not all, areas of the curriculum, but especially science. Perhaps the most common pattern is for the school camping experience to last for one school week, from Monday morning until Friday afternoon, for fifth, sixth or seventh grade classes. Some schools have adapted school camping programs to the secondary level, and some have introduced outdoor education experiences, usually of shorter duration, below the fifth grade as well. Of course, as with any effective field trip, much time is spent in the classroom both before and after camp in correlating the camp program with class activities, and consolidating learning. Effective school camping is an integral part of the total school experience.

Many public school systems as well as private schools across the country have implemented school camping programs. Especially noteworthy is the progress that has been made in such states as California, Michigan, New York, and Texas. Many thousands of children annually attend camp during the school year, usually with their classroom teachers as well as other leaders, as a part of their regular curriculum. New York University's School of Education and other groups are providing leadership and guidance for school systems anxious to get started in the program. Nationwide, the picture is one of rapid expansion of this significant educational innovation.

The most self-evident possibility for extension of the curriculum through

*Reprinted by permission of the publisher from *Science Education* 44:138-42, March, 1960.

school camping is in the area of the sciences. At camp, the subject matter in this field, quite literally in many cases, "comes alive" for the students. The natural environment itself is available to be studied and shared—the sources are primary, although they should be supplemented by books and other secondary materials. Most important, the subject matter has meaning for the child; it is a part of his life. Motivation is no longer a problem.

Almost every area of natural science, if not every one, can be successfully studied at camp—with greater efficiency of learning than in the classroom. Of course, these learnings can be broadened and deepened in the classroom later. The school camp is the laboratory where observations are made first-hand. Ways in which some areas of science may best be studied at camp are presented below. The material is not complete but suggestive; the possibilities are only limited by the limits of teachers' and students' imaginations.

Astronomy is one of the most obvious. The children are at camp "round the clock," and are available to make observations at night. The stars, planets and moon become part of the collective class experience, and children are taught while looking at the sky itself. Facts are learned more easily in a situation such as this, and new feelings are also experienced and learned. There is a spiritual appreciation that is part of knowing the night sky fully, and it cannot be learned from a textbook.

The classroom model of the sun, the moon and the earth makes better sense when children can compare it with an actual sunrise and sunset and the travels of the moon. The spinning of the earth and the moon around the sun begins to have meaning for children in terms of their own lives. Questions arise, again sometimes with spiritual implications, and new learning takes place.

In times like these, we must also turn our attention to man-made celestial bodies. Artificial satellites may be observed, and their study has scientific implications that may lead into many areas such as space travel, rocket operation, jet propulsion, gravity, and friction. In addition, a natural correlation is provided between science and current events. The importance in today's world of education in general, and science education in particular, may thus become clearer to children.

At camp, children are also able most effectively to study meteorology rather than about meteorology. They are living in the out-of-doors, on a twenty-four hour per day basis, and are in an ideal position to make their own observations, using instruments and directly observed natural indications. The whole interesting area of weather and climate is opened to them in a natural, indigenous way. Understanding the weather and even forecasting it becomes important to them, since it has a great influence on their life and program at camp.

The study of soil and water may also be made more meaningful and fruitful in the laboratory that is the school camp. It is natural to ask about the substances that make up "terra firma" when one is at camp, much more likely (and much more relevantly) at camp than in the classroom. This may lead into the whole area of chemistry, for example, or into life sciences.

Another science whose raw materials are part of the camp environment is geology. It is one of the most fascinating to children, when they can be the geologists themselves,—collecting rocks, chipping out fossils and the like. In this situation, the children are clamoring for learning and need only resources—books, charts and the like—to find the facts they want. Perhaps the wisest teacher is the one who doesn't tell them everything, but helps them "look it up."

Botany and zoology are two of the major areas of science that can be studied most effectively in the school camp setting. Plants and animals abound, the children's interests are attracted by them. Not only can plants and animals be studied "in the flesh," but they are in their natural habitats as well. One of the major contributions to children's understanding of life that camping is equipped to make is in just this area, ecology. Once children can understand and get a "feel" for the interdependence of life in a given habitat, including all the limiting factors such as climate, food, shelter and protection, they are much better equipped to study and understand other forms of life. The principles involved—interdependence and balance—have the broadest possible implications for students.

At this point, we begin to see the implications of this kind of study of science for the social learnings of students, for interdependence is a vital principle in this regard. But there is another whole area of scientific learning and experience at school camp, transcending those discussed above, with the most direct and significant social implications. This is the area of conservation. Children at school camp learn about conservation in part by actually doing conservation projects, by talking with resource people whose work is in the field of conservation, and by study. They are concerned with all major areas of conservation—soil, water, wildlife and forests. At all times, underlying reasons for conservation "Do's" and "Don'ts" can be stressed, so that the children learn the scientific bases for what they are doing.

Conservation units include such items as the causes, dangers and control of soil erosion. Learning is consolidated as children actually apply erosion control techniques. They build small dams along streams to impound water and improve fish habitats. They build brush piles for animal shelters, fell trees to thin the forest when necessary, and do other real conservation jobs. Scientific learnings may accompany all of these activities. The environment provides the resources, the laboratory. Of course, the teacher's job as guide and interpreter remains a requisite if learning is to be more than observational and to have real meaning for students.

We have examined a few of the more obvious ways in which science can be more effectively studied using a natural outdoor laboratory. More strictly physical sciences can also be involved, as when a group faces the problem of how to move a large, heavy log that has just been cut. Or, how long it takes a stone to fall from the top of the cliff. Or, how to build and brace that log bridge over the stream. But let us look at the program in the context of an actual elementary school science curriculum.

School camping is perhaps most common at the sixth grade level across the country, and this level provides us with a good example. One state's (New York) Sixth Grade Science Outline lists seven major "problems," at least five of which seem directly related to the kinds of learnings that can be developed naturally through the use of school camps as a laboratory. Certain aspects of the two others, electricity and sound, may also be relevant here but will not be considered in detail. Efficiency of learning is the goal, and units that can be most enhanced through school camping are our primary concern.

The first problem is titled, "Animals Need Food for Growth and Energy." The aims of this unit are listed as:

1. To show the close relation of plants and animals;
2. To learn how animals survive;
3. To find what cells are;
4. To show how animals make use of their food and oxygen.

Suggested approaches are:

1. Find pictures of animals in their natural surroundings;
2. Observe how animals are adapted to their surroundings;
3. Discuss their own pets and animals familiar to the group.

The teaching of this unit can clearly be facilitated through school camping, since it ties in closely with the natural habitats of animals.

The problem "What Causes Changes in Climate and Weather?" has been discussed above. Likewise, we have mentioned astronomy, on which another problem, "Is the Sun a Member of Our Galaxy?" is based. The aims listed for the unit are:

1. To find what is beyond our solar system;
2. To find what are constellations;
3. To show the nature of our galaxy;
4. To find what is beyond our galaxy.

Suggested approaches are:

1. Read legends connected with the constellations and find out how they got their names;
2. Look for interesting articles in newspapers or magazines;

3. Observe the sky on a clear night and try to fix in mind the positions of a few of the brightest stars.

It can readily be seen how many of these kinds of aims and approaches can be enriched and made to "come alive" at camp.

"How Has Man Changed Some Plants and Animals So That They Are Better Suited to His Needs?" is a problem that can be most effectively studied at a school camp which includes a particular kind of resource, a farm. In this situation, children can actually observe the techniques and results of artificial selection, grafting, hybridization and artificially induced mutations. They can become acquainted with farm plants and animals, in part through actually working with and caring for them. Milking the cows, feeding the chickens and harvesting the wheat are some of the kinds of experiences that add new depth to learning about this vital aspect of life. The theoretical aspects become more meaningful in this context. The comparison of domesticated plants and animals with wild ones for purposes of human consumption can be made easily and vividly in this kind of situation.

The final problem is entitled, "Our Health Should Be Safeguarded," and it is in this area that school camping has a special contribution to make in the very nature of things. For the children plan their trip in the classroom before they go. Among their concerns are such matters as, for example, menus, rest and sleep, cleanliness and sanitation, and clothing. These all provide natural opportunities for learning about health. The children usually plan their menus with the help and guidance of the school dietician. She may supply them with the facts about nutrition, such as the kinds of food needed in the basic daily diet, and the reasons for these requirements. Students learn about facts because they need them to use in devising the specific menus for their trip.

Frequently the school nurse is also called in as a resource person. She may discuss with the children their needs for rest and sleep, and the value of rest and sleep to the body, as an aid in their planning of a realistic and intelligent time schedule. Likewise, the need for clean hands at mealtime, the importance of thoroughly disinfecting toilet facilities, care not to spread germs through coughing and sneezing, and similar concerns may be discussed. The values of proper clothing, exercise, fresh air and the like can also be brought into the curriculum naturally in this situation. Of course, for scientific learning to occur, all of these leads must be explored in depth with the children, rather than merely stated or memorized.

But the real essence of scientific learning, especially in the elementary school, involves the scientific attitude and process, which begins with scientific curiosity. For the answer to the scientific challenge of our day does not lie in trying to make every sixth grader a compendium of scientific knowledge. What we must do is inspire young minds to ask questions and to seek answers. We must reward both the asking and the answering. It is in this area of scientific concern that school camping may make its greatest contribution, at least on the elementary school level.

School camping starts with the unfolding of the wonders of the natural world. Students need not "fight" their textbooks. The books are resources, and reward their curiosity with answers, their speculations with support or deeper insights. Teachers help students to ask questions, to reason out answers, and to check conclusions.

The most vital element, the stimulation and motivation, comes from presence of the raw material of learning, life itself. Furthermore, the learning is nonsegmental just as life itself is nonsegmental. There is a natural correlation of subject-matter fields. For the scientific at camp cannot be divorced from the social, the verbal or the quantitative. It is all of a piece. Insofar as life itself is challenging, insofar as children are inherently seekers of knowledge, so can an effective program of school camping tend to enhance the development of our future citizens in the scientific as well as other vital areas of life.

SCIENCE AND OUTDOOR EDUCATION OR "NOBODY CAN REALLY KNOW HOW I FEEL" *

GLENN O. BLOUGH

Dear Mr. Howard:

I wish to thank you for everything you did for us. I would like you to know how much I appreciate going to camp, but I think nobody can really know how I feel.

> Sincerely yours,
> Sharon Birch
> Mr. Egloff's Sixth Grade

By way of explanation, Mr. Howard is the principal of Four Corners School in Montgomery County, Maryland. Sharon has taken part in a week long camping experience that has been designed, along with other objectives to:

1. provide children with many opportunities to experience directly what they are studying
2. influence positively children's attitude toward learning

*Reprinted by permission of the author and publisher from *Journal of Outdoor Education*, Pilot Issue: 8-9, 12-14, Spring, 1966.

3. increase the emphasis on science education and motivate children toward developing increased interest and knowledge in several areas of science
4. make the children's regular school learnings more meaningful through the application of knowledge acquired in the classroom to practical outdoor situations
5. help children recognize the values of our natural resources and learn to use them wisely
6. help children learn to live democratically with other children and adults and to assume responsibilities for the welfare of the group
7. cultivate the children's interest in and appreciation for the out-of-doors which will carry over into later life
8. improve the children's physical fitness.

Sharon is probably voicing the opinions of many children who have participated in a satisfying outdoor education experience and we understand her completely when she says that nobody can know just how she feels.

Whenever a different learning environment is substituted for the usual one, certain factors must be carefully considered. Among them are: What can happen in the new environment that cannot take place in the old one? In other words, why the change? What preparations are essential? What are the expected results? What special emphasis shall be made?

We are considering here only one aspect of outdoor education—an experience designed to further the objectives of the year-long science program. This means that everyone concerned must have the program objectives in mind, must be familiar with teaching procedures that are necessary to attain the objectives and be enthusiastic about the possibilities of an outdoor experience.

What are the objectives of a science program in the elementary school? To help pupils understand that science is a method of discovery as well as comprehension of what's discovered is our aim. In other words we are trying to help pupils understand the methods of science and to use these methods, i.e., methods of discovery, inquiry, problem solving. We also want pupils to understand the meaning and use of scientific attitude, i.e., withholding judgment, using reliable sources of information, etc., and to make these a part of their everyday thinking. We also hope that they will broaden their interest and appreciation for their scientific environment and learn some science information and be able to use it. These, in brief, are our expectations.

Certain teaching procedures are bound to be more successful than others in attaining these objectives. Procedures and methods, whatever they are, must be aimed at achieving the objectives. The activities must be problem-solving centered. The emphasis must be on learning how to learn. The experiences must be interesting and satisfying. The pupils must be learning something that will make a difference to them.

THE OUTDOORS AS A LABORATORY

An examination of the preceding paragraph gives the essence of good teaching of science indoors and outdoors. Experience indicates that an outdoor program has certain unique contributions to make in helping to achieve these objectives.

First, the environment is teeming with materials and phenomena that lend themselves to use by the learners. Problems of plant and animal life are everywhere. Children live in changing weather, look up at the sky at night and are in many ways dependent upon the immediate environment.

Second, the motivation is built in. With intelligent and enthusiastic guidance, most children respond to learning in this environment.

Third, the combination of situation and environment usually generate enthusiasm for whatever task's at hand.

Science programs are most successful in the outdoors if they consider these two important ideas:

The outdoor experience should extend and reinforce the schoolroom experience. In other words there must be careful planning to insure relationship between the indoor and the outdoor program.

The outdoor program should be planned to include the kinds of activities that cannot be done equally well indoors. For example, there is no need to spend time indoors reading or performing experiments—unless it rains! The more formal activities can be done in the classroom where the situation dictates less action.

THE CLASSROOM TEACHER AND THE
OUTDOOR EXPERIENCE

In view of these two considerations, it is important for the regular classroom teachers who know the school curriculum to also be familiar with the outdoor possibilities and ideally they should participate in both. Such a circumstance makes it possible for the teacher, as the year progresses, to say, "Let's consider this further when we are outdoors" and when the children are outdoors, "Who sees any connection between this and our previous study?" Although there are often numerous resource people available in the out-of-doors experience, the teacher and/or someone else who is thoroughly familiar with the school science program must take major responsibility for the outdoor program. Such teachers direct the learning, coach the resource persons and sometimes, if they are prepared, do some of the teaching themselves. It is well to remember that the effectiveness of the resource person depends to a large degree on how carefully his job is thought out and how well his function is communicated to him. Unless there is a strong tie between the school and camp experience, both lose some of their potential.

EXAMPLES OF OUTDOOR SCIENCE EXPERIENCES

The local conditions dictate the selection of the out-of-doors activities. While they vary with the locale, following are examples of problems and activities that tie together the school and camp learnings and can often be done better in the open than in the school.

We are likely to think first of living things as likely subjects for outdoor study. In this connection such problems as these are appropriate: How are plant and animal life interdependent? How do living things get food? How do they protect themselves? How are they adapted to various environments?

Any wood lot, open field, meadow, stream, pond or lake will supply material that will help solve such problems as these. Children who are looking for material and situations for data for such problems about plants will note the effects of shade, too much or too little water, crowding, poor soil, good soil, etc. There is no adequate substitute for first-hand observation here. Here the material and conditions are real. Neither words nor pictures can substitute for them. Discussion on the spot has real meaning. The problems themselves take on extra meaning. If such problems have been considered during the year, pupils will recall their book knowledge and apply it. Let us be reminded that there is a fine balance between giving children enough time and freedom and making sure that they observe the important concepts around which the experience is built.

In connection with animal life pupils will look for homes of various animals, watch animals eat, see how they are adapted for protection, etc. Discovering a bee tree, exploring an old log for insect life, searching in and around a pond for various stages of insect and amphibian life, observing a bird's home in a tree trunk or just sitting quietly in a woods to discover by listening for sounds are examples of observations that may be made.

These are but a few of the many activities that make the study of animal life come alive. They add immeasurably to an appreciation of the interdependence of living things and their adjustment to the environment. No amount of reading, picture study or other substitute for the real thing can take the place of such discovery. Learning by actual observation adds to children's ability to solve problems and the subject matter so learned is certain to be more meaningful and understandable.

The concepts of conservation are at best difficult to teach. True, pupils can pass the test on subject matter learned from a book, but observing the effects of erosion, examining the material on a forest floor, walking through a burned-over area are sure to produce a more lasting result. Conservation learned in the open lasts longer, is real, is important, is more easily understood. When the development of attitudes is important, the method of discovery is important. When the discovery is made on the spot, it is much more likely to result in an improved attitude that is full of meaning.

A study of the earth's surface and the rocks and soils that compose it takes on added meaning when the students are out of doors. Digging into the floor of a forest for many pupils is their first real contact with the cycle that returns dead material back into the earth to be used again. Observing the thin layer of top soil in a field or a cut in the highway sheds new light on the importance of soil conservation. Collecting samples of earth and rock and examining them with a large magnifying glass yields information not easily obtained elsewhere to solve such problem as: "How are soils different from each other?" "How are soils formed?" "Of what are rocks made?"

The use of resource people working in their own familiar surroundings, is an unforgettable experience for many pupils. Individuals from the Forest Service, Soil Conservation Service, Geological Survey and the many other similar areas make excellent contributions to the attitudes and knowledge of pupils. Such individuals always need guidance from the classroom teacher in order to be truly useful but when they are used in the environment with which they are familiar their contributions are much more effective.

Allan Dodd, Assistant Director, Office of Curriculum Development of Montgomery County, Maryland, reminds us that *all* children benefit from outdoor experiences: *City children* who often have no idea of what a natural environment is like, *children from suburbia* whose idea of balance of nature probably doesn't go much further than a picture of a well-manicured lawn with crab grass under control and *rural children* who may live in close proximity to nature but are unaware of what is there and what it all means.

In so short a space we can only begin to consider the relationships between science and outdoor experiences. This relationship is like many others, it must be experienced to be fully comprehended. It is only then that we really understand Sharon's feeling and begin to see that attaining some of the objectives for teaching science in the elementary school may indeed be more effective if we teach where the problems and the materials to solve them meet.

ARITHMETIC IN THE SCHOOL CAMP *

ESTHER P. ROOSSINCK

School camping in the United States is an exploding idea. Over five hundred school systems representing twenty-four states have school camping programs. These programs vary, but there is a general trend toward a one week program for sixth graders. In the type of program this article considers, pupils and teacher together assume direct responsibility for designing, carrying out, and evaluating their plans. These activities are selected by the groups on the basis of being the best way to reach certain educational goals which can be attained better by group living in the outdoors than in a classroom.

This extension of the classroom is designed to provide an environment for the development of concepts through direct experience, and for the application of skills learned in school. Arithmetic, science, language arts, social studies and fine arts are all centered around a core problem. Living together around the clock, pupils and teachers use the entire range of talent found among themselves to solve the real problems of people in communities: food, shelter, clothing, industry, recreation, and wise use of resources for the best general welfare. In solving these problems, each individual can find inspiration, adventure, responsibility, and a new sense of freedom. For the classroom teacher, this is an exciting new classroom, a room with moveable walls which can be pushed out to embrace the whole countryside.

Through camp activities, certain specific objectives of arithmetic instruction can be attained more effectively than might be the case in the classroom. For example, the learner has an opportunity to use his understanding of quantitative relationships in a natural environment. He can use knowledges and skills learned in the classroom to meet social needs. He can define and analyze problems in order to determine the information needed to solve them. Through his own activities he can understand the primitive devices that were invented by men to keep accounts and tell time. He can develop a spirit of inquiry and respect for the orderliness of his natural environment. Furthermore, he can find an opportunity to use the abstractions of a quantitative vocabulary with meaning derived from direct experience. In addition, he can demonstrate quantitative concepts through practical application.

It is with this last objective, the development of numerical concepts through

*Reprinted by permission of *The Arithmetic Teacher* and the author, Dr. Esther P. Railton, Professor, Department of Teacher Education, California State University at Hayward, California, from *The Arithmetic Teacher* 7:22-25, January, 1960.

school camp experiences, that this paper is concerned. Arithmetic concepts are relative and perceptual. Whatever we conceptualize, we perceive as relative to other concepts derived from our unique previous experiences. That is, we see only what we have experience to see. Since our perceptions come not from objects but from us, our ideas about any object depend upon our point of view. Then we act according to our perception of the immediate situation in which we find ourselves. Concepts, then, come from our personal selection and organization of perceptions. Therefore, no one actually sees a thing the same as others see it or has concepts identical to those of anyone else. In order to communicate these concepts, we use abstract vocabulary, therefore, the accuracy of communication is relative to the accuracy with which we have perceived and organized our ideas about quantity, space and time.

This relationship between concepts and experience is demonstrable in school camping. Children ask, "How far is it to camp?" The abstractly expressed or measured distance from one city to its school camp is fifteen miles. This distance was a two-day wagon trip for the pioneers with a load of grist, because they had to make a round-about river crossing. According to one contemporary farmer, the distance is "One good cigar." In fact, the trip takes about forty-five minutes by school bus. One school camper anticipates that distance as the measure of his first prolonged separation from his parents; another thinks of it merely as a field trip to the lake where he fishes with his father. Within the camp, the quarter-mile hike to Mystery Valley is a quick walk, but on a hot summer day when the underbrush is leafy, the same hike becomes a jungle safari. In such instances, school camping affords opportunities for pupils to refine and accurately express their concepts of distance.

THREE KINDS OF QUESTIONS

Children who go to camp ask questions in regard to three kinds of arithmetical concepts. These may be grouped as questions about quantity, questions about space and distance, and questions about time.

The following questions about quantity represent those that children ask while they plan and carry out activities:

How much will it cost to go to camp?
How much clothing shall we bring?
How many people can sleep in the bunkhouses?
How many tables will we need to set for lunch?
How many fires will we need for our cookout?
If each person uses one-fourth pound of hamburger, how much shall we bring?
How many packages of buns do we need?

The next set of questions relates to the campers' concepts about space and distance:

How large is the bunkhouse?
How big is the dining room?
What is the circumference of the tree trunk?
How steep is the slope?
How would a scale profile of the oil well look?
What scale shall we use for our map?
How far is it to camp?
How far is it across the lake?
High high is the water tower?
What is the shortest way to the Grist Mill?
How deep is the top-soil?
How deep is the gravel-pit?
How do I use a compass?

When children seek answers to the following questions, they are forming and revising their concepts about time:

How long will we be in camp?
How long until lunch?
When should we build the fire?
How old is that tree?
What achievements have people made since the tree began to grow?
How much longer will it take to walk than to ride to the lumber mill?
How long ago was the house destroyed at the Abandoned Farm?
How long does it take an inch of topsoil to form?
When did the light we see leave that star?

Many similar questions which involve quantitative, spacial and time concepts arise in varied contexts. They occur while the children are planning the trip to camp, selecting and planning activities, hiking, boating, repairing a bridge, making a terrarium, gazing at the stars, adventuring with compasses and maps, making ice cream, dying cloth with native dyes, exploring the lake shores, cutting ice, skiing, visiting a rural village, lumbering, exploring a mineral deposit, reconstructing the history of an abandoned farm, or cooking over a camp fire.

Examination of one question will show some ways in which a teacher can use it to guide the development and reorganization of concepts to approach reality. In so doing, the children will discover relationships through first-hand observation and activity. For example, sixth grade children frequently ask "How far is it across the lake?"

Because perception comes from the individual, the teacher must try to understand the child's motive for asking. To do this, the teacher must make a judgment as to whether the questioner is seeking information, playing a social role, or hypothesizing. According to the leader's perception of the learner's reason for asking the question, the leader acts on one of three alternatives. He may (1) ignore the question, (2) answer the question, or (3) test the child's reason for asking the question. If he decides that the question is important to the children and in line with educational objectives, he will help the children discover ways of measuring the distance. The question becomes a situation for learning ways of estimating and measuring distance.

DEVELOPMENT FROM A QUESTION

Such a situation may take the form of a conversation between a camp teacher and a group of children standing on the beach. The conversation may proceed something like that which follows:

Camper 1: How far away is that point across the lake?

Teacher: I don't know. How far do you think it is?

Camper 1: A half mile?

Camper 2: No, a half mile is farther than that!

Teacher: Do you see anything that looks like it is a mile away?

Camper 2: Yes, that hill at the end of the lake.

Teacher: How did you get your idea of how far a mile is?

Camper 2: I ride with my father a lot. I look at the speedometer and then pick a tree I think is a mile off. Then I check it.

Camper 3: I know it is a half mile from my house to school. It isn't that far across the lake.

Camper 1: Well, how far is it across the lake?

Teacher: Maybe we can find out.

Camper 4: How?

Camper 2: We can row across with a line and then measure the amount of line we use.

Camper 3: That tree across the lake looks about as far as that tree down the shore. We can measure the distance to the tree down the shore.

Camper 1: You can get a yardstick. That takes too long for me.

Teacher: Maybe there is a faster way.

Camper 2: I could walk there and count my steps.

Camper 5: My legs are longer: I could get there in less steps. How will you know how far it is when you know how many steps you walk?

Camper 2: I can measure my steps.

Teacher: How?

Camper 2: At school we figured out our room was thirty feet long. It took me fifteen steps to walk the length of it.

Teacher: Then how long is each of your steps?

Camper 2:   Two feet.

Teacher: Then let's see how many steps you take to get down to that tree on the shore.

Camper 5:   I know a way our Scout leader taught us.

Teacher: How does it work?

Camper 5:   I can hold a stick at an arm's length and see how much of it blocks out that tree across the lake from my sight. I can measure the stick and measure my arm. It takes two inches of the stick to cover the tree. The stick is at right angles to my arm and two feet from my eye. How high is that tree?

Teacher: Why do you want to know?

Camper 5:   Well, if I knew how high the tree was, I could figure that since my arm is twelve times as long as the stick, the lake would be twelve times as wide as the tree is high.

Teacher: The tree is about sixty feet tall.

Camper 5:   Then the lake is twelve times sixty or seven hundred twenty feet across.

Teacher: How many yards is that?

Camper 5:   Seven hundred twenty feet divided by three is two hundred forty. The lake is two hundred forty yards wide.

Camper 2:   It took me three hundred forty-five steps to that tree.

Teacher: How many feet is that?

Camper 2:   One step is two feet. Three hundred forty-five multiplied by two is six hundred ninety feet.

Camper 3:   That is about two hundred thirty yards.

Teacher: How much difference is there in the answers?

Camper 1:   Ten yards, and that is pretty close.

Teacher: How else can we measure a distance when we can't go directly from one point to another?

Camper 6:   I figured two hundred yards.

Teacher: How did you estimate the distance?

Camper 6:   My casting line is fifty yards long. I figured it would be four casts across the lake if I let all the line out.

Camper 7:   I know another way. It took me ten minutes to row over this morning. It takes me twenty minutes to row a quarter of a mile down our lake at home to where my buddy lives. If it took me half as long to cross this lake as it does to row to my friend's cottage, it is half as far across. One-half of one-fourth mile is one-eighth of a mile. 5,260 feet is one mile, so across the lake is 675-1/2 feet.

Teacher: Could anyone use a compass to find out how far it is without actually crossing the lake?

Camper 8: You could find out the exact direction from this point to the tree across the lake. There are 360 degrees in a circle. The tree is at zero. It is straight north! Then we can hike west, or at 270 degrees, to the end of the lake, go north, 360 or zero until the tree is straight east, (ninety degrees), and come back to the tree. If we pace the distance we have to go north we will have a line overland just as long as across the lake. Here, I'll draw it on the ground.

Camper 9: There is another way in which we won't have to walk so far. I read about it in a book. It is called triangulation. Two sides of a right triangle squared are equal to the square of the hypotenuse. Therefore, we can use a compass to go down the lake one direction until we can sight overland at a right angle to the tree. Then we'll turn and go to the tree. We will pace off each direction. Then we have to square each distance and add them together. The square root of the sum will be the distance across the lake.

Teacher: Will your answer be expressed in steps, feet or yards?

Camper 9: Oh, I forgot to change paces to yards. I'll draw a diagram in the sand to show you how it is shorter than the other way where we'd have to go around three sides of a rectangle.

Teacher: Shall we try it? What else must we learn?

Camper 7: How to get right angles with a compass.

Teacher: You suggested several ways to estimate or find out the distance. Let's take a few minutes to recall them so our recorder can write them down for the camp journal. Which way was easiest? Which way most accurate? Which way do you think it took people longest to discover? Can we use these ways to measure other distances?

Such a discussion leads to taking a compass hike and plotting a scale map of the lake. In addition, a follow-up unit at school or an individual project may be undertaken to investigate the ways man measures distances and the ways in which these methods were developed.

In the group discussion cited above, individuals were thinking at different conceptual levels, building on the discoveries of one another, drawing from previous knowledge and experience, and using their peer audience to test their ideas. To help the children build concepts, the teacher used the open space, the long period, the high motivation and the problem situation which were provided by the camp. In seeking the answer to their own question, "How far is it across the lake?" the children were developing relative concepts of miles, feet and yards; direction, shape and position; various ways to estimate; and the intellectual development of our ways to measure distance. The example demonstrates how relationships were perceptual and how perceptions differed relative to the differences in the past experiences of the individuals.

THE "EXPLORABLE INSTANT" OR WHEN TO OPEN THE CLASSROOM DOOR *

PHYLLIS S. BUSCH

When do you open the classroom door?

Simply, the answer is, "anytime, and often." However, teachers are anxious to know at what given "explorable instant" the students should carry on their investigations outdoors. Once outdoors, what do they do?

The importance of outdoor explorations has been expressed for many, many years, and we all quote, "study nature, not books," but we all interpret this admonition differently. Few today agree with Agassiz' concept of studying nature. There are many who would have differences with Anna Comstock too, although she certainly advocated work outdoors.

So often people seem to redouble their effort even as they are uncertain of whither they go. This is unfortunately true of what passes for outdoor education today. Somehow, the times, together with President Johnson's discovery of the outdoors, turned the light to green and all traffic is converging on the outdoors—usually on the same spot.

Many frightening things are happening which point up a need for knowledge of our environment. Note the serious conflicts which are going on right now, and note, too, that they are the results of an affluent society using applied science (technology)—paving the way to catastrophe because of ecological ignorance.

Everyone is becoming aware of air pollution even as the number of factories, homes, and cars are increasing. Water pollution, resulting in water scarcity, is realized by all. Destruction of natural beauty and the increase of ugliness on the landscape is there for everyone to behold. Excessive noise is taken for granted. Overcrowding of humans in limited space is a fact. Species are disappearing or are on their way to extinction as habitats are bulldozed or filled in, as roads are widened and multiplied, as pesticides are sprayed.

The concerns engendered by problems such as these prompt immediate action—drastic action. In addition there must also be education, a knowledge concerning the outdoors, and understanding of man's habitat and the results of his altering this habitat.

Unfortunately, more is being done in education to misguide than to aid in

*Reprinted by permission of the American Nature Study Society from *Nature Study* 20:6, 9, Winter, 1966-67.

this direction. For example, educators and political figures are giving the impression that going camping is a contribution to conservation. The revolting slums that are developing at campsites all over the country are the consequence. People are told that they need the out-of-doors, the simple life, closeness to nature, peace and quiet reflection. Is this the reason why they demand and get hot showers and washing machines in the wilderness and why they bring cases of beer and radios to entertain themselves? How do you explain that on July 4, 1966, of the 14,500 cars which drove through Great Smoky National Park not enough people came to any of the 12 organized nature walks where trained naturalists were ready to conduct them, in spite of announcements and brochures? Something is wrong. Perhaps we are misinterpreting the desires of the millions who travel the highways to these outdoor areas.

Outdoor educators point out that people need camping experiences and that it should begin with the very young. Many people advocate a week's camping, usually in the sixth grade. Sure it is fun to sit around a campfire and to sing together with one's peers. It is of inestimable social and psychological value but it is not the solution to understanding the objects and events in the universe.

Then there are the elaborate nature centers—starting with costly plans and resulting in elegant dioramas, expensive murals with provisions for special safeguards designed to prevent vandalism. These have a function, a specialized function, but it cannot replace the learning possibilities of guided science and conservation teaching, in which a competent teacher guides inquiry from the classroom to the child's outdoor environment and back.

The occasional field trip with its involved planning also belongs to a special category of limited value, even when it is organized at its best. Yet look about you. The child is surrounded by his outdoor environment and the intelligent teacher understands that he must help his students to understand it. The usual methods indicated above are, at best, inadequate even when successful within their recognized limitations.

The teacher must catch the spark, become truly innovative and initiate lessons for carrying indoor investigations to the wider horizons outdoors. Here is just a sampling of the kinds of inquiries which might occur to a teacher. I call this the "indoor-outdoor-indoor" technique. At best these examples will serve to indicate how, at the "explorable instant," both pupils and teacher will open the door to complete an investigation outdoors. Such problem-solving will result in an increase of science and conservation concepts as well as in experiences in the processes of science.

1. Perhaps you are studying the hydrologic cycle and you discuss cloud formation. You also wish to include some measurement experiences and practice in recording data. You might also wish to point out the instability and constant change of conditions outdoors and you are prompted to make inquiries. "Are

there clouds in the sky today? Many? Are they moving? How quickly? Will this type of cloud be seen here each day? What kind of a cloud record should be kept? For how long? What is the haze outdoors due to? At what time of day is it greatest? Do we have any sources in our neighborhood which contribute to smog? What pollen count do we get near our school? Near our home? Is there any correlation between cloud types, smog, pollen count, industrial activity in our area?"

2. You might be studying flowers. All schools make sure that this comes at a time when the florist has Easter lilies or tulips or gladioli. But you might consider that here is a chance for emphasizing adaption to environment. In the temperate zone many plants have methods of dormancy. The Norway maple and dandelion have fascinating flowers which develop under certain conditions, and they are available everywhere. You might also wish to include at this time some experiences in setting up controlled experiments.

Your inquiries might run along lines such as these. "What is the condition and appearance of the Norway maple before it flowers? When do the buds open? What wind and temperature conditions prevail? What insect life is evident around the tree before and after flowering? Why is there such poor flower development in some trees which are near our bus stop? Can you find rosettes of dandelion before they bloom? When does the dandelion bloom? How do temperature, wind and insect conditions at its time of blooming compare with those of the Norway maple? Do dandelion flowers move? Do clouds affect their opening and closing? Can you design an experiment which can help us to find out whether sunlight has any affect on the opening of dandelion flowers? How could we find out whether the insects which we find on dandelions depend on the flowers or whether the flowers depend on the insect or whether neither depends on the other?"

These are but two small parts of courses of study in general. You can see that once you open your eyes and stimulate your students to open theirs too, the possibilities of outdoor investigations are not only limitless, they become inescapable.

There is no hard and fast rule for when to open the classroom door. The more aware that you become of the urgency of teaching this way, the more opportunities you will see and seize. Perhaps the best advice is not to shut your door, but to leave it slightly ajar. Then you are always ready for the "explorable instant."

AN EXERCISE IN WINTER ECOLOGY *
BROTHER JAMES MURPHY, CFC

The below-freezing temperatures that characterize winter in many areas cause the flora and fauna of these environments to alter their life styles quite drastically. Winter exercises which we use with our students are designed to show how living things survive during one of nature's most trying periods. A prairie or open field is the best location for the exercises, but any outdoor area, even a city park, is satisfactory—provided some animal life is present. If possible, schedule the exercise so that it can be conducted a day or so after a snowfall when there will be clear, fresh animal tracks. The equipment required is a pocket knife and a large plastic bag for collecting materials in the field. Students should be told to come dressed for work outdoors. Beyond that, we give the students several sheets of questions as a guide to the activities, and they go ahead on their own.

Most of the following exercises are self-explanatory, but the suggested rabbit chase does merit some explanation. Catching a rabbit may seem improbable, but it is possible to catch a cottontail if you know a little about the animal and have some faith in the physical capabilities of your students. The rabbit as a species has been able to survive by sheer numbers, protective coloration, and the ability to maneuver at high speeds. The animal's Achilles heel is its lack of endurance. Once a rabbit has been scared out of hiding, all that is necessary to catch it is to keep it moving for about two to four minutes. Even a short rest, and the chase time must start all over again. If the rabbit is not given a chance to rest, it will collapse of exhaustion. It can then be picked up by the scruff of the neck with one hand and a good grip on the hind legs with the other hand. The rabbits can be placed in a burlap bag for easy handling. After they have been measured, weighed, sexed, and tagged for future identification, they should be released in the area where they were caught. If the animals are detained, especially indoors, for more than a few hours they will rapidly lose the vigor that is so necessary for survival in cold weather.

Following are typical handout sheets for the students:

During the winter months the overall life activity of plants and animals in the northern part of this country goes into low gear. Only a few organisms maintain

*Reprinted with permission from *The Science Teacher* 37:59-61, October, 1970.

an active daily schedule for survival; most organisms reduce their metabolism to a bare minimum.

The first activity in the field is to investigate the forms of animal life that are active at this time. The easiest way to do this is to find and identify animal tracks in fresh snow. In studying the tracks, take care not to destroy them. Tracks should be left so that other students may see them. Other evidence of animal life can be found in tree hollows, under logs, and in debris. Return all objects to their original position, so they may continue to serve as a possible source of shelter for animals.

Also note which birds are in the area. Make a list of the animals that are active at this time of year. Compare this list to records of the animals that are found in the area during the summer, and note the organisms that are missing. What similarity exists among the animals found during the winter? List any similarities among the animals found only during the summer. Try to explain the whereabouts of several animals that are not present during the winter. If you scare up a living rabbit, give chase. How close were you to the animal before it moved? Can you explain its reaction? If you chase the animal, it will consider you to be a predator. What does the rabbit do to avoid being caught? If you are able to keep the rabbit moving, it will tire within two to four minutes and can easily be caught without harming it. An interesting study can be done with rabbits that are caught, if they are tagged and released. More complete details on this can be found in several of the books in the reference list.

Find the tracks of an animal and follow them for about ten minutes. Did the animal follow a path or just cut across the terrain at random? Did the animal stop during its movement; if so, why? After following the tracks for some time do you have any information on the animal's source of food and where it finds shelter?

Hibernating insects and spiders of various types may be found under a loose piece of bark or in debris. Insect larvae may be uncovered if you slit down the frozen stalks of some herbs, such as sunflower plants. Larvae may also be found in cocoons attached to plants. What is the source of food for these organisms, and how do they keep from freezing during the winter? You may see abnormal swellings in various parts of plants. Probably these are plant galls. They can be found on a large number of different plants. Make a list of the galls that you find: Record the type of plant, plant part that is affected, and, if possible, determine the name of the animal causing the growth. Use a sharp knife to make a cut in a gall, just off center. If you find a living organism inside, describe it. If the gall is empty, try to figure out what happened to the organism that was inside. Are the animals that cause a gall parasites? An interesting long-range project is to place galls or cocoons in a covered jar and store it in a moderately warm and humid location. Under these conditions you will be able to see the insects emerge from their hibernation.

Observe the plants in the area. Identify any that are green, and try to explain how this is possible. Break several small branches on a tree. Are they frozen? If not, why? Examine the buds at the end of a branch. How are they protected from the cold? See if you can find some small green plants close to the ground. These are usually biennials such as wild lettuce, thistle, and mullein. How does the structure of these plants protect them from the cold and from animals in the area? Examine the lower bark of trees and shrubs; are they being eaten? Why would extensive damage to the bark cause death to these plants? Construct a food web for the area that you are studying. If you have made a food web for the same area during the summer, compare the two and note differences.

REFERENCES

1. Benton, Allen H., and William E. Werner. *Manual of Field Biology and Ecology.* Burgess Publishing Company. Minneapolis, Minnesota. 1956. (Secondary- and college-level laboratory guide in ecology)
2. Mason, George F. *Animal Tracks.* William Morrow & Co. New York. 1943. (Primary- or secondary-level book concerned with the identification of animal tracks)
3. Morgan, Ann H. *Field Book of Animals in Winter.* Van Rees Press. New York. 1939. (Secondary- or college-level natural history book)
4. Mosby, Harry S., Editor. *Wildlife Investigational Techniques.* Edward Brother Inc. Ann Arbor, Michigan. 1963. (College- or secondary-level book that contains a great deal of information on research methods in ecology)
5. Youngpeter, John M. *Winter Science Activities.* Holiday House. New York. 1966. (Primary-level book of information and activities for winter nature study)

NIGHT FIELD TRIPS *

DORIS B. KWASIKPUI

Field trips offer special contributions to the elementary school curriculum because they are related to out-of-school experience, permit firsthand study of actual objects, and sustain interest and curiosity of children. In particular, a science field trip at night can be an effective and appealing learning experience. Boys and girls not only find the night intriguing but also enjoy working together on activities that cannot be done effectively during daylight hours. Night field

*Reprinted with permission from *Science and Children*, Vol. 4, Number 1, Sept. 1966. Copyright 1966 by the National Science Teachers Association, 1201 Sixteenth Street N.W., Washington, D.C. 20036.

study situations that are favorites among children are stargazing, moonlight and
shadow studies, and collecting and observing moths, peepers, earthworms, firefly
beetles and their larvae, and crickets. This article offers some suggestions for the
teacher who wishes to plan and guide such field trips.

A STARGAZING FIELD TRIP

The sky is a laboratory. As long as man has been conscious of his universe he
has gazed at the sky with wonder at the secrets it holds. Likewise children of all
ages are fascinated with the stars. To encourage this natural interest and for
assistance in the identification of celestial objects, it may be helpful to ask a
local resource person to accompany the group.

Have the pupils meet on a moonless night at a location away from the city
lights which interfere with star finding. Each pupil should bring a notebook, a
flashlight, and a home-built telescope or other devices to help in finding stars.

Interesting activities that can be included in this field trip are: (1) distinguishing between the stars and planets, (2) noticing the different colors of the stars
and their intensity, (3) recognizing the configuration of some of the 88 stellar
constellations, and (4) identifying the Milky Way.

A MOONLIGHT AND SHADOWS FIELD TRIP

A night shadow, which is merely an outlined figure of an object made upon
intercepting the light of the moon, is often described as "scary" by boys and
girls. Studying how these night shadows are made helps children to eliminate this
fear as well as to increase their knowledge.

Have the pupils meet at a time and location which will be well suited for
shadow-making on a moonlit night. Be sure that each child is equipped with a
flashlight, a ruler, a steel measuring tape, a chalk crayon, a notebook, and a
pencil.

Some activities that the children can perform are: (1) studying the size of the
area that the shadow covers in comparison to the size of the object casting the
shadow, (2) noting the size and approximate intensity of the light source (moon,
street light, house lamp), and (3) examining the angle of the shadow.

COLLECTING AND OBSERVING ANIMAL SPECIMENS

Children can observe and examine which insects and other small animals are
active at night. Be sure to have the pupils record their observations. If specimens
are to be collected, pupils will need some supplies such as collecting jars with
perforated lids, killing jars, nets, and flashlights.

Night Flying Moth Hunt. On calm evenings, nocturnal moths may be caught easily by simply focusing the rays of a strong light on a white piece of cloth or cardboard. Moths are attracted to the light and can be collected with a net and placed in a killing jar for later study and identification.

Peeper Hunt. Peepers are small tree frogs which are plentiful in many sections of the United States. The best time to observe or collect them is during the breeding season when they inhabit ponds and temporary pools. At other times of the year, peepers live in the trees and bushes, and, because of their secretive habits and protective coloration, they are difficult to discover. By listening carefully for the "peeping" sounds of the frogs, the pupils should be able to locate and catch them easily.

Earthworm Hunt. Earthworms can be cultivated in the classroom to study behavior patterns and life cycles. The best time to collect them in large quantities is on warm rainy nights during the early spring when they come to the surface of the soil.

Be sure the pupils come prepared for this hunt with rubber boots, hat and raincoat, a bucket, and a flashlight.

The activity that the boys seem to enjoy most on an earthworm field is competing to see who can collect the most whole earthworms. However, the environment and behavior of earthworms should be stressed and discussed.

Firefly Beetle and Larva Hunt. Fireflies and their larvae produce one of the most efficient lights known to man. Their larvae shine as brilliantly as the adult fireflies and emit a faint luminescent light as they move through moist earth in the evening.

If the trip begins at dusk during a summer evening the children can observe the remarkable and thrilling sight of a large number of "tiny lanterns" arising almost simultaneously from the ground. Have the group observe how often the luminescence is emitted from the fireflies and their larvae. Some specimens can be collected and observed more closely.

Cricket Hunt. A cricket hunt is a field trip of international favor among children. In Japan, for example, the children collect crickets as pets or purchase them from shopkeepers. The pale-green cricket in the United States may be found in grasses at night from summer to early fall.

Children can perform several activities on this hunt. Some examples are: (1) studying the behavior of crickets in relation to their environment, (2) calculating the temperature through the chirps of the crickets (count the number of chirps in fifteen seconds and add 40), and comparing with the actual temperature, and (3) collecting some to bring back to the classroom for further study.

KINDERGARTEN ROCK STUDY *

DOROTHY MASON

Kindergarten children can begin organized science study if the activities are appropriate to their learning level. A science concept is developed most successfully for young children through a series of experiences which progress from simple observation to observation of a specific "scientific-process" orientation where children make a guess, test, and conclusion—naturally, at a very informal elementary level. Each experience should build upon the last for those children mature enough to organize and retain ideas. However, for children whose attention spans are short and unreliable, each experience should also be its own reward.

For example, the concept that "rocks around us are different in many ways" can help young children gain science skills and knowledge applicable outside the classroom. In kindergarten, children can learn about rocks through a sequence of experiences such as the following:

1. One day on the playground a child brought me a stone and I commented "Oh, what a pretty stone." Soon other children were bringing me "pretty stones."

2. A child who lives on the waterfront then brought "pretty stones from the water" to school. They were put on display in an egg carton on the science table. In the discussion which followed, I elicited the suggestion that "we put the stones back in the water to see how they looked when Michele found them."

3. Further discussion initiated the project of bringing rocks from the children's homes. The resultant display obviously showed how different looking rocks are found at different homes (places) which represented a kindergarten level concept of the origin of rocks. (Kindergarten children need to develop a concept of space near and about them before they can comprehend a concept of "far away.")

4. In picking up stones on the playground the pupils discovered that "pretty stones can be different colors." Each day they found different-colored stones which were collected for the science table. Then again through channeled discussions, the pupils decided to sort the different-colored stones. Papers of various colors were pasted in the bottom of each section of an egg carton. The

*Reprinted with permission from *Science and Children*, Vol. 3, Number 5, February, 1966. Copyright 1966 by the National Science Teachers Association, 1201 Sixteenth Street, N.W., Washington, D.C. 20036.

children took turns sitting at the science table matching rocks from the collection to the various colors.

5. One day, I brought a piece of pegmatite which has large pieces of shiny biotite mica in it. The children were very pleased with the "shiny parts" of the stones and I suggested that they look for other stones that sparkle. A few were brought in each day, and out of this project developed another one: "What do you see in stones?" Fossils, granite, gneiss, striped sedimentary stones, and many other kinds of pitted, spotted, banded, and porous rocks were collected.

6. One day a child picked up a rock on the playground and rubbed it on the concrete sidewalk. It made a mark and he said excitedly, "Look, this stone writes!" He tried other rocks for the same result, keeping those that "wrote" and discarding those that did not. His enthusiasm, which I supported with many comments of praise and approval, was contagious and soon many children were trying rocks on the concrete. Some rocks made darker or different colored writing; some rocks (softer) worked better than others for writing. We used another egg carton to collect rocks that could write in one half and in the other half—rocks that could not write. The "writing rocks" were labeled with a crayon.

7. Another day I showed the children a piece of coquina. They observed that it looked like shells from the beach. I replied, "Yes, it does look like tiny shells, and do you know that this rock can make bubbles?" Kindergarten children adore bubbles; they "bubble" their milk through straws and blow soap bubbles, and they were greatly intrigued with the idea of rocks making bubbles. I showed them a bottle of vinegar, poured some in a thick glass container, added the coquina—result: bubbles! The children immediately wanted to try other kinds of rocks. This was a highly-motivating and dramatic experience in testing and classifying. We placed the vinegar bottle, testing jar, a collection of miscellaneous rocks, and an egg carton on the science table. One half of the carton was given a label with bubbles drawn on it; the other side was given a blank label (no bubbles) and the children took turns testing and sorting. Several of the children were soon able to pick out rocks they thought would be most apt to make bubbles. This entire process of testing for lime content (unnamed as such to the children) was a first experience in the scientific process: collection of materials or data (rocks), formulating an hypothesis ("Maybe other stones will make bubbles"), testing (in vinegar jar), and forming a conclusion (sorting rocks into those that will or will not make bubbles).

As a conclusion and a solution as to what to do with all the rocks we had collected, each child was given an empty cigar box to decorate and then allowed to choose ten (counting experience) rocks that he could put in the box to take home. This further established the organized collecting of rocks.

In their study of rocks the children had experiences in color and texture discrimination, classification, simple technical vocabulary, and the scientific process. Further evidence of learning and its change of behavior as a result of this study of rocks may be cited by noting that on the day the rock collections went home, 30 kindergarten children went home carrying 300 rocks among them and not one rock was dropped, thrown, or lost en route!

SCHOOL CAMPING—A POTENT FACTOR IN GUIDANCE *

MARION J. SACK

Since the fall of 1946 school camping has been part of the curriculum of the Wayne Grammar School in Radnor Township School District, Pennsylvania. Beginning as an experiment with one fifth grade class whose teacher was interested in camping, the program has steadily developed until today, by the end of the sixth grade, each of the Wayne Grammar School children has had four camping experiences. These trips last from three days to a week. They occur during the fifth and sixth grades and are so planned that one comes in the fall, one in the winter, and two in the spring.

After each trip the children and the teacher evaluate their experience. Then the staff themselves come together for an evaluation. In spite of the many difficulties encountered in carrying out the program the staff has always enthusiastically endorsed its continuance. Opportunities for use of the three "r's" in situations where there is a vital need for them; the opportunity to study natural science and natural history in the field; the need for careful planning and foresight; the necessity for knowing what is required in providing a well-balanced diet; the fun of good fellowship; the delight of close contact with the out-of-doors . . . all of these values the staff has found in the camping program. Interestingly enough, however, it is for none of these reasons that the teachers always decide to continue the camping program regardless of difficulties. Again and again they come back to the fact that the camping experience gives them the chance to study and know children in a way that nothing else can.

It is this phase of the camping program, the child study phase, that will be discussed more fully in this paper for our teachers have found that through our camping program we get to know our children more fully than we could otherwise, and, therefore, we are able to give children better guidance.

Guidance we define as anything and everything the teacher does to help the child *know himself* better and, in the light of that self-knowledge, to formulate

*Reprinted from the April, 1953 issue of *Education* by permission of The Bobbs-Merrill Company, Inc., Indianapolis, Indiana.

and carry out *his* plans. In brief, guidance in our thinking is help toward constructive self-direction and independence.

Our camping program requires that the boys and girls plan their own meals, buy all their own food, prepare the meals, and clean up afterward. This, obviously, is genuine responsibility of the first order. It puts the children's work to the acid test of reality. In the planning periods at school, teachers and children, too, become aware of those whom they can depend upon for accurate reports and careful workmanship. Those who are willing to take a chance without checking on an estimate of food or cost; those who are satisfied to "guess" that this will be enough or all right; those who are willing and able to go step by step in gathering their information; those who can organize and those who can't; all such qualities and abilities are brought to light during the camp planning at school. It may be argued, and rightly so, that any good curriculum other than camp does the same kind of sifting and sorting. However, the point to be emphasized here is that this subject matter brings forth an interest and an enthusiasm which causes the varying abilities, work habits, and traits of character to be seen more easily than at other times. The alert teacher is constantly observing the children, taking actual and mental notes and building a knowledge of the child that is invaluable.

The camping experience is always a fruitful place to study human relations. The children are together during the entire twenty-four hours of the day. The teacher sees them in work and play combinations and group situations that would never occur any place except at camp. Moreover, our children work out their own cooking groups, cabin groups, sleeping groups, study groups and play groups for the camping trip. Determining the personnel of these groups is always one of the most difficult of the children's problems. During the process the teacher learns much of the reasons for a child's choice of companions and what his real status in the group is. During this time, too, many opportunities occur for the frank analysis of personality. Frequently great strides are made in helping a child appreciate the reason why he is not popular and another one is, and vice versa. Nothing else in the usual school program—not committee work, nor club groups, nor even square dancing—permits such disclosures of group structure and the individual's relation to it. Teachers have said over and over that the camping experience is worth having if for no other reason than the chance it gives them to see the actual social make-up of the class.

Concomitant with the detailed and thorough knowledge of human relations that camping develops is the discovery of the habits of thought and behavior of the children. Ways of thinking are bared that otherwise would never be uncovered. The teacher realizes that one child's thinking is constructive, another's destructive. This one's is direct while that one's is circuitous. One is optimistic and another pessimistic. Here is one daring and experimental in outlook and there is another fearful and cautious. Frequently, prejudices, often unsuspected by the individual, are brought to the surface. After all, it is one thing to say that all men are brothers, regardless of race or religion, and quite another to live with members of a different race or religion for several days or a week! Here, too, our teachers have felt that this is not a case of the camp program disclosing these things to a greater degree than another part of the curriculum, but of the camp program being the only part of the curriculum which discloses these qualities.

The camp program, too, shows those children who are temperamentally geared to respond to the sensory pleasure of the out-of-doors. The student of mathematics and the book-worm may be unaware of the myriad small sounds of the forest; of the pungent smell of the earth after rain or of the meadow under the noonday sun. The rhythm of the fleeing deer may pass unnoticed; the colors in the rocks be unseen. At camp the child who finds the turtle and the newt, the one who hears the soft whirr of the mourning dove and catches the flash of the humming-bird takes the lead. As a result he gains a respect he never had. Then, because we take a small reference library to camp, the stage is set for the scholar and the child of the earth to come together in mutual respect and with the wise guidance of the teacher each broadens the understanding of the other at the same time that he comes to realize and value his own particular "bent."

Only at camp can we discover the child who is afraid of the dark, or the one who cries for his mother and dreads to face the days without some contact with her. Only at camp is there the opportunity to observe the complete cycle of the day with its round of varying responsibilities, habits of personal needs and the constant action, reaction and interaction of personalities.

In a word, the camp program is our richest source of child study. Knowing children, understanding them individually and as members of a particular group playing varying roles within that group, the teacher plans more effectively for the class as a whole and for each child in the class. The teacher is, therefore, able to help the child know the kind of person he is, . . . his character strengths and weaknesses, his abilities and disabilities, his talents and his lacks, his interests and disinterests.

It should be noted, too, that the camp situation allows children to know the teacher in a way not possible otherwise. This in turn establishes a security which begets confidence and trust. In such an atmosphere the child more readily works with and talks with the teacher.

Because of the mutual respect between children and teacher and because of the teacher's deep understanding of each child, it is possible to provide more effectively the opportunity for experiences which lead the child step by step into an ever-increasing freedom of socially constructive self-direction where guidance becomes less and less necessary.

WOODS, STREAMS, AND UNOBSTRUCTED SKY *

EARL V. PULLIAS

The complex pressures of modern industrial life threaten physical and mental health, the perspective necessary to wisdom, and the fundamental quality of excellence in achievement.

In my judgment, properly conducted outdoor education reduces this threat and hence should be considered not a frill but rather something essential to all other education. A sick, anxious, tense people cannot make a great nation. Effective education at any level must not only heal the wounds that thwart growth but also provide the experience necessary to full personality development.

How then can outdoor education play its major role in the complex, demanding drama of life in industrialized society? Let us examine a few practical ways this aspect of education can contribute to the balanced education of man.

It can provide a regular and satisfying contact with varying forms of the natural world. Woods, streams, meadows, unobstructed sky, mountains, rocks, desert sand—all these compose the physical environment which contributes immeasurably to the growth of body, mind, and soul. To touch these things directly and with interest is a healing and growth-producing experience. Regular interaction with the physical world will take place only if a strong desire is created to spend time in the out-of-doors.

A second phase of a good outdoor-education program is the development of the skills, knowledge, and sensitivity which make outdoor experience satisfying. If contact with natural things deeply satisfies, its priority in a rushed busy life will be high, for we do the things we most want to do.

Skills in outdoor activity must be learned, but it is of utmost importance that they be learned pleasantly. To help students learn the necessary skills without killing interest, or better, to learn them well and yet in such a way that each difficult learning contributes to the joy of the whole achievement; such is a secret of great teaching at any level.

Also, knowledge is important to a satisfying outdoor experience. In this connection I think of my early life on a farm in a beautiful section of Tennessee.

*From *A Search for Understanding*. Wm. C. Brown Co., Dubuque, Iowa, 1965. Reprinted with permission of author and publisher.

I was out of doors much of the day and often much of the night. Doubtless, the constant touch of natural things left some residue in mind and body, but much of the richness was missed because I lacked the knowledge to reach the true meaning of that beautiful place.

Going back years later after a little study of subjects like geology, astronomy, and biology, I found that the intriguing rocks and caves, the heavens, animal and bird life, the streams, the trees, and the seasons with their rain and snow were alive with new interest for me. To be ignorant in the midst of such things is to be like an animal. Doubtless, there is always some unconscious satisfaction, but without knowledge the joy of the mind which is distinctly human is lost.

Even more important than skill and knowledge is sensitivity. But this central goal of all outdoor—or for that matter indoor—education is most difficult to achieve. It cannot be taught in the usual sense of teaching. Direct attempts to teach sensitivity, even though done sincerely and with enthusiasm, may produce dullness instead.

The task is to open up to their full capacity the outer senses and also what may be called the inner senses. This combination is what Robert Frost calls "sight" and "insight." Probably sight becomes increasingly full as insight (the grasp of the relation of what is seen to many other things) increases.

It is a terrible thing to walk blind and deaf in the world of nature. Recently I have been reading a new biography of Helen Keller. This great woman makes one ashamed of his insensitivity. Her magnificent achievement suggests that all children can grow in sensitivity and be increasingly happy in that growth. Perhaps one learns sensitivity most effectively as he associates with someone he admires who is genuinely sensitive.

Outdoor education should strive to cultivate the wisdom to withdraw and seek renewal at the optimum moment for growth and healing.

There is probably a breaking point in the health of both body and mind for every individual. When an individual passes a certain point in stress and his reaction to it, he goes into an area of no return—that is, his powers of self-restoration have been lost or destroyed, growth stops, and healing at best is slow, painful, and often only partial. It is important to develop wisdom enough to withdraw for renewal a safe time before the crucial danger point is reached.

Perhaps most important of all, outdoor education involves a state of mind. Essentially every person needs what has been aptly called "the great good place," after a fable by Henry James. This is a place of retreat suitable to the particular needs of the individual for achieving a creative detachment from practical affairs.

Doubtless, in certain phases of development, the great good place is at best a beautiful, appealing spot in nature enriched by associations of friendship, love, or free zestful activity. But as maturity progresses, it may be created in less externally desirable places. In time, perhaps only a small, almost symbolic representation may be enough to reproduce the great good place so necessary to healing and growth, and it may be that at this stage it becomes largely a place created by the person's mood and attitude.

So one could envision outdoor education that finally might lead to an attitude of mind that would enable one to find his particular great good place in a small garden or back yard or even in the contemplation of a rose.

Perhaps all guidance and growth should point toward the ultimate goal of such inner self-reliance and freedom as would make constantly available all the resources of nature for the replenishment of the spirit. But in the meantime (and that is a long meantime for most of us), planned and somewhat guided outdoor education is needed to lead us gradually toward this goal of a fuller, more self-determined maturity.

ENVIRONMENTAL EDUCATION *
DONALD E. HAWKINS AND DENNIS A. VINTON

It is not surprising that an emerging and universal issue is environmental education. Man is beginning to realize that he does not exist in a vacuum. At one time the natural environment was simply something which man exploited for his own gain—like using a hammer to build a house, or a piece of string to tie a package. However, he is realizing that the environment is far from being something to be consumed—it is a dynamic, changing, and finite entity which depends upon man for continuation, just as man depends upon it for his existence.

Much thought is presently being given to man's ethical philosophy, his interpersonal and inter-environmental behavior, and his value systems with respect to environment and the quality of life. Of prime importance in the world today is a re-evaluation of attitudes toward the environment and a subsequent restructuring of educational programs concerned with man's relationship to the world around him. In fact, educators are beginning to realize that the environment is an ideal classroom.

Because man is the dominant organism on the earth and can, through his technological manipulations of the environment, control much of its condition and consequence, man is the central figure in environmental education. Whether

*Reprinted with permission from *Art Education*, October, 1970, Journal of the National Art Education Association, Washington, D.C.

he is cloistered in a subterranean bunker of experimental laboratories at the South Pole, comfortably nested in a penthouse in the midst of an urban setting, or thousands of miles out in space, the environment is a crucial and significant factor in determining the quality of his life.

Traditionally, subject headings such as mathematics, literature, biology, or geography have been concerned with toxonomical explorations of the universe, rather than relating learning to our immediate surroundings. Since no one subject can do a complete job of describing man and his environment, environmental education ought to be a total look at where man lives, how he lives, and finally why he lives.

Through direct experiences and encounters with his social, physical, and cultural world that this approach provides, the student should gain: (1) A broad understanding of the environment, both natural and man-made; (2) A clear understanding that man is a central and inseparable part of the complex environmental system and that he has the ability to alter the interrelationships of the system; (3) A fundamental understanding of environmental problems confronting man, how these problems can be solved, and the need for individual citizens and government agencies to work toward their solution; and (4) Attitudes of concern for the quality of the environment, which will motivate him to participate in environmental problem solving.

The ultimate goal is for the student to develop an awareness of his environment that will lead to a personal sense of involvement and eventually to the shaping of an environmental ethic to guide his behavior.

The initial step in establishing a comprehensive environmental education program is the identification and refinement of educational goals, objectives, and approaches which will serve to guide all related activities and programs. Environmental education programs should be educationally sound, relevant to the needs of students, and supported by citizens in the community and professional personnel in the schools.

The diverse nature of environmental education suggests the need for a systems approach to planning and development. Although the list of component elements required to establish a workable system may become quite lengthy, most can be categorized in one of three major classifications: curriculum, in-service teacher training, and environmental study areas and facilities.

CURRICULUM

Most curriculum efforts in environmental education have focused on an integrative, curriculum-spanning approach. The focus is on linking those subject areas, K-12, which relate most closely to the environment. Dr. William B. Stapp, chairman of the School of Resource Planning and Conservation at the University of Michigan, has developed a set of guiding principles that should be considered when structuring an environmental education program.[1]

- Span the curriculum, kindergarten through the twelfth grade so that environmental experiences can be presented at every grade level, thereby capitalizing on cumulative effects of the program.
- Link subject areas that relate most closely to the environment, especially science and social studies, so that both the social and scientific knowledge important in understanding and solving environmental problems are properly developed.
- Integrate and correlate the program with the existing curriculum in a manner that will enhance the instructional goals of the school system.
- Focus on the local government, but do not neglect regional, national, and international environment issues.
- Stress attitudes and problem-solving skills. The most important environment impact that most of our urban citizens will have upon our environment is through their action as community citizens.
- The learner should play an active role in the learning process. The learner develops attitudes through personal experiences and thinking and not through the presentation of predigested conclusions..
- Provide a comprehensive in-service teacher education program which would operate throughout the school year and be directed at assisting teachers to increase their understandings, interest, awareness, and teaching skills in environmental affairs and to involve them in curriculum development.

This suggests an interdisciplinary focus for environmental education. Environmental education, then, is not a single subject; it becomes a synthesis of all school experiences, understandings, and skills. Neither is it only the teaching of school subjects outdoors. The teacher uses the environment—natural or man-made, park or urban setting, historical landmark or scenic site—to help teach art, mathematics, science, social studies, or communication by guiding the student to understand the relationships among these subjects, the environment, and man. Thus, the student may find he has learned something about ecology as well as about economics. Similarly, the teacher is likely to discover that any given subject, when related to the study of man's environment, inevitably leads to considerations of other subjects as the exploration widens to include the total

---

[1]William B. Stapp, "A Strategy for Curriculum Development and Implementation in Environmental Education at the Elementary and Secondary Level Based on Environmental Encounters," Unpublished Manuscript presented to the National Consultation on Environmental Education Areas and Facilities, co-sponsored by Project Man's Environment and the Educational Facilities Laboratories, June 3-5, 1970, pp. 14-15.

relationship of man to his environment. To accomplish these objectives, thematic concepts or strands can be developed as a basis for developing curriculum.

The strand approach incorporates both the specific and the investigative approaches into a third approach with which both student and teacher can feel more comfortable. It requires identification and classification, but on a modified basis. It also requires open-ended investigation leading to problem solving. Yet all of its requirements can be taught by a teacher and fulfilled by a student who has little of the rigorous scientific training demanded by the other approaches.

The strand approach makes necessary a reorganization of thinking into unfamiliar patterns, which may at first be difficult. The valuable, unifying characteristic of the strand approach, however, makes whatever initial effort may be necessary unquestionably worthwhile.

For example, the following learning suggestions and discussion questions relate art to five environmental strands—variety and similarities, patterns, interaction and interdependence, continuity and change, evolution and adaptation.

For a detailed treatment of this approach for other subject areas, please refer to: *Man and His Environment: An Introduction to Environmental Study Areas,* published by Association of Classroom Teachers and Project Man's Environment, Washington, D.C., 1970. Available through NEA Publication Sales, 1201 Sixteenth Street, Northwest, Washington, D.C. 20036.

VARIETY AND SIMILARITIES:

Many differences occur among living and nonliving things. A variety of functions, sizes, and structures exist in plants and stars, rocks and animals, processes and people. Yet there are sufficient similarities to permit classification into orderly patterns. These patterns increase one's understanding of his world.

LESSON SUGGESTIONS:

At the site, the student can see the environment in new ways through the focus of different art forms. Asked to interpret what he sees in a creative way and according to his choice of art media, the student will come up with his own insights and feelings about the site, which may never have been brought out through a scientific or mathematical analysis of the environment.

After identifying objects at the site through an analysis of their variety and similarities, students might render the objects in various graphic forms in such a way as to emphasize their variety and similarities.

Students can then observe the great variety of ways their classmates interpret the same environment. Perhaps in pre- and post-site lessons students can study what some great artists have done with similar environments in various art media.

QUESTIONS FOR STUDENT DISCUSSION:

Art focuses upon the environment. What on-site discoveries can you make of subjects that would lend themselves to painting, song, dance, or other artistic interpretations?

What might be revealed about the area with a variety of on-site photographs made into a collage?

What similar elements of this site would recur in a variety of artistic representations of it?

PATTERNS:

Organizational patterns are kinds of structures that may be found in rock formations as well as in social groups of people and animals. Functional patterns include traffic movements and classroom schedules. Spatial arrangements are patterns that often please us. Such patterns occur both in nature and in artistic design.

LESSON SUGGESTIONS:

The pre-site lesson can examine patterns in art works that used the environment as subject matter.

On the site the student can see natural patterns in functional operation and can realize more fully how they influence the patterns of art.

The use of musical patterns as background to an on-site experience could produce an aesthetic experience beyond the capability of the classroom.

In the post-site lesson, the student might consider how patterns of design can be used in tomorrow's environment. He thereby not only learns to appreciate the natural world more fully, but also learns design principles basic to all of man's creations.

QUESTIONS FOR STUDENT DISCUSSION:

Patterns in the environment are also patterns of art—circles, ovals, squares, triangles, stars, spirals, crescents. How many of these can be identified at the site?

How could patterns of leaves, flowers, and plants be arranged to indicate the seasons of the year?

What similar environmental patterns both on the site and in your home or school surroundings have been rendered in art?

INTERACTION AND INTERDEPENDENCE:

Nothing exists in isolation. Each individual is constantly interacting with living and nonliving things: his family, his belongings, his friends, his world. These people and things also depend on the individual in order to function properly. The process is continuous (as part of the life cycle) even after death, for dead life forms nourish the living.

LESSON SUGGESTIONS:

On the site the student can participate in a creative arts lesson that encourages him to wander at will, observe on impulse, and contemplate at length.

Such a lesson can illustrate the principle of interaction between inspiration from the environment and an artist's work of art about his surroundings. An examination of how artists depend on their environment for materials and how the environment depends upon artistic and creative ideas for improvement will give the student a deeper awareness of and appreciation for his surroundings.

QUESTIONS FOR STUDENT DISCUSSION:

Man uses his environment in the creation of art—as subject matter and as material. He uses the sun as a character in stories and songs and as a reflector for sculpture and fountains; flowers provide the subjects for myths and material for artistic arrangements; man sings of trees and uses wood instruments to play the music. What on this site could an artist use for inspiration? What materials on this site could be used to produce art objects?

Can you think of ways that art and the environment interact? What media simply report the environment? What media actually shape the environment? Can you think of any that do both?

CONTINUITY AND CHANGE:

Both living and nonliving things are constantly changing—whether among galaxies and planets or within body cells and body systems. Some things remain the same in spite of change. Matter and energy may change in form, but they can never be created or destroyed.

LESSON SUGGESTIONS:

One lesson might illustrate for the student how—though artistic styles have changed through the years—the environment remains a constant theme.

An on-site lesson can direct the student to observe the everyday changes occurring within the framework of constant environmental processes while he examines what a painter, dancer, composer, or other artist must do to capture these changes.

Post-site study can be directed toward an examination of how both the environment and artistic representatives of it have constantly influenced the inner man—moving, shifting, ever in transition, but always mirroring, deepening, and changing man's feelings of beauty, pathos, and harmony.

QUESTIONS FOR STUDENT DISCUSSION:

How does man's art change as his environment changes?

What materials from the environment has man changed to produce art?

Do ideas about art change as environmental values change?

Do natural resources ever become landmarks? Why do they get this attention?

Dance, music, poetry, painting—all these art forms can express the movement and change of the environment. Which art form would best express the flow of this site?

How can music played on the site change your mood?

EVOLUTION AND ADAPTATION:

Over centuries and centuries of time, living and nonliving things alter and develop in the process called evolution. Probably the greatest number of changes over the longest periods of time come about in order to enable an organism to adapt to the environment. Hereditary factors then preserve the continuing elements. The characteristics that enable the organism to adapt best (for example, the best food finder) are apt to be the traits passed on from generation to generation, thus ensuring survival of the species.

LESSON SUGGESTIONS:

Art lessons in Evolution and Adaptation can clarify for students how man has adapted his creative ideas to his surroundings and evolved art works that reflect and fit his environment. Modern architecture and outdoor sculpture are just two examples.

An on-site lesson can examine any number of ways the environment could evolve through artistic adaptations. In pre- and post-site lessons, students can study how artists have treated evolution and adaptation in the environment. Charlie Russell, the famous cowboy artist from Montana, depicted the Old West as it evolved from the days of the stagecoach to the era of the railroads and airplane. Many artists have revealed their feelings as they lived through the evolution of the landscape and adapted with the environment. These testaments and the works of these artists can be the basis for a number of lesson plans.

QUESTIONS FOR STUDENT DISCUSSION:

How has man's decoration of his body and his home evolved from the past to the present as an art form?

What different art forms have evolved with man's technology? What evidence of those art forms or that technology can be seen on this site?

How is architecture an adaptation of art found in the environment? How has the environment evolved through architecture?

How have architecture and creative planning adapted this site to satisfy your needs and desires?

IN-SERVICE TEACHER TRAINING

The successful implementation of an environmental education program involves the utilization of resources and processes which are not common to most on-going instructional programs. Consequently, the development of a comprehensive in-service teacher training program should be an initial consideration. In addition to school personnel, the training program should seek involvement and input from students, community groups, resource personnel, and specialized consultants.

A variety of approaches may be employed to structure and implement training programs. One approach is to develop a framework with focus on two primary components: process and content. The process component can be divided into general activities such as identification (resources, needs, objectives), innovation and development (case studies of successful programs, development of a model), coordination of resources and personnel, administration, and evaluation. The content component of the training program might include the identification and development of curriculum plans, learning activities, areas and facilities, teacher guides and resource materials.

A number of unique approaches to training are presently being planned and implemented. One such program, an interdisciplinary workshop for junior high school students and educators, was conducted at the Indianhead Arts Center, Shell Lake, Wisconsin, by the Wisconsin Department of Public Instruction and the University of Wisconsin during the week of June 28-July 3, 1970. The workshop was based on the belief that the aesthetic quality of the environment vitally influences its capacity to sustain human life. By exposing the participants to environmental issues, a sense of belonging to the environment was developed.

ENVIRONMENTAL STUDY AREAS AND FACILITIES

A major thrust of many environmental education programs is the identification and development of environmental study areas. The environmental study area concept was first developed by the National Park Service of the U.S. Department of the Interior. Through this program, the National Park Service is making available park lands and facilities to local school districts to support and stimulate environmental education programs. Use of environmental study areas provides actual environmental experiences and encounters and allows students to apply what is learned in the classroom to real life situations.

Ideally, educators and resource managers should work cooperatively to select and plan the use of a site as an environmental study area. A resource manager might be described as a person who administers lands, facilities, and other types of resources. He might, for example, have authority over a park, manage a public reservoir, or be curator of a historical museum. Teachers who select such sites to use as environmental study areas should consult with the resource manager of the site and enlist his aid and expertise, just as resource managers who may have done an initial survey before proposing a site to local educators will seek the cooperation of teachers and administrators in developing the site for environmental education.

Whether the environmental study area is a site provided by the National Park Service, a similar location sponsored by a state historical society or local park authority, or an area selected by school personnel alone, it should have certain characteristics that make it a suitable study area. These include specific educational possibilities, which teachers will need to identify, as well as such physical factors as accessibility, parking areas, rest rooms, etc.

Information concerning the selection, planning, and use of environmental study areas is available in a guide, *Man and His Environment: A Guide to Using Environmental Study Areas,* mentioned previously.

Chapter four
Programs and Practices:
Diversity in Education

INTRODUCTION

The types of outdoor education programs that have developed over the years, both in the United States and in other nations, have reflected a number of uses for the outdoor classroom. In some states, the concept of the school farm or the school forest prevails. In other areas, emphasis is placed upon one-day field trips for the lower grades and the resident outdoor school or school camping for the upper grades. In some instances, the program format is governed by the season of the year.

Financial assistance through the National Defense Education Act and the Elementary-Secondary Education Act of 1965 has enabled various school districts and county school systems to sponsor pilot programs and experimental projects that utilize outdoor instructional areas. These programs have been specifically designed to improve the various areas of science instruction and to create exemplary programs for reaching the educationally and socially disadvantaged youngster.

Still other kinds of outdoor experiences have been designed for youth with special needs such as blindness and mental retardation.

Once again, "variety" is the theme that underlies the types of outdoor school programs that are being conducted in today's world.

SCHOOL CAMP—OUTDOOR LABORATORY FOR ENRICHED LEARNING EXPERIENCES *

GEORGE W. DONALDSON AND HOPE A. LAMBERT

School camping is a lusty youngster. Whereas there were only a few school camps 10 years ago, today there are more than 200 school districts which offer some sort of camping experience. But school camping, like any lusty youngster, has already tended to confuse ends with means. The only justification for schools offering camping experiences to their youngsters lies in the fact that the outdoors offers educational opportunities not found in the classroom.

It follows, then, that the activities in which children engage in a school camp should be directly related to the school experiences of these same children. There is serious doubt that a standard camp program, the same activities for each and every group of children, with only seasonal variations, can meet this criterion. Nor can a purely recreational approach be justified.

Educationally, there is no difference in a teacher and children leaving the classroom to go to the school's library or science center—where experiences not afforded by the classroom can be had—and in their going to the outdoor laboratory, the camp. There is no more reason for taking a group of children into the outdoors when they have no specific purposes of their own for going than there is for taking a class to the library just because the school happens to have one!

OBJECTIVES DEFINED

No new educational medium has ever had a more clear-cut statement of its objectives so long in advance. For 25 years L. B. Sharp has preached the principle:

Things which can best be taught in the outdoors should there be taught.

This principle is as sound today as when it was first propounded. It should form the first criterion for selecting school-camp activities.

*Reprinted by permission from *Camping Magazine* 28:17-21, May, 1956.

If school-camp activities are to be so directly related to the ongoing curriculum of the school, then the first step in deciding the outdoor program for a particular class must be that of asking, "What experiences are these children ready for?" Obviously this question cannot be answered without probing into the experiences the children have already had and then asking, "What things can we do in camp which will add to, enrich, and reinforce these learnings?" The school camp program then comes into proper focus.

SCHOOL-CAMP PRINCIPLES

The following set of principles is offered as a basis for the relationship between a classroom and its outdoor laboratory, the school camp:

1. The school camp is best conceived as the laboratory where teachers and children go to learn about those aspects of the outdoors which cannot be learned in the classroom.
2. An intimate relationship must be maintained between the classroom's aims and subject matter and the experiences offered by camp.
3. Teachers and children will need help from the camp staff in planning for their camp session. Such help should take the form of consultation rather than dictation, because the camp exists to help the teacher and children meet their objectives.
4. The objective of cooperative pre-camp planning should be that of a hand-tailored program for each class, precisely fitted to their educational experiences, needs, and aims.

PRE-CAMP PLANNING

In the Tyler, Texas schools the children, teachers, and camp staff go through the following steps in preparing for each school camp session.

The teacher sets the stage for a teaching unit which will lend itself to the outdoors. Several weeks before camp she may place nature pictures on the bulletin board, or tell stories with nature settings. Whatever the present unit of study, some parts of it can point the way to a natural science unit. The teacher aims to generate questions of general interest and then guide the children as they choose a specific unit such as forestry, weather, soil conservation, or wildlife.

The class secretary may write the suggested subjects on the blackboard. The boys and girls may choose one particular phase—such as weather—and various committees and individuals work on weather instruments, clouds, air pressure, weather predictions, etc. Or one or two committees may make a report on weather, another group on soil conservation, thus sharing with each other a larger picture of the outdoors.

Application of the three R's, plus social development, is the result of this group work. The children may give oral and written reports, make attractive and informative bulletin boards, or tell their story through posters and murals.

One committee may decide to contact a resource person, such as an Agriculture teacher, if they want to know more about farming and soil conservation. They can practice writing business letters requesting printed materials. The search for information naturally gives the children more contact with the vast offerings of the school and public libraries.

With 30 inquisitive minds at work, many questions arise which cannot be answered in the classroom. So the boys and girls keep a list of questions that can best be answered later during the outdoor laboratory period. These questions are the main guide when the class starts scheduling camp activities. Also, the camp staff can see in black and white what the class is seeking and be prepared to give better guidance before and during the camp period.

The camp staff assembles a folder of specific aids for the teacher to help her prepare the children for the regular camp routines. This packet contains cook-out menu suggestions, food price lists, letters for parents, table service diagrams and responsibilities, health inspection sheet, program ideas and banking materials (checkbooks, deposit slips, and balance sheets). The camp staff and teacher "go over" these teaching aids together in a private conference, giving her a chance to ask questions and receive suggestions as to ways she can utilize this information to the fullest extent.

After consultations with the teacher, the counselors visit the classroom. This briefing period is aided by a large chart tablet which describes the steps to follow in making definite camp plans, but the teacher and the class work out the details later. The large handbook is left in the classroom so the children can leaf through and digest its contents at their leisure.

HOW PROGRAM IS PLANNED

Step 1 is to decide why go to camp. The first aim will naturally be to find the answers to questions concerning the Science unit. After familiarizing themselves with the camp routines, other aims—such as learning to live with others, being independent, following instructions, etc.—are mentioned. After all these aims have been listed on the blackboard in the children's own words, they set to work combining ideas, looking for repetitious statements, and making the final draft of specific aims. Thus, language, vocabulary and spelling are not being neglected.

After listing the aims at the top of a program board furnished by the camp, the class starts to think of activities that will best carry out the aims. They can get help from the teacher and from ex-campers, refer to descriptions given by the counselor or the large handbook, or draw on their own experiences. They will be sure to include activities which relate to the unit they have started in class. In order to be democratic, most groups list all the possible activities and the ones getting the most votes are placed on the program board. The counselor can usually be of last-minute assistance if he drops by the classroom about two days before the class leaves for camp. He may spot minor program changes which will make the week more profitable.

Once or twice during the week in camp, the group will take about 30 minutes for a check-up session. They want to find out if their aims are being accomplished and share with each other some things they have learned. Most of the learning experiences they mention during these "round-up" sessions could only have taken place in an outdoor setting.

LEARNINGS GO HOME

As the children board the bus for home, they are leaving the physical camp site—the outdoors—but their mental and spiritual beings have stored away experiences which remain with them. The children will want to share their "fun while learning" experiences with others through plays, skits, puppet shows, written reports, letters, art work, displays and exhibits. Some classes prepare a booklet which contains their pre-camp work on the natural science unit, arithmetic related to camp (cook-out plans, checks written at camp and bank statements), new vocabulary and spelling words, snapshots and a description of responsibilities and jobs they had while at camp. Parents are surprised and pleased to see that Junior's time in this strange outdoor school was well spent and that he did not neglect reading, writing and arithmetic after all.

Teachers say that camping is an ideal way to set the stage for the next unit. Annual rings on a tree stump have been the send-off for a history unit. United States Geography has grown out of a forestry study which included national forests and parks. After doing farm chores, one class wanted to know more about the food in the other countries, thus starting a study of World Geography.

SCHOOL CAMPS
PROVIDE SOCIAL DEVELOPMENT *

ALICE A. KENT

Ten children who have severe hearing losses, and 60 sixth grade boys and girls with normal hearing, took part in a one-week school camp last October. All of the children are pupils in the East Cleveland, Ohio public schools. The

*Reprinted by permission of the publisher and The Alexander Graham Bell Association for the Deaf, Inc. from *The Volta Review* 59:25-26, January, 1957.

experience was a wonderfully gratifying one from the standpoint of creative teaching and social development.

Spring and fall school camping expeditions have become an integral part of school programs in a number of the suburbs of greater Cleveland during the past ten years. Established residential camps are used. On Monday morning the children and their teachers move into camp with their bedrolls and camping equipment and remain until Friday evening. Before going to camp the children are given some preparation for the type of things they will study at camp and are made to understand that it will be a week of learning as well as fun.

Our particular camp was a YMCA camp, and the regular summer kitchen staff, nurse and caretaker were retained. The program was directed by the boys' and girls' physical education directors of the East Cleveland elementary schools. Mothers of campers supplemented the staff by serving as cabin leaders, and teachers were in charge of camp activities.

Specialists were brought in from time to time to give help in specific areas of the program. One evening an astronomer from Case Observatory brought a telescope and slides of the sun, moon and stars. Each child had a look at Mars and the moon through the telescope.

East Cleveland's art supervisor came two afternoons to direct out-of-door sketching classes. After a period of instruction each deaf child was paired with a hearing child and they went off with their drawing boards and colored chalk to sketch a tree laden with fall colors—their art problem for the day.

The music supervisor was on hand for evening programs to direct songs and singing games. One evening she devoted entirely to square dancing and the deaf children were much sought after partners.

A high school teacher, whose hobby is Indian lore, came one evening to display his Indian costumes and demonstrate Indian dances.

From ten to twelve and from two to four o'clock teachers were in charge of the program. During this time the deaf children were not integrated with the hearing children, but were with their regular classroom teacher and supervisor.

The first day in camp the deaf children laid a nature trail for the other campers to follow. This meant identifying ten trees and tagging them with numbers for the other campers to find. They also collected leaves from the ten trees and made leaf prints of them. On Tuesday they made a weather vane and an anemometer and set up a weather station for the entire camp at an out-of-doors bulletin board where hourly checks could be made on the temperature. A notebook was kept with divisions made to classify experiences with animals according to the particular animal groups which they were studying in their science text book in school. Experiences with mammals included finding raccoon tracks near the river, seeing mice in the cabins and finding rabbit fur in a hole in the field. One of the boys even picked up a skunk one night! He had been told what a skunk could do, but now he knows.

On a hike up a ravine where there was a little water trickling down, the children caught wood frogs and salamanders and so they learned about amphibians and their habitat. They counted the legs of a spider hanging over a path in the woods and knew that it was not an insect. They smelled the fragrance of spicebush berries and learned that the pioneers made their allspice from the bush. They saw the nuts and blooms on the witchhazel. They read conservation signs posted in the woods, waded in the swamp in their boots, and chased minnows and water beetles along the edge of the river where they also learned that the willows and sycamores thrive. Because of their keen eyes they were much appreciated partners in the big camp nature treasure hunt that came the last afternoon of camp.

Two deaf children and eight hearing children were assigned to each cabin. Different groups were formed in the same manner at the tables in the dining room.

At the close of camp one of the deaf girls was picked as the best camper in her cabin and one of the boys was named the jolliest camper in camp.

Since these deaf children are in special classes in the same public school which the hearing campers attend, the entire venture has done much to create a better understanding on the part of both children and adults.

THE LONG BEACH PUBLIC SCHOOL CAMP *

KENNETH V. PIKE

Very much in keeping with the needs of children growing up in the highly mechanized world of today is the keen interest of modern educators in the vital learning opportunities offered by the school camp. While many communities are casting about for the necessary ways and means of establishing an outdoor educational program, the city of Long Beach, California, has entered the select ranks of those communities already operating a successful year-round camp. The person best qualified to relate the inspiring account of community interest and cooperation which made the camp possible after nearly a year and a half of the most careful research, thought and planning, is Mr. J. Holly Ashcraft, Assistant Supervisor of Physical Education in the Long Beach Unified School District. His account of the manner in which numerous organizational problems were met would be of considerable value to any group interested in establishing a similar school project.

*Reprinted by permission from *The National Elementary School Principal* 28:24-28, February, 1949. Copyright 1949, Department of Elementary School Principals, National Education Association. All rights reserved.

The present article will deal with camp organization, objectives, programs, and reception by the community.

Organization—Camp Hi Hill is owned and maintained by the city on the north slope of Mt. Wilson in the Angeles National Forest, about fifty miles from Long Beach. The Board of Education supports the educational program, including staff salaries and instructional supplies. The campers themselves pay the cost of food and food services and also carry a seventy-five cent insurance policy premium covering medical, accident, and possible polio expenses. The camping period for each sixth grade class is from Monday through Saturday morning each week. The camp, in its canyon setting, has a major physical asset, in addition to the surrounding mountains, a wealth of forest trees including the bay, live oak, maple, sycamore, alder and big cone spruce, some of which attain a size of four feet in diameter. On the opposite southern slope are found contrasting desert plants including manzanita, yucca, buckthorn, wild lilac and numerous flowering plants. The only means of access, except by Forest Service helicopter, is a mile of gravel road dropping about 600 feet from the Red Box Ranger Station. Here the campers, 35 to 40 in number—a complete sixth grade class and teacher—are deposited by school bus on Monday morning for their introduction to mountain living. It is a mile hike into camp and they arrive just in time for lunch. Accompanying the campers on their bus ride and hike are their classroom teacher, one of the permanent camp staff, who is a credentialed teacher-counselor, and four student counselors selected from the Long Beach City College to live with the campers. On hand to greet them are the camp director and a second teacher-counselor, both credentialed, who together with the caretaker and two cooks complete the permanent camp staff of six people.

Upon arrival, the entire group finds seats on the rocks for a camp welcome and a short discussion on some of the features of mountain living, such as the rocks, narrow trails, rarefied atmosphere, poison oak, and the desire for all to keep healthy while in camp. Following this brief talk the class is divided into four cabin living groups, two of girls and two of boys. One cabin each of boys and girls is combined to form a work and study group. While one group of campers goes to make up bunks and wash for lunch, the other group retires to the shower house to wash in preparation for setting tables in the lodge. The table-setting group then acts as host or hostess and hopper, washes dishes and cleans the dining hall for three successive meals, when the other group takes over.

Having rested for an hour following lunch, each group meets independently to discuss further some of the intricacies of group living in camp. The discussion is followed by a tour of the camp in order to locate facilities, study the camp as an independent community and note program possibilities for the planning meeting which follows the tour. During the counselor-guided, camper planning session, activities are planned for morning, afternoon and evening of each day.

The resulting program is then coordinated with that of the other group by representatives in a central meeting. It should be pointed out that the program thus established does not become the law by which we live. The length of each activity is governed by the camper interest span and the activity originally planned. For instance, a dike building project may suddenly have lost its appeal in favor of some new possibility, such as lumbering of a fallen spruce discovered by the campers while exploring the canyon above their cabin.

The first day in camp is brought to a close with a campfire in the most inspiring setting imaginable—the surrounding mountains, the towering spruce trees, stars twinkling through the branches, the night sounds of wind in the trees and perhaps an owl hooting in the forest, a coyote howling in the distance or a bobcat snarling in the canyon, sounds perhaps strange to a city-dwelling camper but contributing to the feeling of well-being and comfort offered by the protection and warmth of the campfire. The comradeship gained through singing, listening to stories by the director and perhaps a talk from the Forest Ranger assigned to the canyon is immeasurable.

Objectives—The unique opportunity of the school camp to contribute to the education and development of children seems to lie in the general areas of healthful living, democratic social living, basic scientific understandings and appreciations, work experiences and developing worthy skills in recreation.

At Hi Hill, the camp situation affords an opportunity for developing in campers an understanding and acceptance of the needs for sanitation, personal cleanliness and hygiene. Twenty-four hour living with children also makes it possible to teach the importance of maintaining good habits of eating, sleeping, elimination, and relaxed balanced living. These habits and concepts are not acquired by chance in the natural course of growing up. Nor are they developed by establishing a list of rules and requiring blind adherence. Rather, they are established through intelligent discussion of health reasons and needs followed by practice and example. In camp, health practices need no longer be considered the responsibility of the home but become an educational opportunity.

Program—The entire camp program is developed around the democratic processes of group discussion, planning, individual participation and sharing of responsibilities. It is assumed that the best way to teach democracy is to live democratically and that the best way to teach cooperation, understanding, and respect for the rights and personalities of others is to be thrown into a situation where those qualities pay a premium in harmony and enjoyment. The camp situation is ideal for learning to get along well with others. It is not possible here to escape and associate only with those whose company we enjoy.

In camp, too, it is possible to build proper scientific understandings and appreciations, using the outdoors as a laboratory. It is felt that these understandings are basic to proper concepts of conservation and essential to the growth of good citizens and intelligent voters.

When given the opportunity, it becomes natural for children to share in the serving of food, in the washing of dishes, in caring for beds and clothing, in keeping the camp clean, contributing to its beautification and improvement with various conservation projects, and developing some of the basic hand skills through an integrated craft program utilizing native materials. It is sometimes very difficult for an adult to stand by and watch a camper fumble with a particular job; however, to do the job for him robs the camper of the opportunity to discover the relative merits of several different methods as well as deprives him of the personal satisfaction of having done it himself. The counselor's role in camp is one of guidance and suggestion; he lends a hand only when it appears that the job is too difficult and may result in a frustrating experience. Of course in camp, as elsewhere, helping with the "dirty work" makes for easier and better leadership.

The entire camp program is fun. Recreational possibilities permeate much that we do. However, it makes poor educational as well as economical sense to pay a fee and come to camp in the mountains to play softball and other games which can be done better on the playground. Among the recreational assets of Camp Hi Hill are the swimming pool, in season, the relaxing effects of the trails, surrounding mountains, and the general beauty of the camp site. Children will relax and appreciate this beauty if they are not constantly stimulated to other distracting interests. Even learning becomes enjoyable when building stories from evidence found in the woods and preserved in the earth. When learning becomes fun, who is to say where recreation leaves off and education begins?

Whatever the activity planned for the day, whether a trip to explore the source of the camp water supply, a hike to the Mt. Wilson road by a narrow switchback trail, a trip to collect native craft materials, or an all day back pack down the canyon to a public camp site, interesting stories are encountered along the way. It may be the story of a past flood pieced together from the presence in the stream bed of a bent culvert and broken sections of a cement buttress several hundred yards below the road. It may be a geological story explaining the formation of the mountains from evidence laid bare when the fire road was built. The story may be found in the action of the stream aided by frost, erosion and gravity and the resulting effect upon the mountains.

The activity may consist of a camp or cabin improvement project based on a desire to leave the camp site in a better condition than when the campers arrived. Past improvements are brought to the attention of the campers in an attempt to develop an appreciation of the work of others and a desire to do something tangible for the benefit of those who will come to camp later. Each cabin has its own individual craft shop and set of tools. Spare time is spent working with such native materials as yucca, manzanite, acorns, spruce and oak wood. A little imagination, ingenuity and lots of patience may result in the personal satisfaction of having created a "thing of beauty." Very often the letter opener, box, name pins, flower pot holder, or other article is the first one the camper has ever completed with his own hands.

The program is camper planned, no matter how the time is spent. As one camper stated at home, he liked camp because "you got to plan what you wanted to do." Another boy took pride, not before his fellows but in reporting to his parents, that he had made two suggestions that were accepted by the rest of his group in the planning meeting. Perhaps the bubbling account of another camp experience:

> Almost killed myself on the food up there. We had swiss steak, mashed potatoes and spinach. I had five pieces.
> And the manners up there were good.
> I was host and I always gave somebody too much or not enough and sometimes I ran out before everyone had theirs.
> The first day, when I was setting the table, this man (Ferdie) pointed to his head; I still had my sailor hat on!
> And we got to do the dishes. We had soapy water, cloudy water, and clear water. The cloudy water had chlorine in it.
> I know where the bathroom is at home. I woke up in camp and thought I was home and nearly fell out of bed. I was in an upper bunk.

Reactions of Parents to the Camp Plan—In a recent summary compiled by Mr. Anton Thompson, Supervisor of Research for the Long Beach Unified School District, of 341 questionnaires (representing a return of 51 per cent on the first 18 weeks of operation) sent to the parents of each camper inviting their reactions to the camping plan and requesting suggestions for improvements, ninety-nine (99) per cent said they would be willing to send their child to camp again. Four parents failed to answer this particular question and none stated that he would be unwilling to send his child to camp again.

Some very interesting reactions were received in answer to the question, "What things did your child learn?" The learning mentioned most often may be broadly stated as "knowledge, skills, and appreciation of outdoor living; nature lore." Seventy-four (74) per cent of the parents mentioned this outcome in different ways—how to make camp, knowledge of insects, study of the stars, the laws of nature, and so forth.

The second most frequent learning mentioned has been termed "group living; cooperation." Thirty-nine (39) per cent of the parents thought the camping experience had helped their child learn to "cooperate in work and play," and to "get along better with other children."

Third most frequently mentioned learning outcome has been classified "development of self-reliance; living away from home." A total of 48 parents (15 per cent of the group) stated that their children had gained in ability to rely upon themselves or to live independently away from their parents.

Thirteen (13) per cent of the parents mentioned a gain in "manners"—particularly table manners—as an outcome. Other learnings mentioned were "household responsibilities, such as bed-making," "construction skills," etc.

In reply to a second question, "What part of the experience do you feel was most valuable?" more parents (35 per cent) mentioned the value of "learning to live cooperatively with others" than any other outcome.

Almost as many parents (34 per cent) thought that the most valuable part of the camping experience was the development of the child's ability to rely upon himself away from home. Many parents combined this value with the preceding one by a statement along these lines: "The experience of living and cooperating with a large group away from home."

Other values mentioned included growth in skills, knowledge and appreciation that resulted from outdoor living. Enjoyment, household responsibilities, manners and health were also listed.

In the space provided under "Suggestions and General Comments," sixty-eight (68) per cent of the parents—more than two out of three—indicated their support of the camping plan. To quote Mr. Thompson, "Many of these statements indicated such strong support that the cold statistics may not tell the whole story."

With such enthusiastic reception and appreciation, the interest manifested by school districts throughout the country is understandable. Our experience at Long Beach has proved the values received well worth the efforts expended in providing children with a total living experience in a camping situation.

A CASE FOR SCHOOL FORESTS *

WAKELIN McNEEL, JR., AND EDWIN VANDER HEUVEL

Travelers on the back roads in many states may observe a sign at the edge of a woodland bearing the words "school forest." Few of these passers-by know what a school forest is, nor will they question its purpose. Simply translated, school forest could mean education in the woods, or more aptly perhaps, schooling in nature's own laboratory, the great outdoors. In this day of increasing modernization in everything including education, we are apt to get too far afield from the land, and it might be well to reassess the role of school forests in outdoor teaching.

Within the United States there are 3,631 school forests comprising 162,408

*Reprinted by permission of the authors, the publisher, and Michigan Education Association from *Michigan Education Journal* 42:20-22, December, 1964.

acres. Many states inaugurated such forests during the decades of the 1920s and 1930s when consciences were being pricked and people were moved into putting cut and burned-over lands back into usefulness. These early pioneers in the movement saw it largely as an opportunity to enlist the help of school youth in replanting these idle lands of blackened rampikes, often covered with the debris of bygone logging days.

It was felt that youth could learn a great deal about conservation by actual participation in a program which they helped plan themselves. Students would have the opportunity to develop outdoor skills and develop understanding of the interrelationships of living things in their own environment. Participation in projects would help toward an understanding of state and national problems in land use, fire protection, forestry practices, game management, and recreation.

Other groups of individuals such as farmers, sportsmen, or timber owners might see good land use practices demonstrated. More important, and perhaps best disguised, even in the minds of these early leaders, was that these outdoor activities could create certain values and attitudes in youth as they were, in turn, making this land a better place in which to live. Youth was developing when youth was building.

This then was the background for the school forest movement in Michigan. Even before the State Legislature was stirred into action, there were numerous forests that had been acquired by schools in the state. Negaunee, in Michigan's Upper Peninsula, established a school forest in 1925, the project being initiated the year before by a Boy Scout troop. The extension service at Michigan State University became interested, and by 1940 had promoted 14 school forests totaling 560 acres.

Legal recognition of school forests came with the passage of the Municipal or Community Forest Act by the State Legislature in 1931. Now it was possible for school districts, as well as counties, townships, cities or villages to acquire by purchase, gift, or devise, lands to be used for forestry purposes and to be supervised by a locally-appointed forestry commission working with the cooperation of the Michigan Department of Conservation. The law provided that the state could sell homestead tax, swamp, or primary school lands to these local bodies.

Most of the school forests in Michigan were former tax delinquent lands purchased from the state on a 99-year lease basis for $1 and other considerations. In the 1930s, the U.S. Forest Service also made lands within the Manistee and Huron National Forests available for plantings by schools which lacked land. Although the schools did not own the trees they planted, students could participate and use the areas for educational purposes from local land owners or farmers who leased or donated land to a school.

Thirty-three years have elapsed since enactment of the Community Forest Act. The state now has some 627 school forests which are located in 58 of the state's 83 counties, and comprising 67,164 acres. The size ranges from a few acres to more than a thousand acres, the most common being 40 acres. To appraise the school forest situation, a questionnaire was sent to every school recorded as having a school forest with the Forestry Division of the Michigan Department of Conservation.

Replies were received from 330 schools. Of this number, 89 indicated that their forests had been absorbed into other school systems through consolidation. More alarming, 91 schools reported they had no school forest even though the records indicated they did. Thus, data in this article concern the 239 schools reporting knowledge of their forests.

This loss of contact of the schools with their school forest may be due to consolidation and consequent loss of interested personnel or change in emphasis, or a result of new teachers, school administrators, and boards who have no knowledge of the school forest's existence. Several schools even inquired as to the location and description of the properties. In most cases, the county superintendent of schools or the principal was contacted, although teachers often replied when they were in charge of the forest.

As mentioned, one of the first objectives early in school forest work was concerned with getting trees growing on denuded land. Eighty per cent of the schools have planted trees, 14 planting more than 100 acres and one school planting 190 acres. About 6,000 acres in all were planted, with more than 50 per cent red pine—with white pine, Jack pine, Scotch pine, and white spruce following in that order. In all, nine different species of trees have been planted. Free trees are provided for the schools up to a maximum of 5,000 a year. This past biennium, 178,000 free trees were distributed to school districts, and an additional 45,000 seedlings and transplants were purchased by 16 schools.

Three-fourths of the schools carried on some program of timber management. Many of the schools had plantations, and the need for timber stand improvement was recognized, but for a variety of reasons, nothing has been done. Pruning was carried on in more than half the forests; thinning was next commonly done, while some type of selective cutting, including dead tree removal, was accomplished in one-third of the forests. Management practices were more generally and intensively carried out in the Upper Peninsula than elsewhere in the state. Insect control measures, including some aerial spraying, were carried out in 11 per cent of the Upper Peninsula forests, and in 21 and 26 per cent of northern lower Michigan and southern lower Michigan forests, respectively. The higher percentages in the lower forests would be expected as insect problems in southern plantations are apt to be more acute.

HOW ARE FORESTS USED?

A most important item regarding school forests is use. Approximately 70 per cent of the schools (107) used their forests in association with classroom activities, a higher percentage in the more populous southern lower Michigan region than elsewhere. Twenty-eight per cent used them as a source of recreation. Four schools had nature trails, a similar number had research or demonstration plots, two provided school campgrounds, two had arboretums, and three used their forests as a source of trees for school landscaping.

Other uses included hunter safety programs, wildlife habitat improvement studies, roadside parks, studies in forest management, sportsmen's club range, land judging, winter ski and toboggan area, pond construction, combined use with a city for park purposes, and providing wood for the school shop as well as Christmas trees for the school.

Income was obtained from 28 per cent of the forests. Marked regional differences occurred, however. Eighty-two per cent of the Upper Peninsula schools reporting income received it from timber sales of both pulpwood and saw logs.

The Felch School owns one of the oldest school forests in the state. This forest—on a sustained yield basis since 1928—has obtained an average yearly income of about $500, which has paid for construction and maintenance of a school building, school landscaping, and construction of a dam to build a pond.

One year's income of $5,000 was realized on one forest, and five others, also located in the hardwood region of the Upper Peninsula where veneer and saw logs are obtained, reached yearly incomes of $500 and more. The average annual income from those forests reporting income was $64 in northern lower Michigan, and $315 in southern lower Michigan, where 87 per cent of the school forests having income received it from the sale of Christmas trees. One school forest in this region has 300 acres managed primarily for Christmas trees which brings in an annual income of $800 yearly. Other sources of income came from the sale of fuelwood, maple syrup, chemical wood, birch fireplace wood, and from ACP payments.

LACK OF LEADERSHIP HURTS

The key to a successful school forest lies in the supervision and leadership provided. One-fourth of the returns revealed no type of supervision or responsibility whatsoever. Assuming responses came from the most interested schools, it can be assumed that at least 150 school forests in the state lack direction and leadership.

Lack of leadership and consequent lack of use led to the abandonment of certain forests. In several cases forest properties owned by the school were sold or used for building sites.

In summation, then, many school forests in Michigan are yielding a profitable return in the form of educational use—benefiting from the investment of time and energies of earlier leaders. However, in far too many cases the spirit which motivated these people has been lost. The practice of planting trees in those early years of the 1930s and before was beneficial to both students and land, but the consequent growth of these plantations as well as natural timber gave rise to problems in timber management, insect control, and land use which are with us today. Consolidation of schools, loss and retirement of earlier interested persons, and the dropping of the FFA program in many rural schools have all played a role in this story.

A Wisconsin school forest enthusiast, "Ranger Mac," summed up the situation back in 1950 when he wrote: "A successful school forest, like any other enterprise that involves many people, depends on at least one man with conviction of its importance, the courage to crystalize the thinking of others, and the ability to bring about unity of action. Since a school forest is not a short time activity, leadership should look forward into the future, as the turnover in school work is often very rapid. The quality of leadership of the person who directs the school forest activity is evidenced in the way the work is carried on after he leaves the scene. Thus it requires that the conviction and courage be radiated to others, so that the work may be enduring. When this vision is lacking, school forests perish."

MORE THAN A FOREST *

CHARLES O. MORTENSEN

Within the rolling, unglaciated portion of South Central Wisconsin lie 278 acres of oak-hickory: the Madison School Forest.[1] The Society of American Foresters' book on *Forestry Terminology*[2] defines a forest as a plant association predominantly of trees and other woody vegetation. Madison's Forest easily meets these criteria and many more. It has, among other things, a director, a naturalist, a unique staff of part-time naturalists, and the often familiar trails, signs, and buildings. Yet, it is not only these things, important as they are, that separate a school forest from just any forest. The uniqueness of a school forest lies not so much in how we define it, but rather in how we use it and to what ends. Our forest offers special opportunities:

OBSERVATION AND LEARNING

Perhaps above all else the Madison School Forest offers an opportunity to

*Reprinted with permission from *The Science Teacher* 37:69-71, April 1970.
[1]Officially renamed the Col. Joseph W. Jackson School Forest, Madison, Wisconsin.
[2]Meyer, Arthur B., and F. H. Eyre, Editors. *Forestry Terminology*. Third Edition. Society of American Foresters, Washington, D.C. 1958, p. 34.

observe and learn or rather, in the vernacular of today's youth, a chance to see "what the action is." Those who have seen the brightening eyes of young children as they experienced for the first time such things as the plaintive song of the black-capped chickadee, the put-put drumming of ruffed grouse, the unique curved hooks on the seeds of burdock, or the long bole of a tall black cherry will attest to the stimulation provided by observing forest life. But, do children really need to hear the trill of a toad or see pin-sized eggs on a stalk, or even think about their part in the whole? The answer is yes—and not just for the children, but for all of us. Perhaps we will then see and think about more than meets the casual eye, beautiful as it is. Aldo Leopold stated it clearly and succinctly:

> . . . sit quietly and listen . . . and think hard of everything you have seen and tried to understand. Then you may hear it—a vast pulsing harmony— its score inscribed on a thousand hills, its notes the lives and deaths of plants and animals, its rhythms spanning the seconds and the centuries.[3]

That children of all ages be exposed not only to small parts of the whole but also to a philosophy which emphasizes the place of these parts in the total scheme is equally important. Careful observation must be followed by thought if we are to learn from or attempt an understanding of the forest or any other community in our environment. Certainly the foundation upon which to build is through the use of concepts, and children can be exposed to them in the forest as well as in the classroom. The basic idea of food chains takes on a new and fuller meaning when one examines the holes in a leaf only to look upward and see the fat eater or another of the same species firmly in the beak of a downy woodpecker.

Similarly, the idea of interrelationships is basic to observation in the forest. The small hooks on the burs of agrimony seem rather ignoble at first. Yet upon close examination, one discovers that these hooks are remarkably adept at clinging, especially to nappy surfaces. These seemingly delicate hooks, together with the unconscious help of forest mammals, become a very tenacious method of seed dispersal. The relative abundance of squirrels and other fur bearers in the oak-hickory forest may be a partial answer as to why there are more numerous plants with sticking seeds in the oak-hickory forest than in its maple counterpart. Here we have looked at more than the wrapping. Haven't we started to untie the package?

The school forest has "action" to observe and more than enough phenomena to try and comprehend; this resource of the forest we cannot ignore. Shakespeare stated it eloquently when he wrote:

Charmian:
Is this the Man? Is't you, sir, that knows things?

[3]Leopold, Aldo. *A Sand County Almanac.* Oxford University Press, New York, 1949, p. 149.

Soothsayer:
In Nature's infinite book of secrecy, a little I can read.
                                          —*Antony and Cleopatra*, Act I, Sc. 2

ATTITUDE FORMATION

If learning is to become a joy (albeit there is drudgery, too) as it should be, the school forest can play a vital part. Unlocking the mysteries of a fallen tree, of jutting outcrops, animal remains, or newly formed cavities is fun as well as intellectually stimulating. There are countless aspects of the forest we fail to understand. May not the intellectual humility thus gained be transferable to attitudes toward our total environment?

If one learns to care about a portion of his total environment, there is a strong possibility that this sense of husbandry may envelop the total. For example, few youngsters, or adults for that matter, will fail to be awed by the radiant plumage of the scarlet tanager as it leaves its high, secluded perch for a moment's rest on a sun-splashed shrub. Why can't the feeling that here is a thing of beauty, with its summer habitat preserved for future generations, be extended to the desire for a similar type of circumstance within the city. Why can't we rekindle the desire for a river whose rocky shores are washed by clear water rather than by a frothy film or the unnatural excesses of algal bloom? Can the feeling for a purposeful and ecologically sound harvesting of trees be transferred to the urban scene with the concomitant desire for housing which provides more than just physical living space?

Clearly, if the previous questions and the hypotheses they imply are to be more than idle dreaming, we must think creatively and design research which tests their credibility. Until then, we find ourselves in a comfortable, but untenable, position of believing that the hypotheses may be valid because we would like them to be.

Without doubt, a "land ethic," "ecological conscience," "environmental awareness," "a sense of husbandry," or any other words that connote understanding, reason, and responsibility toward our environment denote an attitude needed not only in those who have the power to make decisions affecting the environment, but in our youth as well.

WORK

The opportunity for nonprofessionals to work in resource management is a valuable asset, yet we often overlook its significance. Just as there is no easy road for acquiring a sense of husbandry toward the environment, neither is there one best way. For many, the acquisition of a "land ethic," tragically, may never develop; for others, observation and intellectual activity fail to produce it. For example, when in the course of Madison's unique high school academic credit program water-current deflectors are constructed to help develop a clear bottom and deep pools in a silt-laden trout stream, a tree is seen as something more than beauty or habitat. It can, according to a sound plan, be marked, felled, sawed, and used to build a necessary facility. Work is required—and hard work at that. But so much the better, for lasting attitudes are often the result of attaining difficult goals.

Above all else, a resource management work program gives students and adults alike the opportunity not only to get involved but also to test their depth of commitment in developing or nurturing a "land ethic." Whether the work means a homemaker becoming a part-time naturalist, a logger overseeing felling operations, a teacher supervising the marking of a natural area, a garden club funding and taking part in parochial school tours, or support of another nature, is immaterial. What is important is the common recognition that experience of this type can be basic to awareness and a sound philosophy of land use.

LIVING TOGETHER

Last, but by no means least, the Madison School Forest provides a place for all to live, play, and learn together. Perhaps today, with our often super-fast life, the crowded cities with their inherent tensions, and the widening gap between material affluence and poverty, we need this experience more than ever. A setting which places all in similar living surroundings with a successful experience resting on near total participation is, of itself, useful and rewarding. Further, to let children experience this at an early age is even more beneficial.

The author, along with others, recently witnessed important behavior changes within an assemblage of elementary school students, which may be attributed to living together in the school forest environment. For six of the eight weeks included in the classroom program a group of Indian, Negro, and white fifth- and sixth-grade children representing culturally diverse backgrounds exhibited more than the usual anxieties, conflicts, and lack of student rapport—perhaps reflecting the social disorder and problems facing older generations today. However, after a three-day living, playing, and learning experience in the Madison Forest, a noticeable change occurred. The program jelled, rapport was better, and productive activity was measurably increased. Obviously, without a carefully designed experiment a causal relationship cannot be inferred. Yet, there is a strong possibility that the forest camping program was instrumental, particularly since these children had been living together in a dormitory prior to the school forest experience. Further, a similar situation had followed the same experience during the 1967 summer program.

What about opportunities in other forests, a prairie, or another biological community? Cannot many, if not all, of the above-mentioned aims be accomplished in other areas as well? Yes and no. Yes, it is possible to observe and learn; think critically about natural phenomena; develop a sound "land ethic"; work; study and live together in almost any forest or other natural community. Indeed, many school forests have differing communities in conjunction with or within their boundaries. However, it is not only the natural or physical qualities of the forest that matter; more importantly, it is a "school" forest. If it is true that exposure must precede interest, then tell me who will take Johnny, the small raggedly dressed lad with bright eyes and quick mind and introduce him to the hitherto (to him) unknown forest drama? Johnny is in the fifth grade, and it's his first serious encounter with any community other than the city and its ghetto. Who will help Mary, who has returned from a camp experience brimming with enthusiasm and the need to explore further her interest in natural science and the environment? Her parents pursue professional and social careers which offer little time for helpful assistance. Or Larry, a country boy whose practical knowledge and keen insight concerning ecology need guidance as he explores scientific observation? A school forest can help all three.

A forest belonging to any type of school system—elementary, secondary, or higher—if properly viewed and used is more than a forest. Above all, it may enlighten the student through new knowledge, which may be transferred into creative thinking, generating a new interest in the world about him. This is particularly likely if (and they must be) political, economic, and social considerations are combined with natural history and ecological concepts. Further, it presents unlimited opportunities for teacher and student alike to participate in that all-important aspect of education—"learning to learn." Finally, the school forest is a positive force in developing or nurturing a much-needed "land ethic" among our youth. To do this requires participation by all who share a concern for our environment, whoever they are or whatever their calling. Doing this and more may let us live and think, not apart, but one with our surroundings. To do less will be unfortunate.

MOBILE SCIENCE CLASSROOM *
JAMES A. JOHNSON

Field trips are valuable experiences in many classes and especially in a science class where the entire out-of-doors is a potential laboratory. Science teachers often desire to teach a class with complete freedom from the classroom and with

*Reprinted by permission of the publisher and the National Science Teachers Association from *The Science Teacher* 30:21-22, March, 1963.

the freedom to go where they please and stay as long as they wish while studying their subject firsthand.

Last summer, such a plan became a reality at the New Richmond Public Schools, New Richmond, Wisconsin, where a group of junior high school boys participated in a summer science class which was offered for the first time. This new class centered around a study of elementary lake ecology and was held in a mobile classroom.

An ordinary sixty-passenger school bus was converted to a useful mobile science laboratory by covering an outside one-half of each seat with three-quarter inch plywood forming a counter. This counter was then made stationary by attaching cleats to the underside which fit against the bar on the top of each back rest. During laboratory work, the students could kneel on the bus seats and carry out their work on the counter with ease.

Each student was supplied with a set of science materials consisting of a microscope, hand-magnifying lens, test tubes and rack, dissecting pan and kit, specimen-collecting jars, thermometer, insect mounts, binoculars, and some reference books. This kit of science materials could be stored in a cardboard box on the seat beneath each student's counter. The bus was also stocked with additional items such as dissecting microscopes, animal traps, large jars, slide stains, a small blackboard, and additional reference material which the students could share. They constructed insect nets, clip boards, and insect jars to use during the course. Members of the class brought additional items from home to use for recreation such as waders, fishing poles, swimming suits, etc.

In this manner, the bus served satisfactorily as a mobile science classroom, containing all the material essential to a study of elementary lake ecology.

Each morning the students gathered at the school, boarded the bus, and drove ten miles to Bass Lake, a typical small Wisconsin lake. The instructor obtained a bus driver's license to act as the bus driver, thus eliminating the expense of a regular driver. Here, at Bass Lake, each morning for a period of six weeks, the class conducted a study of elementary lake ecology. This was accomplished in five phases.

The first phase included a study of the physical features of the lake. Students mapped the lake, measured its depth, took temperatures at various depths, and sampled the types of soil and sand found on the shore and at the bottom. Hypotheses were made about the possible formation of the lake and about its future. Running charts were kept on the water level and temperature to detect trends. Throughout the summer students kept extensive notebooks to record their work.

The second phase involved a study of the microscopic plants and animals found in the lake. The students observed many algae forms which are an important plant food found in lakes. They examined samples of soil and water with microscopes, using staining procedures when necessary, and classified the protozoans and tiny plants found during their work. Familiarity with various scientific words and their identification in the experiments proved to be of considerable value also.

The third phase of the class consisted of a study of the insects found in and near Bass Lake. Each student collected, classified, and mounted all the insects he could find.

The class then began work on fish found in Bass Lake by catching, dissecting, and classifying the various specimens. During this phase, Norman Hicks, St. Croix County game warden, spent a day with the class discussing fishing regulations and conservation of wildlife. This proved to be a valuable and interesting experience for the class.

The Bass Lake project concluded with a study of the higher plant and animal forms found in the area. Each student made a collection of leaves from trees found near the lake. Some small animals were trapped also. One day was spent visiting an animal farm nearby. Throughout the summer, an attempt was made to point out the relationship between the various life forms and their environment.

CONCLUSION

All in all, this new approach to the study of science, at least for this group, was considered successful and valuable by the students and the instructor. Student interest was extremely high and considerable learning processes were evident throughout the project.

The mobile classroom idea certainly holds promise for many kinds of science classes and perhaps some nonscience classes. The state of Wisconsin now provides state aid for approved summer programs and thus makes this type of class financially possible for most schools in the state. The author urges educators to try this particular program which provides an interesting approach to science education.

OUTDOOR EDUCATION AS A METHOD OF TEACHING READING *

JEANNE SMITH*

"Poison ivies, meet at the big tree wearing bathing suits." . . . excited hums. "Ticks, report to the archery field." . . . wide grins. "Bears, wear your hiking boots and report to the recreation hall." . . . eager anticipation. "Beavers, report

*From *The Journal of Reading* 12:229-233, December, 1968. Reprinted with permission of the International Reading Association and Jeanne Smith.

to the faculty cottage for reading." . . . puzzled frowns . . . cold, icy stares. How dare you try to teach us to read here! Some fun this camp is!

Some not-so-eager beavers were a little late for their appointment at the faculty cottage—no doubt on purpose. Others tramped onto the porch sighing "Ick! Here we go!" "I know. See Sally run." "Ugh! Books!" At last the entire Beaver ten was seated and ready for the dreaded reading lesson.

"Beavers, I'm sorry to disappoint you, but there *are* no books for you to read here." . . . sighs of relief . . . puzzled faces. "If you look and listen you will be able to learn the words that you need to know in order to enjoy your life at camp and become a good camper. Then, when you go to the archery field, when you hike through the Round Mountain woods, when you go boating or swimming in the river, you will use these words and learn more about what they mean. Your teachers and counselors will expect you to use this language. The more you use the words you learn here, the better are your chances of becoming a good camper and a better reader."

Without making it particularly apparent, the trap was set for a systemized plan of teaching reading, using outdoor education as the bait—outdoor education as a method of teaching reading. How could a child hate reading when it was helping him to learn about living in the outdoors? There was a great deal of language that he needed to know about camp and it could be presented in such a way as to assure interest, attention, and maximum participation.

RATIONALE FOR EXPECTING GAINS IN READING ACHIEVEMENT

In describing the "pioneer" reading program conducted in connection with Title I at the Irvington Outdoor Education Center in Flemington, New Jersey, it will be necessary to consider the philosophy of the camp and the rationale for the reading program.

The camp attempts to give the child a week away from home providing him with new and varied experiences; a well-balanced diet with a good variety of foods; and the opportunity to experience cooperative, democratic living and to share responsibilities in an outdoor setting.

Cases have long been observed where outdoor education has brought about complete reversals in the behavior patterns of children. The child with little interests wants to try everything; the uncooperative child suddenly becomes most cooperative; the withdrawn child sings out freely, perhaps even screams out in the true camp spirit; and the exhibitionist fades into the background. In short, children who are referred to as "problems" by their teachers at school will very often go unnoticed as such at camp.

If we accept this premise concerning the child's behavior, and if we keep in mind the importance of behavior in learning, then it seems valid to say that some children *cannot* and *do not* learn in a school setting. With this concept in mind, it was felt that outdoor education could be most effective as a method of teaching reading to these children with the provision that the reading activities would not resemble "school work" and that they would be a functional and integral and intriguing part of camp life. Reading and personal experience were to go hand in hand and be accompanied by exploration, observation, and discovery. Yet how could this be accomplished?

PROCEDURES

Criteria for selection of participants were achievement test scores, socio-economic status, and interest. Children who would be entering sixth, seventh, eighth, or ninth grade in September were chosen on a townwide basis. Children with low achievement in the area of reading and language were given priority.

Form A of a teacher-made test was administered on the first day of class. Twenty-five multiple choice questions were included under four headings—archery, boating, forestry, and swimming. The alternate forms of the test were constructed to provide an item-by-item balance in difficulty. Questions checked the child's concepts of words as well as recognition of them. The following are examples of test items:

Archery	———— Quiver	A. for stringing the bow B. for carrying or holding arrows C. to miss the bull's eye by an inch
Boating	———— Stern	A. the back of the boat B. the front of the boat C. the middle of the boat
Forestry	————Erosion	A. makes the earth rich B. is caused only by water C. is the loss of topsoil
Swimming	————Exhale	A. breathing out B. breathing in C. holding your breath

CHILDREN MADE AWARE OF OBJECTIVES

Children were encouraged to know and keep in mind the objectives of the reading program, the primary objective being to know and improve oneself. They were happy to learn that there were no passing or failing grades and that if their test scores improved at all, they could be proud of their accomplishment.

The children were pleased when warned not to compare themselves with their peers, for it would seem that the child who has a greater knowledge of camp life through scouting or a similar previous experience would most likely score high on the pretest. However, this did not mean that the child with limited camp experience could not do as well on the post test.

METHODS OF READING INSTRUCTION

Reading lessons were presented largely through the use of the overhead projector with the use of teacher-made and student-made transparencies. The value of this media in capturing the interest of the students cannot be overestimated, for without the overhead projector this type of program might not have succeeded at all.

The campers were pleased to take a one-half hour respite from the other vigorous camp activities to come to reading. They were delighted when given the opportunity to create their own transparencies. Little emphasis was placed on grade level when preparing materials. It was felt that interest and content would be more important. Concepts were presented in the simplest terminology possible.

Learning of skills was incidental and opportunities for such were numerous. Here are but a few examples of incidental learnings:

- During a forestry lesson, the concept *conservation* was discussed only after having considered the syllabication, pronunciation, and meaning of the root word *conserve*.
- The meaning of the prefix *re* was studied when learning about a type of bow called the *recurve* bow.
- The difference in pronunciation of the words *breath* and *breathe* and the reason for this difference were discussed.
- Differences in pronunciation of a *bow* in archery and the *bow* of a boat were noted.

After having been introduced to these concepts as a part of reading instruction, children were armed with questions to ask teachers and counselors. For example, the archery teacher would be asked about the "anchor point" and the boating instructor would be questioned on how to "feather" the oars. In this way teachers of specific activities were reinforcing vocabulary and concepts gained in reading and vice versa.

Children eagerly devoted free time to role playing as they enacted "The Celebrated Jumping Frog" after having spent hours searching for the ever-escaping contestants.

RESULTS

At the dinner table children could be heard discussing enthusiastically what they had tried or discovered that day. They were talking over many of the terms that they had learned in reading! They chatted happily about taking the post test on the final day and on that day they approached the test with an air of confidence. They looked forward to hearing the test results which were related individually during the final moments of camp. Children who had the good fortune to return to camp for another week were still as enthusiastic about the reading program and therefore helped to "sell" it to the newcomers. Often these repeaters assisted at instructing the newcomers.

CONCLUSIONS

1. Outdoor education can be used effectively as a method of teaching reading, for it offers a relaxed situation and an opportunity to present material which is meaningful to the child in that situation.
2. Children learned that reading does not always have to be an experience which can cause anxiety or an experience which is unrelated to life. It can be meaningful in a given life situation.
3. Attitudes toward reading were excellent. Little resistance, if any, was shown.
4. Comparable gains were made by both boys and girls.
5. Mean gains were highest for groups comprised of sixth graders. Second in achievement were seventh graders. Smallest gains were evidenced from eighth and ninth graders' scores.
6. Gains were significantly higher for campers returning to camp for a second or third week.
7. It seemed that language gains were more noticeable than gains in reading skills, per se.

The question may be raised as to what value will be found in this type of program if there is no carry-over in the school. Favorable attitudes gained toward reading can be transferred and the annual summer regression of reading achievement scores can be prevented when children are given a type of program which will interest them.

Perhaps this type of resident camp program would be workable on a four month a year (fall-spring) basis, incorporating not only language arts but also social studies, math, and science, using outdoor education skills as the basis for the curriculum. This is a challenging and exciting area awaiting innovation and experimentation.

BIBLIOGRAPHY

1. Gomberg, Adeline W. "The Lighthouse Day Camp Reading Experiment with Disadvantaged Children," *The Reading Teacher 19* (1965):243.
2. Herzog, Arthur. *Learn, Baby, Learn.* United States Department of Health, Education, and Welfare, July-August 1966, 2, 4.
3. Isenberg, Robert M. "Education Comes Alive Outdoors," *N.E.A. Journal 56* (April 1967): 34-35.

4. LaBrant, Lou. "Broadening the Experiences of Deprived Readers," *Education 85* (April 1965): 499-502.

5. Weiner, Morris. "Outdoor Education Can Help Unlock the School." *Educational Leadership 24* (May 1967): 696-699.

URBAN GEOGRAPHY FROM THE AIR *

KENNETH E. COREY

This discussion is presented in an effort to document a specific, ongoing geographic field experiment and to promote the exchange of ideas and experiences.

The utilization of the air field-trip teaching method at the University of Cincinnati differs considerably from other similar documented activities in that it employs a single large aircraft rather than several light planes. The use of the larger plane presents some unique advantages worth recounting.

Such flights began in the mid-1950s, and have continued successfully to the present. The first air trips were designed to illustrate soil conservation and natural physical geographic phenomena and to allow for observation of the same. Over the years, however, the trips gradually have changed in character and purpose. The prime emphasis no longer is directed to observing the "land." Today the air field-trip is designed to offer the student the rewarding experience of piecing together and organizing the "total landscape panorama."

THE SINGLE PLANE AIR TRIP

Both Richason and Taylor indicated that one of the major problems involved in making their air field-trips effective was the inability of the course instructor to accompany all of the students during the flight. They believed that the advantages of maximum observation for all passengers outweighed this deficiency. Keeping both of these points in mind, officials at the University of Cincinnati contacted Piedmont Airlines for charter flight arrangements. This airline was selected because it features the F-27 "Pacemaker," a high-wing, two-engine aircraft. This plane allows the instructor to accompany all of the students making the trip. What is equally important, all 36 passengers have a completely unobstructed view of the earth below. With the permission of the pilot the instructor is able to narrate over the plane's speaker from the cockpit, thereby providing a detailed, running account of all significant landscape features

*Reprinted by permission of *The Journal of Geography* and The National Council for Geographic Education from *The Journal of Geography* 65:332-333, October, 1966.

appearing on both sides of the plane. This approach eliminated the interruptions of the student's observation which were formerly necessary because he had to reorient himself to a flight plan map. In addition, the instructor is able to maintain a continued level or pace of student interest through narration. When traveling between points to be observed, the instructor can elaborate on phenomena just seen, as well as prepare the class for upcoming observations.

AIR FIELD-TRIP DESIGN

The following notes on air field-trip preparations are offered so that others may benefit from our trials and errors in using this unique field method. For several years past, the programming of the trip has been begun by contacting Mr. Odegard, County Agent for the Hamilton County (Cincinnati), Ohio Soil Conservation District. Mr. Odegard has arranged a preliminary planning flight through the courtesy of the State of Ohio's Department of Commerce, Division of Aviation. This reconnaissance flight has permitted the departmental faculty an opportunity to vary the air field-trip from year to year. Because the detailed route of the trip has been kept variable, the class has been able to observe recent changes in the landscape. This factor is especially important in metropolitan areas where large-scale redevelopment and expressway activities are occurring. Preliminary flights have averaged approximately two hours flying time. Once the route of the air field-trip has been determined for any given year, the only remaining step is conducting the flight.

TRIP IMPLEMENTATION

The air field-trip is scheduled on a Saturday morning during the first two weeks of May. The trip is not required, but is rather an optional activity of the department in which all students are encouraged to participate. Students in both the introductory physical and cultural geography courses receive special encouragement to participate in the trip, for specific lecture and slide references are made throughout the normal activities of instruction. Most of the trip participants are drawn from these two courses and a third course—The Geography of the Cincinnati Region. This advanced field methods and research applications course uses the metropolitan region as its laboratory. Finally, the roster is filled by students from other geography courses and by graduate students from the Division of Community Planning. It is often a group with relatively diverse backgrounds, experiences, and interests—not necessarily a geographically sophisticated group.

The 35 air field-tripping students and their instructor assemble at the airport ten minutes before take-off for a map prospectus of the exact route to be flown. Here the trip participants are informed of the details and specific features which are to be observed. Take-off time is set at either 8:30 or 9:00 a. m. in order to take advantage of morning shadows which tend to aid in relief differentiation. These times also take advantage of the airplane's availability during a lay-over period between scheduled flights.

Once in the air, the students concentrate on listening to the narrative and on observing and interpreting the features below. Because the F-27 has extra-large panoramic windows, even the aisle passengers have no problem with visibility. Flights last between 40 and 45 minutes and cover approximately 90 miles at an average altitude of 1,500 feet and an average speed of 180 miles per hour.

CONCLUSION

The annual Cincinnati Region air field-trip performs the following functions:

1. Both the beginning and advanced student are afforded an overview of a "total landscape." Observation of the natural physical base is stressed equally with observation of settlement features and urban agglomerations.
2. This bird's eye perspective, coupled (both preceding and following this flight) with classroom tools such as small-scale maps, aerial photographs, and three-dimensional models should serve to expose the student adequately to the multi-faceted method of geographic analysis. Spatial understanding is the goal that is sought by utilizing this battery of teaching techniques.
3. The student is given an opportunity to see his local region first-hand and remain informed as to contemporary landscape changes.

The result is a meaningful and flexible air field-trip which does not require an exorbitant expenditure of time either for preparation or implementation.

DISTANCE, WEIGHT, HEIGHT, AREA AND TEMPERATURE PERCEPTS OF UNIVERSITY STUDENTS *

MALCOLM SWAN AND ORVILLE JONES

INTRODUCTION

Educational objectives, particularly in science and mathematics, include the development of our understanding of the world in which we live. Hence, attention to the development of percepts or mental images of intervals and quantities of distance, weight, height, area, and temperature seems in order [1].

*From *Science Education* 55:353-360, July, 1971. Copyright © 1971 by John Wiley & Sons, Inc. Reprinted by permission of John Wiley & Sons, Inc.

If teaching activities using such intervals and quantities are to achieve results, students must be provided with background reference intervals and quantities they can fully understand and visualize.

Comprehension of distances between or across cities and continents, for example, appear to have meaning to the degree the learners can visualize shorter intervals of distance such as "one hundred feet," "twenty-five meters," etc. Without some experiential basis for understanding these units of measure, comprehension and retention are likely to be minimal.

A similar condition exists in regard to other quantitative measures such as volume, weight, height, time et al. Children, and some adults, with few first-hand experiences on which to base a "gallon concept," find references to the per gallon cost of milk difficult to understand. Learning abstractly that three thousand or more gallons of fuel oil may be required to heat a home is even more incomprehensible. Reading about the heights of various trees is probably of little consequence to a child who is weak in height percepts. Telling a child who has vague time percepts to "wait a minute" or "come back in a half-hour" results only in confusion. Memorizing the number of square feet in an acre may be a futile exercise to the learner who lacks a clear mental image of what an acre looks like, or lacks understanding of what the term "acre" signifies [2].

In many science or mathematics classes, discussion frequently centers about such quantitative and interval concepts. Some examples might include: a distance of one hundred or X-number of feet; or a weight of five or X-number of pounds; or a height of fifteen or X-number of feet. When quantities such as these are used in a communicative situation, considerable doubt may exist concerning the degree of understanding or lack of understanding that takes place between the writer and reader, or speaker and listener. The extent to which communication occurs depends on the degree to which the users or learners of a given quantity have had similar experiences and perceptions.

PURPOSE OF STUDY

This study was undertaken to determine the accuracy of the percepts of intervals and quantities of prospective teachers, using both English and metric units, and to test these hypotheses:

(1) University students preparing to become teachers have inaccurate or invalid percepts of intervals and quantities of distance, weight, height, area, and temperature. (Note: The researchers arbitrarily judged an estimate smaller than 75% or larger than 125% of the actual interval or quantity to be inaccurate. A return of more than 50% inaccurate student responses to an item was considered as being supportive of this hypothesis.)

(2) Students' percepts expressed in English units are more accurate than those expressed in metric units.

(3) Accuracy of students' percepts in one area such as distance or weight, etc., is not significantly different from the accuracy of their percepts in other areas.

(4) University students intending to become teachers have little understanding of the relationships or ratios between commonly used English and metric units of measure. (Note: Students' estimates varying 25% or more from the actual ratio were arbitrarily judged indicative of "little understanding" and supportive of this hypothesis.)

PROCEDURE

Immediately on arrival at the Lorado Taft Field Campus (a branch campus of Northern Illinois University), the subjects were given a 5 x 8 card listing certain items pertaining to distance, weight, height, area, and temperature (see Fig. 1). The researchers reviewed the items one by one, so that everyone would be responding to the same item simultaneously.

The subjects were instructed not to discuss their estimates with other persons. They were further asked to provide a response to each item even though they lacked a clear idea of the quantity involved. (The researchers inferred, however, that each individual had some sort of mental image of the quantity because it was thought that students would certainly recognize that the distance intervals, for instance, were less than one-half mile but still greater than one yard.) Some of the students, however, disregarded these instructions and left blank spaces on the inventory card, particularly in regard to the metric units of measure. Consequently, some of the results in this study are probably more conservative than they would be in actuality.

Approximately 50% of the 392 college students participating in this study were majoring in elementary education. The remainder were mostly secondary education students with a variety of subject majors. Included in the latter grouping were a few graduate students majoring in outdoor teacher education.

The estimates of the students were tabulated and analyzed and provided data for the construction of frequency polygons and computation of the various statistics provided in the next section.

RESULTS

DISTANCE INTERVALS

Two distance intervals were used in the study (items 1 and 2 in Fig. 1). The first of these was a distance of 212 feet, or 64.7 meters, between two small buildings (Taft and Browne House), and the second was the width of a building 24 feet, or 7.34 meters (Browne House). Figure 2 illustrates the responses of the subjects in estimating the distance of 212 feet.

The mean of estimates for the first item was 215 feet, just three feet more

PERCEPTS OF QUANTITIES AND INTERVALS

1. Distance between Taft and Browne = _____ft. _____ meters

2. Width of Browne = _____ ft. _____ meters

3. Air Temperature = _____ °F. _____°C.

4. Weight of wood block = _____# _____ Kilograms

5. Weight of rock = _____# _____ Kilograms

6. Height of Tree = _____ft.

7. Height of Tower = _____ ft.

8. Acreage of plot = _____ acres

9. Two adjectives best describing weather: _____, _____

10. Two adjectives best describing river view: _____, _____

Figure 1. Reproduction of an answer card used by Northern Illinois University students to record their estimates.

than the actual distance. Sixty-four per cent of the estimates were judged to be inaccurate because they were either under 159 feet or over 265 feet [see note under hypothesis (1)].

Only 253 of the 392 subjects in the study estimated this distance in terms of meters, and their mean estimate was 101 meters. Approximately 80% of the estimates were inaccurate; i.e., they were above or below the correct figure by more than 25%. When the estimates were examined to determine the understanding of the ratio of meters to feet, the results were as follows:

(a) The correct ratio of meters to feet is .306; but the mean ratio of meters to feet in the estimates was .445.

(b) Seventeen students, 6.7 per cent, indicated that a foot was a larger unit than a meter.

(c) About one-half of the students who responded to the item in terms of both feet and meters had a substantially correct ratio; whereas nearly two-thirds of them were within 25% of the correct ratio.

The mean of the estimates of the building's width (Browne House) was 23 feet, or 12.7 meters. Nearly one-half, (47%) of the students gave an inaccurate estimate when using feet. Of the 237 out of 388 students estimating in metric units, 55% gave inaccurate estimates. The mean of the ratios between meters and feet [see result (a) above] was .546. Nearly 41% of those estimating in both English and metric units were incorrect by more than 25% and nearly one-third were incorrect by more than 50%. Twenty of the students indicated that the

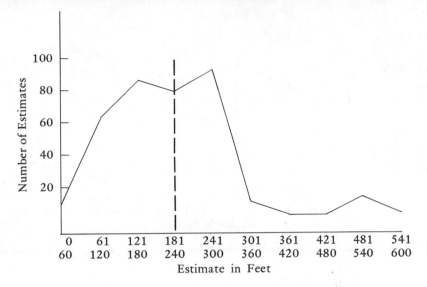

Figure 2. Northern Illinois University students' estimates of a distance interval of 212 feet.

foot was a larger unit than a meter in this case. Relevant to distance estimation, these data and the fact that a significant number of students made no attempt to estimate in metric units seem to support hypotheses (1), (2), and (4).

WEIGHT

Students were asked to lift or "heft" two objects (1) a rock weighing 17.5 pounds, or 8 kilograms, and (2) a block of wood weighing 13 pounds, or 6 kilograms (see items 4 and 5 in Fig. 1). Figure 3 illustrates the estimates for the block of wood using the pound as the unit of measure. The mean of the responses was 11.3 lbs. and the median was 10 lbs. Eighty-two per cent (295 students) gave inaccurate estimates; that is, their estimates were off by 25% or more. Nearly one-half (48%) of them missed the actual weight by more than 6 lbs. Sixty-four per cent of the students estimated low and 25% were high. Only 181 of the 392 students gave a kilogram estimate. The mean estimate was 21.6 kilograms, with ten of the most extreme estimates being excluded. Two-thirds (66%) of these kilogram estimates were considered inaccurate. When comparing each student's estimates in pounds and kilograms, the results were as follows:

(a) On the average, one pound was perceived as equivalent to 2.64 kilograms.
(b) Thirty-five per cent of the students perceived the pound to be a larger unit than a kilogram. Sixty per cent of the students missed the correct ratio by more than 25% and one-half of them missed it by more than 50%.

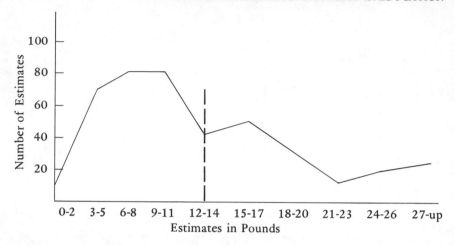

Figure 3. Northern Illinois University students' estimates of the weight of a 13-lb. block of wood.

Similar results were obtained in the estimates of the weight of the rock, but more students overestimated than underestimated. The mean of the estimates was 20.3 lbs. and the median was 18 lbs. Several students thought the rock weighed more than 50 lbs. Fifty-eight per cent of the students were incorrect in their estimates by 25% or more, and nearly one-fourth of them missed by 50% or more.

The kilogram estimates for the rock were as incorrect as with the block of wood. The mean estimate of the 181 responding students was 31.3 kilograms. Two-thirds of the 181 students missed the actual weight by more than 25%.

In this case the students perceived the ratio of pound to kilogram as one pound being equivalent to 2.43 kilograms, again nearly the reverse of the actual situation. Thirty-seven per cent of the students perceived the pound to be the larger unit of measure, and more than 61% of them missed the correct ratio by 25% or more. These data, and the fact that a significant percentage of the students did not even attempt to estimate in kilograms, appear to provide additional support for hypotheses (1), (2), and (4).

TEMPERATURE

Students were asked to estimate the air temperature using both Fahrenheit and centigrade scales. Figure 4 illustrates the accuracy of the Fahrenheit estimates. The estimates ranged from 17 degrees below the actual temperature to 14 degrees above it. The mean error was 4.5 degrees. Fifty-four per cent of the estimates were within 5 degrees of the actual temperature, hence arbitrarily judged by the researchers to be accurate. About the same number of students overestimated the temperature as underestimated.

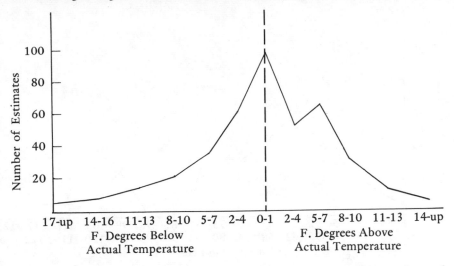

Figure 4. Northern Illinois University students' estimates of the air temperature (error of estimates).

The mean error of the centigrade estimates was 15.6 degrees. Twenty-six per cent of the students gave a higher figure for their centigrade estimates than they did for their Fahrenheit estimates. Eighty per cent of the students' centigrade estimates were high; and only 17% of the students gave comparable answers on both scales.

HEIGHTS

Figure 5 illustrates the estimates of the height of a tree 65 feet tall. The mean of these estimates is 71 feet and the median is 64 feet. Sixty-four per cent of the estimates were within 25% of the actual height. As many students (179) underestimated as overestimated (177). The range of estimates was from 30 feet to 200 feet.

Estimates of a 60-foot tower, located some distance from the tree were considerably more accurate. The students appear to have been aided by two-foot-long segments of the tower's superstructure. Although the range of estimates was from 18 to over 200 feet, the mean was 59 feet. More than 100 of the students estimated correctly the tower's height.

ACREAGE

The students were high in their acreage estimates. Many students remarked that they had never seen an acre of ground, perhaps because most of them were from urban areas having limited open spaces. The mean estimate of the .22 acre plot was .75 acres and the median was .75 acres. The range of estimates was

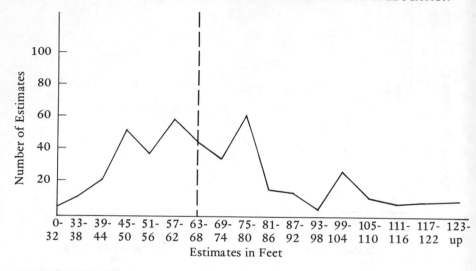

Figure 5. Northern Illinois University students' estimates of the height of a 65-foot tree.

from .05 acres to 5.0 acres. Seventy-one per cent of the estimates were in error by 50% or more.

IMPLICATIONS AND CONCLUSIONS

This study appears to support the hypothesis that university students intending to enter teaching have inaccurate and invalid percepts of intervals and quantities of distance, weight, height, area, and temperature, using both English and metric units of measure. In most instances, the majority of the estimates in English units were in error by more than 25%. Among the exceptions were the height and temperature estimates. It is quite possible that some of the students had heard weather reports prior to arrival at the branch campus.

The results indicate that percepts of such intervals and quantities are less accurate when using metric units than English units. The results also indicate that students' percepts relating to height and air temperature are more accurate than those relating to distance, weight, and acreage. Relatively few of the students perceived the proper relationship between kilogram and pound and between Fahrenheit and centigrade scales. However, a number of students gave estimates that indicated that they understood the relationship between foot and meter.

VIEWPOINT

We believe it is essential in communicative situations for teachers and students to have comparable percepts. One is forced to question the kinds of outcome relative to the teaching-learning process in which these intervals and quantities are involved and in which there is no commonality of understanding. How can teachers be expected to communicate with pupils and be effective in the teaching-learning process if their own percepts are inaccurate, unclear, and invalid? Considerable evidence exists which supports the notion that percepts can be clarified and reinforced through direct, first-hand experience [3]. Thus, it seems not only highly desirable but essential that students at all levels of the educational ladder should have direct experiences to clarify and reinforce these interval and quantity percepts which they will use in and out of school, and throughout their lifetime.

REFERENCES

1. Blough, Glenn O., Julius Schwartz, and Albert J. Hugget, *Elementary School Science and How to Teach It.* New York: Dryden Press, 1958, p. 158.

2. Hammerman, Donald R., and William M. Hammerman, *Teaching in the Outdoors.* Minneapolis: Burgess Publishing Co., 1964, p. 39.

3. Russell, David H., "Concepts," *Encyclopedia of Educational Research.* New York: MacMillan Company, 1960, p. 326; Peter Spencer and Marguerite Brydegard, *Building Mathematical Concepts in the Elementary School.* New York: Holt, Rinehart and Winston, 1952, p. 29; Malcolm D. Swan and Orville E. Jones, "Pre-service Teachers Clarify Mathematical Percepts Through Field Experiences," *The Arithmetic Teacher* 16 (8): 645 (1969).

OUTDOORS WITH TITLE III *

CLARKE L. HERBERT

When Mr. Britton took our class outside and taught us French under the maple tree next to Founders Hall, it was education of a sort, and it was outdoors. But it was not exactly outdoor education. Outdoor education connotes instruction about the natural environment through direct and immediate experience, usually with emphasis on conservation and ecology.

One researcher reports that the first program in outdoor education was conducted in Michigan in 1940 when some teachers took their pupils to a camp to teach them by direct observation and experience. Now more than 700 schools in at least 40 states conduct various types of outdoor education programs.

The U.S. Office of Education has encouraged the development of outdoor

*Copyright 1966, Department of Elementary School Principals, National Education Association. All rights reserved. *The National Elementary Principal* 46:71-75, November, 1966.

education through grants of funds for planning and for operating projects under Title III of the Elementary and Secondary Education Act of 1965—the PACE program of Projects to Advance Creativity in Education. At the end of the second application period in February 1966, twenty proposals for programs in outdoor education had been approved. These include eight operational projects and twelve planning projects for which almost $1,170,000 in federal funds has been granted for the 1966 and 1967 fiscal years. Summaries of eight operational projects, based on their application proposals, follow.

NEWTON OUTDOOR EDUCATION PROJECT

One of the more comprehensive projects is located in Newton, New Jersey. The town is in mountainous Sussex County about 50 miles northwest of New York City. The project serves fourteen school districts in a rural area of about 500 square miles, as well as six metropolitan districts in the suburbs of Newark.

The project is centered at a School of the Outdoors—a facility leased from a private, nonprofit foundation. It is situated near the middle of the county, next to a strip of state lands available for many uses and accessible to the new Delaware Water Gap National Recreation Area. This site, which is a wildlife and nature preserve, serves as an area for field study and trips, school camping, and Saturday and summer enrichment programs. Facilities are available for in-service teacher institutes and for research. A library, a museum, and an exhibit and materials center are also housed at the center.

The Newton Outdoor Education Program includes a number of different types of activities:

The *Rolling Nature Center* is a small van with sides which open to reveal a varied collection of nature materials. The van, with a staff of trained personnel, visits cooperating schools once each month. Children in these schools learn about the nature materials in the van, hear talks by the staff, see films and filmstrips, and go on field trips.

A *Living Heritage Museum*, located at the project center, is being developed to display student exhibits illustrating New Jersey's natural resources and their uses.

The *outdoor recreation program* teaches the skills for participating in outdoor, leisure-time activities the year round. Instruction is given in fishing, fly casting, cycling, and camping in the spring; swimming, boating, canoeing, and riding in the summer; hiking, hosteling, shooting, and archery in the fall; and skiing, skating, and tobogganing in the winter.

In the *teacher and counselor training program* a course in outdoor education is given in the Newton Adult School for two hours a week for a semester. Each class is limited to 20 persons, and graduate credit is available. Teachers and counselors also receive training through a weekend institute in outdoor living which is conducted at the center. Senior counselors for the program are recruited from cooperating colleges, and junior counselors are trained through an experimental program in cooperation with several departments of Newton High School.

A *camping program* is being developed with the goal of eventually providing at least three days of camping for all children in grades 4 through 8.

The *Saturday enrichment program* is held at one school and at the center. Activities on the school grounds include nature studies, gardening and beautification programs, nature plot and trail activities, club programs, folk dancing, outdoor sports, humanities programs, and observation and field study trips. Activities at the center include development of the Living Heritage Museum, instruction in riding and other sports, nature studies, forest and wildlife management, farming, camping, arts, crafts, music, and trips and field study.

The *summer enrichment program* is expected to include activities for the talented in natural science, creative arts, crafts, and humanities, as well as programs for special groups, such as potential dropouts, the retarded, and the emotionally disturbed. Resident programs will be conducted at the center and day programs at selected schools and the center.

The personnel of the project consists of the director; assistant director, program; assistant director, research; center director, camp; center director, school; seven teacher-counselors; consultants; specialists; 16 senior counselors; and eight junior counselors.

PROJECTS IN IMAGINATIVE NATURE EDUCATION

"Projects in Imaginative Nature Education" (PINE) of the Mid-Hudson Regional Supplementary Educational Center in New Paltz, New York, is seeking to develop an awareness of the interest and beauty of the natural environment, the interrelationships of man and nature in the area, and man's responsibility for stewardship in the use of natural resources.

The site of the project is 125 acres located west of New Paltz. On this site, there is an outdoor orientation center, and there are many nature and observation trails, including self-guiding auto trails. There teachers and students may camp for several days to learn firsthand about the area's plants and forests and about the wildlife.

The project also provides speakers and teaching materials for the schools and for the general public. Naturalists visit public and private schools in the area to give talks and to show specimens and slides or films. To supplement classroom instruction, a number of teaching materials are being developed by the project. These include color slides of flora, 8 mm films recording local natural resources and seasonal phenomena of nature, and tapes of nature's sounds. Speakers are available to address service clubs and other community organizations, and local naturalists and professors give evening lectures open to the public in schools and colleges throughout the region. Leaflets on many phases of conservation, nature interpretation, and ecology, as well as guides for the auto tours, are also made available.

The project was planned by a committee of teachers, school administrators, community representatives, and conservationists working over a period of two years. The services of the project are provided the year round and are available to an adult and student population of more than half a million located in six counties in the Mid-Hudson area.

HIGH ROCK NATURE CONSERVATION CENTER

As many as 300 students a day from public and non-public schools in New York City and New Jersey visit municipal High Rock Park on Staten Island throughout the school year to study nature and conservation. The 72 acres of the park include hills, ravines, marshes, and ponds. Four fully winterized buildings provide space for classroom instruction and the project's administration.

Classes are limited to 30 to 35 students. Each lesson consists of a classroom period and a nature walk. During the classroom orientation the instructor gives the students an overview of man's relationship to nature with the aid of appropriate slides, films, and filmstrips. Then trained tour instructors conduct groups of 10 children on the nature walks, pointing out examples of phenomena discussed in the classroom orientation—erosion control, ground cover, the ecology of specific plants and animals, and the like.

JUNIOR EXPLORERS' LEARNING CENTERS

Average-income neighborhoods ring Akron, Ohio, between the richer suburbs and the poorer inner city. Seven elementary schools in the middle band of neighborhoods have been selected to serve as Junior Explorers' Learning Centers where children from the inner, middle, and outer city may mingle in a creative summer program.

Eighty pupils in the fourth, fifth, and sixth grades attend each of the seven centers for six weeks from 9 a.m. until noon. Buses provide transportation to and from the center and for field trips to the city's seven parks. Each of these parks is distinguished by some special feature—cave formations, Indian fortifications, burial mounds, fossils, an example of forest succession, or a canal, railroad, river valley, or dam. As a "School in the Woods," these parks give the children an opportunity to observe nature.

A science field teacher conducts the "School in the Woods" portion of the program. He takes small groups of children to the parks for two- to three-hour tours at least twice a week. He guides their observations, prompts questions, and leads the children through the steps of the scientific method. In the classroom he prepares the children for the field experience and conducts follow-up lessons with continuing reference work, experimentation, and related projects such as construction of a terrarium.

In addition to the science field teacher, each center is staffed with a team teaching leader and two classroom teachers. Three half-time teachers at each center serve as resource persons and teach music, art, and physical education. A librarian aids all of the centers. The project is supervised by a director with the assistance of a clerk-stenographer.

MOHICAN SCHOOL IN THE OUT-OF-DOORS

The Friendly House Settlement Hidden Hollow Camp is situated on 360 acres southeast of Mansfield, Ohio. The natural features of the site include three streams, a waterfall, and soil and rock formations. About half of the land is wooded. Facilities include a main lodge with a dining room, kitchen, and assembly room; two winterized dormitories; a museum building; and an observatory, built by the Richland County Astronomical Society, which is equipped with telescopes, maps, and a library. There is also a swimming pool.

This camp has been leased by the Springfield Local School District of Richland County for the Mohican School in the Out-of-Doors. Here, during 30 weeks of the year, 2,200 to 2,500 sixth-grade pupils from nine school districts in Richland and Crawford Counties and two parochial schools in Mansfield are brought with their classroom teachers to receive instruction in conservation, natural science, and astronomy. Each week, 60 to 80 children arrive after lunch on Monday and return home the following Friday.

A director and three teachers staff the program. Students from Ashland College serve as counselors. A member of the permanent staff visits the children's schools a few weeks before the pupils come to the outdoor school to answer questions, show slides, and explain the program to teachers, students, and parents.

FERNBANK SCIENCE CENTER

The Board of Education in DeKalb County, Georgia, has leased the 50 acres of primeval Fernbank Forest for 48 years. In this great natural resource, located in the midst of the more than a million people of the Atlanta area, the Board is creating a center to teach natural science. The center is designed to serve everyone from preschool children to retired persons—including the mentally and physically handicapped and the economically deprived. The instructional resources of the center are available to more than 75,000 students and their teachers in the city school system of Atlanta and the county school systems of Decatur, Fulton, Rockdale, and Gwinnett Counties. The resources of the center are also available to students and teachers in nearby systems and in non-public schools.

Existing trails in the area are being developed further to provide observation points and outdoor teaching stations which can accommodate groups of 30 to 40 people. Instructional material is prepared for each trail and station. Trained instructors conduct each group of visitors to selected sections of the forest, or individuals may make similar use of the trails and observation points. Specific programs have been developed for groups of various ages.

Later phases of the project include construction of a planetarium, observatory, and natural history museum. Other museums for zoology, paleontology, entomology, geology, and botany are planned. Also contemplated is a scientific library which will contain periodicals and reference books not found in high school collections. Conference facilities will be constructed so that scientists may conduct seminars for elementary and secondary school children as well as for various cultural groups. Plans for the future also call for individual research laboratories in which teams of two students may work on special projects in the biological and physical sciences.

OUTDOOR SCHOOL IN CONSERVATION

Last April, 38 pupils in the sixth and seventh grades in Alberton, Montana, lived and studied conservation at the Ninemile Ranger Station of the U.S. Forest Service. The station is a training center for the Lolo Forest which encompasses a large part of Montana and has been used for training Forest Service smoke jumpers. Alberton is a small community of around 1,000 inhabitants in the mountains of western Montana, about 30 miles west of Missoula.

The children, most of whose families are employed by logging companies, pulp mills, or the railroad, lived and ate in Forest Service facilities. Each of the five days they spent at the station was devoted to the study of a different subject—geology, ecology, meteorology, timber resources management, and soils and wildlife. The class met for two hours in the morning for lectures given by teachers and by specialists from the University of Montana, Montana Fish and Game Department, U.S. Soil Conservation Service, U.S. Fish and Wildlife Service, and U.S. Forest Service. In the two-hour afternoon session, the children were divided into groups to go into the field with their counselors for study and collecting specimens. Back in the laboratory, they conducted individual research projects and analyzed the materials they had collected.

Another outdoor education program last spring was held near Portland, Oregon, on 60 acres of forest. Five hundred sixth-grade pupils from schools in four counties took part. During each of the four weeks the program operated, 125 children and their teachers were transported to the rustic camp on Sunday and returned to their homes the following Friday.

The classrooms of this outdoor school were study plots of one or two acres of ground with a stream. Each plot was provided with a large box containing insect collection screens, butterfly nets, tree measurement tools, plant presses, plaster cast equipment, soil study materials, and reference books. Here, the children spent four hours each day studying weather, soil, water, wildlife, and plants. Guidance was given by resource persons from the Oregon State Forest Department, U.S. Fish and Wildlife Service, Oregon Game Commission, Publishers' Paper Co., Mount Hood National Forest, and the Soil and Conservation Service.

PLANNING OUTDOOR EDUCATION PROGRAMS

In addition to these eight operating projects, twelve grants were approved for planning programs in outdoor education. The following list suggests the variety of programs being developed:

In Coeur D'Alene, Idaho, a cultural and educational summer program is being planned to help seventh-grade pupils make the transition from elementary to junior high school. In addition to counseling services, the program will include physical fitness and health programs, recreational activities, instruction in such areas as nature study, and special assistance to handicapped, disadvantaged, and rural children. A pilot program for 200 to 300 pupils is being planned by a committee.

In Kittery, Maine, a program in the marine sciences is being planned for the children and adults of the community. These are some of the activities being considered: an introduction to marine plants and animals for elementary school pupils; advanced science courses; introduction to careers in the marine sciences; individual projects for high school students; summer institutes and marine science workshops for teachers; lectures by visiting speakers; an aquarium; and a traveling laboratory and museum.

A pilot program is being formulated in Bordentown, New Jersey, which will take all students in the seventh and eighth grades to live for a week in an outdoor setting and study pond ecology.

In Seattle, Washington, plans are being made to develop outdoor learning centers on 586 undeveloped acres.

Plans are being made in Avon, Connecticut, for a mountaintop science center that will include a planetarium, observatory, weather station, and seismograph to serve all levels of instruction and to provide research facilities.

At a marine science station being planned in Inverness, Florida, living specimens will be collected and delivered to schools and junior colleges. Marine plants and animals will also be displayed at the station along with exhibits illustrating the geological, meteorological, chemical, and physical characteristics of the oceans.

A center is being planned in Perry, Florida, to instruct the students and teachers of six counties in the interrelationships among human beings, natural resources, cultural patterns and characteristics, and societal resources.

In Falmouth, Massachusetts, a center is being planned to stimulate interest in oceanography. A pilot project to produce exemplary oceanographic teaching aids is also being studied.

A center under consideration in Charlotte, Michigan, will be used as a laboratory for outdoor education, conservation, and rural life.

An outdoor education center being planned to serve the community in Albuquerque, New Mexico, will provide instruction in a natural setting and a number of artistic and cultural activities.

Administrators and teachers in Abington, Pennsylvania, are investigating the use of a bird observatory and a nature center to improve the science curriculum.

Plans are being developed in Lima, Pennsylvania, to use an arboretum and a state park for field observation, study of conservation, experimental planning, bird census and study, and practical horticulture.

SIXTH GRADERS TAKE KINDERGARTNERS ON AN OVERNIGHT *

EILEEN H. ALLISON

"What our kindergarteners need is a one-to-one relationship with an older child." This statement by the teacher of forty five-year-olds led to a month-long experiment in pairing sixth grade students with kindergarten children on a one-to-two basis. The ultimate goal of the experiment in the children's minds was an overnight camping trip. The long-range goals in the teachers' planning were enhancement of self-image, growth in communication skills, increased motivation for learning, and an opportunity to share nature's lures together.

PRECAMP LEARNING

The precamp activities extended over a one-month period, with the first two weeks concentrated in the sixth grade. These experiences included:

*Reprinted from *Instructor*, © May 1969, the Instructor Publications, Inc., used by permission.

Activities to expand understandings of behavior—Role-playing developed in which sixth graders took the roles of peers and of kindergarteners in many situations in order to better understand behavior patterns of young children and themselves. Study and discussion concerned the basic human needs for affection, achievement, and acceptance.

There was observation of kindergarten children as a group in their classroom and as individuals in the cafeteria and on the school grounds. Discussions with the kindergarten teacher concerned physical and emotional behavior of five-year-olds. Compositions by each sixth grader included names of two five-year-olds he preferred for buddies, with reasons for their selection.

Experiences in science, crafts, music, and arithmetic—Science experiences in the classroom focused on plant life and conservation. Native plant specimens were brought into the classroom for the students to identify, classify, and research for interesting facts such as survival uses. Classification categories for *plants which make seeds* included trees making fruits, trees making cones, vines, shrubs, herbs. Categories for *plants which do not make seeds* included ferns, mosses, and rushes. Pictures of specimens from science books were blown up on the opaque projector for use in teaching the kindergarten children.

Vocabulary development activities evolved when students discovered the need for learning new words in order to talk and write about conservation. Their list of words included *deciduous, evergreen, foliage, ecology, landslide, gully, gorge, erosion.* The class developed a bulletin board to explain vocabulary.

Craft experiences were those that would be easy enough for five-year-olds to enjoy doing or at least involve some steps in which they could participate. Those selected (and practiced to proficiency by the sixth grade) were blueprint design, drawing with colored chalk and buttermilk, spatter painting, plaster casting, and weaving.

Music, fun, and games preparation included the compilation of a camp song booklet from which the children selected a number of "must learns" for the trip.

Food planning within a limited budget provided lessons in arithmetic and nutrition. Using newspaper ads they made a checklist on: foods we'd like most to eat; foods we've suggested that provide a balance in the basic nutrition groups; estimated quantities for seventy people; costs. Compromise and monetary limitations produced menus which included such favorites as the meal-in-one dinner, raisins, "s' mores," bacon-and-egg breakfast.

Preparation experiences for both groups—Sixth graders as teacher aides used plant specimens, bulletin-board displays, and vocabulary cards to help the young children learn to identify common trees and shrubs.

Volunteer sixth graders went to the kindergarten room to teach camp songs. Individual sixth graders had get-acquainted sessions with their younger buddies.

Final organizational preparations included securing ten high school and college students to accompany the group. On the morning of the trip teams were organized so there was a chain of responsibility, with one high school or college student over two sixth graders, each of whom was over two kindergarteners.

CAMP-OUT HIGHLIGHTS

The morning two-hour hike along a nature trail gave the children their first opportunities to identify, observe, and teach each other. The air was filled with questions and answers.

"Is that three-leaved plant poison oak or blackberry vine?"

"See the stickers? It's blackberry; don't worry."

For the afternoon craft period, a table was set up outdoors for each activity. Pupil teams moved from table to table of their choice.

The evening hours were full of food, campfire smells, laughter, and music. Each team of one college student, two sixth graders, and four kindergarteners slept at one campsite.

Breakfast was a two-course affair with cereal and milk at each campsite followed by bacon and scrambled eggs at one large campfire. Then each team went on its own "treasure hunt" hike. The sixth graders had pencils and checklists of plants to credit each younger child for all plants he identified along the trail. Contests and games were enjoyed before the partnership teams were disbanded to allow time for one last challenging hike for the sixth grade.

EVALUATION

Back at school both groups presented an informal assembly, sharing experiences and learnings with the rest of the school.

There were bulletin boards displaying crafts and creative writing. A hall board was titled *Camping Is Living and Learning Together.* Those words well summarize the month-long experience.

TOUCH AND SEE NATURE TRAIL *

JOSEPH GARVEY

A cooperative, imaginative project that offers unsighted children an opportunity to explore the wonders of a woodland area has been developed by the National Arboretum in Washington, D.C. The Touch and See Nature Trail is a

---

*Reproduced with permission from *Science and Children*, October, 1968. Copyright 1968 by the National Science Teachers Association, 1201 Sixteenth Street, N.W., Washington, D.C. 20036.

1640-foot walk wandering through trees, flowers, and other plant growth of a forest. The trail is neither a fragrance garden nor a texture path as some of the gardens for the blind are constructed. It is a nature trail through the woods just as it is for those who walk a sighted path.

A visitor passes along a rope-guided path from station to station where the surrounding highlights of nature are described in Braille and print. The "point of interest" might be a rotting stump, a large white oak, or the fallen tree trunk that can be "climbed" by hand to suggest a feeling of height. The station signs call particular attention to features in the woodland that are continually changing as part of the cyclic program in nature.

The decision to construct a Braille trail was based on the Arboretum's interest in helping an individual discover for himself the peace and beauty of his natural surroundings. Planners insisted that the trail wind through the interior of the woods where the sounds of man and industry are muted.

After the site for the trail had been selected, the path was marked by a series of stakes along a center line. Whenever a natural feature did not meet the path, the path was altered to accommodate the feature—the result, a crooked path where the visitor is relatively secluded at all times. The selection of station areas was based on the versatility of what was available. For example, at the site where a witch hazel overhangs the trail, the marker states that the plant is a fragrant fall flower and is located only in this part of the Arboretum. The marker also mentions that the plant has an oriental variety that blooms in the late winter.

Another example of area selection is that of a huge oak tree with a "saddle" or "crotch" prominently displayed. After an inspection of an old contour map dating back to the year 1935, it was discovered that this tree actually had been plotted by a survey team. On the surveyor's map, the tree was 12 inches in diameter. Today that tree is 36 inches across. The visitor is invited to reach around this mighty giant and estimate its growth in the years since 1935.

There are, of course, many features to point out—the forest floor, the sound of dry leaves underfoot, the steep grades, the damp smell, a rotting tree. A rotting tree is a feature that is made to order for the Touch and See Trail. The tree is still standing erect and tall long after it stopped growing. Only the oaks would be able to stand so long in a dead condition. The tree bark has fallen back at its base, dry, hard, smooth wood not yet decayed above and below hip height, soft, pithy, damp decaying wood is exposed. All of these features are suggested for observation on the station marker. Not only is the tree a prime example of wood deterioration and decay, but it is also an excellent place to note the presence of insect life. Insects are living in abundance near the ample food supply. While feeling this wood, the visitor may touch a woodbug or beetle.

Presently, the trail contains 24 stations which feature woods, inhabitants, or other phenomena. It is a modest beginning, but in time the trail will be expanded and altered. Arboretum trail planners had to be conscious of the time it takes to read Braille and investigate the subject.

For individuals who may be interested in developing their own nature trails for the blind, some of the details of design follow.

The rough standards which hold the markers were cut from trees being removed at the Arboretum. A rough-cut board 14 x 10 x 1 inches screwed onto the standard acts as a platform for the Braille and print. Ann Chapman, from the Columbia Lighthouse for the Blind, acted as consultant to the project and indicated the appropriate angle and position for the board. Since the Braille is read with the fingertips, a near level position of the oak board was most desirable. Nevertheless, it was necessary to slant it slightly to encourage rainwater to run off quickly. Screwed on top of the board was an aluminum sheet (gauge, .025) 12 x 9 inches and painted a flat black color. The print was photographed from a lettering machine onto plastic paper and the Braille was made up on regular lightweight plastic Braille sheets by the Library of Congress in Washington, D.C. The plastic has the advantage of being waterproof.

Actually, during the experimentation with the signs, Miss Chapman made up sample Braille on laminated plastic, stiff paper, and aluminum foil. All seemed to do reasonably well under tests.

The plastic paper with print and the plastic paper with Braille were spray glued and pressed to the aluminum plate. The metal plate serves as backing for the Braille and print copy. This method allows for easy plate reconditioning or changing.

One-half inch Manila hemp is used as the guide rope throughout the trail. It blends well with the ruggedness of the woods and literally ties each station together. The rope is strung between 4 x 4-inch posts placed at eight-foot intervals. Every eight-foot interval is cut and knotted so that if a section needs replacing, the entire trail would not be affected. This system is particularly practical when altering trail directions. The Arboretum staff soon discovered that Manila rope really shrinks in wet weather, so it was necessary to leave plenty of slack in the line. A seasoned sailor would already know this. "Landlubbers" learn the hard way. Crooked posts were the result of shrinking rope. The guide ropes are positioned on either side of the trail and are specifically there to lead the visitor from station to station.

The trail leads down a slope covered with hardwood trees to a meadow at the end of which is a small pond. Miss Chapman thought the visitor should be encouraged to roam freely at this point. How to do this and keep the visitor informed of his safety was the topic of discussion under the warmth of a late April sunshine. Eventually, the staff decided to put a gravel band around the safe area of the meadow—an excellent solution. The station sign informs the visitor that this is a meadow area where he may walk or run freely until he steps on the gravel strip which outlines the "safe zone." In the meadow area, the warm sun contrasts to the coolness of the forest trees. Here also in the meadow the visitor's attention is drawn to a willow tree and cattail plants inhabiting a marsh area. The footpath here is typically soft and boggy.

On the return trip, the spines of the American holly leaf are singled out. Trumpetvine and the dogwood are also encountered after a relaxing stroll back to the midpoint of the path. At this point, the "climbing" of a fallen tree is suggested. A fallen dead oak of modest size is lying near the return side of the trail. The reader at the fallen-tree station is encouraged to walk his hands one over the other for the length of the tree. In so doing, the feeling of size, roughness, and that first crotch can be envisioned.

All along the Touch and See Nature Trail, the total cycle of forest life, death, decay, and nourishment is told. But the greatest observation, of course, is that the forest is alive, busy with activity; a beautiful interrelated, coordinated activity, interdependent, and self-sufficient. The complete picture of nature in balance is a lesson worth repeating and relearning time and time again.

OUTDOOR EDUCATION FOR THE MENTALLY RETARDED *

DAVID A. MORLOCK AND BARBARA MASON

How does a dandelion grow? Although this question is in itself academic, it points up the infinite opportunities nature provides in developing the learning process. The subject matter is familiar, concrete, and everchanging, laying the fundamental groundwork for developing learning concepts. A program of outdoor education was implemented at Dixon State School in order to provide experiences and simultaneously to take advantage of the immediate, surrounding environment as a learning situation. Such a plan was unique, as the very structure of an institution for the mentally retarded in itself prohibits diversity of experience. Frequently children are exposed to fragments of information with minimal opportunity for application of this knowledge in familiar constructs. They need concrete experiences in relating ideas and objects in order to develop structure basic to learning.

GOALS

The primary goal of the outdoor education program was, in essence, to provide multisensory stimulations which would enable each child to acquire knowledge and experience relationships, at the same time providing the reinforcement essential to learning.

*From *Education and Training for the Mentally Retarded* 4:84-88, April, 1969. Reprinted with permission of The Council for Exceptional Children.

The inclusion of a large number of residents was a secondary goal which was also incorporated into the design. There were approximately twice as many children in the Outdoor Education (ODE) program as had been enrolled in the regular school program. This was possible because physical facilities were no longer a deterring factor inasmuch as the out-of-doors was now the classroom, and summer college student workers could assist the special education staff. Many of the residents enrolled had never attended school previously.

Another goal inherent in the project was to provide an innovative method to lessen the monotony of the twelve month education program both for the teaching staff and for the residents.

As most staff members were not indoctrinated in the basic concepts and techniques of outdoor education, the staff participated in a course at Northern Illinois University, Lorado Taft Field Campus, for a three week period. This course was designed to provide a background in philosophy and the theories of outdoor education, thus enhancing the special educator's knowledge in the area.

METHOD OF PROCEDURE

With knowledge that summer college students would be available and that specialized training for the teachers could be obtained, a survey of the institution facilities was made. Factors other than the program itself had to be considered: weather, accessibility, physical needs of the children, and transportation. The program center selected was an unused nine room farmhouse and a barn which were within walking distance of the cottages in which the children lived. Minor additions were essential—such as outdoor sinks for washing and electrical outlets in the barn and outside for an electrical piano. A bus used primarily for special education trips was procured. This bus was also used for transporting some of the children who were physically handicapped and/or in the event of inclement weather. The farmhouse accommodated supplies and served for night storage as well as emergency shelter during disagreeable weather. The arts and crafts center was located in the barn with the exterior used as a display board.

During the time when the physical facilities were being prepared—organizing, cleaning, and moving equipment—the teachers involved in the program were receiving intensive training in the basic concepts and procedures of ODE at Northern Illinois University. The course content was specifically oriented towards the following:

1. History and meaning of outdoor education.
2. Curriculum content.
3. Outdoor resources and their utilization.
4. Learning and teaching processes relevant to ODE; concepts of motivation, problem solving, inquiry, discovery and involvement.

5. Organization and scheduling.
6. Instructional materials.
7. Resource materials: texts, pamphlets, and journals.

In after class hours, while enrolled in the course, the teachers developed the course curriculum for the ODE Program specifically designed for the needs of the Dixon State School.

The project was of eight weeks duration with two daily sessions. Each child attended class for three hours per day. The number enrolled was governed by the available staff in order to maintain the ratio of one teacher and one to four college workers per 16 to 20 children. Children ranging in age from preschool through school age were eligible; however, 400 was the number which could be accommodated according to our staff ratio. Residents were recommended by the cottage personnel and/or the teaching staff. As it was apparent that the number of children recommended would exceed the limit, a screening process was set up by several teachers and college student workers. This consisted of one half to one hour daily observation of the applicants in a classroom setting for a three week period prior to the implementation of the ODE summer program. The criteria for acceptance were:

1. Toilet trained and/or time toilet trained.
2. Sufficient attention span and ability to handle physical objects (crayons, colors, etc) for a short period of time.
3. Behavior within manageable limits.

Flexibility in selecting applicants was essential if children who desperately needed the experience were to be accepted in the program.

CURRICULUM

The program had seven basic themes: animals, birds, plants, trees, rocks, water, and weather. Each week instruction was oriented primarily toward one of these categories, implemented by specialized instruction relating to the subject (i.e., music, art, physical education, and discussion). The basic learning situation was the natural habitat, with its wide array of material. The resulting diversity of experience as well as its integration provided an opportunity for the students to commence forming a conceptual framework which was not possible in the ordinary setting.

As each curricular concept was somewhat broad, further refinement was effected by specifying areas to be stressed in each of the themes. They were as follows:

1. Language development—story telling, music, drama, sensory development (i.e., listening, watching), imitation, naming, discussion, and performing skills (reading, counting, writing).

2. Physical development—individual and group exercises, purposeful activities (planting seeds, pulling weeds, watering), and exploring the physical environment (farmhouse, home living concepts).

3. Social experiences—field trips, juice time, sharing equipment, group activities, and responsibility for specific projects and for care of equipment.

4. Creative activities—arts, water play, sand, drama, or dress-up play, music, finger games, rhythm band, and dancing.

5. Self-care—washroom activities, eating and drinking, personal safety at the institution and on field trips, and obeying rules.

6. Understanding the environment—attention to form, size, color, space, quantity, and development of discrimination (tactile, auditory, visual, taste, odor), as well as the development of perception.

Teachers were assigned the task of developing specific implementation in the curriculum for each theme which would incorporate or stress the above areas. In addition, they were to provide opportunities for developing social skills and for building interrelationships. Many of the activities had inherent potential within them for language, social, and emotional development; however, certain activities were specifically designed to enhance these concepts.

STAFF AND RESIDENTS PARTICIPATING

The staff consisted of eighteen teachers, three ancillary specialists in art, music, and physical education, and seventy-four college student workers. The latter were not specifically assigned to given teachers, rather each was assigned a group of residents who were participating in the ODE program. The primary advantage to this type of assignment was continuity of programing. Upon returning to the cottage, the students attempted to implement the core curriculum daily with parallel activities.

Approximately 400 residents were enrolled: 296 trainable, 70 educable, and 22 physically handicapped.

EVALUATION

Subjective evaluations, in the form of written reports, were made by the teaching staff, student workers, and cottage personnel. There were three areas which were reported improved—language development, socialization, and behavior. There was total agreement among the evaluators that the children's behavior was greatly improved in their daily living. Improvement in socialization and language development was noted. Increased motivation to attend school was demonstrated in that physical complaints and procrastination were almost totally absent. In general the results indicated no discernible immediate improvement in academic skills, except in a few isolated cases.

A facet of the program was the assignment of a student worker to a group of children on an eight hour basis in order that he might provide continuity for the program. This aspect was successful in that the student workers were knowledgeable of the activities in which the children were presently engaged and were thereby able to provide further expansion of the day's learning.

An interesting side effect occurred. Some of the children in each cottage who were neither enrolled in the school program nor assigned to a student worker were included in the carryover activities by the student workers and residents who were participating in the program. As a result, these children received vicarious learning, particularly in the area of music and games. The primary observable gain for this group, however, was in the area of socialization, specifically group interaction and behavior.

The staff members directly involved in the program were requested to point up negative features and make recommendations. As with any program which is in its embryonic stage, unanticipated problems were soon apparent; however, solutions of these problems were found in the initial phase of the program.

The following recommendations for future programs were made on the basis of this year's experiences:

1. Each class should be more homogeneous in terms of chronological age, developmental level of functioning and developmental potential.
2. The program should be eight weeks long, or consist of two sessions of six weeks duration.
3. There should be frequent planning sessions between teachers and college student workers.
4. A garden should be planted prior to inception of the project to show the children what they may expect from their own gardens at some future time.
5. The physical education equipment should be increased.
6. The class time of arts for trainable children should be reduced from one hour to one half hour.
7. There should be better organization, particularly in the residents' arriving and being dismissed.
8. Specific goals, methods of achieving the goals, methods of procedure, and duties should be more succinctly defined, since the student workers lack basic knowledge in these areas.

SUMMARY

The general consensus of the staff was that the project was successful in that (a) the curricular concepts were implemented, (b) the number of residents served exceeded the normal school population as well as improved the teacher-child ratio, (c) the mode was exciting and stimulating, and (d) there were definite gains in language development, socialization, and behavior.

Chapter five
International
Outdoor Education

INTRODUCTION

O utdoor education as we know it in Canada and the United States has roots which can be traced to Europe. The British "Tented Schools" prior to World War I and the German School Country Homes of the twenties and early thirties are but two examples. Schullandheime and Sports Schools continue to flourish in Germany and Austria, while France has its Snow Schools, and Australia and New Zealand boast a variety of school camps. Great Britain has extensive Field Studies programs and Outdoor Pursuits Centers.

International outdoor education is perhaps best characterized by its great diversity, running the gamut from investigation of the local community to day-long treks to the mountains including skiing and rock climbing, to one or two weeks of residence in an outdoor center with the emphasis on social development and physical fitness, to detailed study of the natural environment, to scientific expeditions and school journeys out of the country.

A close relationship has developed in recent years between outdoor educators in the United States and Canada resulting in an exchange of information and expertise, and attendance at conferences and workshops in each country. On the international scene there appears to be growing awareness of what is happening in outdoor education. Recent sessions on outdoor education in Europe, Australia, and Canada have helped to generate this awareness. In addition, Northern Illinois University has conducted a series of foreign study tours expressly designed to examine outdoor education in foreign lands.

While not all-inclusive, the articles in this chapter provide a broad overview of what is happening in outdoor education in various parts of the world.

SOME INTERNATIONAL ASPECTS
OF SCHOOL CAMPING *

BY BEN SOLOMON

With the rise of school camping in America and the accelerated interest of educators in outdoors education it might help some to study what other countries have been doing for many years in this more or less pioneer field of learning-in-the-open.

Contrary to belief in some quarters, America did not originate nor were we the first to experiment with regular curriculum instruction outside the classroom, more particularly in the outdoor areas and woodland places. European countries have been doing it for years and have gained a great deal of experience in solving administrative, financial, program leadership, and other problems. It is plain common sense to study their experience, their methods and results as a direct aid in helping solve the many problems local education authorities are sure to meet with here in the States.

Ministries or Departments of Education, National and Provincial, in England, Scotland, Wales, Australia, Tasmania, Union of South Africa, British Honduras, and other countries, have created and operated school camps in various ways for many years before the modern movement in America began. Their parliaments have passed important laws relating to this type of education and in some cases

*Reprinted from the September, 1952 issue of *Education* by permission of The Bobbs-Merrill Company, Inc., Indianapolis, Indiana.

federal funds are made available to help local education authorities add school camping to their regular year-round academic curriculums.

There are five specific types of help an American school superintendent desirous of operating school camps can secure from a study of what foreign countries are doing in this field.

1. In the first place, a study of their experience will help any educator garner ideas, both general and specific, which might be incorporated into his own plan. They've been at it a longer time, started much earlier than we, and have much to teach us.

2. They, too, have met in the beginning with many serious problems and have found practical ways of solving them. This doesn't necessarily mean that solutions to problems here in the States must be the same but certainly working plans would be helpful in many ways.

3. Some of their program ideas, activities, and special fields of work point the way very definitely along paths that we might follow. They also indicate some directions in which school camping of the future might develop.

4. They have already amassed much printed matter, research and studies and many charts and forms exceedingly interesting to any educator, most of which are available upon request.

5. Just as the various countries in different geographical areas of the world, in different climates, with widely varying problems and needs have evolved different plans, especially in facilities and programming, so can our different 48 states, also with varying needs and conditions, select those things which are more applicable to their particular needs and environment.

THEY STARTED LONG AGO

Since the beginning of this century and before, throughout the Scandinavian countries and particularly in Germany, it has been common practice for whole classes or smaller groups to go out on teacher-led trips, on school journeys, not particularly as a recreational holiday, but specifically for the learning value inherent in such excursions. These trips sometimes lasted two and three weeks and were considered part of the school curriculum and were taken during school time. The instruction on these trips was integrated with the classroom lessons and to this day, in England, they are valued so highly as curricular activity that a special organization known as the School Journey Association (1) carries on a year-round program aimed at increasing and developing this type of schooling in the outdoors.

In Scotland, the Educational Institute of Scotland, and the Association of Directors of Education have concerned themselves with the organization of school camps near Edinburgh and special arrangements were made for the school children to attend the Edinburgh Festival. School camps have been developed since 1939 all over England, Scotland, and Wales, for a variety of purposes, the most important of which was a curriculum instruction. The healthy growth of school camping in Great Britain was accelerated by an act of Parliament passed in 1939 which created the National Camps Corporation (2) and gave it a grant of funds which it was to use to build and equip camps and to assist local education authorities in the acquiring and operation of school camps. The Act empowered the corporation to purchase land and build camps and to make loans to local education authorities which were repayable out of the camper's fees. The Act has been working well since its passage and to date England, Scotland, and Wales operate nearly 100 camps all year round, including the summer vacation season. Children are taken to camp for a period varying from two weeks to an entire year. The corporation's charges to the local operating authorities are on a sliding scale depending upon the number of children taken to camp. The parent camp corporation is entirely responsible for the maintenance of the camps and the domestic services, whereas the teaching, discipline, and entertainment of the children is the responsibility of the local authorities. Included in the facilities in addition to the normal dining, sleeping, and play buildings and areas, is a separate hospital building staffed with two nurses, and the general capacity of each camp is up to about 275 children. A similar organization, Scottish National Camps Association, (3) has the responsibility for administering the camps in Scotland and an interesting report has been issued about this program by the Scottish Education Department at Glasgow, called "Education in Scotland in 1948." More than 100 applications for camps from local boards of education, both in Scotland and England, for 1951 were received, and the indication is that the number will be higher this year. These applications come mainly from school systems, but in some cases are received from accredited play centers, junior clubs, and youth groups.

In Australia, there has also been rapid and important growth in school camping and outdoor education. Canadian-born Gordon Young, after graduation from Springfield College in Massachusetts, came to Australia in 1939 and introduced all-year-round school camps in New South Wales. The movement since then has grown in a very healthy fashion, and today with the backing of the Australian National Fitness Council, (4) Western Australia, Victoria, Queensland, and the island of Tasmania have made this movement part of their educational systems. Already there are scores of camps with over one hundred thousand campers, and the movement bids fair to become a regular integrated part of the whole Australian primary and secondary school system.

PROBLEMS

The problem in Great Britain of creating facilities, of acquiring land and building camps, of the year-round maintenance, kitchen staffs, foods and feeding, were all taken care of through the setup by Parliament of the National Camps Corporation, whose function it was to take care of these things. In Australia the sponsorship and backing by the National Fitness Council did a similar job for that commonwealth, and the fact that half of the money loaned to the local education authorities has already been repaid from their camper fee incomes indicates that the plan works well. A copy of the lease agreement between the National Camps Corporation and the local board of education can probably be secured by writing to them at the address given at the end of this article.

As to counselor training, in nearly all countries the school camps are used in the summertime or school vacation period as leadership training camps for the teachers. In fact, in 1951, the British Ministry of Education sponsored its 65th camp training course for teachers and youth leaders. This is a ten-day training period stressing camping techniques, living out in the open, and especially methods of teaching in the outdoors. This is indeed something that we could well follow in this country.

PROGRAM

There are some revealing and interesting facets relating to the programs in these foreign school camps which should give school men some interesting ideas about present and future programs in American school camping.

I have mentioned the leadership training courses in these camps during those periods when the school children are not using the facilities. Some of these training courses are designed for high school seniors with the aim of making them counselor assistants at the regular school camps. In Australia, where sheep and wool are of great importance to the economy of the people, one camp is given over entirely to the special study of sheep and the entire sheep-wool industry. In England some of the camps specialize as school harvest camps, which the Ministry of Argiculture sponsors. Here, of course, only the older boys and girls are used, and great care is taken to see that the campers are well taken care of in every respect. There are also special camps for the physically handicapped, and children are transported, wheelchairs, crutches and all, to the countryside to continue their school studies. In another case one camp is set up entirely as a music camp, and the School Music Association of Australia, in cooperation with the National Fitness Council, formed orchestras and chamber music groups quite successfully during the experiment. It is now being established as a regular part of the school's music education curriculum. In the Union of South Africa one camp was set up especially to teach children to fight soil erosion, and the campers were transported from school to camp for two weeks each to build soil and conservation works. This camp also is being made a permanent school organization.

Australian university students are the latest to catch the school camp idea. Today the National Union of Australian University Students, representing six state universities and three colleges, holds meetings in a school camp located on a subtropical beach in southern Queensland. The student congresses in Tasmania and in Victoria are also held in school camps. Thus, the "campus in camp" has become quite popular.

A feature of British school camping is the emphasis the local school authorities place upon "lightweight" camping, wherein the campers live out in the open, entirely on their own, sleep under canvas, and cook their own meals. This has been made practical through the cooperation of the school superintendents with the officials of the Camping Club of Great Britain and Ireland, from whom they have secured lecturers and instructors in camping techniques.

There is also a Central Bureau for Educational Visits and Exchanges (5) which specializes in making such visits available and practical for school groups.

Certainly among these various program activities and ideas now being practiced in other countries, we can garner some thought to enrich our own school camping programs and to meet the needs of the community and the children.

PRINTED MATTER

Although I have no way of knowing at this moment how much printed matter is available below upon inquiry I feel confident that a request to any of the addresses by American educators would receive a cordial reception. I suggest, therefore, that you send for a copy of the Act of Parliament, which created the National Camps Corporation and particularly for the lease agreement the corporation uses. You might also write for their forms and annual reports, and for any other handbooks and printed matter they may have available. Some of the material is free, while the rest would be at nominal cost. Here are important addresses for your correspondence.

1. School Journey Association of England
   89 Waddon Park Avenue
   Croydon, Surrey, England
   Hon. Secretary, Mr. James Hallam

2. National Camps Corporation, Ltd.
   72 Victoria Street
   London, S. W. 1, England

3. Scottish National Camps Association
   11 Drumseugh Gardens
   Edinburgh 3, Scotland

4. Australian National Fitness Council
   Canberra, Australia

5. Central Bureau of Educational Visits and Exchanges
   (Same address as School Journey Association.)

6. Ministry of Education
   Parliament Building
   London, England

7. Director of Education for Glasgow, Scotland

8. British Information Services
   30 Rockefeller Plaza
   New York 20, New York

9. Australian News and Information Bureau
   636 Fifth Avenue
   New York 20, New York

10. Commonwealth Council for National Fitness
    Canberra, Australia
    L. F. Johnston, Government Printer

WORLD PERSPECTIVES IN
OUTDOOR EDUCATION *

N. J. MacKENZIE

During a 1968-69 sabbatical year, I had the opportunity to visit many countries around the world, observing a variety of programs in outdoor education in schools, colleges, and in the community at large. This comparative educational approach resulted in a broadening of my perspectives, and revealed two very impressive features about outdoor education. They are:

(a) A rapidly expanding growth in programs on a world-wide scale.

(b) A great diversity in emphases and organization.

Both of these features are based on an increasing recognition of the many-sided values of outdoor education in today's world. The reasons for this are various but they generate from several concepts concerning the nature of the individual, society, education, and the environment. Some of these concepts are:

*Reprinted with permission from *Journal of Outdoor Education* 4 (3):3-9, Spring 1970.

(1) *Continuing Education*—a lifelong on-going concern of the individual extensive in "time" from childhood to old age.

(2) *Education-oriented Society*—reflecting a community-wide opportunity and responsibility for education by all peoples, agencies and institutions—extensive in "space" throughout the length and breadth of society. Education is no longer considered the sole preserve of any one group or institution. In part it must be a cooperative pursuit—it is no longer feasible to operate independently. And it isn't simply a matter of making room for all agencies, industries, governments, schools, colleges, camps, churches, and families under the umbrella of education. But rather, it is a matter of ensuring that all, either directly or indirectly, will exercise educational roles in a society that, by virtue of desire and necessity, is becoming increasingly education-centered.

(3) *The Individual-in-Society*—an integrating concept to bring individual and society into a reasonable harmony. This concept might also suggest a guideline to help avoid the potential dangers of a child-centered, individualistic culture of the West on the one hand, and that of a society-centered culture of Eastern Europe and the Soviet Union on the other. Extremes and misinterpretations in either direction can lead to distortions: the East where the welfare of the individual may suffer from the over-concern for building a better future society; or the West where social and cultural structure and the environment may suffer from the demands of egocentric individualism.

The needs of the individual, and needs of "society" may, hopefully, be integrated. We must have sufficient faith to shape a society within which individuals will have a real opportunity to achieve their unique fulfillment. At the same time, we must endeavour to produce individuals who will be motivated to contribute to a healthy society. Some of these needs that are particularly associated with education would include:

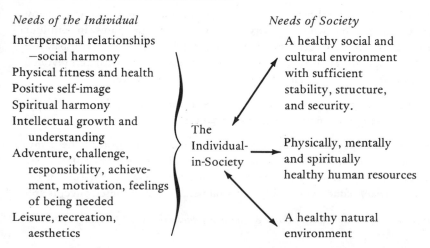

Needs of the Individual

Interpersonal relationships
—social harmony
Physical fitness and health
Positive self-image
Spiritual harmony
Intellectual growth and
  understanding
Adventure, challenge,
  responsibility, achievement, motivation, feelings
  of being needed
Leisure, recreation,
  aesthetics

The
Individual-
in-Society

Needs of Society

A healthy social and
cultural environment
with sufficient
stability, structure,
and security.

Physically, mentally
and spiritually
healthy human resources

A healthy natural
environment

We may have to re-evaluate what is growth and what is progress in individuals and in societies. Our problems and needs are not essentially on the moon, or even in getting there: that is, they are probably not even mainly technological. Our problems and needs are social and environmental, political, and economic, moral and aesthetic.

(4) *Outdoor Education*—a concept that in its practice can contribute vitally and significantly toward the fulfillment of all three concepts above. It offers the whole outdoor natural environment as a medium for education, and is limited by neither time nor space. No one segment of society, whether individual, agency, or institution, has a monopoly on either the outdoors or education. Nor does it seem that outdoor education can become the exclusive stepchild of any particular aspect of education, whether of field studies, outdoor physical pursuits, conservation, or the military.

Thus outdoor education is taking its place around the world as an increasingly important part of Continuing Education; as an increasingly important concern of a society that is growing more education-oriented; and as a vital integrative force in fulfilling both the needs of the individual and those of the society in which, for better or worse, each of us must function: that is, the integrated needs of the individual-in-society.

• • •

The rest of this article will illustrate these concepts and perspectives in outdoor education with a few examples drawn from around the world. It is impossible, of course, and even presumptuous in a short article, to try to do justice to the great diversity of programs and emphasis. However, I have tried to identify certain of these emphases as they have impressed me. None is mutually exclusive, and in trying to compartmentalize them there is inevitably an element of unfairness. However, I think it is helpful in understanding the roles of outdoor education to look at various countries, institutions and schools, as each selects from the broad spectrum of outdoor education, those emphases that seem to them, because of a particular time, interest, place or circumstance, to be of special concern.

The following examples are drawn mainly from schools, and they will not dwell upon the organizational structuring involved. As far as the schools' use of time is concerned, outdoor education around the world takes place during single or double class lessons, out-of-class time, half-days of school, full days, overnights, weekends, extended trips, and residential outdoor experiences from three days to one month.

A. *Social Emphases*—a healthy social environment

New Zealand and Australia both place priorities on social growth in their "School Camping" programs. In both countries, ten-day residential camping has evolved as the major pattern. The main emphasis is placed upon experiences in communal living and social community action, with each one pulling his weight.

The programs are typically broad and cut across the curriculum, with the activities used as means toward the social ends. Many "Down Under" educators feel that outdoor education provides a great opportunity to improve relationships between staff members as well as between staff and students. I visited one secondary school camp in New Zealand where the headmaster's role for the ten days was that of cook for his students!

In New South Wales, the camping programs are conducted both on school time and out-of-school (vacation camping) using National Fitness Camps and State Education Department camps run by the Physical Education Branch. In order to enrich the social emphasis, pupils, mainly 10-12 years old, are brought together on a quota basis from all over the State—three or four from this school, one or two from this class, with a mixing of rural and urban children. The Branch has tried everything from three days to sixteen days at camp, but found ten days best because:

(a) It takes ten days to provide time for social development and change.
(b) General fitness was found to be higher after ten days than after five days.
(c) The organization and travelling involved make it hard to justify a shorter period.

The Department of Education in New South Wales feels that camping is the Branch's "greatest selling card" and because of the overall educational values, hopes that every child will have this experience at least once. Total attendance in their eight camps was 28,000 in 1967.

Many programs in other countries also put a high, if not a top priority upon social education. For example, the Outdoor Pursuits Center in the West Riding of Yorkshire, England, brings in secondary pupils from a variety of schools for periods of ten days to three weeks. The pupils are deliberately grouped so that all in each group are "strangers." Gradually individual interests and concerns are integrated into social groups—recognizing and valuing each member of the group. Evenings are almost always devoted to social (co-educational) activities and the tables at mealtime are co-educational. The headmaster (and staff of 35) feels that three weeks is better than ten days or two weeks.

B. *Conservation Emphasis*—a healthy natural environment

In Sweden, interest and concern for the environment has risen "like an explosion" over the past five years or so. The Swedish ban on DDT and other chlorinated hydrocarbons was probably the first imposed by any country. This concern for environmental education has been reflected in the schools, as Parliament has asked the National Board of Education what they are doing in outdoor education (e.g., biology, geography). A National Board of Education Committee has been set up to study the whole matter of environmental education. Upon completion of the Committee's report and recommendations, the Board will look at the implications for curriculum change in the schools.

Likely results will include many outdoor residential schools (which Sweden does not now have) plus day trips, and much more will be done in Teacher Education. A special Nature Conservation Week for all Swedish schools was planned for September, 1969. It was reported in a Swedish magazine that conservation education was becoming as important in Sweden as sex education.

It appears that "Environmental Education" in Sweden will not include physical activities such as skiing, skating, and orienteering. Nor is it likely that these will be integrated; it is felt that school classes, "open-air" days, and the February sports holiday suffice for outdoor physical pursuits.

In Ontario, Canada, the various Regional Conservation Authorities have Educational Divisions. As part of their educational programs, some of these Authorities are providing residential facilities and other outdoor opportunities for the pupils of schools in their respective regions as cooperative projects between schools and the environment.

C. *Physical and Fitness Emphasis*—healthy human resources

Great Britain has seen a great expansion in outdoor education in the schools since 1950, through a variety of forms. This has included "Field Studies" in geography, history, biology, and latterly some "Environmental Studies" involving a more integrated approach, but the most popular and extensive development has been the growth in "Outdoor Pursuits"—for example: sailing, canoeing, rock climbing, hiking, camping, skiing, and orienteering. More and more Education Authorities are acquiring residential Outdoor Pursuits Centers for their schools, often in the rugged physical environments of North Wales, the Lake District, and parts of Scotland. These Centers cater mainly to secondary school pupils, often 14-15 years old, and encampments usually last for 10 to 12 days. One of the main aims of these centers is to introduce pupils to outdoor physical activities in preparation for leisure and recreation later.

A growing trend is noted in British schools to include outdoor pursuits as options offered within the class physical education program at the upper secondary school levels. Also, the traditional "games afternoon" each week has become much more diversified, to include outdoor pursuits that will lead to lifetime interests.

Sweden introduced its "Open-Air Days" in the 1940s. This was put into the curriculum as eight whole (school) days per academic year for all grades, to be used for outdoor physical education activities in the countryside. In 1968 the requirement was converted to hours (42 per year) to allow greater flexibility. The schools usually use one day per month, and engage in various types of skiing, orienteering, ice activities, cross country, or swimming. Russia uses a similar approach: the schools go to the country for six "Health Days" per year, and ski, swim, and hike.

France has several hundred residential camps called Vacation Camps, which are used from July to September as holiday camps for swimming, climbing, and sailing. These are also used from December to April as residential centers for ski instruction for pupils aged five years to fourteen years—the famous "Classes du Neige." School classes attend for one month, with half the day for studies indoors and half the day for ski instruction. Priority is given to city children—for example, 20 per cent of all Paris pupils attend one of these at least once in their school careers.

Several other countries provide full-time skiing weeks for secondary school pupils (e.g., Czechoslovakia, Austria 100,000 pupils per year—and Switzerland), all in school time. Some thirty-five Special Ski Schools are operated in Austria. Top skiers are taken to these at 15 years of age and continue for five years of schooling. Cross-country skiing is compulsory in Russian schools, from the third or fourth grade up, in addition to the regular physical education periods, and typically, pupils will go to parks for 3 to 5 kilometers of skiing. Besides the fitness and leisure aspects, these skills have significance in Russia for military preparedness. In Edinburgh, Scotland, 1,000 pupils per week receive year around instruction on a quarter mile long artificial ski slope made of nylon.

In Sweden, all schools have a special holiday "Sports Week" in February or early March for winter sports. Half the schools close one week, and the other half the next, or the country's sports (especially skiing) facilities would be over-run. The schools usually distribute information and brochures on what opportunities are available around the country, as the whole community gears up with special programs. The Finns also have a "Sports Holiday" of one week in the late winter, especially for skiing. Their physical education programs in schools are outdoor-oriented, both summer and winter.

Israel's physical education programs do not involve much outdoor education as yet, but all girls and boys in high school have a period per week, plus one day per month, of pre-military training—"Gadna"—in which outdoor pursuits, for example hiking, camping, fitness training, and orienteering, are stressed.

An increasing number of Physical Education Teachers Colleges around the world now take their students 850 miles to the northern mountains for two weeks of skiing in each year of the two year course. Loughborough College of Education in England take their first year physical education students for ten days to their center in Wales for rock climbing, canoeing, camping, and map work. Further opportunities are provided in second and third years for specialization in these or in sailing.

Phillip Smithells, Director of the School of Physical Education at Otago University in New Zealand has said, "To me, more of the objectives of physical education can be reached at once through camping than outdoor pursuits can help to provide this foundation for recreation, fitness, and leisure."

D. *A Positive Self-Image*—healthy human resources

Special mention should be made here of the many Outward Bound Schools and their growing influence upon education in countries such as Britain, New

Zealand, Australia, the United States, and Canada. The program was designed to help young men discover latent abilities in themselves, and extend their personalities through a 26-day period, using the mountains, the sea, or rivers and lakes as the main media. These schools direct their efforts towards Kurt Hahn's "Six Declines": the decline of Physical Fitness, Skill and Craftsmanship, Self-Discipline, Memory and Imagination, and Compassion. They try to re-focus away from modern materialism, to a humanization of the individual as part of a close-knit group.

The spirit of adventure and challenge in the outdoors lies at the heart of Outward Bound thinking, not for itself, but related to character growth. The extreme toughness for toughness' sake approach is changing to a sounder educational philosophy of enhancing the personality. Through motivation and guidance, young people are encouraged to stretch themselves, to come to believe what they are capable of when given a challenge. It is quite possible that if more of our young people were impelled into the adventure and challenge of the outdoors, they would be less likely to turn to less desirable adventurous pursuits.

E. *Intellectual or Academic Emphasis*—healthy human resources

A good example of the intellectual is the Field Studies Council Centers in Britain, with residential courses in aspects of geography, geology, botany, or zoology. The courses are often quite specialized—for example, courses on "Mosses and Lichens," "Insects," etc. Most directors of these Centers feel that in order to do the necessary depth work, they must keep specialized, and not integrate with Outdoor Pursuits. These centers cater to upper secondary school pupils as well as to any interested individual or teachers. Some Education Authorities operate their own Field Studies Centers, and there has been a slow movement to get some Field Studies into the Outdoor Pursuits Centers.

F. *Spiritual Emphasis*—healthy human resources

Many private, agency and church summer camps make deliberate efforts to provide for spiritual growth using the outdoors as an environmental stimulus. The serenity and beauty of the natural world can help to bring man back to the basic fundamentals of life, and offers a leavening influence upon spiritual relationships—between man and man, and man and God. A spiritual emphasis in all aspects of life may yet prove to be the vital catalyst essential to integrate the individual-in-society.

● ● ●

In addition to these emphases, another permeates many programs in many countries—that of using the outdoors to assist in the general education of children. These programs involve many areas of the curriculum, and embrace a cross-section of emphases. They provide a wide background of experience and motivation to present and further learning, and counter the visual emphasis of indoor education. Many school programs in the United States, Canada, Britain, and West Germany, for example, would be included here. One of the thousands of "Schullandheime" in West Germany has the following motto: "In this House, the spirit of tolerance prevails, the pupils and teachers proceed together, in work and free time, in duty and freedom, in community requirements, in experiencing the local environment, to understand our people past and present, and to give more understanding for other peoples and countries."

Integration—"Environmental Studies"

The advantages of an integrated approach to outdoor education are coming to be recognized in a variety of ways, although it is neither necessary nor desirable to "integrate" at all times. An interesting example of this approach is a trip planned by some secondary school boys from London, England, to Greenland in the summer of 1970. A team of three staff members will go—a geographer, a biologist, and a physical educator. It will be a six-weeks' trip with canoes (kayaks) used as a major means of transportation in order to move about a coastal area for field studies. The physical educator is an expert in outdoor pursuits—canoeing, hiking, camping. The geographer and the biologist (as well as the boys) are currently working with the physical educator to learn the living and travelling skills they will need in order to carry out the field studies aspects of the project.

Learning to travel and live safely in a particular outdoor environment is fundamental if broader activities are to be included in any program. Many teachers never use the outdoors for science, conservation, social, or other purposes, partly because they do not have the basics of being safely and comfortably at home in the outdoors. An integrated team approach can be an administrative asset here to the staff, as well as provide a more natural approach to pupil learning, which should not always be compartmentalized.

A new Specialist Course in "Environmental Education" planned for the I. M. Marsh Teachers' College in Liverpool reflects some of the interest in England in the integration of Outdoor Pursuits and Field Studies; i.e., not limiting the outdoor education of the pupil. The course will emphasize two mountain pursuits and two water pursuits—skiing and rock climbing, sailing and canoeing—and the geography and biology of these environments. It is hoped that these specialists would fit into schools or school systems, to assist in a team effort of teachers using the outdoors more effectively.

● ● ●

These examples, drawn from several countries, indicate the wide range of purposes and options in outdoor education. Obviously not everything can be emphasized at any one time or in any one situation. Over a period of time, pupils and adults will have increasing opportunities to experience a wide spectrum of emphases—emphases which are continually and equally sensitive to the needs of the individual, and those of his society.

FIFTY YEARS OF OUTDOOR EDUCATION IN THE FRANKFURT, GERMANY SCHOOLS *

OSWALD H. GOERING

On June 20, 1970, a large number of people interested in outdoor education met in the newly built general meeting room of the Wegscheide chapel. Their purpose was to celebrate and commemorate the 50th anniversary of the resident outdoor education center called "Schullandheimdorfes Wegscheide" (School Country Home village "Wegscheide") and the outdoor education program of the public schools of Frankfurt, Germany.

Those who attended this historic meeting on this beautiful sunny, summer day could not help be impressed with the facilities and program that were now being brought into focus. From what was once a troop training center during World War I had emerged a modern educational center. Instead of troops preparing themselves for battle and destruction, today school children are learning how to live and study harmoniously with each other in this beautiful outdoor setting.

The Wegscheide is one of the largest resident outdoor education centers in Europe, probably in the world. A total of 25-30 classes with their teachers can be in residence at the same time, being housed in sixteen different buildings. This facility is sometimes referred to as a children's village, "Kinderdorf," and one certainly gets this impression as one enters the grounds. Even though the teachers with their classes operate their programs independent from other classes, the area is organized as a village having its own mayor, post office, and church. A central kitchen prepares the food which is taken by the school children to their own houses where it is eaten.

The Wegscheide is located about an hour's drive southeast of Frankfurt in a wooded mountain area known as the "Spessart." It is surrounded by large forests and even though there may be 800-1000 people in residence at one time, one is hardly aware of them for they are usually out (in small groups) hiking and exploring in the wooded areas.

The administration of the Wegscheide can be justly proud of their facility and program. Only traces of the former uses of the area now remain and children are having much needed wholesome experiences. The Wegscheide has achieved its

*Reprinted with permission from *Journal of Outdoor Education* 5 (3):6-9, Spring 1971.

great respect because of the idealism, personal interest, and hard physical work of many people. Today it stands as a monument to their efforts.

HISTORY

1914   The German Government acquired approximately 9,000 acres near Bad Orb. This mountainous, heavily wooded area was to be used as a troop training facility. Barracks were built on the highest point of the property. Today's houses named Taunus, Spessart, and Rhonlhaus were formerly used as horse barns. Two neighboring villages, Villach and Lettgenbrunn, were evacuated and used for target practice by the artillery. Four months after its establishment, World War I broke out. The area saw much activity from then on until the defeat of the German armies. After World War I, these facilities, like many similar ones in Germany, stood empty.

1920   The war brought about much suffering in Germany. There was a shortage of food and the general physical condition of the people, particularly the children, was very poor. The superintendent of schools of Frankfurt, Rector August Jaspert, was very much concerned and began looking for an area that he could use as a children's health center. In his search he came upon the Wegscheide. During the first year it was used primarily for the underprivileged and undernourished children of Frankfurt.

1921   In this year the graduating classes of the Frankfurt public elementary schools participated in a resident outdoor education program at Wegscheide. Here they lived, worked and studied with their teachers for a full week. In 1921 a total of 6,063 students attended. This was the beginning of a program that was to grow steadily until the dark clouds of the Third Reich loomed over Germany.

1936   The wooded areas in the southern part of the Wegscheide were once more taken over by the government for military purposes. The villages of Villbach and Lettgenbrunn were again evacuated, this time to be used for target practice by the German air force.

1938   The schools were now afraid that the Nazis would want to take over all of the Wegscheide and so they transferred the ownership of the Wegscheide from the schools to that of a charitable foundation with its own board. Such charitable foundations were protected by law against confiscation.

1939   The 1938 action only delayed the take-over of the facility by the army which confiscated it in 1939. The Wegscheide now became a prisoner-of-war camp. From this time until the end of the war in 1945, prisoners from Belgium, France, Italy and Russia were interned in the places once occupied by children. Approximately a half mile south of the Wegscheide, in a quiet wooded area, is a cemetery where 1,530 Russians (victims of a typhus epidemic) are buried in a mass grave. During the war other government actions affected the boundaries of the Wegscheide, reducing it considerably in size.

1945 After the war the Wegscheide underwent another change. As the soldiers left, their places were taken by the refugees who came streaming from the eastern parts of Germany, now being taken over by Poland and the Communists. At the peak of its term as a refugee camp, there were over 3,000 refugees living there. At the west entrance of the Wegscheide is a small cemetery used by the refugees which serves as a reminder of this time. The last of the refugees did not leave the Wegscheide until 1955.

1946 One of the buildings in the valley, the Talheim (little home in the valley) was returned to be used as a children's home to be operated by the Social Affairs Administration of the city of Frankfurt.

1949 For the first time after World War II, students from the schools with their teachers again came to the Wegscheide. Some of the facilities were still occupied by the refugees.

1963 The Talheim, the house used as the children's home in the valley, was in such bad need of repair that it was decided to sell it.

1949-1969 During this period six to seven thousand students with their teachers each year come to the Wegscheide for a three-week stay. During the summer a program similar to American summer camps takes place with children from all parts of Germany, other European countries, and from as far as the U.S.A. in residence.

1970 Celebration of the 50th anniversary of the Wegscheide and its outdoor education program.

PRESENT PROGRAM

Today the Wegscheide has facilities to house and feed approximately 1,000 people. This means that from 25 to 30 classes with their teachers can be in residence at the same time. The classes come for a three-week stay in this beautiful school country home located in the heavy wooded mountain area called the Spessart. Nearby is the famous Bad Orb which is widely known as a spa for heart treatments.

The name Wegscheide translated to English means "the parting of the road." The term "Wegscheide" refers to an important crossroads, not far from the school country home, where, during the Middle Ages, two important trade routes crossed.

During their stay in the school country home, the children and their teachers together perform all of the necessary tasks required in the orderly operation of the community. Children are involved in such tasks as the cleaning and repairing of the roads as well as the daily living duties that deal with room and board. They are involved in the workings of the village and, thus, get a first hand experience in community living with peers.

The mornings are usually taken up with two-three hours of classwork and may include subjects like biology, geology, meteorology, astronomy, language, music, drawing, and sports. In the afternoons the classes usually go for walks in the woods surrounding the area. They may also go sightseeing, participate in sporting competitions, go swimming in the swimming pool, or just play or dance.

EDUCATIONAL AIMS

The Wegscheide offers an ideal situation for the development of social behavior as many classes and teachers come into close contact. Here nothing is "learned" but "experienced." Social virtues are developed through practice. The various classes join together for some activities and entertainment. Sporting events, various competitions, amateur dramatics, demonstrations and participation in dancing and singing events are jointly prepared by the pupils and staff. In these cases the classes and the various groups work together. However, each class or group is independent in its own right. It is the individual teacher who decides, in cooperation with his students, the activities and schedule for their stay at the Wegscheide. The only parts of the time schedule that must be observed by all are the meal times and bed time.

As noted above, the early primary purpose of the Wegscheide was to improve the physical and mental health of the school children. This is still important today for the children who live in the inner city. Many of the children of Frankfurt never leave the city and frequently they are said to learn a foreign language quicker than the geography of the areas nearby such as the beautiful Spessart mountains.

Years of experience have taught Frankfurt educators that the Wegscheide also offers great opportunities for educational purposes. Weeks of living and working together in a peer community, eating together, sleeping with classmates under the same roof are important educationally. There is more to be learned than the "stuff" contained in the usual courses. This realization has brought many new subjects into the school curriculum of Germany. The Wegscheide offers opportunities for study in areas which the school cannot offer such as arts and crafts, work on projects, photography, and astronomy. Opportunity to study stars is good "because one can see the stars out here in the country."

The teachers and students get some assistance from the Wegscheide staff. The help of an educational leader is available; a comprehensive library is also available to both the students and the teachers. There are well designed workrooms available. The Wegscheide also has its own infirmary with a doctor and nurse in residence. The Wegscheide has its own post office.

The time table observed by all classes in residence is as follows:

7:30 a.m.   Reveille
8:00 a.m.   Breakfast

12:00	Lunch
1:30-3:30 p.m.	Rest hour or hiking
3:00 p.m.	Coffee
6:00 p.m.	Dinner
8:00 p.m.	Evening assembly on the top of the hill
9:00 p.m.	Bedtime

SUMMER PROGRAM

During the summer the program at the Wegscheide resembles that of the summer camps in the U.S.A. Children come from all parts of Germany and from many foreign countries for either an 18 or 36 day period. Children ages 11-13 are accepted in this program. The cost is 95 German Mark ($25) for the 18 day experience and 184 DM ($50) for the 36 days.

The camp is in operation from about July 10 to August 14, with the 18-day children either terminating or beginning their experience on about July 27. The children in Frankfurt apply for admission at the schools where they are in attendance. The price includes transportation, and a special train is operated for this purpose on the days when camp opens and closes.

The children are divided into boy or girl groups of about 25 to a home under the supervision of adult teachers. The food is plentiful and tasty. The rich wooded areas offer opportunities for exciting exploration hikes. The children's village also has well constructed playgrounds. A doctor and nurse reside in their own clinic and assume the responsibilities for the health of the campers.

The Wegscheide is, as a charitable foundation, a nonprofit establishment within the administration of a nondenominational welfare organization. It is financially maintained by the city of Frankfurt am Main, and is supervised by the Department of Institutions and Foundations of Frankfurt and of the President of the Administrative District of Dormstadt.

REFERENCES

Schenk, H., "50 Jahre Frankfurter Schullandheim Wegscheide," *Das Schulland-heim*, No. 75-76, pages 31-34, Fall, 1970, Hamburg.

Glass, Theo, "Frankfurt's Kinderdorf im Spessart," *Frankfurt Lebendige Stadt*, No. 1, March 1967, Frankfurt.

Glass, Theo and Others, *Unsere Wegscheide*, Johannes Weisbecker, Frankfurt.

Stiftung Frankfurter Schullandheim Wegscheide, *The Frankfurt "Wegscheide" School Country Home*, Information Sheet, Frankfurt.

OUTDOOR EDUCATION IN DENMARK *

THOMAS SCHMIDT

An institution like the school will—if it does not consistently analyze its functions, seeing them in relation to the surrounding world—stagnate in its practices. It can imagine that it prepares the children to fulfill the obligations of society, but by virtue of its formalization and stagnation, and because society continues to develop, it actually teaches the children to serve the community of yesterday. This, presumably, is the great dilemma of the school during these years.

Should the school prepare the pupils to live in a society like the one we know? Should the school prepare the pupils to live within social systems and norms that we do not know today? Or should the school be a society in itself—the pupils here and now? Should it be an "either-or," or a "both-and?"

In the old days it was very simple: the community found its expression in the school, and the school was reflected in the community. If we interpret the demands of modern society we must give the children a school for the "here and now" as well as one preparing them to an unknown, coming society. The purpose of the school must be:

1. to develop the abilities and talents of the children, i.e., to assure their vigorous development;
2. to strengthen their character, i.e., to instill educationally appropriate attitudes;
3. to teach them useful knowledge, i.e., proficiency and knowledge that is learned functionally, thus being profitable in other connections.

Specifically, two activities, orientation and camp-school, are means by which the objectives of the school can be fulfilled, these being interpreted in the text above. The school as an institution has, as long as it has existed, been affected by both internal and external powers in an attempt to prevent stagnation.

The idea of camp-school was such an idea which has exerted its influence on the Danish public school since the early thirties.

The camp-school will for a short time move the children from the classroom and the world of books to living life and the tangible world. It does not introduce new subjects that have to be pressed into an already crowded schedule, but it takes the children out into nature, bringing them in contact with

*Reprinted with permission from *Journal of Outdoor Education* 4 (3):19-21, Spring 1970.

reality and giving the teacher means to show the connecting principles of subjects such as geography, biology, and history.

The pupils observe the surroundings, work on the observations through papers, drawings, discussions, and calculations. Books become a supplement. Meeting reality becomes the main purpose, and at times the children have fun doing healthy sports in the fresh air, living a wonderful life with friends and teachers.

However, this institution has also felt internal and external influences. Due to the development of society in the last ten or fifteen years, several teachers have been impelled to put more and different values into the excellent opportunity that a stay away from the school and its milieu implies. The camp-school now has different primary purposes than this praiseworthy objective which is to show the connection between the subjects and, in a manner of speaking, bring them down to earth. These other primary purposes have been determined by the personality of the teacher, his fields of interest, the needs of the pupils, their age and stage of development as well as various other social, educational, and psychological factors relating more or less consciously to the purpose of the school.

What primary purposes should direct a camp-school? After analyzing the description of school camps the following can be stated. These examples reflect the detailed teacher-programmed camp as well as the pupil-planned and administered camp. The examples are isolated. In practice, of course, they will overlap and mix, and combinations can and do occur.

1. *Nature oriented camp.* Purpose: to explore the connection between geographical and biological factors in nature, and to assess the consequences of human intervention.

2. *Historical camp.* Purpose: to study the historical basis for contemporary cultural, occupational, and social conditions.

3. *Social-Political camp.* Purpose: to study the connection between the existence of the individual citizen and the functions of society.

4. *Occupation-oriented camp.* Purpose: to study the individual in relation to occupation and production, to learn the process of production, and to state what factors influence this process.

5. *Economics camp.* Purpose: to practice economical and administrative responsibility through planning and management of the group economy, i.e., traveling, staying, shopping, and cooking.

6. *Music-creative camp.* Purpose: through stay in stimulating surroundings to arouse creative activities and musical ways of expression.

7. *Social camp.* Purpose: through stay in an unknown milieu to practice adjustment, understanding, acceptance, and cooperation in relation to the individuals of the unknown milieu.

8. *Education-oriented camp.* Purpose: through placement in different educational surroundings to learn the conditions of education.
9. *International camp.* Purpose: together with groups of different nationalities to encourage communication and create human contact.
10. *Work camp.* Purpose: to undertake the execution of practical and constructive work on building or rebuilding.
11. *Exercise camp.* Purpose: through physical training to feel the necessity and well-being of physical care of the body accomplished either by hiking or gymnastic exercises.
12. *Group dynamics camp.* Purpose: to acknowledge one's own place and function in the group, and the influence exercised on others and one's self.
13. *"Have a good time" camp.* Purpose: in pleasant surroundings to associate with friends, relaxed and without obligations.
14. *Observation camp.* Purpose: to give the teachers the opportunity to observe the attitude and behavior of the pupils, concerning the application of appropriate study methods. This makes it possible for teachers to place the pupils at a level where they can fulfill their requirements.

It is obvious that the arranged purposes are not always accomplished satisfactorily, neither is the profit achieved always identical with the one expected. Analyzing the course of a camp might perhaps explain this. One thing is certain, camps are an educational necessity in our accelerated time.

Specific local arrangements are different but several problems have to be taken into consideration. Influential factors are time, duration, place, subsidy, supply of teachers, number of camp-leaders, and wages. The problems will be illustrated for the Copenhagen area.

Camps are usually placed in the spring or fall-terms. The application to the granting authorities is sent in about one month before the time of the camp stating the number of persons participating and the purpose of the camp. Possibly an application to the Danish Railways for free transportation is enclosed.

Usually the authorities grant only one camp a year in seventh, eighth, ninth, and tenth grade; if more camps are wanted the funds must be provided by the children and the teachers themselves. A camp-school usually lasts 8 or 9 days, occasionally divided into periods of 2 or 3 days. The estimated grants cover room and board at a youth-hostel, various entrance-fees, and transportation excluding Danish Railways. At the moment the amount is about $3 a day for each person. If the camp-school takes place abroad the subsidy is only $1 a day, because this is considered more as a "have a good time" camp than as a relevant part of the education.

Among the teachers the attitude towards camp-schools is often faltering. One of the reasons given is that teachers do not get a bonus for undertaking the work-load of preparing, accomplishing and ending a camp, though this is a job that demands attention 24 hours a day. This attitude is, however, slowly changing.

Every camp consisting of both boys and girls must have a man as well as a woman teacher, while it is not always considered necessary to bring along a matron if only boys are attending.

The places most frequently used for camps are holiday-settlements, of which Copenhagen has about 60 distributed all over the country. In addition youth-hostels are frequently used, these often being specialized in receiving schools. However, we have a very wide selection, as we are granted means to rent the cottages of other schools. This gives us a varied and more profitable program every year to the delight of both pupils, teachers and parents, who afterwards are often invited to watch films, pictures and exhibitions, and to listen to reports on the camp-school.

THE FIELD STUDIES COUNCIL (ENGLAND) *

J. D. CARTHY

Thoughts of what the postwar world would be like were uppermost in the minds of Francis Butler, Dr. Eric Ennion and Professor Tansley when they determined in 1943 to establish what was then called the Council for the Promotion of Field Studies. Their intention was to provide living accommodation for anyone who wished to study any aspect of the environment. The first Centre was established in 1945 on the Suffolk bank of the river Stour at Flatford Mill near Colchester in the beautiful buildings once owned by the uncle of the great painter John Constable. A Warden was in charge, a person with a wide knowledge of natural history who could aid any visitor with information about the surroundings.

But in the postwar period two things became obvious, firstly that it was unlikely that Centres of this sort could be run economically and, secondly, that a greatly increased interest in field studies was being demonstrated by schools and universities. It was plain that the sort of practical experience given by courses in the field would become an essential part of teaching biology, geography and geology. Nothing could have been more obvious than that the Council should supply the facilities for these studies, transforming itself into the more frankly educational organization. Today the Council has nine Centres in which last year 15,000 students stayed for one week courses.

From the first the Council, renamed the Field Studies Council in 1955, has

*Reprinted with permission from *Journal of Outdoor Education* 4 (3):15-18, Spring 1970.

remained independent of the Governmental Education system. It is a charity and finds its funds almost entirely from the fees paid by the students. For about ten years the then Ministry of Education made an annual grant but this ceased in 1964. The great majority of the students are supported by their Local Education Authorities, receiving their fees and travelling expenses in full or in part; in this way the Council may be said to be indirectly aided by the State educational system. A number of Trusts and Foundations, such as the Carnegie Trust, the Drapers' Company, the Pilgrim Trust, and the Goldsmiths' Company, have made grants to the Council for specific projects, most of them buildings.

The Centres are as follows, in order of their opening:

Flatford Mill Field Centre, East Bergholt, near Colchester, Essex. (1946)
Malham Tarn Field Centre, near Settle, Yorkshire. (1947)
Juniper Hall Field Centre, Dorking, Surrey. (1947)
Dale Fort Field Centre, Haverfordwest, Pembrokeshire. (1947)
Preston Montford Field Centre, near Shrewsbury, Shropshire. (1957)
Slapton Ley Field Centre, Slapton, Kingsbridge, Devonshire. (1959)
Orielton Field Centre, near Pembroke, Pembrokeshire. (1963)
The Drapers' Field Centre, Rhyd-y-Creuau, Betwys-y-Coed, Caernarvonshire. (1967)
The Leonard Wills Field Centre, Nettlecombe Court, Williton, Taunton, Somerset. (1968)
The Epping Forest Conservation Centre built by the Corporation of the City of London in the Forest for which it is responsible on the North-Eastern edge of the capital. This will be wholly managed by the Field Studies Council and will be its first day-centre.

The typical Centre is a house large enough to house about 60 students and some 10 members of staff (4 teaching, 6 domestic and administrative), with the necessary domestic arrangements, laboratories, and a library. As the Centres serve a range of ages, dormitories are avoided and as far as possible no more than four people are allocated to a room. There are, however, rather fewer single rooms at the existing Centres than we would like to have.

Each is under the direction of a Warden assisted by three other teaching staff. These people are all graduates in biology, geography, or geology; some with previous experience of teaching in school, others coming direct from University. On the domestic side, there are at least three permanent staff who are supported during the season by temporary staff, both students from Britain and girls from other countries in Europe.

Many of the Centres are near sites of great natural and scientific interest. The house by Malham Tarn, in which Kingsley wrote part of "The Water Babies," is a good example. It is on a carboniferous limestone plateau on the Yorkshire Pennines, not far from the famous features of Malham Cove and Gordale Scar.

Karstic features are shown here better than anywhere else in Britain. The Tarn itself has interesting features as a calcareous lake with an abundant fauna of fish and invertebrates, as well as breeding birds such as grebe. The first Centre to be purpose-built was The Drapers' Field Centre, situated on the edge of the Snowdonia National Park of North Wales, an area renowned for its biological and geological interest.

In all the Centres courses last from Wednesday to Wednesday. They commence at the beginning of March, the season lasting until the end of October. There are three main groups of courses: those taught by the Centre Staff (Centre-taught); those run by teachers from schools, universities, and colleges for their own students (independent); and those taught by a specialist invited by the Warden to come and run a course (specialist). The subjects range widely; they are mainly ecological and geographical but in addition courses on art and archaeology are popular. An increasing number of younger children are taken on general environmental study courses. During the 1969 season, the breakdown of students by subjects was as follows:—

Biology	8,458
General and Environmental Studies	419
Geography and Geology	6,076
Art	407
Archaeology	203
Others	204

A large proportion of the students come from schools; they are aged about 16-17 years and are taking their course for the Advanced Level of the General Certificate of Education. Many of the examining boards responsible for this Certificate encourage field studies for those taking a biological or geographical subject; some insist on this kind of work. Other courses are arranged for students from Colleges of Education—the teachers of the future—and for teachers who are in service. University students constitute another group. Finally there is a steady proportion provided by amateurs who come on courses out of interest and not necessarily with any previous knowledge of the subject. The distribution of students in 1969 into these categories was as follows:

"A" Level	10,254
Other forms	268
Colleges of Education and Teachers	2,378
Universities	1,474
Amateurs	1,153

The pattern of a course is one of daily field work after a short introduction to the work for that day. Then in the field students are encouraged to measure and count, to collect figures rather than specimens (of either living things or rocks).

The potentially harmful effect of taking students weekly to particular sites is well realized, and the fact that other groups, not staying at the Centre, also visit these places makes it the more essential that the greatest care is taken not to damage the environment. After returning to the Centre, the students write up their results and carry out experiments to test hypotheses which they have put forward during the day. The results for the day are drawn together by lecture and discussion in order to put them into the broader picture of the concept of ecology, or of the origins of landforms or whatever it may be that the students are studying. It is often difficult to get students to stop work in the evening; they frequently show diligence which amazes their teachers. In essence an ecological course will consist of the study in some depth of living communities, considering the distribution of animals and plants, the environmental factors, variation and adaptation, the structure of the communities, and productivity and energy flow. A geographical course will include maps and map use, investigation of the landscape both from the physical and cultural aspects, study of the environment as a whole, and introductions to special techniques. Implicit in all courses is the recognition of the problems raised by man's use of the natural environment and the importance of conservation and planning.

It is rare for courses to be repeated two weeks running for changes in weather and season demand alterations. The variety of courses held in any Centre is indeed very great, for in addition to these main courses there are many others dealing with, for example, population dynamics of sea-birds or estuarine fish, spiders, weather and plants, even mathematics and physics out-of-doors are just a few subjects. This is to say nothing of industrial archaeology, stained glass, and flower painting. Generally at least two and often three different courses are going on in a Centre at one and the same time with the students mixing and gaining the bonus of educating each other.

Staff courses are held annually to which research workers and teachers are invited to talk and to lead field expeditions in order that the Council's teaching staff can be kept up-to-date with new trends, not only in their science but also in teaching method and syllabus content.

While the Council is essentially a teaching organization, members of staff are encouraged to do research; a good teacher with a deep and personal interest in a particular problem can excite students into a realization of what investigation means and show them the kind of question they ought to be asking of the environment. Therefore a number of members of staff are registered for higher degrees. The Council's annual publication "Field Studies" is a scientific journal of high standing which provides a place for the publication of this and other work concerning the areas around the Centres.

However, thanks to grants given by the Natural Environmental Research Council, the Institute of Petroleum, and the World Wildlife Fund, it has been possible to employ staff whose work is purely research. In this way the interesting distribution of plants of the Breidden Hills near Shrewsbury is being studied, and a very active Oil Pollution Research Unit which concerns itself with oil and intertidal life is based on the Orielton Field Centre. Though not intended as teachers, all these research workers have been swept into teaching where their special skills make valuable contributions.

A new venture is the Epping Forest Conservation Centre, to deal on a daily basis with large numbers of younger children (9-14) from schools in the surrounding areas, as well as older school students. It will also provide a place for student teachers to practice their craft as well as furnish accommodation for people who wish to work on the many conservation problems which loom very large in a natural area like this so close to London. Amateur naturalists will be able to use the Centre and its library, and their meetings will be welcomed in the lecture theatre. A permanent exhibition on conservation will be there for the public to see and an information desk will be manned throughout the day. A nearby Forest Museum will be integrated into a general scheme to inform the general public about the Forest which they have come to enjoy. The opening of the Centre will be one of the major events in the British contribution to European Conservation Year 1970.

The prospect in Britain of greatly increased numbers of students in sixth forms and in higher education means that inevitably the Council will have to expand in the years to come. This must be so despite the fact that there are at the moment 186 other residential centres in Great Britain run mainly by local authorities. The demand for field work at all ages is already very great. Indeed, it cannot be met and it will grow. We hope that the Council will continue the role it has made for itself, that of initiator and leader of outdoor teaching in this country.

OUTDOOR PURSUITS WITH EDUCATIONALLY SUB-NORMAL PUPILS IN NORTHUMBERLAND COUNTY, ENGLAND *

GEORGE H. SLEE AND ORVILLE E. JONES

The County of Northumberland Education Committee operates nine residential field study and expedition centers and three hostels that can be used by county schools, colleges and youth associations for outdoor activities. Experience in a variety of activities for pupils of different levels of ability is

*Reprinted with permission from *Journal of Outdoor Education* 5 (3):13-15, Spring 1971.

provided from Monday to Friday of each week, while colleges and youth groups, in addition to schools, use the premises and equipment on the weekends. In the field study and expedition centers, generally, each group operates under supervision of the Center Warden, but some groups develop and carry out their own program of activities. The hostels are used during the week by school groups which provide their own staff and program and on weekends by youth associations.

In the paragraphs which follow is a description of one of the most interesting outdoor pursuits programs carried on under auspices of the Education Committee, that provided by Gallowhill Hall Residential School, which has 80 educationally subnormal boys aged 9-16.[1] Because Gallowhill is isolated from any community, school authorities became concerned three years ago about the lack of social integration afforded the boys, particularly with reference to leisure time adjustment in the period immediately following the leaving of school. Evidence seemed to indicate that even when there was a Youth Club available to the youth after leaving the school, few were able to take part in club activities without being the "odd-one-out." With this concern in mind, the school authorities introduced the Duke of Edinburgh Scheme and Scouting Program into the school curriculum and enlisted the cooperation of the Chief Constable. He made available to the school a number of Police Cadets who assisted in expedition training one afternoon each week.

At this time, George Slee, the County Principal Organizer of Outdoor Pursuits, recommended to the school head teacher a twelve-month program. Experiences to be provided the older boys aged 13-15 years during this period of time included basic movement and way finding, rock climbing and canoeing, campcraft and outdoor living, and half-day and one-day expeditions. He also recommended that the group spend one week at each of four field study and expedition centers located in different environments. The experiences and training provided at each of these centers would lay the foundation for future leisure time skill and attitude development. Attendance at a center was in a group of 12 boys, a teacher, and two police cadets. Structuring of the program at the center was the duty of the Center Warden.

Between visits to the various centers, the boys received training on the school grounds and in the local environment one day per week and during some weekends. Any special clothing and equipment needed by the boys was provided by the school. The twelve-month program culminated in a standing camp in the Border Forest which is located near the Kielder Center. This was the first time the boys had camped away from the school.

---

[1]Children unable to take advantage of education in the normal schooling—e.g., emotionally disturbed, poor home circumstances, broken homes, uncoordinated physically, etc.

The Gallowhill staff indicated that improvement in technical skill demonstrated by the boys was noteworthy, and the increase in self-confidence remarkable. Effect on behavior in the school was highlighted since discipline became less of a problem. Many boys found new interests, previously unknown to them.

Subsequent to this initial twelve-month experimental program, additional activities have been introduced. These are discussed below.

Accident Procedures: Close to the Gallowhill School is a typical moorland/ crag area. The basic skills of first aid are practiced in a real situation, and realistic accident procedures evolve and are developed. Practice with a Thomas stretcher led the school to design and build its own rescue stretcher for use in the school base area. This experience helped the boys to work together as a team and created an awareness of the need to care for others in a potentially dangerous area.

Rock Climbing: The school has no gymnasium, but use of the afforested grounds created an outdoor gym. A quarry on the grounds was cleared of undergrowth and vegetation. Top rope climbing was initiated. Basic rock climbing techniques were taught and short climbs introduced. Safety ropes were used at all times. Not only did the boys increase their manipulative skills, they also increased their appreciation of the trust and interdependence between rope mates.

Sailing: The boys from Gallowhill were introduced to sailing in 1968 at Derwent Reservoir, which is situated on the Northumberland Durham Border south of Hexham, when a new member of the staff with sailing experiences was appointed. There has been increasing interest in this activity. At the present, 12 boys each session enjoy sailing.

Canoeing: Close to the school is Bolam Lake, and it is used during the outdoor activity days for canoeing. Initially four canoe kits were available for use and three boys received instruction each week. (The fleet has been increased to eight.) Part of the winter activity included instruction in the construction of canoes. A BAT mould was hired, and as of this date nine canoes have been built and made available for instruction and practice.

Skiing: Eight boys and one leader have regular training sessions on the county artificial ski slope. This group travelled to Norway in January, 1971 to take part in the Education Ski Venture along with 200 other children who follow a program of ski training, local study, and Anglo-Norwegian social activities. Since the inception of these activities, several members of the staff have gained certification in the respective skills. These have provided additional opportunities for boys in the school, and have broadened the range of opportunities.

In closing it seems imperative to the authors that one testimonial about the value of the outdoor pursuits program at Gallowhill should be provided the readers.

Headmaster E. O. Williams said:

Since embarking on the outdoor pursuits programme much progress has been made particularly with the more disturbed pupil. As has already been mentioned, the original motive was to give the Special School child an opportunity on leaving school to pursue leisure time activities with other pupils in his age group. Inevitably, because of lack of social courage, the Special School child fears to join youth centres and other youth activities, and in order to compensate his inefficiency in this field his attitude tends to become antisocial.

In simple terms what we are trying to do is to provide the means for a boy to gain these skills and so enjoy the opportunities afforded in the County area. The confidence gained and the therapy these pursuits have provided, have reflected in academic work, for the happier and more stable the personality, the more the incentive to improve in all fields. The pupil's outlook has naturally been broadened beyond that of his own school community which can so very often be a false community.

What the programme has done with the excellent support of the County Authority and its advisory staff, is to open up new horizons of pleasurable activities enabling our boys to partake as fully as they are able in a purposeful life both in and out of school. A lad is able to gain achievement in such skills as mentioned without the traditional academic barriers. Achievement breeds confidence.

. . . The benefits to the child, and the results in achievement will undoubtedly be beyond many traditional educationalists' hopes.

OUTDOOR TEACHER EDUCATION
IN NEW ZEALAND *
DUDLEY WILLS AND E. A. SCHOLER

In New Zealand, outdoor education includes field trips for biology, ecology, and similar types of classes, farm visits, and school camping and is a rapidly expanding area of education.

The training of educators in this area, however, has not yet been accepted as an integral part of the teacher training curricula. Whereas some institutions in the United States have been able to initiate such teacher training programs, New Zealand must rely on existing teacher training programs, workshops, and institutes presented by the Physical Education Branch of the Department of Education.

All students majoring in Social Studies at any of the teachers' colleges in New Zealand are required to do field work that is closely allied to outdoor education.

*Reprinted with permission from *Journal of Outdoor Education* 5 (3):10-12, Spring 1971.

These field experiences consist of trips to various places of historical, archeological, and current interest. They may be for a period as long as two weeks. Comprehensive notes are kept together with all information concerning the sites visited.

Some of these students also spend what is termed a "section," consisting of ten days, at one of the outdoor education centers or school camps. While in attendance the students assist with different groups and understudy members of the staff so as to have a working knowledge of actual camp procedures. After the experience, the students return to classrooms to present evaluation and critique of their experiences.

Currently, practice is to conduct an in-service training session for the teachers whose classes are scheduled to attend encampments at the outdoor education centers during the school year. These in-service training camps are conducted by specialists from the Physical Education Branch, Department of Education, with assistance from additional experts as required for a comprehensive camp program. These sessions provide on-the-site training as the teachers organize and operate their own camps with the assistance of these specialists. The latter are available to teach a variety of outdoor skills which the teachers will need to use in their camps later during the school year. Through these in-service training periods the Physical Education Branch has been able to develop a corps of well-qualified teachers capable of operating their own camps with specialists in a stand-by role. Trained specialists, however, are the only personnel used for the more rugged camping experiences in the bush.

The only other training for outdoor education is that given in certain courses offered by colleges and universities. Four schools offer such training: Auckland Secondary Teachers College, Christchurch Secondary Teachers College, Deinedin Teachers College, and the University of Otago School of Physical Education. In all four institutions outdoor education is a segment of the regular physical education course of study. The inclusion of this training is primarily dependent on the interest of the individuals responsible for curriculum development.

For many years the staff of the University of Otago School of Physical Education has been vitally interested in outdoor education and camping as well as physical fitness. Philip Smithells, Director of the School, emphasizes the camping experience in the school's curriculum in this statement: "Through camping . . . we feel that more of the aims of physical education can be reached *at one time* than through any medium of which we know. . . ."

Every Otago student must attend at least one camp during his time in the School of Physical Education. While development of physical education skills is the primary objective of the camp, the following is noted in the syllabus for campcraft certification: "In New Zealand we have nature in greater available abundance than most anywhere in the world, but there are many who are barely aware of it, and many others who desecrate it as any camping ground or beauty spot shows. Through camping we hope to change this picture."

Campcraft certification includes units on water supplies, maps and compass, bush craft (survival techniques), first aid, facilities and equipment, recreation, nature study (including flora, fauna, geology, geography, stars, and weather), and perhaps most important, the unit dealing with the integration of outdoor education into general education.

The primary purpose of the typical school camp program in New Zealand is to provide opportunity for students and teachers to live together in a special environment and to share the unique experiences offered by this environment. This experience of living, planning, working and enjoying experiences together undergrids the whole camp program. However, since the camps are held during the school year, there is a major emphasis on the educational role of the camp program. The Program allows sufficient time for a variety of recreation activities, but the main program themes are concerned with the learning experiences in this environment.

These include:

I. Bushcraft
   A. Camp Crafts—back packing; fires and fire lighting; clothing and equipment; safety precautions; first aid; food preparation; tent pitching.
   B. Survival Skills—bush travel and navigation; hazards of the outdoors; shelter; living off the land; what to do if lost.
   C. Map Reading, Compass Work, Orienteering—This is introduced at appropriate levels and culminated in field competition in which teams find their way across country.
   D. Elementary Climbing—An introduction to simple climbing skills.
II. Natural Science
   Local plants; animals; conservation; forestry; farming; weather; ecology; collections.
III. Language
   Diaries; logs; stories; camp magazine; letters home; reports.
IV. Social Studies
   The locality, its development, population, production, economy, people.
V. Health Education
   Camp sanitation; preventing illness; water supply; nutrition; first aid.
VI. Music and Drama
   Camp songs, concerts; evening entertainment.
VII. Field Mathematics
   The application of measurement to local terrain.
VIII. Physical Education
   Swimming; games; confidence courses; hikes; fitness for survival.
IX. Private Study
   Time is provided for students to write up their diaries, read, study the natural science collections or discuss experiences.

Though great attention is given to what may be learned *in* the outdoor environment, it should be emphasized that in New Zealand learning *through* these experiences is of even greater significance. Camping is a special climate for learning and program planners take advantage of this, but the important learnings are associated with being together, cooperation, self-reliance, thinking, planning, doing, and sharing. These experiences are truly educational for they bring about changes in the habits and attitudes of the students that can have a profound effect on their lives.

Back in the classroom, the astute teacher has several months of fascinating work awaiting his eager class. The natural science and environmental studies can be continued and developed; further language work around camp themes will be accepted eagerly; camp music and drama will come alive again and a highlight will be the class presentation and demonstration for parents.

This small country of only 2¾ million people has made tremendous strides in the development of outdoor education as an integral part of the school curriculum. Teacher education is quite specific and is directly related to the needs of the teachers who will be working with programs at the outdoor education centers. Of special interest is the supportive help available from specialists. These include not only those from the Physical Education branch of the Department of Education but agencies and clubs such as the Mountain club of New Zealand and the National Park Board. The majority of teachers have been exposed to basic environmental concepts in their training and enjoy sharing a knowledge and appreciation of the New Zealand countryside with their pupils through an integration of education skills.

AUSTRALIA ADOPTS SCHOOL CAMPING *

H. C. GIESE

Despite the excellent conditions which exist in all states in Australia for the development of camping facilities and the fact that youth organizations and kindred groups have long recognized the value of camping in their training and recreational programs, camping as an integral part of the school program is of only recent development in the Australian education scene. As a result, facilities for school camping are still at a stage where only a very small proportion of Australian school children can obtain camping experience.

Further developments must necessarily be viewed in relation to the require-

*Reprinted by permission of the publisher, the American Association of Health, Physical Education, and Recreation, from the *Journal of Health, Physical Education, Recreation* 23:16-18, November, 1952.

ments of State Education Departments for more school buildings and facilities to provide for an increasing school age population, to extend both the school-entering and school-leaving ages, to decrease the number of children in the classroom unit, and also to meet the backlog of developmental works occasioned by the war and the immediate postwar years. For these reasons the growth of school camps in Australia over the next decade will not be as spectacular as some enthusiasts would desire.

HOW SCHOOL CAMPING BEGAN

In 1937, a Director of Physical Education was appointed in New South Wales. One of the first tasks which he undertook in planning for the development of a comprehensive program of physical education was the selection of suitable areas for subsequent development as school and youth camps. The New South Wales Department of Education, in accepting the full implications of a modern physical education program, was the first education department in Australia to accept the principle of school camping and to plan and establish facilities which would enable large numbers of children to have this experience as part of their school program. Further impetus to the school camping movement in this state and also generally throughout Australia, was given in 1941 by (a) the allocation of funds to State National Fitness Councils for the development of permanent camp facilities; and (b) the allocation of a portion of the National Fitness grant to State Education Departments for the conduct of school camps.

After World War II, some Education Departments (Western Australia and Victoria) took over military camp establishments which they adapted for use as school camps.

At the present time all State Education Departments in Australia have accepted the principle of school camping as a part of the school program and, within the limits of facilities and staff, are operating camps on a part- or full-time basis.

New South Wales has five camps, two of them operating on a year-round basis, while the Health and Recreation Camp at Queenscliff (Victoria) and the Bellerive Camp (Tasmania) also operate on a year-round basis with permanent staff in residence. In the other states (Queensland, Western Australia, and South Australia), where school camps operate at present only intermittently by arrangements between the State National Fitness Council and the Education Department, National Fitness Camps are used for this purpose. (See Table 1.)

ORGANIZATION OF THE CAMPS

The only camps which were planned and built as school camps are those in New South Wales, and these would not lose by comparison with school camps in any other country in the world from the points of view of location, environ-

TABLE 1

Permanent National Fitness and State Education Departments Camps in Australia

Name of Camp	Control	Where Located	Present Capacity
New South Wales			
Broken Bay	Nat'l Fitness Council	Seaside	200
Point Wolstoncroft	Nat'l Fitness Council	Lakeside	100
Lennox Heads	Nat'l Fitness Council	Seaside	120
Narrabeen	Nat'l Fitness Council	Lakeside	30
Commodore Heights	Nat'l Fitness Council	Seaside	50
Victoria			
Mt. Evelyn	Nat'l Fitness Council	Country	100
Queenscliffe	Education Dept.	Seaside	100
Queensland			
Burleigh Heads	Nat'l Fitness Council	Seaside	600
Yeppoon	Nat'l Fitness Council	Seaside	50
Lamington	Nat'l Fitness Council	Country	50
Hartley's Creek	Nat'l Fitness Council	Seaside	120
Magnetic Island	Nat'l Fitness Council	Seaside	50
South Australia			
Mylor	Nat'l Fitness Council	Country	50
Christie's Beach	Nat'l Fitness Council	Seaside	50
Western Australia			
Point Peron	Nat'l Fitness Council	Seaside	100
Brickley	Nat'l Fitness Council	Country	50
Albany	On loan from Comm. Dept. of Health	Seaside	50
Esperance	On loan from Goldfields Fresh Air League	Seaside	50
Tasmania			
Bellerive	Education Dept.	Seaside	100
Collinsvale	Nat'l Fitness Council	Country	20

ment, staffing, facilities, and layout. Problems of organization and administration, particularly in relation to preparation of food, dining and recreation facilities, and arrangement of educational programs, are greater in camps in other states where military camp establishments or other buildings have had to be adapted for this purpose.

With the differences in education method and practice among the various states, it is understandable that there is no uniform pattern as to the nature of the camps. Camps in New South Wales and Victoria are either boys' or girls' camps; in other states, boys and girls are brought into the one camp. There is little doubt on the one hand that segregation into boys' and girls' camps does minimize organization and staff problems; but it is felt by some authorities that this gain is offset by loss of valuable social training.

AGE GROUPS

There is no standard procedure in Australia at the present time as to the ages of children to be brought into camp, each state having developed its practice to meet its particular needs and conditions.[1]

In Western Australia, complete one-teacher school units (three or four schools at a time), principally from remote country areas, with teachers and in some cases parents also, are brought into camp. Tasmania follows a somewhat similar practice, concentrating on the small schools from rural areas and bringing in teachers and parents as well. With the few camps that have been held in Queensland, children have been brought for the most part from the far southwest (Charleville and Goondiwindi) to the Burleigh Heads National Fitness Camp. In 1950 a plan was approved to bring some 800 children between the ages of 11 and 14 into eight school camps. These children are drawn principally from remote small schools and from correspondence classes.

It can be appreciated, from this brief statement, that the pattern, already clearly indicated in these states of concentrating on the needs of rural children and particularly those from remote country areas, will continue to be followed.

In Victoria and New South Wales, on the other hand, children brought into camps are between the ages of 10 and 14 years, and, as far as possible, country and metropolitan children are mixed in the one camp.

CAMP PROGRAMS

One would expect some variation in the nature of the programs conducted in the various states. All states make provision for a considerably expanded physical education program, including swimming, and for nature studies, bush crafts, and handicrafts associated with the camp environment. Some reference is made to the study of ordinary school subjects in Victoria, Queensland, Western Australia and, in at least one state (Western Australia), the morning session is given over to these studies.

The objectives of camp programs generally are to assist the child to (a) learn to swim and master elementary watermanship skills; (b) if the child can swim, obtain suitable graded life-saving awards; (c) master the technique of two bush

---

[1]No uniform pattern has been arrived at in Great Britain as to the ages at which children should be brought into camp for the experience to be most effective.

crafts (map reading, compass bearing, fire-making, camping out, etc.); (d) obtain a knowledge of local flora and fauna; and (e) continue his experience in handicrafts, particularly those associated with the camp environment.

HEALTHY LIVING AND SOCIAL TRAINING

It is now generally recognized that among the most important objectives of the school camp program should be the inculcation of sound habits and attitudes towards healthy living. The whole of the camp program and environment is directed towards this end. There are also opportunities in the well-planned camp program for experiences in community living which should foster a spirit of service and fellowship, for training in shared duties and responsibilities, and for the development of resource and initiative. In effect, the camp can provide group and individual experiences which can make a valuable contribution to education in citizenship. Those in charge of school camps in Australia are fully aware of these values in the camp program, and are gradually convincing the educational administrator that the camp program should not attempt to reproduce the normal school program enriched in certain areas, but should build up its own curriculum based on social training, physical and health education, nature studies, bush crafts (orienteering), and handicrafts.

HEALTH AND DENTAL INSPECTIONS

It is general practice at all school camps to have a school nurse in attendance for routine and emergency cases. In those states where children are being brought from remote country areas and even inner industrial areas, there does seem a splendid opportunity for carrying out a thorough health (including medical and dental) examination and, in cases where treatment is of short duration, treatment also.

If all children in the 10 to 11 or 12 years age-group are eventually to be brought into camp, it is reasonable to expect that during this period they might be given one of their school medical and dental examinations. Under existing conditions, this service could very readily be put into operation. The camps could then, with every justification, be called "Health and Recreation" Camps.

There is some evidence to suggest that, in several states (Western Australia and Queensland in particular), where limited services in this connection have been developed, the next few years will see some striking developments in the provision of medical and dental services in camps.

EXTENSION OF EXISTING FACILITIES

At the present time camp facilities in all except one state are being used to their fullest extent. The addition of new and improved facilities would in several

TABLE 2

Additional School Camps Required

Name of State	Approximate Number of Children 10 Years of Age	Approximate Number of Additional Camp Units (200 Campers) Required
New South Wales	36,000	12
Victoria	22,000	8
Queensland	16,000	6
South Australia	9,000	2
Western Australia	8,000	2
Tasmania	4,000	1

states enable additional children to be catered for, but would not make a substantial change in the present situation.

It is quite obvious, for reasons noted earlier, that the building of new camps will, in the future, be a slow process. This should not, however, preclude the possibility of making plans for further development of the scheme.

Bearing in mind the fact that there is now fairly general acceptance that camping experience should be obtained in the period 10-12 years of age, it would appear that consideration in the future will be given to offering this experience in any one year to all 10-year-olds, or 11-year-olds, or 12-year-olds. Experiments and observation over the next two or three years in existing camps might indicate which of these ages is the most suitable for this experience.

If this principle is accepted, additional school camps will be required in the various states as indicated in Table 2. The figures for the numbers of camps required are based on a camp period of 21 days,[2] which means that over a school year it should be possible to conduct at least twelve full period camps. On this basis, and with camp units of 200 campers, which are now regarded both from economic and administrative points of view as being the most suitable units, it should be possible for each camp to handle approximately 2,400 children each year. It is on this basis that the future needs of each state in this connection have been assessed.

TRAINING OF TEACHERS

At the present time, in states where school camps are in operation, teachers

---

[2]It is suggested that at least 21 days is required, if the camp experience is to be socially and physically effective.

with special training in physical education are appointed to the specialist staff. As has been noted earlier, it is the practice in some states for general teachers to come in with the children. When this occurs, any special abilities which such teachers may have are used in the camp program.

A strong case can be made out in favor of using the teacher trained in physical education as the basis of the specialist camp staff. This will apply more particularly when physical education courses have been extended to four years and more emphasis has been placed on this aspect of education during such training courses.

SUMMARY

School camping, as a part of the educational program, has, in the short period of a decade, made a significant contribution to the Australian education scene, and must be regarded as an important achievement of the National Fitness Movement. If developments along the lines foreshadowed in this article can be continued, there is no doubt that school camping will play a major part in assisting in promoting the health and well-being of Australian youth.

AMBASSADORS ON SKIS *
WILLIAM B. LEE

Ambassadors on skis? Why not? What could be a more accurate description of American boys and girls studying, skiing, eating, playing, and sharing life for two weeks with French children in a French Alpine community?

The French call the program Classe de Neige, literally class in the snow, and the fortunate Americans are sixth graders attending the Department of Defense Dependents Schools in France, those for children of military personnel.

The French inaugurated the Classe de Neige in 1953 as a fresh air program with less than 100 students from Paris. This year, more than 40,000 children from all parts of France will participate in what must be the most extensive program of outdoor education in the world.

Americans joined the program in 1962 with 50 students from two schools, and this winter more than 800 students from 14 schools will participate.

One American and one French class, each of about thirty youngsters, share an

*Reprinted by permission of the publisher, the American Association of Health, Physical Education, and Recreation, from the *Journal of Health, Physical Education, Recreation* 37:39, 61, March, 1966.

approved hotel situated in one of the many villages scattered throughout the French Alps. Often the village selected is isolated from major ski areas and would normally be closed during January and February were it not for the Classe de Neige. To be selected, the hotel must provide adequate sleeping and study facilities, meet exacting standards of cleanliness, and serve wholesome food.

Pencils, paper, and selected texts are transported to the hotel where regular classes are held six mornings a week in an improvised classroom, often the lobby of the hotel. Quite naturally instruction centers around the immediate experiences of the youngsters. The first English lesson assigned is a letter home recounting the train journey or bus trip and telling of arriving safely. The second might be to describe the hotel, the mountains, or a snowflake, and the next to interview the village priest, the mayor, or the student's favorite French friend. The best of the writing is compiled in a class newspaper, a record to be shared with parents and a souvenir to be enjoyed in future years.

Mountain topography and its varied life furnish rich raw materials for science lessons. The students find it particularly interesting to study and compare the differences between Alpine flora and fauna and those near the base or in their home states.

Students receive ample opportunities to know and participate in the panorama of village life: To observe the skimaker, to marvel at the woodcarver, to watch cheese being produced, to purchase souvenirs at the general store, and to browse in the local museum.

Every afternoon on a slope near the hotel, the youngsters practice the ancient Alpine sport of skiing. The instructors, licensed from the Ecole de Ski Francais, very seldom speak English, obliging the highly motivated children to assimilate quickly the basic ski vocabulary in French. With daily intensive practice, ski progress is more rapid than one would anticipate, and at the end of the two-week period, many earn certificates for skiing skill. When comparing American and French children, the instructors rate the Americans as daredevils.

Perhaps the most meaningful experiences grow out of the continual personal contacts with French boys and girls. Meals are eaten together and present an informal setting for the appreciation and absorption of cultural diversity. The Americans are surprised that the French do not drink milk for breakfast, but soon learn that this is compensated by eating cheese at the end of a meal, and if breakfast is not as copious as an American one, supper is later and snacks more frequent.

After dinner, programs feature birthday celebrations, community singing in both languages, or an occasional American evening with popcorn, square dancing, and perhaps a travelogue.

Sunday is a special day, with no classes and no ski instruction. The afternoon might include a tramp in the woods, a bus excursion to the nearest large city, perhaps Geneva, or a local ski meet.

Total per student cost of the Classe de Neige is about $65, including round-trip transportation, room and board, ski instruction, and rental of all ski equipment. Fund raising to help maintain the school is usually a community affair with students baking cakes, sponsoring variety shows, and washing cars. Parent groups conduct raffles and sell Classe de Neige stock certificates to the community. On many bases the local officers club or noncommissioned officers club may award scholarships to needy students.

How do Americans rate the Classe de Neige? An exciting educational experience is the unanimous reaction of American students, teachers, and chaperons. The opportunity to learn to ski is the reason most often given by the students, followed closely by their pleasure in becoming acquainted with French boys and girls and their enjoyment of French cooking. The teachers report the satisfaction of getting to know the children better in a pleasant, out-of-school situation. They marvel at the high academic motivation of the children and their social growth in group living. A shy, retiring student in the classroom often emerges as a leader in the Classe de Neige.

Parent chaperons gain a firsthand appreciation of the strenuous art of dealing with groups of exuberant twelve-year-olds and a deeper understanding of the problems of the schools. For some of them, this was their first extensive exposure to French culture. One stated that he thought he and his child learned more in this two-week period than they normally would have during their entire three-year tour of duty.

What were the French impressions of this cross section of American life transplanted into provincial France?

The hotel owners were pleasantly surprised. At first they were apprehensive about receiving Americans but later reported that the American children were neat and well behaved.

Most of the observations, however, came from the French educators. They were astonished to see the amount of parental involvement in education— American parents aided in planning the trip, in raising funds, and even accompanied the class as chaperons. Many of them had paid their own way and several officers took leave to be with the class.

The mingling of colored and white children amazed many of them who, by newspaper and television reports, are thoroughly informed of America's desegregation problems.

They also noted a sense of self-discipline in the American children. Although this is one of the goals of American education, we often wonder if we are successful in achieving it. The French educators seem to think so.

Chapter six
Environmental
Education: Crusade
for the Seventies

INTRODUCTION

The seventies have been designated as the environmental decade. Seldom has a cause burst on the world scene with more fanfare than the concern for environmental quality. Whether one's concern is for cleaner air, unpolluted water, controlled population, esthetically designed communities, unspoiled wilderness, or an environmentally literate citizenry, the cause has been advanced in true crusade fashion by business, science, industry, and government.

The media have had a heyday saturating the public with visual and written messages running the gamut from prophet-of-doom prognostication to patent recipes for saving the environment. Behind all of this verbal and visual bombardment, however, is the stark reality that man has indeed degraded his environment and must now face certain consequences.

One of the more positive results of the crisis proportions of the problem is the fact that industry has tooled up to provide cleaner burning gasolines, air and water fit for human consumption, and materials that can be recycled.

The current concern for environmental quality triggered a flurry of activity not only within industrial ranks but in government and professional organizations as well. A narrative of just a small sample of activity makes a rather interesting chronicle. The President of the United States established a Council on Environmental Quality. Congress enacted the Environmental Education Act. A number of state-wide and regional conclaves were held as a result. Various educational agencies have developed curriculum models for environmental education. The National Park Service launched the National Environmental Education Development (NEED) Project and the National Environmental Study Area (NESA) Program. In addition, a special program to prepare teachers to utilize the out-of-doors effectively for environmental education has been inaugurated by the U.S. Forest Service. The National Education Association established an Environmental Task Force. The American Association of Health, Physical Education, Recreation established Project Man's Environment. Various institutions of higher education have developed undergraduate and graduate programs focusing on environmental quality. Activity has been regenerated among organizations which, traditionally, have worked actively to prod the general public to greater environmental awareness: the Izaak Walton League, the Conservation Foundation, the National Audubon Society, the Sierra Club, the National Wildlife Foundation, and the Wilderness Society.

A natural outgrowth of the environmental movement was the creation of a number of new organizations such as: Environmental Protection Agencies, Friends of the Earth, Student Councils on Pollution and Environment, (SEEK) Services for Environmental Communications, Inc., Environmental Action, Student Environmental Consulting Service, Zero Population Growth, Environmental Action Coalition, National Ecology Foundation, Ecological Action Environmental Institute. Thus was the environmental education movement launched—on a sea of words which generated a wave of organizations to help man solve a multitude of environmental problems which were plaguing him.

WHY THE EXCITEMENT ABOUT ENVIRONMENTAL EDUCATION? *

WILLIAM M. HAMMERMAN

The lead story in a Chicago newspaper last month reported that "Eleven area companies were charged by the federal government with polluting rivers and waterways." The action was announced by the United States attorney general, who also authorized initiation of the first federal grand jury to investigate water pollution in that area.

The legislature of a western state recently passed a law that requires that adopted courses of study shall provide for instruction in "protection and conservation of resources" and "man's relationships to his human and natural environment" in appropriate grade-levels and subject-areas, grades one through 12. Additional legislation established a conservation education service in the department of education to encourage and assist school-districts in developing and maintaining conservation education programs.

A conservation education advisory committee recommended in its report to a state board of education that preservice teacher training *must* include, as a minimum, "one three-unit course in the philosophy, politics, economics, sociology, and ecological aspects of conservation . . . such a course to be a requirement for graduation."

Local citizen groups have been formed to correct blighted neighborhood areas, to campaign for more open spaces, and to petition for stricter pollution control laws. Student organizations have conducted ecological "teach-ins" and dramatized the problems of air pollution by burying an automobile.

Reports of this nature are now everyday occurrences across this nation, though ten years ago such news items were seldom heard. Along with these developments has come a flood of articles in the popular magazines dealing with the quality of our environment. Last fall a new professional journal—*Environmental Education*—appeared, devoted to discovery and dissemination in the emerging field of multidisciplinary conservation communications. The aim of most environmental education programs is to produce a citizenry that is knowledgeable concerning our biophysical environment and its associated problems, aware of how to help solve these problems, and motivated to work toward their solution.

*Reprinted with permission from *Washington Education*, March 1970, pp. 12-13.

Many people, including educators, ask themselves, "Why all this excitement about environmental education?" Some answer, it is simply a matter of survival. More and more people now see and sense what some scientists and environmental experts have been reporting and predicting for years:

- Poorer-quality air space as evidenced by smog.
- Lower-quality land and water areas because of various types of pollution and poor use and management policies.
- Alienation of people living in the larger metropolitan areas, resulting in degenerating human relations.

In brief, an overall threat to the quality of man's way of life and his relationship to his planet is certain unless he modifies his life-style and behavior patterns.

Combined with the survival factor has been a cumulative effect of earlier events that has caused people in the United States to value their natural resources and to be concerned about the quality of their environment. In *The American Environment,* Roderick Nash traces the history of conservation in this country through a selection of readings, one as early as 1832. During the Progressive period of the twentieth century, the first major thrust of the American conservation movement occurred. Some of the same factors as are seen today—a growing population, urbanization and industrialization—created a climate for Americans to be concerned about their environment. Scores of articles, pamphlets and books that treated resource management were published. This was the period of a White House Conference on Conservation, the National Conservation Commission, and the North American Conservation Conference. Men such as Gifford Pinchot, Jay N. Darling, Robert Johnson and John Muir were well known for their efforts to communicate this growing concern to the public.

During the 1930s and 1940s, the writings of Aldo Leopold, Hugh Bennett and Robert Marshall, plus events such as establishment of the United States Soil Conservation Service, the Tennessee Valley Authority, and the Civilian Conservation Corps, helped to create an ethic for man-land relations and a readiness for Americans to be concerned about their environment. The dominant theme of the *quality* of man's environment was nurtured to new heights by Rachel Carson's *Silent Spring* (1962), Stewart Udall's *The Quiet Crisis* (1963) and Paul Ehrlich's *The Population Bomb* (1968). As in Fairfield Osborn's *Our Plundered Earth* (1948) and *The Limits of the Earth* (1953), modern man finds himself an endangered species on a "spaceship" that must find both a means of survival and a style of living compatible with the optimum development of both man and his environment.

A major issue of the 1970s—politically, socially, economically, and biologically—is the environment. Only recently, the President of the United States created a Council on Environmental Quality to study this problem area and provide guidance. However, regardless of the number of special commissions, legislative controls and appropriations of emergency funds regarding various environmental concerns, an informed and educated citizenry will be needed if any long-enduring changes are to take place.

For years, some educators have been utilizing various natural areas as a laboratory for achieving the goals of education. One state reported a 32 per cent increase in the number of children participating in a resident outdoor school program over a seven-year period. The outdoor education concept received great impetus through Title III of the Elementary and Secondary Education Act of 1965 which funded approximately 110 outdoor education projects over a three-year period. Environmental education experiences were designed to take place in the inner city studying types of air pollution, aboard a floating laboratory ship to study oceanography, at a resident outdoor center to learn about renewable resources that sustain thousands of people, and at a school-yard arboretum to observe ecological habitats. More than 150 projects sponsored by Title I of the Higher Education Act have resulted in environmental education programs related to conservation, beautification, land use planning, and community services.

Other groups have recognized the need to educate the younger generations, if an environmental ethic is to be cultivated and perpetuated in our society. "Project Man's Environment" has been developed by the American Association for Health, Physical Education, and Recreation in cooperation with other National Education Association affiliates and associated organizations. To guide the project, a number of goals have been developed as guidelines:

- To alert man to environmental problems and the need to work toward their solution.
- Assist citizens in developing ethical standards and behavioral patterns which match man's personal identity to a good-quality living environment.
- Stimulate and foster an environmental consciousness among the educational sector, our nation's youth, and the general public.
- Integrate efforts in outdoor education, conservation, and environmental education, and interpretive naturalism with innovative approaches to teaching about man's relationship with his environment.
- To utilize urban parks and open space, recreation and wilderness areas, and other cultural and natural environments for educational experiences involving school and college students, adult education, and the leisure consumer.

The National Park Service is attempting to foster environmental awareness through its "NEED Project" (National Environmental Education Development).

In this K-12 program, curriculum materials are being designed to stress appreciation for the environment, knowledge about uses and abuses of our resources, and the development of the will and ability to take responsible action.

The Visitor Information Service of the United States Forest Service and the Audubon Society's Urban Nature Centers are but two more examples of agencies and organizations that recognize the fact that an educational effort is a must in order to sustain a quality environment. Our educational endeavors, at all levels, must incorporate the "Direct Experience Approach to Learning" when appropriate and thereby provide a "DEAL" for the learner as he internalizes the ABCs of environmental behavior: Awareness behavior leads to concern. Acquisition of knowledge behavior leads to commitment. Action behavior results in change.

Georgia state legislator Julian Bond recently warned higher education administrators that "revolution" on American campuses will not end until universities become centers for the study "of how to make men behave better." Bond said:

> The pollution of the air and water is not carried out by fools or idiots but men educated at the best scientific and technical centers. . . . The ability to shape a society that spends nearly one hundred billions of dollars on conquering space and dominating the globe militarily comes from men of genius, not from men whose minds are limited. Instead of solving his problem, educated man in America has instead poisoned the air and water, raped the land, and colonized whole races of people both here and abroad.

As man enters the latter portion of the twentieth century, he stands at a fork in his environmental road to a good life for the future. Are the schools and other education-oriented groups ready to prepare today's first-grader (age 6 in 1970) for his post-collegiate world (age 21 in 1985) or for the turn of the century (age 36 in 2000)? If we are to succeed in man's quest for survival and a good-quality environment, educators must make their contribution by designing:

- A basic conceptual framework for environmental education that will be relevant in both the 1970s and the year 2000.
- A K-12 sequence of experiences that causes the student to become aware and committed to take appropriate action in order to maintain a good-quality environment, including a complementary series of direct learning experiences in various outdoor laboratories that range from the school-yard and nearby park to national parks, forests, and wilderness areas.

The schools of tomorrow must impart more than a body of skills and knowledge. There is a growing appreciation that it is not enough to give people tools without defining the context in which they will be used. Let it not be recorded in the annals of future historians that man failed to recognize the one true "non-negotiable" demand—the ecological parameters of his environment.

WHAT *IS* ENVIRONMENTAL EDUCATION? *
GEORGE E. ARNSTEIN

One reason why the present surge for a better environment is so widespread is that each supporter sees his own segment and thinks that everybody shares his special vision of the good life. On closer examination, in the heat of political combat, this apparent consensus may turn out to be illusory. Here are some illustrations.

● Those who want better health may want to ban persistent pesticides like DDT on the grounds that they accumulate in the food chain and eventually end up in the human body. But farmers have found that they can greatly increase food production through preventive spraying with DDT which kills crop-destroying insects.

Both sides advocate a better environment.

● Those who fear malaria now favor the draining of swamps which breed mosquitoes that transmit malaria. Duck-hunters like marshes because they are home to the ducks which are part of our heritage and also a favorite target of hunters. There are federal agencies given orders and money to drain marshes; there are other federal agencies with orders and money to preserve marshes.

Both sides are confident that they are contributing to a better environment.

● Backers of the supersonic transport praise the comfort and speed of the new commercial plane, invoke American pride and leadership, and note that there are thousands of jobs at stake. Opponents cite the supersonic boom, the unknown consequences of high-altitude vapor trails, and ask if high-speed travel truly is a necessary ingredient of our high standard of living.

Both sides favor a better environment, especially if it is defined to include a high material standard of living.

● Members of traditional conservation societies want to maintain and expand wilderness areas, bird refuges, and save the California Condor. While there are few opponents of this view per se, there are spokesmen who say that we have much more urgent priorities than to put large chunks of public funds into the creation of public parks and to save a variety of vulture.

● At least one state legislature has considered a bill to outlaw the internal combustion engine. Most Americans would rather fight than switch back to bicycles.

*Reprinted with permission of the author and the Dembar Educational Research Services, Inc., from *The Journal of Environmental Education*, 3(1):7-9, Fall 1971.

Both sides defend their own version of environmental quality.

What these examples are meant to illustrate is the great range of concepts, all of which are presently subsumed under the heading of environmental quality.

In the matter of environmental education we have much the same situation. There are those who think it is an expanded version of conservation education. They are right; environmental education certainly includes the concepts of traditional conservation, sometimes referred to as classical conservation: preservation of our natural resources, use of techniques of soil conservation, contour plowing, windbreaks, afforestation, expansion and preservation of wilderness areas.

The schools have been doing a pretty fair job of teaching these concepts and values for half a century, although the increasing shift to our cities has brought with it some lags. Conservation education tends to be too rural and not enough urban. It needs updating but its basic concepts and ideas are sound. There are some new textbooks and some new ideas coming to the fore. They are part of an honorable and sound tradition which should be encouraged and helped to meet the needs of our increasing urban and suburban population.

There are those who think environmental education is a new version of science education. They are right. Environmental education surely must have scientific content, and new curricula are being developed. A report to the Environmental Studies Board of the National Academy of Sciences singles out the Science Curriculum Improvement Study (SCIS) at the University of California at Berkeley (1:30). At the same time it notes the need for a high priority Junior Environmental Education Program (grades 7-9) to follow in the footsteps of SCIS which is for kindergarten through grade 7.

The programs have a strong bent toward science. Especially noteworthy is the deliberate attempt to build the program around things which can be handled and touched. It is a deliberate attempt to get away from abstract learning and to emphasize tactile, visual, manipulable learning—which then leads to abstractions.

This is science education, it is part of environmental education, and it also contains welcome elements of reform of educational methods and techniques.

There are those who think environmental education is an expanded version of outdoor education. They are right. Man and his relationship to nature is an important part of environmental education. We ought to welcome almost any educational experience which will take the students outside the four walls, the boxlike environment in which they spend half of their waking hours.

As we become more and more urban, this is even more important than it was in the days of our agricultural past when there was neither television nor air pollution.

There are those who think that environmental education is an enlargement of biology into ecology, a modification of geography into something broader and deeper, an addition to English courses so they will include a composition on how we left our picnic area unlittered. All of these advocates are right, and they should be encouraged into broadening and modifying existing educational programs.

There are those who think that environmental education is the constructive use of field trips to national landmarks, to the environmental study areas being set up by the National Park Service, to the use of the American countryside (and urban settings) to tie together nature, history, and an appreciation of our heritage. They are right.

There are those who think that environmental education is something to be added to the curriculum, a special unit on the environment analogous to the way certain states have legislated units on the evils of alcohol, tobacco, or drugs.

They are wrong because this approach is perfunctory and it doesn't work. It fails to get to the heart of the matter, which is what environmental education really means or should mean.

The pervasive and conscious examination and understanding of man's relationship to nature, influenced by our growing population which produces congestion, and which, in turn, calls for a change in values and attitudes.

A change in values is an uncomfortable experience. It means the rejection of the inherited conventional wisdom and the adoption of a new stance. It represents a challenge to what has gone before and an opportunity to deal with what is yet to come. Here are some illustrations of values which have changed in our recent past:

● The thirteenth amendment to the Constitution abolished slavery. This means that there used to be a day when the majority thought slavery was desirable or at least tolerable.

● Women did not have the right to vote. For the past 50 years they have had this right—and it represents a reversal of inherited values. The battle for women's rights is still going on, of course.

● We used to prohibit trade unions as conspiracies of working men. Today just about everybody thinks unions are and ought to be permitted, even though there may be charges of excessive power.

● We used to have laws on certain beaches calling for tops on bathing suits for women and men.

● Benjamin Franklin said that a penny saved is a penny earned. Today's credit card economy runs counter to Poor Richard's Almanac.

● We sought to tame and exploit the North American continent by fighting Indians and burning forests to clear the land. Today we have guilt feelings about our treatment of Indians and seek to conserve what is left of the forests and our wilderness areas.

● We used to justify education which was separate, then went to separate but equal, until the Supreme Court said that separate could not possibly be equal.

● We used to believe in free curbside downtown parking. Only grudgingly have we accepted parking meters and other restrictions.

● President Nixon, in his State of the Union message, pointed to another change not all of us are ready to accept: "We still think air is free. But clean air is not free, and neither is clean water."

● Similarly, in discussing economic growth, the President said: "The critical question is not whether we will grow, but how we will use that growth." He then called for quality rather than quantity.

It is in this sense that environmental education must get to the heart of the matter: It must deal with values and attitudes, and these values must be based on understanding of how we hope to manage the environment.

It is in this sense that environmental education cannot hope to be successful as long as it is part of a society which still worships the "Holy Grail of a rising Gross National Product" (to borrow a phrase from former Secretary Udall).

If adults pollute and destroy, then is it realistic to ask teachers to expose the evils of pollution and despoliation? As long as advertising favors smoking, big cars with high-compression engines and leaded gasoline, can we expect the schools to overcome the deliberate and expensive assault staged by our sophisticated media? As long as we favor throw-away bottles, can we hope to persuade children that litter and waste are extravagent and expensive and ugly?

One of the hazards of the Environmental Education Act recently passed by the Congress is that it may raise false hopes. If it merely leads to add-on teaching units with up-to-date label of environmental and ecological education, it may merely widen the credibility gap and may increase youthful cynicism about adult hypocrisy.

The real thrust of effective environmental education must begin with adult awareness. This probably now exists at a fairly high level. What does not yet exist is the realization of just how expensive and pervasive the pursuit of environmental quality will be.

If we want clean rivers, the answer lies only partly in first, second, and third-stage treatment plants. Most of the answer lies in preventing some of the effluents in the first place. Effluent charges are considered the most effective way of doing this because it avoids much regimentation, leaves the polluters a choice of paying the price of pollution or saving money through prevention or through their own clean-up efforts.

If we want to have cleaner air, part of the answer is to stimulate research on alternatives to the internal combustion engine, and part of the answer is through disincentives. In practice, this means a higher tax on leaded gasoline than on unleaded gasoline, a higher excise tax on big cars than on small cars, the use of service charges to assess those who produce many harmful emissions, and to keep low the charges to those who produce few harmful emissions.

There is a whole arsenal at our disposal, not necessarily through absolute prohibition but through incentives and disincentives, through taxes and service charges. Incentives cost money; disincentives and service charges produce revenue, although the purpose should be—from an educational point of view— not so much to raise revenue as to create awareness and to change behavior.

It is in this context that we need to work toward a pragmatic definition of environmental education, which must be relevant to young people as well as to adults. Some of the witnesses testifying on the Environmental Education Act of 1970 touched on questions of awareness and values, but the majority of the witnesses had their eyes firmly on their own tree, while overlooking the forest as a whole.

The significant thing about our current ecological crisis is that it may be the last one, that it is taking place at a point in history when we are witnessing unprecedented changes. Not the least of the consequences of change is that adult knowledge may be obsolete, that the very concept of seniority is now open to question, that not all experience accumulated over years of living will be valid.

The Environmental Education Act can lay the groundwork for an effective program of environmental education. The new law can provide leadership, authority, funding, and encouragement, especially by putting the focus on powers of observation, by seizing on existing and latent motivation, and by encouraging us to arrive at a better understanding of the potentially harmonious relationships between man and nature.

Whether we can rely on education to bail us out of our present impasse is something that now looks doubtful, but not impossible. What is important is that we view environmental education in a context which is broader than that of the birdwatcher, the salesman of air filters, the anti-litter crusader, or any one of the other fragmented advocates, each of whom may be honest, bold, high-minded but also must have the vision to see the environment as a whole. That, if we hope to survive, is what environmental education should be all about.

REFERENCE

1. *Institution for Effective Management of the Environment*, Part I, January 1970, p. 30.

THE LIVING WORLD:
THE PHYSICAL ENVIRONMENT *
WILLIAM B. STAPP

As our spaceship Earth moves through the universe, it is imperative to keep in mind that the earth is a closed system. We have on it all of the air, water, and land we will ever have. Space and resources are finite, yet since 1950 we have

*From *Childhood Education* 47(4):179-81, January, 1971. Reprinted by permission of William B. Stapp and the Association for Childhood Education International, 3615 Wisconsin Avenue, N. W., Washington, D.C. Copyright © 1971 by the Association.

added one billion people to an area faced with unprecedented environmental problems.

As we enter the 1970s, we must realize that open land is being reduced. Large- and middle-sized communities, many within complex urban regions, have evolved to where people are concentrated on a small portion of our land surface. (In the United States over 70 per cent of the population resides on 1½ per cent of the nation's land.) Consequently, the independent rural-oriented living that once characterized our heritage is no longer a dominating influence on the lives of the great majority of the world's people.

Man has but a short time to learn to become trustee of his inherited land, air, and water and to live in harmony with his environment. On how well and how soon he learns this lesson rests the fate of our planet earth.

As ecologist Pauline Gratz clearly indicates . . . our urban as well as rural areas are being plagued with complex biological-physical-social problems, such as indiscriminate use of pesticides, community blight, air and water pollution, traffic congestion, lack of comprehensive environmental planning, and lack of institutional arrangements needed to cope effectively with environmental problems. While these problems are legitimate concerns of community governmental officials and planners, responsibility for their solution rests, to a large extent, with citizens.

As consumers and voters we are increasingly being asked to make decisions that affect environmental quality. We can help determine sound policy as we ask informed questions, at the proper time, of the right people; as we elect representatives to policy-making bodies; and as we cast votes on community issues and support appropriate legislation directed at resolving environmental problems. To perform these tasks effectively, it is vital that we be *knowledgeable* concerning the biophysical environment and its associated problems, *aware* of how we can help solve these problems, and *motivated* to work toward effective solutions.

The foundation for strong citizen action rests, to a large degree, on what happens in our schools. Many current programs in conservation education focus primarily on basic resources and neglect the community environment and its associated problems. Moreover, they fail to emphasize the role of the citizen. Today's youth will soon be the citizens and voters whose decisions will affect not only the immediate environment in which they live, but also that of the larger world. *They* will make the choices and cast the votes about recreation, transportation, beautification, water needs, and control of air and water pollution. Therefore, it is critically important that citizens of all ages examine their way of life to determine the degree to which it reflects a commitment both to protect and to enhance the environment. As a simple example, citizens can be active in solving traffic congestion not just through the political process but by walking, bicycling, or using rapid transit rather than their cars. If the car must be used, then driving pools should be formed. How much are our youth and adults willing to sacrifice personally in order to provide a high quality environment?

To obtain insight into approaches a school system might consider in assisting children and youth to become more sensitized to the environment and more inclined to participate in coping with environmental problems, basic learning principles might well be reviewed. What would happen if we really moved into action these too-often-voiced, too-seldom-practiced concepts:

● Learning best takes place through the active involvement of the student. What he does he learns, not what the teacher does. We know that reaction to excessive direction of the teacher is likely to be apathetic conformity, defiance, or escapism. We know that inquiry-approaches stimulate intrinsic motivation, a sense of excitement and discovering for oneself.
● What is learned is most likely to be available for use if learned in a situation much like that in which it is to be used and immediately preceding the time when it is needed.

● ● ●

● Behaviors that are reinforced are more likely to recur. It is therefore important to link school programs with activities in the home and community so that desired behaviors will be reinforced by the home, school, church, and youth organizations.
● Learners are more likely to throw themselves wholeheartedly into a project if they themselves have a meaningful role in selecting and planning the enterprise. Children are more likely to become involved in environmental issues if they are aware of how they can affect decision-making.
● Most effective effort is put forth when tasks fall in the range of challenge—not too easy and not too hard—where success seems likely but not certain.

These learning principles tell us that at each school level students should be provided meaningful encounters with their environment. Some examples of topics the encounters might focus upon, in addition to land, water, and air resources, are environmental design and planning, transportation, solid waste disposal, and recreation. A class could select with its teacher environmental encounters to extend a study already under way or to serve as the central thrust of a major new teaching unit.

In the earlier grades emphasis should be centered on developing interest, awareness, understanding, and respect for the environment. In the later years emphasis should be on "honing" problem-solving skills: defining the environmental problem or issue, becoming informed about the problem, stating alternative solutions, developing a plan of action, and implementing that plan. The critical focus must be that at each level the learner become *personally* involved in positive action toward the solution of environmental problems to which he has been exposed. . . .

In a school system that revolves its environmental education program around this encounter-approach, a twelfth-grader may not have been exposed to all aspects of study of the environment. But through the advocated inquiry-approach he would have been helped to develop greater sensitivity (total awareness), more sophisticated problem-solving skills, and a heightened motivation to participate in coping with environmental problems than would the product of more conventional approaches to instruction. He should see more clearly too the importance of relating ecologically economic, social, technological, esthetic, and political information.

SUMMARY

If we are to bring urbanized man to a fuller understanding of his environment, our schools must embark on a comprehensive environmental education program. The program should be aimed at helping our youth to be more knowledgeable concerning the environment and associated problems, aware of how to help solve these problems, and motivated to work toward their solution—making tomorrow NOW.

ENVIRONMENT AND THE SHAPING OF CIVILIZATION *

LYNTON K. CALDWELL

Can we really elect to have a high-quality environment? Does the structure of American society—pluralistic, democratic, historically biased in favor of an "everyman's *laissez-faire*"—permit the shaping of its environment in any way other than by combat and compromise? The question is not whether conflict of interests in the environment can be eliminated. There is no prospect, in a finite world, that they will be. A second practical question is how to raise the levels of information and social concern at which the process of bargaining and accommodation occurs. To improve the human environment, both man and politics must be improved. Men make politics; political institutions influence human behavior; and behavior is heavily influenced by attitudes, beliefs, and values. Purposeful shaping of the environment involves the purposeful shaping of outlooks on life. The quality of the future environment depends, therefore, upon the shaping of attitudes, beliefs, and values through present education.

Some aspects of human conduct are expressions of psychophysical nature. As

*Reprinted with permission of the author and the Dembar Educational Research Services, Inc., from *The Journal of Environmental Education*, 2(2):6-8, Winter 1970.

a civilizing animal it is natural for man to substitute reason and culture for subrational drives, but rational behavior may serve irrational motives. It is, therefore, important to our welfare to understand the nature and effect of physiologically conditioned behavior. If man is a territorial animal, and if he displaces onto the environment aggression generated in his social relationships, knowledge concerning these circumstances could greatly assist development of feasible strategies for effective environmental policy. Yet not all men nor all societies project impulses against the environment. The improvement of man can proceed through education, in the broad sense, while efforts are made also to improve the psychophysical endowment of the human species.

What are the implications for an educational process that will help build better environmental relationships in the future? The structuring of the entire process of formal education around man-environment relationships is not necessarily indicated. Many of the attitudes, beliefs, and values that would improve prospects for better environments in the future are equally suitable to help society to set goals and establish priorities for the future. Education limited to information is of little help. The question becomes one of what attitudes, beliefs, and values the system inculcates. In the broadest sense, the issue is what kind of civilization the process of education will produce.

Within this broader context of educational policy an increased and, in some measure, new focus on environmental relationships and policies will be necessary. This basically ecological aspect of research and teaching has long been neglected to our detriment and to our increasing peril. Recent moves to establish centers or institutes for environmental studies in numbers of colleges and universities indicate intention to remedy the neglect. Through the organization of new courses of study and the reorganization of old ones, higher education is better equipping today's youths to perceive and to assess the meaning of environmental change. Only a beginning has been made and much more needs to be done. It is especially important that basic environmental concepts be built into secondary education where they have heretofore generally been lacking. Education is more than schooling, but it is through formal systematic mass education that the greatest single impact on attitudes, beliefs, and values can be made.

In a techno-scientific age there is no end to the need for learning. Planned, systematic education now continues through adult life and is increasingly civic as well as vocational in character. With the displacement of traditional culture by techno-science, we are confronted with the necessity of working to obtain our civilization. We can no longer merely inherit it. To preserve the culture of the past, whether in art, ethics, historic sites, landscapes, or social institutions, requires unremitting effort. It also requires reappraisal; for not all we inherit is necessarily good.

In the new world struggling to be born it is we who must struggle. The disintegration of traditional culture is a grim and tragic process. We see its consequences in starkest relief in catastrophes that have befallen the ancient civilization of China. Fortunately for us of the Western World, the concepts of self-actualization and of the evolution of man and society are embodied in our culture. Yet, although these internalized concepts may have helped to spare us the misfortunes of China, they have not helped us to be self-actualizing in all respects. Why have they not been more effective in guiding public effort toward better environmental decisions? The explanation lies perhaps in the complexity of our culture and in the particular ways in which these concepts are expressed in our society. More certainly, our educational system has not equipped people to make well-considered environmental choices.

We are not yet able to explain why some societies adopt ecologically valid goals and practices and others do not. Simplified explanations are likely to be wrong, but it is possible to draw certain general conclusions from the courses that contrasting cultures have taken, without fully understanding the causal factors. For example, although no simple explanation seems adequate to account for the decline of Chinese civilization, the inadvertent overstressing of the environment by sheer numbers of people seems to have been a critical factor. The ethos of China, less complex and more dogmatic than the ideologies of the West, was more congenial to harmony with nature. Yet neither philosophy, bureaucracy, nor science enabled China to avoid the environmental impoverishment that followed a slowly increasing but unremitting pressure of man on the land. In the West, science and technology enabled society to achieve a more productive and better balanced relationship to the natural world even though, paradoxically, the dominant attitudes toward nature tended as much toward hostility as toward harmony. Industrialization and the colonization of the Americas relieved in Europe the inordinate stress of man on his environment that accompanied the decline of Chinese civilization. But we have no assurance that the combination of culture and technology that, with obvious exceptions, has worked well for the West will continue to do so in the techno-scientific society of the future.

Two obvious aspects of the historical threshold over which all society is now passing are exponential increases of people and of power. The danger in destructive or misguided attitudes toward nature has become greater today because of the greater means to translate attitudes into action. Guided ignorance in the form of dogma appears to have been a factor in the decline of old China; unguided knowledge in the form of technocratic optimism appears to have been the characteristic danger to the West. Today, the establishment of guidelines for knowledge in the application of science and technology to the human environment is a task of urgent importance everywhere. The task is urgent because until it is accomplished there will be no adequate basis in theory or principle upon which to base public and international policies for the custody, care, and development of the human environment.

In America, we have no corpus of ecological doctrine in our public life comparable to that which now influences or governs our economic decisions. Our public life is shaped by particular interpretations, or misinterpretations, of self-actualization and freedom to change that tend to contradict the concepts that they are presumed to exemplify. These misinterpretations although deeply rooted in American society are neither uniquely nor necessarily American. They may be changed, and they must be changed, if the shaping of American civilization is to enlarge the public happiness and welfare. Among the attitudes that misinterpret the meaning of human freedom the following are especially familiar and especially harmful to the quality of civilization and its environment; first, an uncritical bias for growth; second, techno-economic determinism; third, cultural relativism; and, fourth, self-centered individualism—the "everyman's *laissez-faire.*"

These attitudes share certain negative characteristics significant for the environment-shaping process. None of them imply or require self-restraint or control, none suggest individual or collective accountability, none concede the existence of criteria for evaluating the use of the environment that are independent of individual interest or preference. All of these attitudes suggest resistance to any general pattern of environmental development in society or to any meaningful standards of environmental quality, per se. They do not preclude the imposition of social control where a clear and present danger to individual well-being can be proved. But they severely retard the establishment of general principles of ecological policy upon which more specific standards can be based. More critical attention to their effects is therefore needed.

The "growthmanship" attitude is deeply embedded in American culture. Whether our national obsession with quantitative growth can be transformed into qualitative growth, or growth within a self-renewing or an internally dynamic homeostatic system is conjectural. The most problematic growth of all is that of numbers of people. In America there are grounds for cautious optimism that the national enthusiasm for numbers may someday be displaced by a concern for the quality of human life generally.

Techno-economic determinism, or the "you can't stop progress" attitude, is still firmly ascendant in American life—despite critical attack from both science and aesthetics. Supersonic transport and airports unlimited are only current examples of a national tendency. It is curious that people vigilantly jealous of their rights in relation to government will permit their privacy, convenience, and even health to be jeopardized by costly and unnecessary technological innovation that yields little, if any, social benefit. More strange is the tendency of science-oriented, rational people to accept the metaphysical dogma of technological inevitability. It is, as we have emphasized, a contradiction to the tacit belief of Americans in the self-actualization of the human personality. It is an example of compartmentalized thinking against which education has not yet provided sufficient protection.

Cultural relativism has permeated the social sciences and has strongly influenced ethical and religious thought. The value of a demonstrably valid set of ecological principles by which public policy could be guided would be very great. It could provide a common ground for greater consensus. But it would encounter objections from those who hold that science has nothing to do with values, and that one man's values are as good as another's. Our slowness in exploring the biosocial interface in science has kept us from providing an adequate and convincing answer to arguments over relativity or priority among values in the environment. Political accommodation among conflicting interests therefore tends to occur at too low a conceptual level to give adequate weight to scientific knowledge or ecological wisdom.

The *laissez-faire* attitude toward the rights of individuals in relation to the environment has suffered some attrition through public action on behalf of public health and safety. Land-use planning and zoning, and emerging pollution control legislation, further constrain individual behavior in relation to the environment. We are beginning to lay a foundation for a legal doctrine of public rights in the environment, as distinguished from the specific and discrete prohibitions that have hitherto characterized our environmental policy. Yet at the local level of government and throughout large areas of the country where pressure on the environment has not been felt acutely, the right to exploit the environment for personal advantage is still very broadly construed. Here again culture shapes environmental attitudes. The psychology of the frontiersman is still vigorous and when reinforced by techno-scientific capability can be a very potent force, usually in ways harmful to environmental quality.

A characteristic common to all of these foregoing attitudes is that each of them is highly dysfunctional to the effective public control of applied science or technology. They derive from viewpoints formed mostly in the prescientific world, although cultural relativism reflects to some degree an inclination to be scientific. Relativistic thinking that dismisses weight of evidence and insists upon incontrovertible proof of the validity of one environmental attitude as against another has abandoned science for a philosophical fetish. In actuality these attitudes do not appear as clear-cut or consistent categories of belief or behavior. They are interwoven in the fabric of our social, political, and economic life, and this is why it becomes so difficult to change them. It is why environment shaping becomes culture shaping, and why attack upon the environmental abuses of our industrial society readily becomes an attack upon certain aspects of the structure of the society itself.

These remarks began with an allusion to the concept of two worlds—the familiar but no longer viable past and the future which, more than a transition from the past, appears to bring a change of state in the human condition. Related to this concept is that of two cultures, popularized by C. P. Snow. Each of these concepts is expressive of the change that science has brought into the world. Both imply discontinuities in culture: chronological, intellectual, and emotional.

The truth of these interpretations of present history is perhaps more poetic than rigorously factual, more qualitative than quantitatively demonstrable. A truth may be substantial without being universal. And it seems true that the *means* to shape the environment of civilized societies belong largely to science; whereas the purposes of men, the standards of beauty, order, aesthetic satisfaction, welfare, and even of some aspects of health belong to the humanities. This separation between the custodians of means and ends in our society creates weakness and discontinuity at the point of social decision. It is in the process of public policy making that the respective contributions of the "two cultures" are needed to form a mutually comprehensible and coherent unity.

The size and complexity of modern society require specialization. In the absence of integrative forces, occupational differences tend to fractionalize society. Communication across occupational lines becomes difficult, and no common set of assumptions or values provides a meeting ground for differing interests. The openness of modern society is deceptive. Freed from barriers of class and caste, it is more subtly fragmented by techno-scientific specialization and by the progressive isolation of the traditional culture from techno-science.

Here perhaps lies the answer to the question of why contemporary Western techno-scientific society has not dealt more effectively with its environmental problems. Means and ends are separated. The wholeness of man and of society requires a synthesis or integration in orientation toward the world and life that conventional education has not provided. Thus, as we earlier observed, contradictory tendencies of modern American society are built into its social system. And it is this schizoid tendency that most of all makes it difficult for the United States of America to develop a guiding set of environmental policies or to employ more than a fraction of the potential power of science and technology on behalf of human welfare.

Science has placed in the hands of man knowledge and power that makes him responsible for his future; it has not given him the moral compulsion to act responsibly. The substantive values that science and technology serve are articulated in the humanities, but are seldom amenable to scientific verification. It is at this interface between science and the humanities that environmental policy, if made, is made. And it is at this interface also that higher education can contribute to resolving what some observers have called our environmental crisis.

How this task can be accomplished in the colleges and universities is yet to be discovered, and it must also be acknowledged that education alone will not solve our problems. There is no master blueprint equally applicable to all institutions or to all aspects of the educational task. But these elements in that task are universal: first, it is primarily one of synthesis—its basic data will be derived largely from the established disciplines that individually are unable to bring together knowledge relevant to environmental policy in a comprehensive or coherent system; second, its concern is not merely with the appearance of things, but with the purpose, quality, and worth of man-environment relationships; third, it reinforces rather than dilutes efforts in the separate sciences and humanities because it establishes or clarifies their relevance to life; fourth and finally, it emphasizes a truth that is too often forgotten—that through education the civilization of the future is shaped.

Past generations of Americans, and men generally, have understood education as preparation for life. It is that, but that is its smaller dimension. Its larger dimension and equally important task is to shape life as well as to help prepare for it. In some degree education has always done this, but often without conscious effort or intention. If man is to be the master of his own ingenuity, and not its victim, he will have to find better ways to relate means to ends, and to evaluate the ends that science makes available to him. In summation, the major task of education and politics is to shape a world in which preparation for life is worthwhile.

THE *EDUCATION* IN ENVIRONMENTAL EDUCATION *

IRA WINN

Two dominant and interrelated themes are found in the new conservation movement in American education: (1) the integrated or interdisciplinary approach as a substitute for narrow and traditional departmentalized offerings; and (2) the corresponding necessity to implement programs that will give people not only an understanding of the ecological facts of life, but will move them to action in helping to prevent and solve environmental problems. The first theme underlies many problems of higher education. It signals the need for a basic reappraisal of educational structure and better organization and administration of curricula. But it is the second theme that in many ways is the more difficult to act upon, for the planning involved can easily fall into the category of wishful

*Reprinted with permission of the author and the Dembar Educational Research Services, Inc., from *The Journal of Environmental Education*, 1(4):140-41, Summer 1970.

thinking that so often widens and clouds the gap between felt needs and effective educational programming.

Havlick's survey of environmental education opportunities in American higher education indicates that the most serious weakness is "the absence of any vigorous environmental education program in the Departments or Schools of Education . . . very modest and uncoordinated teacher training effort at every institution studied" (2). At the same time, interestingly, the study notes that few students now in the field of environmental education plan to enter teaching. And when they arrive in training, doubtless those few teacher candidates are highly specialized as biologists or geographers. Thus develops the vicious cycle that must be broken before the training of teachers for the new conservation movement becomes adequate for the needs and realistic for the times. The departments of education, biology, city planning and architecture, recreation, agriculture, sociology, etc., will have to work cooperatively or they will fail in the difficult task of environmental education because they deny the interdependence of educational life even as they affirm it for life in general.

THE ENVIRONMENTAL EDUCATION TEACHER

For one thing there are few teacher education specialists who are adequately trained in the environmental sciences. For another, there are few scientists who have a grasp of the difficulties of mounting an effective teacher training program. Commonly, training is seen as the giving of courses—the filling of the pitcher of the mind with facts about the environment that can be learned in the various departments. But what must be quickly learned by environmental educators is an old dictum of Plutarch: The mind should not be seen as a pitcher to be filled, but as a flame to be kindled and fueled. The fact that man does not act simply on the basis of his knowledge accounts not only for the high rate of drug use among doctors or the ease with which advertisers and highway engineers fool housewives and house owners; this fact affects the entire fabric of our being and raises questions about our perception of the way the world really works and what we are prepared to do about it. The purpose of this article is to offer some perspectives for effective training programs in environmental education, to set the sights and raise some standards, and to point out some of the pitfalls that lie along the way.

It would be utopian to assume that most university education in the near future will take a fully integrated tack. Interdisciplinary seminars, however, can be set into the more general departmentalized framework and thus serve as a vitalizing force and a link between subject specialists. Of course, the environmental education major, whatever his particular subject specialty, will take a broad spectrum of course work involving both physical and social sciences and the humanistic studies which raise fundamental questions of esthetics, values and ethics. Most important during the upper division and graduate years, inter-disciplinary seminars and symposia should be made a part of the requirement for all subject majors in fields involving the environment. In fact, this is no more than to say that at least a 1-year seminar on environmental problems should be made a part of the minimum requirements for a university degree.

CASE STUDIES

The educational dialogues of the new conservation must be strongly problem-oriented. Environmental educators should lean heavily on the use of case studies in order to bring field realities into the classroom and to cause diverse subject specialists to rub shoulders and broaden their perspectives. The decisional character of case study is of particularly vital significance to environmental education (3). The approach not only forces cross-disciplinary thinking in the course of problem solving, but it is strongly directed toward consideration of fundamental value problems inherent in the development of democratic political life. Illustrative is the recent study by Erickson and Reynolds of the ecology of the Quabbin reservoir (1), a case analysis that moves thinking and discussion beyond the preliminary level of problem description and data collection, where so much of education today lies stagnant. The focus on judgment (the solution of the case problem) helps the participants in the case discussion to adopt the reflective-questioning attitude so vital to the new conservation. As the authors conclude, "The ecological system of a reservoir includes our own sociology. If it is scientifically possible to dredge a reservoir, for example, is it sociologically wise to 'dirty up' a fisherman's favorite lake? If it is scientifically feasible to reduce nutrient levels in a reservoir by strict surveillance of sewage disposal and fertilizer use in areas surrounding a reservoir, is it politically feasible to do so? These are obviously questions that the biologist and engineer cannot answer—but it is often within the framework of just this kind of question that their proposals must be built" (1).

The teacher candidate who is nurtured through such an interdisciplinary sharpening process will be primed to enter into the modern currents of inductive teaching. Those trends are now beginning to revitalize teacher education as a force for social change. First, the goals of teacher training for environmental education need to be written from an operational standpoint, rather than in terms of glittering generalities and traditionally vague objectives such as "appreciation of nature" or "understanding the importance of conservation." A more appropriately written lesson goal for the new conservation might be: "Students will be able to point out political factors influencing decision on a given park localization or choice of freeway routing"; or, "Students will be able to find examples of environmental contaminants in home or neighborhood store and be able to explain to their class and the owner the reason for their danger." The student teacher in environmental education should thus become proficient in lesson planning for behavioral change. While there will still be room for a general statement of objectives, incorporating a rationale or a general philosophy, modern educational experience dictates a break away from the common fixation on lesson planning at the abstract level. The second point of departure from tradition is the need for stress on practice of problem solving techniques and innovative approaches that both stimulate intellectual curiosity and practical wisdom. Peer teaching critique sessions, perhaps using video tape, can be "traded" for factual knowledge with subject specialists in the sciences and in other areas where schools of education will likely be in short supply.

The use of combined teams and visiting consultants will further the healthy exchange of ideas as well as give the necessary substantive boost in what will constitute a mutual learning phase over the next few years. Social science teacher trainers should have little difficulty adapting to the political, economic, and sociological side of environmental education, while science trainers will easily learn to handle approaches to the physical aspects of environmental problems. But the real trick is to combine these forces with all the other esthetic and value perspectives that make up the whole of the new conservation and life in general.

ADOLESCENCE OF ENVIRONMENTAL EDUCATION

During the coming (and inevitable) 3-5-year period of adolescence and early adulthood of the environmental education movement there will be need for special and summer projects, federally and privately financed, to develop training programs and new educational techniques and to set standards for assessing progress. As the Report to the President's Council on Environmental Quality has noted not only is there "excessive reliance on traditional classroom methodology," but environmental projects in the past have lacked evaluation and articulation, and it is nearly impossible to tell what works best and why (4).

This admission of past deficiencies, this need to experiment anew and to borrow in order to build a new field of knowledge is not as gloomy a course as first it may appear. The new conservation has the advantage of not being bound by the constraints of traditional subject organization and methodology. And the changes in teacher training will help force corresponding reform in the secondary schools, as physical, social sciences, and recreation are brought into better articulation. Financial support seems to be steadily increasing, and, hopefully, the foundations and goverment agencies concerned will increase their aid in order to institutionalize and expand environmental education centers in the universities. Naturally, failures can be expected to occur, if only because the field is still emerging from its infancy. But in a more basic sense, learning is a form of borrowing and profiting from error, and often the best learning occurs in the act of teaching others while teaching oneself.

What larger outcomes can be expected from such an educational reform movement? Properly administered, what should result is not only a transformation in the structure of education but new perspectives, new perceptions, new actions by the general public (5). The awakening of the citizenry to the delicate ecological fabric of life will bring into being a political body much more resistant to the blandishments of the hucksters, aware of long run consequences of short run plans, and alive to the dangers of patchwork approaches to problems of food supply and population, energy sources, underdevelopment, pollution, and other social issues. Students of the new conservation will inevitably be activists, oriented toward involvement in the world community and its problems. Thus will be created or recreated that which gave heart to Tocqueville as he weighed the promise of the American scene—a community of publics, now engaged in thinking about the nature of their education and their environment, questioning the kinds of cities they are living or going to live in, and concerned about the kind of life they are leading. Are we, those most concerned with environmental education, fully ready to accept these changes?

REFERENCES

1. Erickson, Paul A.; Reynolds, John T., "The Ecology of a Reservoir," *Natural History*, 78:(no. 9) 52, November, 1969.
2. Havlick, Spenser W., "A Glimpse and Analysis of Environmental Education Opportunities in American Higher Education," *Environmental Education*, 1:(no. 1)21-24, Fall 1969.
3. Hunt, Pearson, "The Case Method of Instruction," *Harvard Education Review*, 21:177-178, 1951; Winn, Ira, *The Case Study Reform Movement in American Civil Education: Educational Implications of Political Apathy*, doctoral dissertation, University of California, 1966, pp. 109-166; Oliver Donald; Shaver, James P., *The Analysis of Public Controversy*, Harvard Graduate School of Education Report, chapters X-XI, 1962.
4. Rockefeller, Laurance and others, "Report to the President and the President's Council on Environmental Quality," pp. 13, 31-32, August, 1969.
5. Winn, Ira, "Public Parks and Private Lives," *Natural History*, 78:(no. 8)20-26, October, 1969; Ferry, W. H., "The Technophiliacs," *The Center Magazine*, Center for the Study of Democratic Institutions, Santa Barbara, 1:(no. 5)45-49, July, 1968.

THE CHALLENGE OF
ENVIRONMENTAL EDUCATION *
J. ALAN WAGAR

I am not an environmental educator. Rather then a researcher concerned among other things with studying the effectiveness of communicating environmental information and concepts to the public. As such, I am an analyst who stands somewhat off to the side and examines what the problems are, how current efforts are working, what seems to be needed, and how improvements might be made.

From my slightly detached point of view, I conclude that we face an environmental crisis and that the challenge of environmental education is no less than that of preventing disaster for the human race.

Our environmental crisis comes from an arrested mentality that still assumes the environment can absorb any insult we can hurl at it. But along with this caveman mentality we have a modern technology and a command of energy that permit us to commit environmental errors that may not be reversible.

For example, two-thirds of the world is already hungry, but as a species we are reproducing as if the earth had no limit. The land that must support these populations has often been abused beyond repair. We are dumping such poisons as lead, asbestos, radioactive materials, and pesticides into the environment. Perhaps of greater importance, we are adding carbon dioxide and particulate matter to the atmosphere in great quantities. The increased carbon dioxide could conceivably cause the earth to warm enough to melt the ice caps and thereby flood most of the world's major cities. Or, the particles in the air might block out so much of the sun's heat that the earth could experience another ice age.

Some may think I am too pessimistic: after all, they could reason, despite the doomsday predictions over the centuries, man has survived all of his problems so far. Furthermore, it is his great skill in problem solving that has made man the dominant species on earth—a species that now numbers more than three-and-a-half billion and poses a major threat to any species that gets in his way.

Although contemporary problems are enormous, a host of specialists are waiting to save us with schemes of many kinds. In view of all this talent, what is so important about environmental education?

*Reprinted with permission from *Today's Education*, December 1970, pp. 15-18, with permission from the author and the National Education Association.

In its simplest terms, environmental education is merely education for living effectively in an environmental situation that is turning out to be quite unlike what we have thought it to be. Our way of life is less and less appropriate to survival, and the task of correcting the situation is enormous, involving no less than a restructuring of some long-accepted attitudes in the American way of life. Essentially, we are talking about changing basic cultural values.

In trying to cope with the environmental crisis, we should avoid the witch-hunt approach of seeking "greedy corporations," "profiteering sub-dividers," "corrupt politicians," "misguided agencies," and "unscrupulous advertisers" upon whom to pile the blame. These people are not blameless and should not escape our scrutiny, but they are not so much the *causes* as they are *agents* for the rest of us. They can often claim—with some justice—that they are only practicing the good American virtues of progress, economic growth, free enterprise, and providing the public with an abundant life.

The blame comes home to roost. The causes, rather than being out there with "them," are right here with "us" and with some of our most cherished values.

Let me illustrate by reviewing some problems that spring from just four of our basic values: growth, laissez-faire, economic efficiency, and specialization.

First of all, we have an obsession with growth. This value made sense when a few settlers faced a nearly empty continent with vast spaces to be filled and rich resources to be tapped. In such an environment, an accelerating growth rate was feasible, even desirable.

But the earth is finite, and the end of growth is inevitable. Sooner or later, various limiting factors, such as lack of food or space and the diseases, parasites, and predators that flourish when a species is crowded, must slow down and eventually stop growth.

In all growing systems, there tends to be a slow start, a period of rapid growth, and finally a slowing and cessation of growth as various limiting factors are reached. When natural populations reach the levels at which limiting factors take effect, they can remain stable or they can become nearly extinct. (The latter occurred to the deer of the Kaibab Plateau, which became so numerous that they destroyed their food supply and then starved to death.)

Human populations, however, have a third alternative. Within limits, they can use technology to remove the limiting factors. This is exactly what has happened in the United States. Technology has so effectively removed the limiting factors encountered with population growth that we have come to believe in the possibility of an ever-expanding economy and ever-increasing growth. This belief, however, is complete nonsense in a finite world. If we avoid one limiting factor, another, perhaps more subtle, will take effect.

Currently, the limiting factors seem to be getting ahead of technology, and we are beginning to see that the effects of a growing economy include increasing smog, a vanishing countryside, the generation gap, death on our highways, crowded and substandard schools, growing restrictions on individual freedom, urban congestion, rising taxes, and a host of other problems.

At the same time that past growth has made future growth less and less desirable, it has also made some of our other values less and less effective. Our laissez-faire philosophy, for example, holds that the efforts of individuals to achieve their own self-interest will predictably lead to the common good. In pioneering times this assumption was often correct and workable because it provided the incentive for people to undertake the many tasks that needed doing.

But now there are many more of us, and we have growing access to mechanized energy that permits each of us to move about more and more. We occupy space directly by rushing about in automobiles, boats, and other conveyances and indirectly by requiring great factories, power plants, highways, transmission lines, and so on. Because we are all neighbors now, the decisions of one person affect many others. If one man decides his self-interest is best served by raising hogs or by installing a gravel crusher in his backyard or by gouging a mountainside or by filling an estuary, the effects on the neighbors are direct and highly disagreeable. As a friend of mine phrased it, "Not only are there more of us but each of us has bigger elbows."

Closely related to laissez-faire is the idea of economic efficiency. From the point of view of either the individual or of an organization, the cheapest way has usually been the best way. For example, in the interest of economy, waste products were normally just dumped into the water, into the air, or onto the land—regardless of their effect on others or on the total environment. In other words, dollar costs were the only costs recognized by the specific person or organization making a decision. The same reasoning has even been applied to public services. Many highway departments, for example, have been charged *by law* with the building of highways at the lowest dollar cost, even if somewhat greater dollar investments would do less damage to scenery, farmland, small communities, or fish and wildlife habitats.

Our passion for specialization grew as times became increasingly complex and the way to success lay in doing only one thing at a time. We purposely narrowed the view so that each specialist could delve deeply and solve problems of great difficulty in one small area of inquiry. But such specialization has more and more drawbacks. As John Muir pointed out long ago, you can't do just one thing at a time because there are always side effects.

When we lived in a very spacious environment and each of us had access to very limited amounts of energy, the side effects didn't gang up on us but were generally dissipated into harmlessness. People could rightly claim that "the solution to pollution is dilution." But now, when the side effects of our activities have become some of our major problems, we are stuck with experts who are so specialized that they are often unaware of side effects.

Many examples come to mind. The people who designed color TV were engineers, not medical scientists or geneticists, and they didn't know that some sets produced dangerous levels of X-rays until after thousands of children had been exposed to them. Chemists, not ecologists, developed insecticides, and only after the damage was far advanced did they recognize that some insecticides were concentrated and passed along in biological food chains until they are now threatening eagles, falcons, ospreys, pelicans, and other species with extinction. Similarly, the specialists who developed automobiles weren't thinking of smog. The specialists who mechanized farming and thus cut down on the need for farm labor were not thinking of the consequent migration to the cities, which resulted in urban congestion with all its attendant problems.

The complexity of our society and technology is such that we must continue to rely on experts. But every expert must be sensitized to anticipate side effects and to recognize their growing importance. Part of every educated person's knowledge must be the idea that professional blindness to environmental consequences is no longer tolerable.

I have been saying that such values as growth, laissez-faire, economic efficiency, and specialization—values woven into the very fabric of our economic order—are also at the root of our fastest growing problems. If we don't modify these values, we face disaster.

On the other hand, disaster would be just as certain if we followed the suggestion of various campus radicals and summarily threw out the complex of values, technology, and organization that holds society together. Romantic as living without this "establishment" might be, we are far, far beyond the point of no return. To illustrate, it has been estimated that the entire earth would support only 10 million people at the hunting and gathering level of technology. North America alone might support two million. Currently, we have more than 100 times that many—vastly more people than can be maintained without all the technology and organization implied by the word *establishment.*

The upshot of all of this is that we don't have much room to maneuver. We must change our value system at a nearly explosive speed yet without destructive violence. In a society where government is by consent of the people, massive education offers us the only hope of avoiding disaster.

To meet this challenge, environmental education must involve far more than plant and animal identification for grade school kids. The crucial task is to provide every man, woman, and child in the nation with a deep ecological awareness of how all the things in our environment are interrelated.

Now that most of us live in cities, we are far removed from such realities as photosynthesis, soils, and food production. Many city people grow up thinking of milk as something technology provides to us in cartons. To them it has no relation to cows, grass, soils, sunshine, and acres of land. Yet these are the citizens who vote on crucial environmental issues. Environmental education has become essential for responsible citizenship.

Let's look at the needed changes in attitudes. Perhaps the starting point is to recognize that the earth is finite—a limited sphere. Having accepted this idea, we must recognize that unlimited growth is neither possible nor desirable and seek an approximately stable relationship with our environment. This will call for recycling as much of our material wealth as possible instead of using it and then discarding it. Currently, instead of a circular flow in which things are used repeatedly, we have a one-way flow—from resources through various processors and factories to consumers to junkyards. This one-way flow is depleting our resources and gorging our junkyards.

As part of a revised value system, we need to accept a new outlook on social accounting so that such things as clean air, safe streets, open spaces, and diversity are prized along with next year's automobiles and gold-plated plumbing fixtures. Often we will have to pay higher prices that cover *all* the costs of production, including repair of any damage done to the environment.

Within our present institutional framework, we can do this simply by changing the rules (and, of course, enforcing them), so that profit is taken out of doing the wrong things and incentive provided for doing the right things. A tax or charge on pollution and other environmental damage would create incentives for producers to find cheaper alternatives than dumping things into the environment and paying the charge. Such procedures would immediately bring technology and ingenuity to bear on problems in great need of solution.

There are sound scientific principles that determine the limits within which human populations, their environments, and their technologies can remain viable.

Attaining widespread understanding of the relationships between people and the environment is going to require massive education, involving all of the mass media. Fortunately, this is already taking place. Scarcely a day goes by without news coverage or a new magazine article on environmental problems.

Something deeper seems to be needed, however. All segments of the public need information that helps them see the nature of the problem and that helps them develop attitudes appropriate to the world as it is today.

To ask for change in deep-seated attitudes is stern medicine, and most people won't take it unless it is sugarcoated. Therefore, we need to place much of the burden on television. We should have prime-time programs that are dramatic and enjoyable enough to hold noncaptive audiences of all ages. Such programs could undoubtedly capitalize on the drama and even terror of what can happen if we don't change our ways. And, as I have mentioned, the villains must include our own inappropriate attitudes, not just convenient scapegoats.

To supplement and complement the mass media, the schools must introduce the basic concepts of ecology in the early grades as is already done in some places. Similar coverage must continue right on through college. This will require some tooling up, for at present there is a dearth of teachers equipped to do this. We also need to ask some searching questions about the content and effectiveness of the programs that do exist.

Since most of us cling to our basic attitudes unless we are under great stress, perhaps we won't change until the stress gets much greater. But by then we may have lost many valuable options.

What I am suggesting is that we have two basic choices. We can limit our growth and other impacts on the environment voluntarily, in which case the limiting factor is an *attraction* consisting of a life-style that provides space, abundance, freedom of many kinds, and a broad variety of alternative opportunities. Or, we can continue to grow and pollute and congest until stopped by *hardships*—limiting factors that are not of our own choosing. Instead of attractions, these will be constraints and repulsions, such as limited food, space, and resources; intense pollution; epidemics; greatly restricted alternatives on where we live and what we do; or a social pathology that paralyzes most of our efforts. Technology might deal with some of the problems, but only by imposing its own set of restrictions and problems.

As a species, we will probably survive, even if we take no action, just as scattered and impoverished people survive on deserts that once supported rich agriculture and major civilizations. However, if Homo sapiens is truly a thinking being, we should seek much more than merely to survive environmental disaster. Attaining this "something more" is the challenge of environmental education.

WHAT THE WORLD NEEDS NOW: ENVIRONMENTAL EDUCATION FOR YOUNG CHILDREN *

JEAN KLUGE

Change has long been equated with progress in our country. Finally, we are beginning to see that, at least as far as our environment is concerned, change does not always mean progress. We are aware that our high standard of living has resulted in misuse of our natural resources. Fortunately, we have begun to look around us, to face the problems, and to take action against those who abuse these resources and add to the deterioration of our environment. Our change in attitude is progress—progress toward safeguarding our children's future. Chances are that before we committed ourselves to preservation of our natural resources, we looked around to see what was happening, what the problems were, and how we could help to solve them. To be really committed to this cause, it was necessary to become involved to a high degree with the subject, to observe directly the relationship of forces on objects and man to his surroundings.

We can help children to become involved with their environment in much the same way. We can help them to be aware of such problems posed by the changes that result from too many people living beyond the means of our available natural resources. In becoming familiar with his world, whether it be a city or prairie, the child begins the process of observation. This initial step, so important to future involvement in preservation of what is vital to sustained healthy life, precedes the ability to relate ecological effects to man-made causes. Just as we help the child to understand his role in the environment that we set up for him in the classroom, so can we encourage him to look beyond his immediate surroundings to forces and conditions affecting these surroundings.

Children don't learn about their environment just by looking at it. They explore it by touching, tasting, listening and smelling, as well. With the help of adults, they can begin to piece together information that they have discovered for themselves. Be it city or country, a child can benefit from many experiences in gaining knowledge about his environment. The beginnings of cause-and-effect problem-solving, attitude formation, awareness and appreciation are rooted in these early life experiences.

*Reprinted with permission from *Young Children*, 26(5):260, 262-263, May, 1971. Copyright © 1971, National Association for the Education of Young Children, 1834 Connecticut Avenue, N. W., Washington, D.C. 20009.

RETENTION BY DISCOVERY

A child will more fully retain his firsthand knowledge of a dandelion through his discovery of one by the side of a building than through the words and illustrations in a book. He needs to feel it to know it is fuzzy and to smell it to know it has an odor. Lengthy explanations and naming objects or processes are not necessary in promoting environmental awareness in young children. Help them to see how things are similar, how things change, how objects and systems depend on or help each other, and also how things live in and adapt to their environment. Even big cities have trees! Help the children to really look at one by touching it, by making crayon rubbings of the bark, by feeling the leaves that grow on it, or just by trying to put their arms around it! How is it like other plants—perhaps a dandelion or a bush nearby? How is it helpful to us, especially on a hot summer day? Who perhaps uses it for a home or other source? What conditions allowed it to grow there and not somewhere less suitable? What kind of attitudes can we help form about living things and their relationship to other living things, particularly man? That same tree can be looked at throughout the year, perhaps involving the children in a kind of personal relationship with it.

The leaves or rocks a teacher places on a "nature table" inside of the classroom without the outdoor experience will not be as meaningful as those found by the child in their natural setting. Questions enhance his observations. "What can you tell me about this puddle?" might prompt some children to note qualities such as, "wet, shiny, splashy," while others may notice that the puddle wasn't there before. The youngest child may comprehend only the simplest observable attributes or qualities without responding verbally to questions.

NATURAL VS. MAN-MADE OBJECTS

A focus for a preschooler's observations may be to classify objects into two categories: natural versus man-made. A city child's collection bag would yield far more man-made materials than the country child's. Both children can learn to classify their collections, thereby establishing some basic relationships between objects necessary to the child's ordering of his world. Conceptual learning comes about naturally when a child directly experiences his environment. The look on Roger's face was one of discovery and delight as he patted the snow with his bare hands, exclaiming, "It's cold!" It was easy for him to make a snowball "bigger" than mine. He learned what "melting" meant when he brought his snowball inside to keep it until he went home. At juice time, he wadded up a white paper napkin, patting it like he did the real snowball, making it "round." It was easy for him to represent a snowball after his first-hand experience with a real one.

Walks or bus rides to different areas can prompt some observations of the impact of man on the environment.

Recently, our group of preschoolers took a bus ride into the business section of town to visit the pet store. As we rode, we noticed more houses closer together and an occasional apartment building. Four-year-old Judy said, as she pointed to the apartment building, that there were "a lot" of people living there. Who lives on the big open field next to our school? "Cows and horses" was the reply. Can we run and play freely on the sidewalk downtown without holding a teacher's hand? Where is there a lot of space to play? While driving down a city street, we asked if the children saw any trees or birds. We asked them to close their eyes and tell us what they heard.

Eventually the observations begin to form mental patterns. The world becomes an ordered system and not just a disjunct conglomeration of objects. Hopefully, the child will become familiar with many features of his environment, developing an admiration for some aspects of it and a healthy adjustment to other aspects.

The beginnings of problem-solving are rooted in recognition. Indeed many of our present-day environmental problems that grew to the crisis stage went unnoticed far too long. We can't expect young children to think in terms of devices for improving air or water quality, but we can help them to develop an awareness that will be the basis of intelligent action in the future.

As the teacher shifts her focus from trying to elicit specific responses from the child to observing how the child interacts with and responds to the environment, she will be able to encourage and enhance his learning as well as to create new situations for further discovery. The adult who looks and learns along with the child reinforces his discoveries with her own curiosity and enthusiasm. A feeling of pride in his successful encounters can lead to the child's further sensitivity toward his environment and, ultimately, to responsible actions for maintaining or improving that which is vital to our existence.

MAKING TOMORROW NOW: BUILDING A QUALITATIVE ENVIRONMENT FOR ALL CHILDREN *

MATTHEW J. BRENNAN

In the United States today, we are witnessing a cultural revolution. For the first time in our history as a nation, our people are becoming concerned with the deteriorating quality of the environment in which they are forced to live. We are rapidly approaching a crisis—not the "quiet crisis" about which former Secretary of the Interior Udall wrote but a noisy, clamoring crisis in which men will struggle for space in which to live and play, air fit to breathe, and water fit to drink, not to mention food that is not contaminated by poisons and additives of one type or another designed to enhance its appearance or preserve it from the processes of oxidation and decay.

Concern for the quality of the environment was first voiced by scientists, then by social scientists, now by people in all segments of society. As in all social crises of the past, the American people have turned to education for solutions. Yet for reasons that elude understanding, education in America is not prepared to offer solutions. Although our heritage as a nation is closely bound to the outdoors—to the natural environment—our educational system does not reflect this tie. Where the environment has been studied, man has not been considered as a part of it.

In developing a strategy for education for an environment of quality, let us make one major assumption. If man is the only living thing which can consciously transform, manipulate, control, preserve or destroy his environment, then a knowledge of *how* he affects his environment and, perhaps even more important, of the *consequences* of his actions should be an essential element of human understanding. It is not, and the reason it is not represents a failure of American education.

What is environmental education? It is that education which develops in man a recognition of his interdependence with all of life *and* a recognition of his responsibility to maintain the environment in a manner fit for life and for living—an environment of beauty and bounty in which man lives in harmony.

* From *Childhood Education* October 1970, pp. 2-5. Reprinted by permission of Matthew J. Brennan and the Association for Childhood Education International, 3615 Wisconsin Avenue, N. W., Washington, D.C. Copyright © 1970 by the Association.

The first part of environmental education involves development of understanding; the second, development of attitudes—a "conservation ethic."

Understanding the environment and man's activities in it certainly involves the sciences. Indeed, an understanding of the chemistry, geology, physics, and biology of the environment is basic. But many scientists have themselves learned that decisions regarding man's actions in and use of his environment and its resources are not always made on the basis of scientific knowledge. We have the knowledge to solve most of the new environmental problems—population, pesticides, pollution, poverty of the environment (I call them the "P" problems). But decisions are being made, and will increasingly be made, on the basis of social desirability, economic feasibility, or political expediency (have you noticed how many politicians have suddenly become environmental protectors?). The social sciences must therefore also be an important segment of environmental education. And since natural beauty, esthetics and the ennobling elements of the environment are receiving increased attention, the humanities must come within the purview of our program.

Most important, we can no longer segment our subjects. Discussions of population, pesticides, pollution and poverty of the environment are by nature interdisciplinary. How can you separate the scientific, religious, and social aspects of population; the scientific, esthetic, and social aspects of resource use; the scientific and esthetic aspects of wilderness preservation?

TOTAL ENVIRONMENTS FOR EDUCATION

We are really talking, then, about a new kind of education—I call it *education for the total environment*—which involves understanding of the *external* environment. But, if we are to accomplish the second part of environmental education—the development of a "conservation ethic," an attitude of responsibility for the environment—then our education must involve the *inner* environment of the child as well. We know that life styles and attitudes are formed at an early age. The reasons why people "conserve" are internal, and we will fail if we do not develop in children a good inner environment. Why should the child who has not been conserved be concerned about wilderness, California condors, or Antarctic penguins? Where is esthetics taught in our schools?

To attain our objective—education for the total environment—we must develop *total environments for education*.

Obviously, the most efficient laboratory for experiences in search of meaning in the environment *is* the environment. Yet, in most schools every element of the school facility but the surrounding environment is used. Our teachers are trained to use textbooks, guides, machines, media equipment, indoor laboratories—but never the real laboratory just outside the school. In most schools, the teacher is discouraged from using the surroundings as a laboratory. He can make

TNT in the laboratory and be fully covered by insurance if the school blows up. No parental permission is required. Yet, if he wants to take his class out-of-doors he needs both parental permission and insurance against injury. Is it any wonder the average American knows little about his environment?

The outdoor laboratory must become an essential element of every school facility, extending eventually into the community. Here learning can go on naturally. Here the child can fail without penalty—and learn from his failure. Here he can become part of his environment and his environment a part of him—it will conserve him; he will conserve it.

A STRATEGY FOR ENVIRONMENTAL EDUCATION

What understandings are we talking about? Three great conceptual schemes govern all of life on earth, including man:

1. Living things and environments are in constant change.
2. Living things are interdependent with one another and with their environment.
3. Living things, or populations of living things, are the product of their heredity and their environment.

Although these concepts are complex in nature, an understanding of them and their relationship can be developed quite simply, in this way:

Since man is the principal agent of change in the environment, we can look for rapid changes as a result of his activities. Children can be taught to look for change. *Change* results in a new environment—when man adds poisons, builds dams or roads, or kills predators, new environments are created. Now we must look for *consequences,* since all living things are dependent on their environments. What effect does the change have? Can we predict it? Did we foresee polluted water from detergents that gave us the whitest washes in the world? Did we foresee DDT in the tissues of Antarctic penguins when we sprayed the forests and farms of America to control insects? We must expect consequences when new environments result from change.

Finally, we must try to determine how living things will survive in the new environment. Not all living things have been adapted for life under changed conditions. Our list of endangered species is long. Perhaps man may be on the list; some scientists believe so. Can man survive the pollution, poisons, crowding, noise, etc., that he has introduced into his environment?

As educators we must believe that education for these three basic concepts of life on earth will give man the understanding necessary for his life as a member of the planet earth environment. Your role? If you, teachers and parents, could make a contribution to the success of a space program, you would start working on it now. But in the program for an environment of quality, you not only can make a contribution; you hold the key. Only you can develop programs of education for the total environment. Only you can develop total environments for education. Will you start making tomorrow NOW?

ENVIRONMENTAL ENCOUNTER *
VICTOR A. SCHLICH

A sixth-grade classroom in the Intermediate School at Yarmouth, Maine, buzzed with discussion about the location of a sewage treatment plant in a mythical community. Pupils were clustered in small groups, each representing a segment of the community population: real estate developers, laborers, shop-keepers, housewives, professional men, industrialists, sportsmen, farmers.

Their teacher, Gordon Corbett, interrupted the talk while he placed a cutout of the treatment plant at a river's edge on a colorful map board. This was where the groups had voted to spot the plant. Then Corbett pointed out that the resulting effluent might cause some problems.

"For example, it could produce an algae bloom farther down the river," he said. "Would that make you change your minds about the location?"

The buzzing resumed, only to be punctured suddenly by a shrill voice from the rear: "That's another town. We don't care about them." That set off a roar as the class plunged into debate on one of the more fundamental issues of our time—the complicated adjustment of men, not just to each other but to the total environment.

Elimination of a narrow perception of the environment is a primary objective of the Regional Environmental Education Program (REEP), originated in Yarmouth and since expanded to the surrounding communities of Cumberland, Falmouth, Freeport, and North Yarmouth. This is how the program's coordinator Wesley Willink describes its purpose:

"We are trying to create a better understanding of the ecological situation in the individual pupil's community, what it is and how it got that way. Through this program we are looking for ways to stimulate individual commitment, not to find scapegoats for existing pollution."

Though its responsibility for developing citizens is firmly established, education frequently is criticized for being out of step, of not being relevant to what students see here and now. This is one criticism that cannot justly be directed at the program.

*From *American Education* 7:23-26, August/September, 1971. A publication of the U.S. Department of Health, Education, and Welfare.

REEP addresses itself to environmental conditions that are both "here and now" with relation to its students. It involves itself at all levels, from kindergarten through high school. Thus far the major emphasis has been put on the elementary grades, but special projects also have been devised for junior and senior high schoolers. Environments to be studied are selected to conform with established levels of ability and comprehension.

Kindergarten and first-grade pupils consider the environment in the immediate vicinity of their school. Second-graders and third-graders move out into the neighborhood around the school. Fourth-graders and fifth-graders use the whole community as their environmental classroom. Sixth-grade pupils consider the entire region.

Within each study environment, pupils examine 12 basic environmental themes. Six deal with the natural environment, six with man-made.

Classroom presentations of the study environments open the REEP schedule in the fall; these are followed up by carefully planned field trips. During the winter, when cold weather curbs outdoor activities, members of each class discuss what they saw on their field trips and seek to develop possible solutions for the environmental problems they encountered. One problem is chosen and used as the basis for an action plan, which is put to work in the spring.

HOW DOES IT WORK?

After a field trip around the school property, one first-grade class came up with several suggestions for improving that particular environment. For example, the pupils suggested that pipe be added to a roof run-off drain so that water would be carried to nearby trees and not dumped in the yard. They also made a somewhat less elaborate suggestion that grass be planted in a section of the playground that had been worn thin by the school bus.

"Our most difficult job is to get children so involved in a situation that they themselves actually do something," says Willink. He was asked what first-graders could do about any of the problems they encountered during their inspection of the schoolyard.

"For one thing," he said, "*they* can plant the grass, and that's just what they did. When the teacher told us what the children had said, we bought them some seed and they planted it." The first-graders also devoted several art periods to drawing color pictures of their suggestions, showing each problem in its "before" and "after" state.

"The point to be made," said Willink, "is that the children and their teacher looked at a situation that needed correction, discussed what could be done about it, decided what action they could take, and then went ahead and did it. I call that an excellent example of problem solving."

Proper preparation of teachers is crucial to a program such as REEP, and

Willink devotes time during each school year to this task. He constantly stresses the need to integrate the environmental education program into regular classroom programs. He does not want it added like just another layer on an already heavy cake.

Teachers are encouraged to think of the program as a series of "environmental encounters," adding an environmental emphasis to existing course content and stimulating their pupils to investigate, to ask questions, to determine solutions, to plan actions, and most important, to act. Willink works with the teachers to show them how they can devise encounters suited to their grade levels.

"Environmental encounters are readymade blueprints aimed at encouraging pupils to master problem-solving techniques that will carry over to other courses and into their later lives," says Willink.

The same message is carried to the citizen volunteers who have become an essential element in the program. The volunteers are used primarily as teacher assistants on field trips. Some, after field experience, assist in the classroom presentations as well.

REEP WANTS YOU

The staff at Yarmouth Intermediate School has found that recruiting volunteers is a stimulating process that capitalizes on a valuable educational resource while providing an opportunity to explain the program to the community. REEP especially concentrated on arranging meetings with women's organizations, and it was from these groups that most of the initial corps of volunteers came.

"We train our volunteers in much the same way that we train teachers," says Willink. "Once they have had the program carefully explained to them, we take them on field trips. Each goes on trips similar to those taken by the pupils, but we cover the salient points in greater detail."

Every volunteer is given a copy of REEP's guide for the grade level at which she will work as well as a written outline of the field trip listing the points to be emphasized. The ideal situation is to have enough volunteers so that each class can be broken up into groups of about five pupils each.

Field trips are the core of the environmental education program. Pupils are urged to observe, to listen, to touch, to question. From these experiences comes the foundation for problem solving and individual action backed by a basic appreciation of the interrelationships among natural and man-made elements in the environment.

From the second grade on up, field trips are made by school bus, considered by REEP personnel as "our classrooms on wheels." At predetermined stops the study groups get out to walk a street, to go into a field, or to examine a pond.

Every effort is made to stimulate discussion and to give the children a sense of participation.

During a walk down a suburban street from the main highway to the ocean shore, study groups from a fourth grade stopped frequently to discuss particular aspects of their surroundings. Willink halted his group at the edge of the highway and called attention to a huge maple. He asked if anyone noticed anything unusual about it.

"It's lopsided," said one girl.

"Do you know why it's lopsided?" asked Willink.

"I'm not sure, but maybe it's because of all those wires up there." She pointed to a welter of telephone wires strung from a pole just a few feet from the tree.

"That's right. We need those wires, but when they come close to a big tree like this it's easier sometimes to cut the branches than to move the pole. Can anybody tell me how to solve this?"

"Put the wires underground," volunteered a boy.

Willink explained that this indeed was a solution, that it was, in fact, already being done in other communities.

Another field trip—this time with sixth-grade pupils—involved a visit to a pond. Willink carried with him a small test kit to measure the amount of dissolved oxygen in the water. Step by step he led his group through the procedure, with each pupil taking part. When the completed test indicated a dissolved oxygen content high enough to support fish, Willink told the group, "This means your suggestion to stock the pond with trout will work. Next fall, we'll get busy on that." It was a happy group that trudged back to the road.

POLLUTION SOLUTIONS

A bus carrying another sixth-grade class stopped just short of a bridge crossing a notoriously polluted river. Willink asked what caused the pollution. With one voice the pupils named an industrial plant upriver from them. Willink was not satisfied.

"How about other industrial plants that may be dumping wastes? How about sewage from the various towns along the river? How about sewage from our own town?"

He reemphasized that the purpose of REEP was not to provide scapegoats for existing pollution. Plants and factories guilty of polluting our air and water have to be called to account, he told the class, but so do other possible sources of pollution, which sometimes may be the consequences of alternative preventive actions. In short, students must learn to see the picture in its entirety.

Given that goal, the key man in the REEP operation is the coordinator, as he works full time in three basic areas. First, he helps teachers develop environmental encounters that are directly related to the traditional subjects, thus linking academic achievement with awareness of environmental problems and a search for solutions to those problems.

Second, he works with the administrative and teaching staffs toward using the school facility itself as a teaching resource. He thereby involves the students in an environment they cannot help but find real and relevant.

Third, he enriches the curriculum by conducting inservice workshops for teachers and volunteers, by purchasing and distributing related teaching materials, and by frequent consultation with teachers and pupils.

In these endeavors Willink sees the school as not only having an impact on its students but as helping adults become more aware of the community's environmental problems and as providing a focal point for citizen interest and concern. One of the methods he uses with upper elementary grade pupils to show why every citizen has a stake in the problem is to involve them in playing "Man in His Environment," a game developed by a commercial concern and a committee of educators.

Here the teacher plays the role of a real estate developer who comes to town and proposes a series of projects likely to have a significant effect on the environment. The pupils are broken down into small groups representing various segments of the mythical community.

As the teacher unfolds and explains each development, the pupils huddle with each other. They discuss the potential impact of the project on the community—favorable and unfavorable. Then they vote on whether to accept or reject it.

"No group can cast a vote unless its members are able to provide logical reasons for casting such a vote," says Willink. "This compels them to do some serious thinking about each proposal. The end result is much like the workings of a town meeting."

Although the bulk of the emphasis thus far has been on grades K-6, two model field trips have been developed at the junior high level. One involves the history of the community, including visits to historical spots in each town; the other deals with the recycling of waste products.

A start also has been made at the high school level. Students in one particular civics class, for example, met several times at the REEP resource center to discuss with Willink and several outside speakers an encounter titled "Identifying Community Environmental Issues." During these meetings speakers and students reviewed methods by which the local government regulates environmental issues and they talked of the relationships among private organizations interested in environmental problems.

The civics students compiled a list of community environmental issues as seen by a second group of students. From this list they assigned themselves specific issues for personal investigation, to be followed by a report of their findings.

The action plan was to prepare a general report for presentation to their fellow students and to the community.

SUPPLYING THE TOOLS

REEP operates out of a classroom and a small attached office in the Intermediate School at Yarmouth. The classroom has been converted into a combination training and resource center. Here are stored such teaching aids as mounted animal specimens, samples of resource products, and a variety of printed material, films, and scientific testing equipment. Also on hand are such mundane items as picks and shovels for action projects.

From the resource center Willink periodically visits the five communities participating in the program to lead classroom discussions, join in field trips, and meet with teachers and citizen volunteers. He also serves as a sort of purchasing agent. "Just the other day I provided some white paint for a school in Freeport," he says. "The pupils painted various games on the blacktop yard and marked where their class lines should form."

Federal funds are channeled into REEP through the Maine Environmental Education Project, with the regional program serving as a demonstration project for an expanded Maine program due to begin this fall. Federal funds are used only to purchase supplies and to pay for teacher scholarships at the Maine Conservation Camp at Bryant Pond.

Because of REEP, 5,500 pupils in five Maine communities are becoming increasingly aware of the complex environmental interrelationships within a particular community and among the communities within a region. They know that events in one community can affect the environment of the others, and probably will. And as they learn, they may be launching a social action movement.

Says Willink, "When children get involved they create adult interest, and it would appear that we are now reaching entire families throughout the area."

WHITHER URBAN
ENVIRONMENTAL EDUCATION'' *

BARBARA J. REID

Environmentally, the cities of North America may be the products of man's worst failure to date in dealing with his surroundings. In terms of both natural resources and the quality of life, our cities are deteriorating. Seventy per cent of Americans now live in metropolitan areas, and it is estimated that 90 per cent will do so in 20 years.

The overpowering results of man's technology are polluting the air through the factory, the automobile, and the private furnace; and polluting the streams to such an extent that during last year's drought in Northeastern America the residents of New York City could not drink the water of the mighty Hudson which flows next to it. In 1966 ten million families in America were estimated to be living in deteriorated or substandard housing (4). Urban sprawl continues unabated with little or no attempt at city or regional planning. Our population growth is taking place at the fastest rate in those urban areas that can least afford it. Transportation systems are clogged by commuters, and freeways through the cities continue to be built without considerations of either their effect upon the residents of the area or the land itself.

Growth rates that are projected by planners, etc., are taken as fact, and systems are designed to accommodate such growth in population, automobiles, housing needs, and other areas without ever questioning the assumption that such growth may not be desired. For example, it is no surprise to those within the city that the transportation systems are incredibly clogged at the present time. Yet, we continue to build functional and aesthetically displeasing freeways to accommodate even more traffic jams. This does not have to occur, and citizens are beginning to realize this. In sum, the most basic questions about the use of natural and man-made resources are not being asked on a broad scale.[1]

Educationally, the inner city can also be deemed a failure in many ways. The urban deprived are of course the most obvious example of this failure. In New York City alone 65 per cent of all Black People and Puerto Ricans drop out of high school (3). In some school districts in Chicago the rate is the same, if not

---

*Reprinted with permission of the author and the Dembar Educational Research Services, Inc., from *The Journal of Environmental Education*, 2(1):28-29, Fall 1970.

[1]For a good discussion of this see Marine, Gene, *America the Raped*, Simon and Schuster, New York, 1969.

worse. This amounts to about one thousand students a month (3). Children in metropolitan areas are not all deprived economically and socially, but many if not most are deprived educationally in the sense that they are not aware of the basic ecological relationships of the world around them. They are not in most cases aware of nature in the wilderness sense or of the ecology of the city—both in terms of people and nature. The traditional educational curricula of the U.S. does not include questions that deal with the environment—man's relationship to it and the results of the relationship in the past. Because of the failure of the urban schools in many of the most rudimentary concerns, educational innovation is becoming a concern for most urban educators. This innovation is taking place in terms of curriculum, educational techniques, teacher training, classroom organization, and a restructuring of the schools in relation to parents and to other community organizations across a broad spectrum.

It is hoped that the growing student and citizen environmental action will encourage the development of environmental education on the part of students, teachers, and all citizens. Future international conferences such as the 1972 United Nations Conference on the Environment will also provide forums for educational concerns. It is hoped that those involved in educational innovations and those concerned with environmental education can come together to forge a new program for the urban child.

It is often assumed that taking the city child out of the city and into nature will suffice. The following comment by Gerald Schneider of the Audubon Naturalist Society of Washington, D.C., gives a different point of view:

> The strength and the backbone of the conservation movement and love of nature have come from naturalists, and still do. But the naturalist, to paraphrase the philosopher Rousseau, may be a slave and a serf to his own pretensions, unable to separate that which is his value from that which may be someone else's value. As such, he may try to project his values on the urban child and find his values rejected because the child lacks the experience to base nature values on (2).

The question must be asked whether an urban child, in learning about trees and the natural food chain, takes this knowledge back into the city as something relevant for his everyday life of concrete, ghetto (or suburbia), air pollution, overcrowding, and museum-protected open space.

The answer *may* be to focus the attention of the city child on his most common experience—neighborhood planning in the city, waste disposal, water supply, man's growth within the city, and how the city came to exist in the first place. A sense of partnership with the world of nature and human beings that surrounds the city child may have to be established before he can feel a partnership with nature "out there." Partnership can be defined in many ways, but it may be that a sense of continuity with the development of both man and the structures he has created is more specific.[2] For the city is a man-made environment and it may be preferable to deal with the resource base on which it depends and the functionally pleasing improvements that can be made in terms of the city itself. "Since nature as it exists now is largely a creation of man, and in turn shapes him and his societies, its quality must be evaluated in terms not of primeval wilderness, but of its relation to civilized life" (1). Aesthetics become extremely important in a man-made environment. Nature left to its own devices may be aesthetically satisfying, but the same can scarcely be said of the cities.

REFERENCES

1. Dubos, Rene, *So Human an Animal*, Charles Schribner, New York, 1968.
2. Conference, *Man and Nature in the City*, Bureau of Sport Fisheries and Wildlife, U.S. Department of the Interior, Government Printing Office, Washington, D.C., 1969, p. 68.
3. *New York Times*, December 29, 1968, p. E11.
4. Schussheim, Morton J., *Toward a New Housing Policy*. Committee for Economic Development Supplementary Paper No. 29, 1969, p. 9.

NEW HORIZONS FOR ENVIRONMENTAL EDUCATION *

WILHELMINA HILL AND ROY C. WHITE

As man reaches out into space, probes the depths of the ocean, and tries to renew the environment for living in its cities, environmental education is reaching for new dimensions. The improvement of the quality of man's surroundings, reduction of pollution, and accomodation to population increases and problems require studies in depth. A high priority is essential for educational programs that deal with new developments and problems related to man and the new technology.

Quality control of the environment is one of the basic needs of mankind. Preservation and enhancement of our natural resources go hand in hand with

*Reprinted with permission of the authors and the Dembar Educational Research Services, Inc., from *The Journal of Environmental Education*, 1(2):43-46, Winter 1969.

[2]For a good discussion of the new biological and anthropological discoveries and its justification of the sense of continuity see Ardrey, Robert, *The Territorial Imperative*, Dell Publishing Company, New York, 1966.

resource use developments that will benefit people. Survival on this planet is dependent upon man's willingness to cope with these problems.

Some of the most serious pollution problems with which we are now faced are in the areas of air pollution, noise, water pollution, and landscape desecration. Due to technology and population increases, some of these kinds of pollution are becoming extremely serious and difficult or impossible to control.

When twentieth century man ventures into space, lands on the moon, or explores the ocean resources, he must cope with new environmental conditions and problems. Wherever people have clustered into urban centers, large or small, environmental problems have been encountered. And these people represent approximately three-fourths of the population in our country.

The new environmental education is resulting from the crucial needs and problems of man in relation to his environment. It is people centered and includes urban as well as rural areas. Natural resources—their uses, preservation, and enhancement—are considered in their relationship to people.

School children as well as adults require many opportunities to become *aware* of such natural resources as forests, lakes, or swamps. Outdoor education centers, such as the one at High Rock on Staten Island, New York, offer opportunities for children of New York City to visit a nature area with the guidance of naturalists. At such a center, inner city children often see many birds and animals other than the pigeons, starlings, and sparrows or even rats that inhabit their home neighborhoods. One little girl reported, "This is the first time I've seen all the way around a horse." From first-hand knowledge and experience, children may gain not only *knowledge* but *appreciation* of their natural resources.

Responsibility for improvement of the environment and for attaining real action may often be learned effectively through actual experiences. Through *participation* in school ground and neighborhood conservation or beautification projects, children learn skills and develop interests in environmental improvement. Conservation then can become a way of life.

A striking illustration of pupil participation in conservation was carried out in the Shore and Marine Environmental Program at the Sandy Hook State Park in New Jersey. Among other activities, the children planted large numbers of used Christmas trees from New York City along the barrier beach. The trees were planted at such an angle as to catch sand and start the building of sand dunes. The project director, Richard Cole, reports that during a recent storm the part of the beach where the trees were planted withstood the wind and waves best.

Environmental pollution problems may be studied entirely through the use of textbook or lecture methods. Not so in the classes of Dr. Phyllis Busch of Project Spruce at Pine Planes, New York. When providing instruction about air pollution in inner city classrooms of mid-Hudson New York State, she takes the children into the streets and city squares. There they note the degree and types of air pollution, take samples on moist blotters or cloth, observe the sources of pollution, and consider ways in which it could be controlled or reduced. On rainy days the sampling may be made by similar methods on window sills. Every child has a role to play in these *problem solving* activities. In such *discovery* methods of learning, textbooks, reference books, magazines, films, television, and many other media are used as appropriate for the learners. The teacher's contributions are of value. However, the pupil is central, and the out-of-door resources, teachers, and communication media are the means to help him learn about the natural environment and his relationship to it.

Oceanography and marine science are meriting increased attention by students. The ocean world—its resources and its problems—is being probed as never before as a source of food, minerals, water, and energy. While students study the ocean, management problems related to uses and pollution are increasing.

Orange County children of California have been learning about the ocean's characteristics, resources, and pollution problems through an oceanography center at Santa Ana. The floating laboratory ship, Fury II, leaves Newport Beach harbor at Balboa Island daily with groups of 30 or 40 children and their teachers. The junior high school groups have 4-hour and the senior high 8-hour cruises. They divide into six or seven groups to study and record findings about plankton, water temperatures at various depths, sea birds, seals, types of pollution carried by the tides, and kinds of things netted from the ocean floor. Some of their findings are recorded and reported daily to science people in the area as valuable information.

A training project is being carried out on a vessel anchored in the Washington, D.C. area. Here 120 unemployed, disadvantaged young people are being given training to prepare them as oceanographic aides. This project is sponsored by the U.S. Office of Education under the Manpower Development and Training Act.

Approximately 15 oceanography and marine science centers have been funded through Title III of the Elementary and Secondary Education Act. They are helping many school systems develop new or improved education programs in this rapidly developing resource area from the oceans of the world.

In the Bureau of Higher Education, fellowships have been and are being awarded in the support of graduate studies in Oceanography and Marine Science. Last year approximately 49 fellowships were awarded in this field.

As an outcome of the increased focus on environmental education, some curriculum guides have been produced or are in the process of development. The state departments of education of South Carolina, Louisiana, and Colorado are among those which have published such guides.

The ecological approach to environmental education is believed to hold considerable promise. Some progress in this direction has been made by an experimental planning project in the Arlington and Alexandria, Virginia, public schools. Outstanding ecologists from the Smithsonian Institution and local universities have been working with the school people on this project.

Concept development is important in environmental as well as other curriculum areas. Various forms of generalized knowledge have greater significance and more likelihood of retention by the learner than factual knowledge only. These concepts and generalizations can be designed to run through the environmental curriculum as threads or strands in a more or less spiral order.

People concerned with various aspects of environmental education have been identifying and publishing basic concepts and understandings which could be useful in curriculum development. A special issue of the *Grade Teacher* on ecology contains one article that identifies four basic ecological concepts as well as other materials gleaned from outdoor education programs in Minnesota, Missouri, Idaho, and Connecticut. A fairly recent doctoral dissertation at the University of Montana (by one of the authors of this article) presents a comprehensive treatment of "conservation understandings associated with community resources."

In concept development, it is well to keep in mind that one cannot teach concepts to people. Concepts develop within the individual as the result of his educational experiences.

Curriculum workers are as much concerned with human society and the quality of our environment as with the use of natural resources. As technology increases in sophistication, there is an apparent decrease in the quality of our environment. No longer can conservation education be concerned only with problems relevant to the proper use of natural resources. It must also become more concerned with social and health problems resulting from a rapidly increasing population and from an affluent society.

The educational community can, and must, provide action oriented programs of environmental education for young people. The students of today must become more cognizant of the consequences they will face tomorrow if the environment is allowed to become more polluted and the quality of the environment is allowed to deteriorate further.

Since all people are affected by their environment, it seems essential that all people become more aware of their environment and their relation with it. Therefore, environmental education does not lend itself only to a single subject, but may be incorporated into the total curriculum. It is important, however, that this incorporation into the total curriculum not place the teaching of environmental education in a subordinate position, as has sometimes happened in the past.

Many subject areas offer opportunities for the integration of environmental educational concepts. However, to accomplish this effectively, consideration must be given to another aspect of the educational spectrum, that is to teacher education.

At the present time many colleges and universities have courses related to environmental education available for teachers, or other students. Few of these institutions require or recommend that these courses be studied by prospective teachers. If we are to have young people educated about the relationship of man with his environment, we need classroom teachers who are somewhat knowledgeable about concepts of human ecology. To accomplish this goal, colleges and universities should accept the challenge of improving their curricula in environmental education. This could be done by providing expanded and improved programs in environmental education and requiring that some courses in this field be studied by all prospective teachers, along with expanded summer programs for experienced teachers.

Through the Education Professions Development Act, funds have been made available for proposals related to the education of teachers, including the area of conservation and environmental studies. Universities, states, and local school systems may apply for financial aid through this act. Fellowship programs, both at prospective and experienced teacher levels, provide an opportunity for full-time educational programs in a variety of fields, including those closely related to environmental education.

One Experienced Teacher Fellowship Program in Outdoor Education and Conservation was held in New Jersey. Currently a Prospective Teacher Fellowship Program in the same field, leading to a Master of Arts Degree, is being carried out through four cooperating institutions: Trenton State College, Glassboro State College, Montclair State College, and the New Jersey State School of Conservation.

The momentum thus far gained for contemporary environmental education cannot be increased only through curriculum development and teacher education. There is still another facet of the educational community that must be considered before a comprehensive environmental education program can become fully operational. The schools in a community usually reflect the educational philosophy of that community. If this is a valid assumption, we need to alert parents and other residents of a community about the urgent need for including environmental education in the school curriculum. School administrators, school governing bodies, and parents must support the environmental education program if it is to be effective. Unfortunately, community support for environmental education is sometimes lacking.

Many *community resources* can be incorporated into an environmental education program. Resources such as people, places, and things are available in all communities and if properly utilized can enhance the curriculum. Resource people residing in the school community may be available—and willing—to assist teachers and administrators with their environmental education program. Persons knowledgeable about conservation may be enlisted to serve as classroom visitors or assist with trips to natural areas. Thus, two kinds of community resources—people and field study sites—could be included in environmental programs.

Some outdoor education projects currently receive assistance from employees of state and national conservation agencies. These personnel may be employed by fish and game departments, state and national forests and parks, and public health agencies. College and university professors may also be available to assist with local environmental studies. Each community could identify available resource personnel for its geographic area.

Field study sites may be in a wide variety of areas, school grounds being the most accessible. Much study of the students' environment can be undertaken on the local school grounds and surrounding neighborhood. These areas, where available, should be used as extensively as possible.

In many environmental education programs, field study sites, whether large or small, are selected away from the school. Some schools take their students to national parks and forests, while others go to local parks, lakes, or vacant lots within the community. The students may stay at these field study sites for a few hours to a full week, or longer. Seasonal changes in the environment are observed by students in some programs as sites are visited several times in a school year.

Some programs involve the students during several weeks of the summer. The Summer Ecology Program at Deer Lodge, Montana, provides the opportunity for Powell County High School students to study ecology for four weeks in the out-of-doors. The students in the summer outdoor education program at Cedar Rapids, Iowa, have continuing classroom activities during the following school year.

Some programs furnish children the opportunity to live in an outdoor area for several continuous days. Such experiences are provided for students near Golden Pond, Kentucky, at "Land Between the Lakes." Other students from Marshfield, Wisconsin; Alberton, Montana; and North Bend, Washington, also live at outdoor camps for several days at a time.

Other environmental education programs limit the field experiences for children to short visits to outdoor sites, or to several visits to the same area during the school term. This type of program can be observed at Media, Pennsylvania; Newark, Delaware; and Missoula, Montana.

The variety of outdoor education programs reflects the philosophies of the communities and indicates the resources available within communities. It is encouraging to observe that many schools are providing diverse opportunities for their students to gain experiences related to their environment. It is also obvious that many schools are utilizing resources within the community to enhance their environmental education programs.

The U.S. Office of Education provides a wide variety of services and administers fiscal aid assigned to it through federal aid legislation. A good many of these programs are available for environmental education. Some have been used for developing a substantial number of conservation/environmental projects. The resources of others are just beginning to be applied to this rapidly developing field.

Title I, of the Elementary and Secondary Education Act is the Nation's largest Federal aid-to-education program. Each year since 1965-66 more than $1 billion has gone to serve underachievers from low-income families. More than 16,000 of the Nation's school districts participate.

Because of Title I, ESEA, many children who have never before had an opportunity to walk in a forest or see wildlife in its natural habitat are now having these experiences. Dozens of camping facilities are operating all year round, serving children from low-income families from the impoverished areas of the inner cities. Hundreds more operate during the summertime. There are nature and conservation camps, day camps, sleep-away camps, laboratories and science camps operating throughout the country with the support of Title I, ESEA.

In addition, during warm weather, some classes are also held outdoors—in places like Tiffin and Springfield, Ohio; Memphis, Tennessee; and Garrett, Maryland.

The outdoor camping programs are, generally, operated by local school districts—from Los Angeles and Seattle, to Detroit and New York City. In addition to the camps there are mobile science laboratories through which students are exposed to those areas of science which can be most directly related to their environment—marine biology, astronomy, and earth science. A typical project of this type serves the island, Martha's Vineyard.

Title III, ESEA, which funds innovative center projects, has made possible the funding of approximately 110 outdoor education projects. These have included such varied projects as the Oceanographic Education Center at Falmouth, Massachusetts; Suffolk Environmental Biology Center, Port Jefferson, New York; and Conservation and Environmental Science Center for Southern New Jersey at Browns Mills; the Program of Outdoor Education for southern Idaho (office at American Falls), the Napa Experimental Forest education center in California; an ecological oriented conservation project at Missoula, Montana, which includes habitat improvement; and Project Introspection, dealing with the cultural, historical, and natural resources of the Virgin Islands.

Over a period of 3 years, Title I of the Higher Education Act has provided funds for over 150 programs in areas of environmental education, including planning, beautification, land use, and conservation. These grants are available for community services and continuing education projects through designated State agencies and are to utilize the resources of colleges and universities to help solve problems relating to the quality of the environment.

Other Office of Education programs which have environmental education aspects or opportunities include:

Elementary and Secondary Education Act, Titles II, V, and VIII

Bureau of Research (especially Small Projects of the Regional Research Program)

Health, Physical Education, and Recreation program (Bureau of Elementary and Secondary Education)

Manpower Development and Training Act

Office of Construction Services

Chapter seven
Teacher Education
Out-of-Doors

INTRODUCTION

Over the years institutions of higher education have paid increasing attention to the significance of preparing teachers to carry their instructional programs beyond the four walls of the classroom. Outdoor education for teachers focuses primarily upon three areas of emphasis: (1) utilizing the out-of-doors to facilitate effective and efficient learning, (2) relating curriculum content, i.e., abstract textbook knowledge to the practical reality of firsthand learning experience in the larger community classroom, (3) gaining additional insight and understanding of child development and behavior in a total-living situation.

Developments in teacher education have assumed various patterns. Some institutions of higher education use a resident internship at an outdoor school as a supplement to the regular student teaching experience, while others incorporate outdoor education into the on-going professional course work of the pre-service teacher. Some 200 colleges and universities offer specific courses in outdoor education. It is even possible at a few select institutions to pursue graduate work in outdoor education.

Of recent significance is the impact of the Elementary and Secondary Education Act upon newly developing outdoor education projects, and the critical demand this has created for teachers and administrators trained in outdoor education.

THE TEACHER OUT OF DOORS *

LAWRENCE H. CONRAD

Nearly everyone who has ever tried learning out of doors is delighted with the idea. They say first that it's fun; second that it's simple and natural; and third that both the experiences and the knowledge we take from them are unforgetable. Yet the progress of outdoor education has been slow; and the reason is lack of suitable teachers. It is a fact still that many teachers are better behind a desk than anywhere else and that in teacher education we have not yet managed to any appreciable extent to involve our candidates in experiences which would enrich their lives and give them something genuinely big to communicate.

Wherever we have broken the pattern of lecture-and-textbook learning, we have had reason to applaud the result. Yet until the present moment, we have not grown bold enough to declare that direct learning, in contact with the realities of life, is the most vital and valuable part of any teacher's equipment.

We have all along been aware that one teacher becomes great and inspiring through his intimate relationship with life, while another, equally studious and equally learned, becomes merely a bore. The difference is often that the one teacher has many and lively contacts with reality, while the other has kept his nose constantly in a book. Yet we have permitted the accidents of life to fall as Fate might direct, and we felt powerless to guide or to influence them. In a study of students in three New Jersey State Teachers Colleges, one investigator found that 60 per cent had never attended a real session of court; gone up in an airplane; visited a hospital for the insane; hiked a distance of ten miles; been the main speaker at a meeting; printed a photograph; or earned money by making something with their hands. More than 80 per cent had never been down in a mine; had never gone hungry for 24 hours; nor been present when someone was born or when someone died. These students may have gone on to sound training

*Reprinted by permission of the publisher and the National Association of Secondary School Principals from *The Bulletin of the National Association of Secondary School Principals* 31:36-41, May, 1947.

and to successful teaching. Yet their contact with the realities of life would seem slender from this report; and their knowledge, accordingly, might appear theoretical if not superficial. Only a very small part of their training as teachers is aimed deliberately at involving them—their persons and their lives—in the experiences of human beings on this earth.

JUST BEYOND THE CLASSROOM

To say that teachers colleges are not equipped to provide such experiences is to think very narrowly of the process of teacher education. There is a whole vast area of extramural living and thinking which we have not yet begun to incorporate into the field of teacher preparation. It is the area of outdoor learning; it lies just beyond the classroom; it sets in just after the bell rings; it is more interesting, more attractive, more compelling than is the area to which we have devoted our total attention. It is important first because the things to be learned out there are frequently more real and more useful than the indoor things; and second because reflection and growth and human relationships—the best parts of education—are easy and natural there, whereas they are difficult and rather stilted indoors. One's body and one's whole being are together involved in the educational process when it takes to the woods, the fields, the open country.

If educational experiences in the open air are good for boys and girls, it is doubly important that their teachers have such experiences both for their own sake and as preparation for guiding and directing programs of outdoor learning in their work as teachers.

Every teacher of every subject would do a better job if some of the training sessions, at least, could be held in the open where pertinent *realia* can be seen and touched in a state of nature; where relationships among things are undistorted; and where the artificial repressions of the classroom may be relaxed. Any good teacher shows up better under such conditions. And regardless of what is being studied, the guidance and leadership of a walk in the open, or a gathering, or an exploration constitute the best educational situation to be found. Every teacher should have this technique as a substantial part of her training.

The best way to get it, by all odds, is through an organized session of educational camping. For in an educational camp, the teachers and prospective teachers can have some contact daily with youngsters of the age group for which they are trained or are training; the daily life can be natural and real; and certain human qualities sometimes lacking in school teachers can take root and grow while the sun and the air and the elements and the informal companionship of others are getting in their work.

In one of the camps, a mere ten-day session for prospective teachers has drawn comment of the highest enthusiasm. The immediate comment, made while still in camp, is that all of education should go in this direction—which indeed it is doing. But later, after the experience has been digested and integrated, the students express the conviction that all teachers everywhere ought to have the chance to develop the ingenuity, the self-reliance, the independence, and the inspiration that are to be found in a well-regulated camping experience. Prospective teachers found themselves growing so notice-ably *as people* that in a mere ten day session a number of them became actually human in outlook and attitude. Some saw in the simplified pattern of camp life an understandable prototype of human society, so that no social problem thereafter could be quite as puzzling as most problems had been before. And all agreed that the term "integration" as applied to school work had never come to life for them with a tangible meaning until they saw themselves in a group of learners using all their resources of knowledge and skill and assisting each other for an entire morning in an adventure of learning. No bells, no departments of subject matter, no switching of instructors, no academic formalities; but a constant cooperation in which even the smallest contributions count greatly, as they often give to the thinking of the group a new center or a new focus.

The unifying principle in the whole process of teacher education may well be found in a single camp session. Here, truly, the relationships of all the subject-matter fields may be seen; the elements vital to a sound teaching method may be found and approved; and an educational philosophy may be formed in the presence of simplicity, reality, and the seriousness of the real problems of youth. More and more attention is swinging, in the profession of teaching, to the importance of this one completely natural element in the building of leadership qualities in a teacher. Superintendents and boards of education are careful to inquire whether candidates for teaching positions have had camping experience. They would be happy to learn that such experiences were actually incorporated into the teaching-training program.

Outdoor education is widely recognized in our school systems. Our elemen-tary school explores the woods and fields in quest of knowledge. Our junior high school studies the farms and factories, the power houses and dairies in the vicinity. Our high school blueprints all of the services and agencies in the life of the community. Further, we carry on field trips to study housing, prisons, the various branches of the government; and to acquaint students generally with situations that lie outside of books. Visits to museums and to the theatre are now commonplaces of school life. Yet these expeditions are still in the hands of the very few teachers who can handle them. Many of our teachers are at a loss, once the comforting school building has receded into the background; and some even experience the panic of wondering what to *do* with these youngsters! Yet the parents all trust that every teacher knows what to do with boys and girls in any situation.

One preparation for conducting outdoor experiences, whether in the country or in town, is to have experiences of one's own during which adjustments have been made to the personal and social relationships that are brought into being by the absence of a school building. Hence journeys, explorations, and field trips are indispensable in the preparation of teachers. And all of the better colleges are coming to accept the inevitability of this training.

Outdoor education restores the natural situation in which primitive man first learned, and so it brings into play two forces that are difficult to establish in any formal classroom: the quick enthusiasm and joy of learning; and the constant awareness of the steps by which we learn. The student in the out-of-doors is filled with curiosity and wonder as he comes upon things he cannot identify or does not understand; so his need is real and present. Whatever he learns will give immediate pleasure, therefore, and may be appreciated on the spot. Nor is the process of outdoor learning either remote or involved. More than is the case in any textbook, the learner sees what he is getting, and the steps by which he is getting it. This is seen in the fact that soon afterward he will undertake to point out to others every single thing he has ever learned through the use of his senses. The learner becomes the teacher by the natural desire to communicate, by the joy he takes in his knowledge, and by his recollection of the clear steps of his own advancement in learning.

REDUCING STUDENT RESISTANCE

The resistance which students are able to offer to their teachers is traditional and legendary. The antagonism has been furthered by the fact that students and teachers are on different sides—of the desk, perhaps, or a lectern. Even the teacher who walks up and down the aisles has a retreat—and the students well know it—to the other side of the desk, should any crisis arise. Though we have remodeled the furniture of the classroom and have unscrewed the benches from the floor, the old enmity remains. It may be the oldest enmity in the world—students and teachers. The teacher is there to ask the questions, and the student is there to be wary in answering them.

How much the classroom itself has to do with this division of labor, we may never know. But it is a fact that, when teacher and class move out of doors, there comes a marked increase in friendliness reflected back and forth across the barrier. For of course the barrier—if it is a piece of furniture—has disappeared. Somebody has to walk along with the teacher. Everyone has to walk near the teacher, if comments are to be exchanged or questions asked. But with only this slight change in relationship, quite a change in atmosphere occurs. A group in the out-of-doors customarily arranges itself in a rough circle in concentric circles. It is not often easy to tell which person in the circle is the teacher. Even if you listened to the talk, you might not know for a time. For once outside the classroom, the students, as if by some magic, commence to ask the questions; and the teacher has to spend a much higher percentage of time giving answers.

Watching such a group, you would see no sullen docility—which is never entirely absent indoors. Instead, you would see informality and freedom from all artificial restraint. You would see more friendliness—between student and student, and between student and teacher—than the walls of a classroom would ever encourage. You would hear less cant, less jargon, less stilted school-teacher talk than you had ever heard before from such a group. You would hear less hair-splitting, less affirming of the obvious, fewer lofty-sounding remarks. You would see and hear practically no bluffing: no teacher trying to impress students with his vast knowledge; no students trying to get credit for work they haven't done. For here some of the students are always around behind the teacher's back, from which position even a very faint Bronx cheer can be pretty disconcerting; and the students are usually so crowded together that a well-placed elbow in the ribs is enough to bring to a halt any student's try for an "A" that he hasn't earned. The outdoor situation helps to bring to the fore all of the real and worthy elements in education; and reduces greatly the unnatural and artificial ones that have grown, sometimes, into real evils in the indoor classroom.

Outdoor education makes no effort to supplant the traditional teacher-student relationship, nor does it hope to do away with the classroom or with the schoolhouse. Employed in the situations for which it is designed, it will do some of the work of education better than heretofore. Employed with regularity under appropriate conditions, outdoor education and its methods will affect profoundly the whole educational process. Indoor education is noticeably improved when groups and classes begin circulating out of doors, or setting out on trips together. The contact with reality brings a wholesome spirit to circulate all through the school. Relations between teachers and students show a healthy improvement. All book-studies are enriched by the references which outdoor parties bring into the classroom. And life itself becomes—as was the original intention—the chief study in the public school system.

TEACHER PREPARATION NEEDED

But somehow the teachers do have to be trained. There is no special virtue in just going out of doors—except that the air is always better. The teacher has to know what to do when he gets out there. He has the almost terrifying problem of keeping the minds busy—and the hands and bodies—of a group of lively, eager, and curious young people. It is not enough for him to have studied how youth act when seated in rows. He must have his training in child behavior reinforced by hour-long, day-long, week-long companionship with them in learning; and if it is to be natural, it must be in the midst of nature.

Institutions for the preparation of teachers need, therefore, to supplement their indoor program with as many outdoor facilities as can be arranged and made a part of the training period. The first need is for classes in all subjects that will make occasional intelligent use of the area in which the college is situated. Next, a systematic program of field trips for making organized studies of more remote subjects and areas. And finally, a brief period of camp life in contact with young people of the proper age group, for every teacher-candidate; and the requirement that some success be attained in this fellowship of learning before the teaching certificate is issued.

The schools of tomorrow will educate the pupil by means of experiences, rather than by means of lectures and readings. They will bring the pupil and the world together for study. Hence the teacher will have to know both the pupil and the world, not as fictions dealt with in books but as living realities that have been met and learned together, on the same ground. In the face of this certainty, teacher education must turn—not tomorrow, but today—to the outdoors and to reality. Thousands of teachers old and new will be making that turn during the present school year.

FIRST-RATE TEACHERS NEED FIRSTHAND EXPERIENCE *

DONALD R. HAMMERMAN

All students majoring in elementary education at Northern Illinois University participate in three outdoor-education experiences at the campus near Oregon, Illinois. These experiences occur at the sophomore, junior, and senior levels, and are an integral part of a student's professional preparation for teaching.

In an attempt to determine the extent of college students' background of first-hand experience, the author administered a basic experience survey to 92 sophomores. A factor to be taken into consideration was that a large majority of the students at Northern Illinois University come from the metropolitan Chicago area. The students were under no pressure to answer one way or the other. Their responses had nothing whatever to do with their grades; in fact, they were not even required to sign their names.

SURVEY RESULTS

The results were quite startling. Roughly, only half of the students had ever

*Reprinted by permission of the publisher and the National Commission on Teacher Education and Professional Standards from *The Journal of Teacher Education* 11:408-411, September, 1960.

been close enough to a snake to hold it in their hands. Close to one-third of the respondents had never seen an eclipse of the moon and more than half (59 per cent) of the students had never viewed a solar eclipse. Fewer still, only one out of three could actually locate the North Star in the night sky. A little less than half of the students (42 per cent) indicated that they had ever followed the tracks of an animal to see where it had been or where it was going.

Only slightly more than half (58 per cent) of the students had ever been intrigued sufficiently to determine the age of a tree by counting its rings. Only two out of five students had ever found a fossil.

The highest rated experience was that of catching a fish. Four out of five students had experienced this.

Only one out of four students could identify any bird by its song alone. Students mentioned 21 different birds in responding to this item. Cardinal, robin, blue jay, crow, and bob white were the five birds mentioned with greatest frequency.

Only one out of four students had ever in his lifetime walked more than 10 miles on a hike.

These figures suggest that a large proportion of persons entering the teaching profession have rather limited backgrounds of outdoor experience. Can such people bring a wealth of meaningful learning to their own pupils? Perhaps it is as important for prospective teachers to have direct experiences in science, mathematics, and the social studies as it is for them to study these subjects from textbooks.

Following their initial exposure to outdoor education, 76 of the 92 sophomore students involved in the basic experience survey were asked to list a new experience—one thing that they had either seen or done for the first time in their lives at the Field Campus. The answers were interesting.

Learning to use a compass led the list of new experiences, with almost half (31) of the students mentioning it. Eight students found a fossil for the first time, and seven saw their first wild deer. Learning to distinguish one tree from another was listed as a new experience by seven students. Trees mentioned in this category as being "new discoveries" were oak, honey locust, and hackberry. Making a plaster cast of an animal track was a new experience for four students, while three others saw the bones of a dead animal for the first time. Three of the students also listed looking at the moon through a telescope.

Two students made a terrarium for the first time. Seeing vines growing up a tree, "took a squirrel's nest apart," others. "Learned to use my watch as a compass," was also mentioned by two. Seeing tracks of various animals, seeing a fire started with flint and steel, petting a deer, seeing a blue jay, chopping down a tree, "took a squirrel's nest apart," and "just sat and listened to all the sounds" were each mentioned by one person as being a new experience. One student even went so far as to state that she did everything "during the past few days for the first time."

KINDS OF EXPERIENCE

It might be well at this point to examine rather closely the kinds of outdoor-education experiences which contribute to the professional program of teacher preparation at Northern Illinois University.

During the two and a half days in which sophomore students are in residence at the Field Campus, emphasis is placed on developing an initial concept of outdoor education. Students spend considerable time sharpening perceptions, reawakening senses which are largely unused in on-campus academic work. Students are led to explore the unfamiliar and are encouraged to search for answers to the mysteries of the natural world. As was indicated in the survey following up the basic experience inventory, many students are confronting natural wonders for the first time in their lives.

Since sophomore students are concerned with the nature of the learning process, the main focus of the experience is directed to concept formation and problem solving.

In order to have a better understanding of the steps involved in problem solving, a class of sophomore students developed the following plan of action. The class divided into small groups of two or three students. Each group was to identify a problem to be solved, devise a plan that would lead to the solution, try the plan, and evaluate the results. Students identified such problems as: "How large is an acre?" "How do we go about identifying wild flowers?" "In what direction does the river current flow?" "How would we go about mapping the creek on paper?"

To further illustrate the manner in which these activities were carried out, one of the reports which students submitted appears [below] :

DEFINITION OF THE PROBLEM

In what direction does the river current flow?

THE PLAN

1. Watch the direction of river flow from the dining hall.
2. Look at a map in the library.
3. Talk to a resource person.
4. Throw objects into the water and observe them.

THE TRIAL

1. We observed the river from the top of the bluff. It seemed to be flowing north.
2. We went to the library and looked at two maps. We found the origin of the Rock River to be at Fond du lac, Wisconsin. It empties into the Mississippi River at Rock Island, Illinois.

3. We talked to a resource person. He reminded us of the dam that we had seen previously south of the Lorado Taft Field Campus. We then recalled that the water went south over the dam.

4. At the river's edge we again observed the direction of flow. This time our opinion was that it flowed in a southerly direction.

5. Pat W. lowered her foot into the water and reported that the force of the current felt as though it were flowing to the south.

6. Each member of the group threw several sticks into the water. The sticks landed various distances from the shore. All sticks took the direction of south as they floated.

7. Joan M. placed a four-foot stick in the water, holding it straight but loosely enough so that the current could be felt. The stick gradually floated upward and southward.

CONCLUSION

Problem solved. Considering our observations of the map, the dam, and finally, our experiments, we came to the conclusion that the direction of flow of the Rock River is from north to south.

SECOND-YEAR EXPERIENCE

Students return for the second experience in the outdoor teacher education sequence during their junior year. This experience is for three days. The main focus is upon content areas of the elementary curriculum—mainly, ways and means of supplementing subject matter through firsthand observation and direct experience in an outdoor classroom.

Junior students usually spend a session investigating the kind of outdoor learning activities that will add meaning and understanding to mathematical concepts and principles. Such activities as measuring the height of trees, pacing off distances, using shadow measurement, figuring the width of a river, staking off an acre, and using a compass fall into this category.

Another area that bears investigation is social studies. An old abandoned cemetery lends itself well to historical research. A wealth of local history is inscribed on tombstones. Students eagerly seek the answers to such questions as: When was the first burial here? What is the date of the last burial? What nationalities are represented? What is the youngest death recorded? Is there evidence of infant mortality? Who lived the longest? Can any conclusions be drawn as to the relative size of families?

After an hour or so of gathering data, the group meets to share information and to see what inferences can be drawn from known facts.

Geography is another aspect of social studies which affords opportunity for study in the out-of-doors. Learning activities which may be pursued in this area are recognition of land forms, mapping the terrain, and discovering uses of the land.

Science, of course, is a natural for learning outdoors. Becoming acquainted with trees, birds, rocks, flowers and insects; making collections; observing weather; discovering the stars; developing appreciations and understanding of natural phenomena; and recognizing the interrelatedness of living things are some examples of activities.

Language arts, naturally, is a common thread running through every area of study. Students cannot escape recording observations, sharing discoveries, or summarizing conclusions. One aspect of the language arts which holds great potential in an outdoor setting is in the realm of creative expression. Many college students, when exposed to the stimuli of the great outdoors, find to their amazement that they posses worthwhile creative abilities. An example appears [below] :

Eagle Dreams

They say an eagle nested once
Upon the heights of yonder tree.
How dazzling to the mind of man!
How insecure!

We can be sure
He rested there to dream
The dreams that seem
As lofty as his house.

But now, the tree is dead.
The bird has fled
Not to regret the ruin of his old abode,
But wandered to more fertile lands
Where eagle dreams unfold.

THIRD-YEAR EXPERIENCE

The culminating experience for all elementary-education majors occurs when as seniors they return to he Field Campus for a full week. A class of elementary-school pupils is also in residence for the entire week carrying on a program of school camping. This supplementary student-teaching experience for the seniors is in addition to the nine weeks of regulation student teaching which they do in the public schools.

The main function of the student teachers during the week is to plan with and teach the pupils in an outdoor school situation. In addition to their instructional responsibilities, student teachers also supervise children at mealtimes, during rest hour, and in the bunkhouses. This affords the prospective teacher an opportunity to observe children under a variety of conditions and in a setting unlike that of the schoolroom. The values of such an experience involving both pupils and teachers in a total living situation are easily observable but difficult to measure.

The first-rate teacher who would bring meaning and understanding to learning, which must, of necessity, be carried on mainly at the verbal level, should first be well grounded himself in a variety of direct experiences. Secondly, he should possess the outdoor knowledge and skills that will enable him to vitalize teaching and learning both inside and outside the classroom.

COLLEGE EXPERIMENT IN THE OUT-OF-DOORS *

HOWARD A. OZMON, JR.

All sophomores in the New Jersey state colleges take a one-week course in outdoor education at the New Jersey School of Conservation.

The school is in the northern part of the state, in Stokes State Forest (12,429 acres of land). This area is bounded on the north by High Point State Park (10,935 acres) to make 23,364 acres of land which can be used for educational purposes. The school, originally developed during the 1930s as a CCC camp, is now owned by the Department of Conservation and Economic Development. Its present educational program is under the supervision of the State Department of Education.

At Stokes there is every opportunity for learning experiences. Classes are conducted in forestry, wildlife, geology, conservation projects. and many other aspects of outdoor living, by a regular staff of instructors located at the school. In addition, teachers from the state colleges go to Stokes to give classes in their own specialized field as it relates to outdoor education. English teachers come to discuss Thoreau, Whitman, and Wordsworth. Teachers of philosophy hold classes on Rousseau's *Emile* or deal with some of the other naturalistic philosophers. Art teachers give instruction regarding outdoor painting. Mathematics is shown to have some relationship to outdoor life as teachers discuss land boundaries, surveying techniques, and so on. There is really no subject taught in the college curriculum which cannot be related to outdoor education in this fashion.

Philosophers and poets, as well as many religious men, have taught that it is necessary for man to leave his civilized life periodically in order to spend time in some sort of a retreat, on the sea or in the forests or deserts. Man is a unique

*Reprinted by permission of the publisher, the American Association of Health, Physical Education, and Recreation, from the *Journal of Health, Physical Education, Recreation* 33:30, April, 1962.

kind of animal due to his ability to think, but he is still part of the animal scale, and many thinkers believe that man begins to understand his basic nature best when he places himself in the type of environment that portrays him not as a machine (which is often a civilized conception of man's nature) but as a highly developed and very complex kind of animal. Thus, at Stokes, every attempt is made to place the students in a natural environment where they can begin to understand their basic relationship to nature. There is a provision against making unnatural noises, like the sounds of radios or car horns. How refreshing! For a week, at least, students are encouraged to listen to the song of birds, the gurgling of brooks, and the sounds in the underbrush of animals going about their daily tasks. At Stokes, students learn how to follow tracks in the woods, how to camp out, how to be self-sufficient in the matter of food and shelter. The advantages of having to undergo this kind of training are many. Students learn how to fend for themselves, how to adapt to a new environment. There is a wealth of knowledge to be obtained first-hand about animals, flowers, trees, terrain, and weather. For the first time, students may begin to realize what life was like for the early American settlers. They may begin to understand, too, how an army conducts itself on a campaign, making use of the natural resources of the area, drawing plans for the rationing of food, spotting dangers, and learning survival measures in medicine and shelter.

One of the primary reasons why this kind of program for college students is of such importance is that more public schools in New Jersey are becoming aware of the need for elementary and secondary school pupils to receive outdoor education. Many of these college students will become teachers in school systems where entire classes will go out on overnight, weekend, and sometimes even week-long nature excursions. In order to make these trips profitable experiences the teachers who accompany the classes should themselves have had some prior experience with outdoor living. This is the kind of training which the school at Stokes offers.

Another important part of the program at Stokes is its role in giving prospective teachers some idea of the need for conservation. Too many of our natural resources are being depleted through waste and carelessness. The program in outdoor education at Stokes is designed to make participants aware of the serious nature of this problem. By giving future teachers an interest in conservation, they can help see that our natural resources are used more wisely today and through their teaching can help to see that they are protected through future generations.

INDEPENDENT STUDY AND
OUTDOOR EDUCATION IN COLLEGE *

WILLIAM L. HOWENSTINE

College involvement in outdoor education has most often been linked with one or both of two objectives. On the one hand the study of the philosophy, methods, and organization of outdoor education has been seen of direct value to future teachers or other youth workers who would be prospective participants in outdoor education or recreation programs during their professional careers. Exemplifying this link is the outdoor education program at Northern Illinois University in which all students majoring in Education participate. On the other hand there has been an involvement of college students in outdoor education programs because of the general value of work experience in providing a maturing perspective on one's academic studies. As an example of this approach one might cite the Extramural Program of Antioch College in which college students are required to alternate periods of academic study on campus with successful periods of professional work off campus; many of these students (without regard to possible future employment as teachers) have found their work experience in an outdoor education center.

A third link with outdoor education, which has been tried recently by Chicago Teachers College, North, is that of independent study. It has long been known that motivated and responsible students could progress very rapidly in their studies without the aid of the traditional procedures of the traditional college class. In recent years there have been a number of attempts across the country to develop new structural approaches to independent study.[1] For purposes here "independent study" may be defined as a program of learning which releases students from the requirement of traditional class attendance in a conscious attempt to place relatively greater responsibility upon the student for the achievement of his own education.

It was this new element of independent study which was especially incorporated with the outdoor education program of Chicago Teachers College, North. With the cooperation of the Camp Reinberg Association, Palatine,

*Reprinted by permission of Ray Page, Superintendent of Public Instruction and editor of the *Illinois Journal of Education*, the *Illinois Journal of Education*, and the author from *Illinois Journal of Education*, 55:25-27, December, 1964.

[1] For example, Antioch College, Yellow Springs, Ohio, has carried on such studies and has published the account of the attempts and their evaluation in several bulletins.

Illinois, a trial program was initiated in May 1963, when nine CTC-North students went to Camp Reinberg to spend the May-August Trimester in residence in a work-study program. Five more students participated in the program in the September-December Trimester, and in the Trimester beginning May 1964, twelve students participated. After some modifications during these few trimesters the essential elements of the program now stand as follows:

1. *Faculty supervision.* Overall guidance of the program and policy formulation is in the hands of a standing faculty committee operating with the approval of the administration. One of this committee serves as the active coordinator of the academic portion of the program when students are at Camp Reinberg. Individual instructors are responsible for the independent study arrangements in the particular courses in which they have students enrolled.

2. *Student selection.* Up to twelve students are selected for the program each trimester according to the policies established by the faculty committee. Factors considered in selection are grade point average, priority of application, sex, class level in college, and previous work.

3. *Academic program.* Each student participant is required to carry some academic course work; this averages about twelve credit hours per student although some students have taken as many as sixteen. All students must take the course entitled Field Experiences in Human Development. Other courses elected are dependent upon the needs and interests of students and faculty. (Faculty participation is voluntary.) An attempt is made to ensure that there are a number of courses offered which have a direct relationship to the work of the students or the setting of the camp. However, fully 50 per cent of the courses have no direct relationship to either the work or site. Some of the courses (other than Field Experiences in Human Development) which have been commonly included are: Urban Ecology; Spanish; History of American Institutions; Conservation of Natural Resources; Recreational Games; American English—Writing; and Studies in Human Personality. Each student is responsible for contacting his instructors in the courses in which he is enrolled, with regard to assignments and other course requirements. In most cases the students have conferences with instructors every one or two weeks. In addition to readings, written assignments, and conferences, frequent use is made of tape recordings of lectures, special assignments, etc.

4. *Work program.* Student participants work half-time (approximately twenty hours per week) as leaders in the camp's various programs. Since Camp Reinberg operates year-round and involves summer camping, weekend groups, and public school outdoor education programs the college students have an opportunity to work with a great variety of programs, people, and activities. For this portion of their program the college students are directly responsible to the Program Director of Camp Reinberg.

5. *Financial arrangements.* Camp Reinberg provides the college students with

free board and room in exchange for their work in outdoor education. Students must pay for their books and other academic supplies, for transportation to and from camp, for accident insurance, and for their personal expenses. The college provides such audiovisual equipment as tape recorders and is devising a plan whereby faculty members supervising students in independent study (whether connected with the outdoor education program or not) will receive credit for such supervision in their academic loads.

6. *Mechanics of communication.* Camp Reinberg, the location of this outdoor education program, is within an hour's travel time by bus or car from the college. Students are responsible for returning to campus occasionally for conferences, library materials, etc. The faculty member who is coordinator of the academic program is not resident on the camp site, but goes to the camp almost weekly for conferences with students and the camp personnel. Other faculty members visit the camp to confer with students from time to time at the discretion of the faculty members. (This is voluntary and not all instructors involved in the program do this.)

Conclusion. While no thorough evaluation of the program has been completed yet there is considerable agreement on the following. The combination of academic study with the outdoor education experience has been useful in linking the entire program to the on-going college work, giving a sense of serious purpose to all aspects. The emphasis upon independent study has complemented and enhanced the well-known values of direct experience in outdoor education programs. There is some uncertainty about how many and which combination of courses are the optimum for students, but there is little question about the course work itself. Obviously the program serves only a small number of students, but it provides these students with an unusually full and intensive outdoor education experience. Its success thus far would seem to point to the desirability of expansion and particularly to the possibilities in combining academic studies with work experience. Is not a goal of all college education the production of an individual who continues to extend his knowledge and competence with independent study throughout his adult professional life?

Chapter eight
Evaluation and Research

INTRODUCTION

As any educational innovation develops and becomes established in the curriculum framework of our school systems, articles describing various evaluation and research efforts begin to appear in addition to those dealing with program description and philosophy. Evaluation efforts, early in a developing field, usually employ a survey and/or questionnaire design. As the new educational area grows and gains acceptance, emphasis is gradually placed upon more sophisticated designs employing experimental techniques. Studies tracing the historical development and analyzing the philosophical, sociological, or psychological elements also appear in the research literature about the same time.

This has generally been the pattern for outdoor education. Although a few hundred research studies have been completed pertaining to this field, it has only been during the past several years that evaluation studies and research efforts of more sophisticated. design have been completed in larger numbers. In spite of the increase in studies of this nature, very few reports have found their way into the periodic literature. The selections in this chapter represent some efforts that have been made in order to substantiate various gains claimed by outdoor educators.

The future growth and development of outdoor education will depend upon the willingness and the ability of professors, administrators, teachers, and resource people in the field to support or refute the many positive goals they "feel" are being reached through learning experiences in the outdoor environment.

RESEARCH IMPLICATIONS
FOR OUTDOOR EDUCATION *
DONALD R. HAMMERMAN

Programs of outdoor education can make a significant contribution to education by providing a laboratory setting conducive to educational research. Since 1930 approximately 150 studies have been conducted at the masters and doctoral level.[1]

The research dealing with the various facets of outdoor education and school camping is by no means exhaustive, even though the amount of research on this topic has increased steadily over the past 20 years. Many early studies were an attempt to justify resident outdoor education (formerly referred to as school camping) as a legitimate educational function of the public school. The rapid development of resident outdoor education programs in various sections of the country during the forties and fifties was paralleled by a corresponding preponderance of research devoted purely to the administrative and organizational aspects of operating an outdoor education facility. Research studies which were basically proposals for the implementation of a specific resident outdoor school development also showed a proportionate increase. There is, however, a dearth of experimental studies in this area of education, as well as a notable lack of research concerned with the philosophical implications of the outdoor education movement.

---

*Reprinted by permission of the publisher, the American Association of Health, Physical Education, and Recreation, from the *Journal of Health, Physical Education, Recreation* 35:89-90, March, 1964.

[1] These studies are listed in the second revision of the "Bibliography of Studies and Research related to Camping and Outdoor Education," available from the American Camping Association, Bradford Woods, Martinsville, Indiana. Many of the studies were also reviewed in the author's dissertation, "An Historical Analysis of the Socio-Cultural Factors that Influenced the Development of Camping Education," The Pennsylvania State University, 1961.

While it is obvious that a great deal of additional research is needed on this topic, outdoor education's greatest contribution to research may well be in the experimental setting it provides for psychological and sociological study. The resident outdoor school is a self-contained laboratory of human relations. Pupil behavior may be observed rather intensively over a concentrated period of time. Problems dealing with poor relations, group social structure, concept formation, problem solving, etc. ought to be investigated in the total-living situation of the resident outdoor school.

No study in the research conducted thus far has undertaken the problem of constructing a theoretical framework for the various aspects of outdoor education. This is a top priority problem! Significant research should have some theoretical framework as a base. One example of such a framework would be the work of Getzels and Guba at the University of Chicago. These two researchers developed a theoretical framework to explain social behavior of administrators.[2] Studies have since been designed to investigate various hypotheses based on Getzels' and Guba's role theory model. Outdoor education is in need of similar theoretical structure to promote and guide further research.

Educators make many claims for outdoor education. They claim that subject matter is enriched and made more meaningful through firsthand experience in the out-of-doors. They claim that a high degree of pupil-teacher rapport is established in the resident outdoor school situation. They claim that principles of democracy are better learned by living them in the total-living situation. They claim that significant changes occur in the social structure of a group while living together at the resident outdoor school. These claims pose many possibilities for additional research. Each claim needs further investigation and substantiation.

RECOMMENDATIONS FOR RESEARCH

Investigation is needed in the areas of curriculum, learning, child development, adjustment, behavior, instruction, and teacher education as related to outdoor education. Some problems that warrant study are listed below:

1. What changes in the social structure of a group actually do occur in one week of outdoor education?
2. What subjects can best be taught in the outdoor setting? It is inconceivable that all subjects lend themselves to outdoor instruction. Also related to this problem: what concepts, generalizations, and principles of science, mathematics, etc., are gained through firsthand experience in the outdoor laboratory?
3. What evidence is there to indicate that democratic principles are learned in the resident outdoor school situation?

[2] Jacob W. Getzels and Egon G. Guba, "Social Behavior and the Administrative Process," *The School Review* 63:423-441, Winter 1957.

4. Does teacher behavior or role change while in the outdoor school situation? Is teacher-pupil rapport improved?

5. Is it possible for the teacher to gain insight and understanding of pupil behavior that would not have occurred in the classroom?

The main concern in each of the above problems deals with the fundamental question: What evidence is there that such gains do, in fact, take place? The findings of such investigation would have significant bearing on teacher education. For example, what specific outdoor related teaching competencies ought to be included in preservice teacher education?

There also is a need to replicate certain studies. The New York City camping education experiment[3] ought to be repeated with other grade groups in other school systems. Additional data measuring subject matter achievement in the outdoor school as compared to classroom learning are needed. Kranzer's study also warrants replication.[4] Additional data are needed to substantiate the conclusion that desirable social and democratic behavioral changes among sixth graders are effected more readily in the outdoor school setting than in the regular classroom. The claim that sixth grade pupils of ". . . low mental ability may tend to improve slightly in critical thinking as a result of a camping experience . . ."[5] warrants further corroboration.

Outdoor education has brought a new dimension to educational research. The elements of curriculum, method, and administration have broadened in scope. When research points the way, aspects of curriculum content, instructional technique, and administrative procedure as related to outdoor education may undergo change. Theory and practice are not dichotomous. One reenforces the other. The task of research in outdoor education is to bring meaning and substantiation to theory, and to improve practice through experimentation.

[3]New York City Board of Education, *Extending Education Through Camping*, (Carbondale, Ill.: Outdoor Education Association, Inc., 1948).

[4]H.C. Kranzer, "Effects of School Camping on Selected Aspects of Pupil Behavior—An Experimental Study," (unpublished doctoral dissertation, University of California, Los Angeles, 1958).

[5]Ibid., p. 83.

THE ATTITUDE OF CHILDREN TOWARD OUTDOOR EDUCATION *

HOLLY J. ASHCROFT

Outdoor education conducted in a camp environment has an almost universal child appeal. This natural appeal stems from the very nature of the program which seems to satisfy many of the fundamental urges and needs of the pre-teen group. The healthy child of this age is an active, vigorous being who wants to be continuously on the move and doing things. Although he is the product of today's urban and mechanized living, he has the same fundamental characteristics and urges as youth had in our early pioneer days.

The preadolescent is adventurous. He comes to the school camp anticipating new experiences and looking toward new horizons. With this attitude he is potentially a dynamic learner. The skillful teacher takes advantage of this fact and uses the well-established techniques of exploration and discovery and firsthand experiences. In the camp environment, the child utilizes all his senses in the learning process. The new outdoor environment in which he lives for a time becomes the child's broader classroom; in it he learns to observe carefully the intricacies of nature about him, and through direct experience the story of nature unfolds for him in a natural and realistic manner.

The child is a realist. He wants to experience things firsthand; he is not impressed by theory. When he has direct contacts with the outdoors, coupled with effective teaching and guidance, the interrelationship and interdependence of all things in nature become real and understandable.

The child continually seeks status with his peer group. Camp living is small group living, and the child needs and wants to "belong." In order to acquire status and to be wanted by the group, the child learns quickly that he must be tolerant, cooperative, helpful, sportsmanlike, and willing to assume his share of necessary duties and responsibilities. The well-operated camp becomes a child's community where everyone shares in planning, executing, and evaluating the program. These activities bring about a sense of responsibility and a feeling of making a worthy contribution to the community group. Through this method of operation the camp becomes a laboratory that furnishes throughout a 24-hour day significant experiences in democratic social living.

The normal child wishes above all things to be "grown up," and thus be

*Reprinted by permission of the author and publisher from *California Journal of Elementary Education* 26:96-101, November, 1957.

increasingly independent of adults. Strange as it may seem many sixth grade children have never been away from the family home overnight. For many girls and boys, living for a five- or six-day period in camp away from home is a major accomplishment in independence. Being "on their own" and assuming responsibility for themselves are definite steps in the maturing process. For children who experience some homesickness, the school camp often helps to ease the emotional stress, because of the familiar classmates and the presence of classroom teachers.

Children need wholesome, active outdoor living, and the school camp provides an ideal environment in which to attain it. It has been said that children, like trees, grow best in the great outdoors. The change in altitude, proper balance of exercise and rest, carefully planned, wholesome meals, attention to cleanliness, and clean, refreshing air all contribute to children's feelings of health and mental well-being. The freedom from the pressures of urban living, the emphasis on cooperative rather than competitive living seem to change the tempo of the group, and the children become increasingly relaxed as each day in camp passes.

Children need fun. The child's concept of fun is usually quite broad in contrast to that of the adult. If the camp maintains a warm, friendly atmosphere, then every activity, whether it be outdoor science, building a check dam to prevent erosion, washing dishes, star study, or planning projects with his friends are all summed up in the child's meaning of "fun." In such an atmosphere, learning goes on without tension, in an easy, effective manner.

Evidence of the value of school camping and outdoor education can be found by going directly to the children themselves. During January, 1957, a questionnaire was submitted to over 1,500 Long Beach sixth grade girls and boys who had a five-day camping experience between the opening of school in the fall of 1956 and the middle of January, 1957. The final tabulation of data from the 1,500 questionnaires completed by sixth grade pupils and an analysis of them follows:

PERSONAL ENJOYMENT

Nearly 93 per cent of the 1,500 pupils were enthusiastic; 7 per cent reported a "fairly good time"; and only four children said they did not enjoy the camp experience. Nearly 94 per cent said that they would remember for a long time the relaxation and happiness they felt while in camp. Approximately 92 per cent reported that they would never forget the evening campfire experiences.

From a list of 14 choices, pupils were asked to "underline three things you enjoyed most at camp." The following eight received the number of approvals shown.

Nature hikes 1,090   Campfires 318

Living with classmates	632	Nature Study	289
Crafts	438	Meals	264
Mail from home	319	Friendliness of all	227

When asked to write a few sentences on one of eight topics suggested, pupils selected the following topics with the frequency indicated:

I Like Being in the Outdoors	433
Being One of the Gang at Camp	259
Being on My Own at Camp	226
Plants, Insects, Animals, and Man Depend on Each Other and Work Together	121
What My Parents Thought Camp Did for Me	103

The following were typical of the many opinions expressed by pupils:

The gang sure liked living with each other and working with each other and hiking with each other. Living together up at camp helped us to think more of each other and to be more friendly with each other.

My parents thought camp gave me a new experience in the out-of-doors. In a week we saw more, did more, and learned more and learned to get along with everyone.

My parents thought camp did a lot for me, and because I was on my own and there was no one to tell me to make my bed or help clear the table, when I got home I sort of did the things I was supposed to do without being told.

I liked learning table manners at camp because at home my mother is always after me to use better table manners. At camp it was more fun learning table manners than at home. I feel more comfortable when I go over to my friends to eat than before I went to camp.

Plants, insects, animals, and man depend on each other so much that if one of the four were to become extinct all the rest of the four mentioned would also become extinct. We learned about that at camp and I enjoyed that part of camp very much.

I like plants, insects, animals, and conservation because I learned more about them than I would have otherwise. I'm more interested in animals, insects, and plants. I think camp was wonderful.

I like being outdoors because it makes you feel like a man. When you curl up in your sleeping bag you can't help feeling good deep inside.

PERSONAL GAINS

In the study 822 children said it made them feel good to help with camp chores—that they felt they were doing something important; 628 said they didn't mind helping at a camp when all shared the duties.

More than half the children, 773, reported that they felt camping helped them to understand their school work better. Nearly all, actually 1,412, said that one of the best things they learned at camp was to take care of themselves; 1,070 reported that they felt more "grown up" after their camp experience.

In response to one question, 1,324 expressed the belief that the camp experience might help those who had fears of snakes, insects, animals, or darkness.

SOCIAL GAINS

The class was reported by 622 children as more friendly following the camp experience; and 515 thought they were getting along better with others in their class. ·

Relationship of the children to their teachers was revealed by the response of 954, who said they were glad their classroom teacher could go to camp with them and that they felt they knew the teacher better and that he knew them better; however, 416 seemed somewhat less enthusiastic, they said they didn't mind having him go to camp with them.

That most of the girls and boys cooperated in doing their share of the work was reported by 1,308 people. New friends made at camp was reported as a social gain by 1,358 girls and boys.

KNOWLEDGE OF SCIENCE AND CONSERVATION

Nearly all or 1,449 children reported a new realization of the importance of good outdoor manners and practicing conservation; 1,420 had new concepts of the importance of protecting forests against fire. After studying nature, 1,443 reported that they understood better the place and purpose all creatures and plants have in the total scheme of life. New things learned about nature in camp were reported by 1,204 children; the most frequently mentioned included conservation, animals, trees and other plant life.

In responding to a question about new things learned about conservation, pupils listed the following most frequently—fire prevention, contribution of trees and plants to human welfare, water and water cycles, erosion.

NEW INTERESTS

New interests that they might continue as hobbies were reported by 733 children. Most frequently mentioned were woodcraft, nature study, science, rocks and minerals.

Increased reading of books because of new interests was reported by 673 children as an outcome of their camp experience. Books most frequently · selected were about animals, birds, stars, trees, plants, and rocks.

When asked what they would like to learn more about if they could go to camp again, children replied in the following order of preference: nature study, stars, conservation, animals, birds, trees, and plants.

From the responses to the questionnaires to the sixth grade campers it is apparent that the school camp program is an effective method of teaching. It appears to make a unique contribution in enriching the child's experience in the fields of social living, the sciences, independence and self-reliance, and the recreational skills experienced in outdoor living. Forest service personnel have been warm in their praise of the contribution of the camping program to good forest manners and the proper, considerate use of mountain areas.

Classroom teachers who have accompanied their pupils to camp, administrators whose schools have participated in camp experience, and parents who have seen their girls and boys return with new interests and understanding are all high in their praise of the educational benefits and enjoyment for the girls and boys who have participated in the program.

These commendations add to the replies to the questionnaire from the 1,500 sixth grade girls and boys to reveal the attitude of children toward outdoor education.

THE EFFECT OF A SCHOOL CAMP EXPERIENCE ON FRIENDSHIP CHOICES *

O. L. DAVIS, JR.

School camping in most school programs is justified by its peculiar contributions to children's learning about life in the out-of-doors, science, and conservation. Other reasons given for school camping include extending children's interests, providing motivation for learning in the regular school subjects, broadening children's experimental background, and offering a stimulating experience in social living [1, pp. 1-2; 3; 4; 9].

Evaluation of the goals of school camping is difficult. Most descriptions of school camp programs indicate various attempts at evaluation; almost always, examples of children's, parents', and teachers' statements of the values of the experience form a substantial portion of the evaluation [2, 5, 6]. Few objective measures of learning or of the extent goals were attained have been used. In the area of social living, sociometric instruments and statements by children and adults have been reported [1, pp. 36-37; 2, pp. 11-12; 9]. An increase in the

*Reprinted by permission of the publisher and The Payne Education Sociology Foundation, Inc., from The Journal of Educational Sociology 33:305-13, March, 1960.

number of friends has been cited as a value of school camping. Also, some advocates of school camping state that these programs provide opportunities to demonstrate leadership for children who formerly have not had these opportunities. However, the interpretation of the results obtained with the sociometric devices have been reported in subjective terms. The present study was designed to provide some objective data about the effect of the school camp situation on friendship choices. The hypothesis tested was:

After an experience of social living at a school camp, there will be an increase in the number of times children are chosen as friends by their classmates.

Further, this hypothesis was tested by treatment of data for boys and girls separately. Most of the subjects were thirteen years old. At this age, boys and girls often exhibit relatively mature behavior. However, on occasions, many behave characteristically, as preadolescents, i.e., making a clear distinction between sexes by refusing to play together, preferring to work separately, and by taking antagonistic actions toward the opposite sex. At thirteen, boys appear to take a kind of neutral attitude toward girls; girls demonstrate a rising interest in boys but do not choose a boy as a best friend or companion for most activities. Because of the general sex differences apparent at this age, treatment of boys and girls separately seemed desirable.

PROCEDURE

THE SOCIOMETRIC DEVICE

An inventory of children's friendship choices was devised. Entitled "Who Would You Choose?" the form listed 10 open-ended questions which related to various types of school camp activities. The questions were developed after careful consideration of the activities planned for a school camp at which the class to be studied was scheduled to attend. Items were assigned positions on the final form by the use of a table of random numbers. The ten questions, listed in the order of their appearance on the "Who Would You Choose?" form, are:

1. Which of your classmates would you choose to engage in a leisure-time activity with you?
2. Which of your classmates would you choose to be your tent-mate on a sleep-out?
3. Which of your classmates would you choose to invite to a cabin party?
4. Which of your classmates would you choose to be on your side in a team game?
5. Which of your classmates would you choose to help you plan and direct recreation for a night program (such as skits, singsong, etc.)?
6. Which of your classmates would you choose to clean a cabin with you?
7. Which of your classmates would you choose to help you cook and wash dishes for a day?

8. Which of your classmates would you choose to go with you on a nature study hike?
9. Which of your classmates would you choose to be in your cabin group?
10. Which of your classmates would you choose to go on a cook-out with you?

Unlimited choice was given the children in choosing their classmates. Scores were obtained on all questions separately and for the inventory as a whole. A child's score was the number of times he was chosen by his classmates on the particular question or for the test as a whole. The test was administered first during the week prior to the class's leaving for camp. It was readministered during the week following the return from camp. Table 1 shows the means and standard deviations of the number of choices received on each item of both administrations of the inventory for boys and girls separately. Means and standard deviations of the total number of choices received by boys, girls, and the entire class on both administrations of the inventory are presented in Table 2. While no

TABLE 1

Means and Standard Deviations for Total Number of Choices of Pre-Camp and Post-Camp Administrations of "Who Would You Choose?" Inventory

Question	Pre-Camp		Post-Camp		Pre-Camp		Post-Camp	
	M	SD	M	SD	M	SD	M	SD
1.	4.75	2.59	4.94	2.09	5.00	2.12	5.81	3.28
2.	1.88	1.58	2.75	1.64	3.69	2.14	3.69	1.79
3.	6.25	3.70	7.56	4.17	4.94	3.03	5.94	3.33
4.	6.44	4.99	7.81	5.36	4.38	2.85	4.00	1.84
5.	3.62	2.83	4.06	3.11	4.38	3.55	4.44	3.39
6.	3.19	1.91	3.69	1.55	4.25	1.78	5.62	2.26
7.	2.44	1.46	3.44	1.66	3.69	2.34	3.75	2.32
8.	4.56	4.46	6.00	5.21	3.12	2.11	3.44	1.97
9.	4.31	1.99	4.62	1.87	5.81	1.51	6.88	2.55
10.	4.81	2.81	6.31	3.08	3.38	2.26	4.75	2.56

TABLE 2

Means and Standard Deviations for Total Number of Choices Received on Pre-Camp and Post-Camp Administrations of "Who Would You Choose?" Inventory

Class Group	Pre-Camp		Post-Camp	
	M	SD	M	SD
Boys	42.25	20.58	51.25	22.20
Girls	42.62	19.63	48.31	21.71
Total Class	42.44	20.10	49.78	21.71

attempt was made to check the reliability of the "Who Would You Choose?" inventory, sociometric and reputation type data are generally quite stable [10].

SUBJECTS

Subjects were all pupils enrolled in the eighth grade of a campus laboratory school in the Spring, 1957, a total of 16 boys and 16 girls. The composition of this class has remained unchanged throughout the year. Approximately one-third of the children has been in the same group since entering first grade. Seven children were newcomers to the group that school year. The children were, on the whole, from an upper-middle class population.

A school camp at this laboratory school has been conducted as a regular and integral part of the eighth grade's program for 10 years. The camp program was based on a sound philosophy of outdoor education [3; 7]. For this year's camp, planning began in the Fall Quarter, but intensive plans were not begun until March. The class helped set its goals and plan its activities for the ten-day camp session. One of the objectives ranked high for the class was "To make new friends and to get to know each other better." The regular classroom teacher was the camp director. Additional adult counsellors were composed of the class's student teachers for the quarter and other senior-college and graduate students.

One member of the class, a girl, did not attend the school camp.

RESULTS

To test the hypothesis of this study, data obtained from the pre- and post-tests were analyzed by the sign test [8, pp. 68-75]. Since the hypothesis was directional in nature, a one-tailed test was used. The 5 per cent level of significance was used throughout.

Using total number of times chosen for each item on both tests, the hypothesis was accepted:

As a class, the children were chosen more times after camp than before camp (26+, 5-; p < .00005).

Boys received more choices after camp than before (13+, 2-; p=.004).

Girls received more choices after camp than before (13+, 3-; p=.018).

Each question was analyzed separately as further tests of dispersion of friendship choices after the school camp experience. The analyses revealed that the children were chosen significantly more after camp on only four individual questions, i.e., those asking for choices 1) to engage in a leisure-time activity (17+, 6-; p= .017), 3) to invite to a cabin party (20+, 6-; p= .005), 6) to clean a cabin (19+, 9-; p= .04), and 10) to go on a cook-out (22+, 4-; p= .0005).

Boys, however, were chosen significantly more after camp on six of the questions: 2) to be a tent-mate on a sleep-out (p=.003), 3) to be invited to a cabin party (p=.029), 4) to be on one's side in a team game (p=.046), 7) to help one cook and wash dishes for a day (p=.046), 8) to be a companion on a nature study hike (p=.033), and 10) to go on a cook-out (p=.029).

On only one question, number 10, were girls chosen significantly more times after camp than before (p=.003).

The ten questions on the "Who Would You Choose?" inventory were divided into two classes: bisexual, that is, where choice was not limited to the same sex as the respondent by the nature of the activity, and unisexual, where the choice was limited to the sex of the respondent by the nature of the activity. There were three unisexual items (numbers 2, 6 and 9). The remaining were bisexual. A descriptive analysis of the cross-sex choices on this latter classification and a generalization regarding camp activities relating to each question follow.

Question 1. No boys and only three girls chose classmates of the opposite sex before camp "to engage in a leisure-time activity with you." On the final inventory, three boys chose girls and six girls chose boys. Leisure time was provided each day after lunch and before supper at which time the class was encouraged to engage in activities such as fishing, loafing, and nonstrenuous games.

Question 3. Five boys chose girls and ten girls chose boys on this item, "to invite to a cabin party," before camp. Six additional boys chose girls and four additional girls chose boys after camp. Only two girls did not choose a boy, whereas five boys did not choose a girl after camp. During the camp, several occasions permitted invitations by girls and boys to parties.

Question 4. No boy chose a girl either before or after camp "to be on your side in a team game." Girls chose boys frequently on both administrations of the inventory. Yet, during the camp, most of the girls and most of the boys participated together in team games and "choosing sides" was a feature of almost every recreation period. Girls were not automatically chosen after all boys during these games.

Question 5. Only three boys chose girls before and after camp "to help you plan and direct recreation for a night program." Nine girls selected boys before camp and eight girls chose boys after camp. Throughout the camp session, boys and girls worked together voluntarily on this activity.

Question 7. No girl chose a boy before camp but six chose boys after camp "to help you cook and wash dishes for a day." Four boys initially chose girls but only three selected girls after camp for this activity. A team of three, including at least one boy and one girl, performed this necessary camp duty each day during camp.

Question 8. Only one boy chose girls before camp "to go with you on a nature study hike" and only two chose girls for this activity following camp. Nine girls chose boys initially, whereas all girls chose boys after camp. Approximately equal numbers of boys and girls comprised study groups at camp and the camp staff observed boys and girls going together frequently on nature study hikes (to the river to fish, to the quarry for fossils, to the woods for butterflies, etc.).

Question 10. No boy chose a girl initially "to go on a cook-out with you" and only three boys selected girls after camp. Six girls chose boys before camp and eleven chose boys after camp on this item. During the camp session, there were two scheduled "cook-outs" on which occasions opportunities for choice of group composition existed.

No statistical significance is attached to these descriptions of cross-sex choices on the sociometric instrument employed in this study.

DISCUSSION

The results of this study bear out the contention that friendships in a participating class are affected significantly by a school camp experience. After camp, more children were named as friends than named before camp. Such a fact is encouraging in that it substantiates opinions expressed by educators and children who have engaged in school camping projects. Pupils in the class studies here indicated on a self-evaluation form that they had made new friends at camp. Several parents commented to the class teacher that their children seemed to "like" more of their classmates and/or more classmates seemed to "like" their children than before camp. The goal of better human relations was apparently achieved in this particular school activity. Another indication of this was that children significantly chose more of their classmates after camp than they did before camp (p=.004). Boys chose more of their classmates after camp (p=.038) as did girls in the class (p=.011). This evidence may be viewed as indicative of increased "good feeling" within the group, yet it further demonstrates that friendships were widened.

A possible source of contamination of the data arose from the fact that the teacher and class discussed its goals for camp in the pre-camp planning and one of the goals selected was that of making new and better friends. This fact may have prejudiced the results in that the children may have felt they had to report more friends after camp to prove that camp had been successful to them.

Friendship choices were more diffused following the camp period, but was the basic pattern changed which already was established in the class? To suggest a possible answer to this vexing question, Spearman rank-order correlation coefficients [8, pp. 202-213] were calculated for the results of the two administrations of the inventory. Obtained correlations of .78 for the boys, .64 for the girls, and .80 for the class as a unit, all significant beyond the .01 level of significance, indicate a rather high similarity in the results of the two administrations. Thus, while some children "lost" friends and most pupils "gained" friends, the basic friendship pattern of the class may not seriously have been altered during the school camp period. While the school camp may not have had a marked effect upon the basic friendship structure of the class, it apparently did afford opportunities for a widening of friendships.

Reductions in the number of stars and isolates in a class is often indicative of dispersion of friendship choices. Stars and isolates in the class were selected by an impartial referee after the total nominations for each S on each administration of the inventory were ranked in a frequency distribution. Four Ss, having received from 79-71 choices before camp, were named as stars. After camp, seven pupils received more than 71 nominations, but only four were named as stars, having received 80 or more choices. Two of the four post-camp stars were ones identified before camp. The two new after-camp stars were ranked fifth and seventh (67 and 61 nominations, respectively) in the class before camp. The two before-camp stars who failed to maintain this status after camp were ranked fifth and sixth on the final tabulation and received 77 and 74 nominations respectively, more essential. In this paper we raise a few questions and review some pertinent data only on extent and type of differences among students.

An interest in diversity at some levels of schooling has a long history in American Education. Much attention and study have been concentrated on all kinds of exceptional children in the elementary school years, and increasing emphasis is being given to the education of the talented and superior in both the elementary and secondary choices than they received before camp. Thus, data about stars are not conclusive; apparently the school camp experience had the effect of reshuffling the relative order of the most popular children, but not radically.

Three children, all boys, were identified as isolates before camp. They received only 6-8 nominations each and were ranked 30-32 in the class. After camp, two of these boys were still classed as isolates, having been chosen 7 and 12 times, still ranking 31st and 32nd in the class. The pre-camp isolate not so identified following camp still ranked 14th among the boys, his pre-camp position, and 28th in the class. Like data about the stars, those concerning isolates are inconclusive. The camp was probably not such a significant social experience to disturb the long-set pattern of behavior of the isolates in the group nor the attitudes of the class toward the isolates.

The one S, a girl, who did not attend school camp received 48 nominations before camp, ranking 13.5 in the class and 6.5 among the girls. After camp, she was chosen only 27 times and ranked 26.5 in the class and 14th among the girls. Only those girls who were this S's best friends during the year chose her after camp. No S changed position within the class as much as this girl did.

An analysis of the responses to the questions on the inventory is very interesting. Boys tended to perceive the situations in which friendship choices were to be made in this study as unisexual. Girls, while present at camp and while they participated in these activities by choice of the boys, were not selected extensively in the test situation by boys. Since girls did receive more nominations overall after camp than before, they may have chosen each other more often. While boys received more choices overall and on six of the questions separately, and while girls seemed to choose boys more often after camp, girls' choices cannot be given credit for the increase in the boys' post-camp nominations. Further generalizations about cross-sex choices in school camp situations must await evidence from future research. Observations from the discussion here might profitably be used as hypotheses for such study.

While the school camp had the effect of widening friendships in the class studied, this fact does not, in itself, justify a school camping program. The major goals of the school camp are identical to those of the regular school curriculum. The learning environment and the materials of instruction at camp differ. Yet, to know that friendships have been widened through a school camp experience is an important fact, for such a climate of feelings seems conducive to the realization of the major aims of instructions.

No evidence is presented to indicate that changes in friendship choices as a result of a school camp experience are greater or less than those occurring as a result of other activities.

SUMMARY

Friendship choices of an eighth grade class before and after a school camp experience were studied.

Friendships within the class were more diffused after camp. Considered separately, boys and girls were both chosen more times after camp than before. Boys were chosen more times after camp than before on six items on the sociometric inventory while girls were chosen more times after camp than before on only one item.

REFERENCES

1. DeWitt, R. T. *An Experiment in Camping Education.* Nashville, Tennessee: George Peabody College for Teachers, (n.d.).
2. DeWitt, R. T., and Wilson, G. M. (Eds.) *School Camping at Peabody 1952.* Nashville, Tennessee: George Peabody College for Teachers, 1952.
3. Donaldson, G. W. *School Camping.* New York: Association Press, 1952.
4. Gilliland, J. W. *School Camping.* Washington: The Association for Supervision and Curriculum Development, NEA, 1954.
5. Goodrich, Lois, "As Campers See It." *The NASSPP Bulletin,* 1947, 31, 21-30.
6. Goodrich, Lois. "Parents Size Up Camping." *The NASSPP Bulletin,* 1947, 31, 43-47.
7. Sharp, L. B. "Outside the Classroom" *The Educational Forum,* 1943, 7, 361-368.

8. Siegel, S. *Nonparametric Statistics for the Behavioral Sciences.* New York: McGraw-Hill, 1956.
9. Wilson, Phyliss J. "School Camping and Mental Health." *Understanding the Child,* 1957, 26, 113-114.
10. Witrol, S. L., and Thompson, G. G. "A Critical Review of the Stability of Social Acceptability Scores Obtained with the Partial-Prank-Order and Paired Comparison Scales." *Gen. Psych. Monog.,* 1953, 48, 221-260.

DO PARENTS AND TEACHERS VALUE OUTDOOR EDUCATION? *

ETHEL TOBIN BELL AND HOWARD M. BELL

Those responsible for outdoor education in elementary schools recognize the importance of evaluation as a process of assessing pupils' achievement. The results obtained indicate the degree to which the goals sought are being attained. And by comparing the results secured in making evaluations as they are needed and charting the results, a picture of the outdoor education program is developed.

TYPES OF PARENT-TEACHER EVALUATION

Evaluation of outdoor education has commonly been sought through verbal and written reports from principals and from the teachers who have taken their classes to camp. Parent-teacher associations, community and educational leaders have been given opportunitites to express their feelings about the outdoor education programs in their schools. Pupils have evaluated their experiences throughout the daily camp program and in the post-camp periods through discussion, written reports, and the creative expression of art, crafts, language arts, and letters to camp staff members. Many pupils also have kept diaries of their experiences.

Parents have helped to evaluate the outdoor education programs in which their children have participated. Their help has included the completion of questionnaires, visiting camps and reporting their observations, and voluntarily reporting their ideas regarding the program orally and in writing. Questionnaires have been completed by camp staffs and supervisors and the results analyzed. Many teachers and camp personnel have kept daily logs of programs and

*Reprinted by permission of the authors and publisher from *California Journal of Elementary Education* 26:102-107, November, 1957.

experiences which provide worthwhile evaluations. Specialized evaluation techniques have been used to appraise certain outcomes. Sociograms have been used to determine children's social acceptance of each other after a week at camp. Special tests, check lists, and case studies have been used to determine the degree that the individual's life purposes, values, attitudes, and human relations have changed during a week in a school camp. Various evaluation techniques are constantly being employed to measure the effectiveness of procedures and experiences at the school camp. The purposes of the evaluations are to secure data regarding pupils' growth through camp experiences that can be used as a basis for helping pupils to attain the objectives they are seeking.

WHAT PARENTS AND TEACHERS THINK ABOUT THE SCHOOL CAMP PROGRAM

It is exceedingly difficult to secure an appraisal of all the changes that take place in children during, or as a result of, their camping experience. This difficulty is caused by the multitude of concepts and skills that are furthered through the outdoor education program. However, data valuable for use in making such an appraisal can be collected from the parents and teachers of the children who participate in the program. The teacher is in an especially good position to give valuable appraisals as he has personal contact with both parents and pupils. These contacts with parents and children start with the first notice of the impending trip, and continue through the orientation and planning period, then with the children at camp and in the post-camp evaluation sessions. Many questions arise and are answered during the planning periods. How will the children like the week away from home? Will regular school work be pursued? If not, how will the aims and objectives of education be met? Will the outcomes be desirable? Is it a justifiable expense? Many plans are laid for the new experience. Obviously, the camp experience differs from that of school and family living. Outdoor education as a part of the school curriculum is new to all but relatively few parents and teachers.

Parents and teachers in nearly all of the 100 school districts having outdoor education programs have participated in comprehensive evaluations. Many kinds of questionnaires have been developed to secure adequate expression of feelings and attitudes regarding the values of the programs. Replies from parents have shown a consistently high enthusiasm for, and appreciation of, the program. Both parents and teachers seem to consider school camping an unusually satisfying experience. The outstanding theme running throughout the written comments points to the need for opportunities for every child to attend a school camp for at least one week during his elementary school life.

In reviewing evaluation forms used by several different school districts, it was found that the questions asked by the districts were similar. In reviewing the data collected by the districts, it was found that the opinions on camping expressed by parents and teachers in the various districts were similar.

Questions of the type asked on the majority of questionnaires follow: (1) What did the child learn at camp? (2) What part of the camp experience was considered most valuable? and (3) What are your suggestions for improving the program?

The answers received in response to such questions revealed that from 95 to 99 per cent of the parents would like to have their children attend camp again and would like the program to continue because they believed it provided worthwhile experience.

Tables 1 and 2 show the results of a study made by the Los Angeles public schools to determine (1) What parents think children learn at camp; and (2) What camp experiences parents considered most valuable.

Answers to the question, What Did the Children Learn at Camp? (Table 1), revealed that knowledge, skills, and appreciation of outdoors were reported by the largest number of parents both in 1954-55 and in 1955-56; better understanding of group living was reported by the next largest number.

Table 2 shows responses to the question: What part of the camp experience do you consider most valuable? Learning to live cooperatively was mentioned

TABLE 1

What Parents Think Children Learn At Camp

| Learnings | Parents Reporting Each of Two School Years | | | |
| | 1955-56 | | 1954-55 | |
	Number	Percent	Number	Percent
Knowledge, skills, appreciation of outdoors	551	93	561	89
Group living, cooperation	159	27	214	34
Swimming, archery	148	25	88	14
Camp duties, responsibilities	122	21	138	22
Manners	74	12	75	12
Self-reliance	57	10	——	——
Craft skills	46	8	84	13
Campfire activities	37	6	50	8
Banking, checkwriting	28	5	40	6
Flag orientation	19	3	—	——
Eating different foods	13	2	——	——
No comment	6	1	16	3

TABLE 2

Camp Experiences Considered Most Valuable

| Camp Experiences | Parents Reporting Each of Two School Years | | | |
| | 1955-56 | | 1954-55 | |
	Number	Percent	Number	Percent
Learning to live cooperatively	276	46	280	45
Knowledge, skills, appreciation of outdoors	237	40	217	35
Self-reliance	164	28	198	32
Camp duties, responsibilities	82	14	52	8
None most favorable, all fine	44	7	43	7
Supervised by others than own parents	35	6	---	---
Manners	24	4	13	2
Enjoyment	23	4	16	3
Campfire activities	12	2	13	2
No comment	14	2	32	5

most frequently. However, knowledge, skills, and appreciation of the outdoors were also mentioned with great frequency.

In the suggestions and comments portion of the questionnaires used in the Los Angeles study over 95 per cent of the comments regarding camping were favorable. They included statements such as "Excellent supervision," "Good food," "Chance for learning self-reliance." Suggestions for improvement included (1) a longer camp period; and (2) more and better facilities.

Similar reports have been received regarding the programs conducted in Merced and Monterey counties, the year-round programs conducted by the Norwalk, Bellflower, and Long Beach school districts, and the short-term programs conducted by the Garvey, Wiseburn, Hawthorne, and East Whittier school districts. It is reasonable to expect that similar reports regarding programs operating in such widely separated areas as San Diego, Santa Clara, and Fresno counties are available.

Statements by parents follow:

Sally had an experience which could not have been possible in the city. The ruggedness of the mountains, the closeness of the stars, the outdoor living was a thrill to her. But perhaps even greater was the importance of being away from home for the first time with children her own age.

Our boy learned so much about the importance of trees and how to prevent fires in one week. His Dad doesn't see how you do it.

Betty told us about learning how to fold the American flag and about standing tall as a pine as the flag was raised high about the trees.

I wish more children could be given the opportunity to learn about nature and conservation under such pleasant conditions. The sharing of responsibilities in serving food and the social obligations of nice table manners made a real impression on our boy.

This is the first time anyone has made a point of teaching weather, star study, tree planting, and conservation. These are just the things my son has asked questions about.

Statements by teachers follow:

I'm sure that the noticeable growth in social understanding and the new appreciation of the wonders of nature were among the most important aspects of the school camping program for my class.

I was happy to have the opportunity to spend a continuous period sharing the children's learnings more completely than is possible in the classroom.

The whole staff at camp is an outstanding group of educators. I was impressed by their kind and efficient manner of working with children.

I think the camp was a wonderful experience for all the girls and boys. It seemed to unite them as a group.

Words can't express the pleasures I had the past two years at camp. I know the classes have felt the same.

Enthusiasm runs high. There seems to be a great lack of time to do the many activities that are an important part of going to school outdoors.

Statements by principals follow:

When ten of our staff members and the Parent-Teacher Association president visited Camp last Thursday night we were delighted with the enthusiasm of the children and the progress made. All had learned greater cooperation, several had learned to swim, table manners had improved, and responsibilities had been cheerfully assumed.

I am more impressed each time with the educational and social values of this experience for girls and boys. We are all looking forward to the time when every school may be included annually.

The teachers commented on the careful planning and the evaluation of each activity. The children came back healthy, enthusiastic, and well adjusted.

The setting, the quality of the planned program, the excellent food, the high standards maintained, all contributed to provide a most worthwhile experience for our pupils.

ARITHMETIC OUTDOORS—
IT DOES MAKE A DIFFERENCE! *

HAROLD L. HOEKSEMA

How does the use of outdoor teaching methods influence achievement in arithmetic? An experiment, conducted by the writer, indicated some positive relationships between arithmetic achievement and teaching in the out-of-doors.

Two sixth grades, from Grove Junior High School in Elk Grove Village, Illinois, served as control and experimental groups. After establishing paired groups, matched as closely as circumstances allowed in age, I.Q., sex, and arithmetic achievement, (pretest, California Achievement Test, form W) the experiment began. The control group was taught using the indoor classroom, while the arithmetic program of the experimental group included experiences in the out-of-doors. After a period of four school weeks the experiment was terminated. Each group was then subjected to a post-test. The post-test was form X of the California Achievement Test.

The following table summarizes the results of the experiment:

Comparison of Mean Gains

	Reasoning	Computation	Total
Difference of Mean Gains	.92	4.2	5.04
Standard Error of Mean Difference	.661	1.414	1.718
"t" score	1.391	2.969	2.933
Probability	.10	.01	.01

Statistical analysis of the gains from pretest to post-test revealed that each group achieved significant gains in reasoning and computation. The difference in mean gains (Mean gain experimental minus Mean gain control) was significant only in computation skills. However, when the total mean gain differences (Reasoning scores plus Computation scores) were analyzed, the experimental group established a gain which was significant at the one per cent level of confidence.

*Reprinted by permission of Ray Page, Superintendent of Public Instruction and editor of the *Illinois Journal of Education*, the *Illinois Journal of Education*, and the author from *Illinois Journal of Education* 55:18-19, December, 1964.

Outdoor educators have long expounded on the values of outdoor education as a method to make the learning process more efficient and meaningful. During the experiment, outdoor teaching methods were used only when, in the judgment of the experimenter, such procedures would produce more effective learning situations. The outdoor classroom provides many keys to direct experience in arithmetic problem solving. Units in direct and indirect measurement, area and volume, temperature studies, and ratio, have almost no bounds for direct, purposeful, experiences in the out-of-doors. In addition to direct experience, Julian Smith relates that as a method of teaching outdoor education provides also for: (1) Discovery, exploration, adventure, (2) Sensory learning, (3) Natural motivation, (4) Intense interest, (5) Realism, (6) Problems in context, (7) Active participation.

An informal setting, such as the out-of-doors, provided for more interaction among the students. Students freely discussed methods and compared results as well. Some students spent as much time or more time in calculating and checking their problems outdoors than the group who were working strictly from the textbook. Comparing results, in many instances, indicated that a particular answer was not reasonable; thus necessitating recalculation. Most students were very much concerned about right or reasonable answers.

Although no provisions were made in the design of the experiment to measure changes in attitude or interest, the significant gain achieved by the experimental group may have been a result of increased interest and the formation of positive attitudes toward arithmetic.

The evidence gathered in this experiment does seem to give credence to outdoor education as a valuable adjunct to the teaching of arithmetic. Experiments involving larger populations, and encompassing the many varied aspects of outdoor education need to be designed and performed to further substantiate these findings.

DO IT YOURSELF CONSERVATION AND ITS EFFECT UPON ATTITUDES OF PROSPECTIVE TEACHERS *

GEORGE M. LAUG AND THEODORE E. ECKERT

The teaching of conservation and ecology in the public schools and colleges has been receiving increased emphasis. It is also true that in public schools in

*Reprinted by permission of the National Association of Biology Teachers from *The American Biology Teacher* 24:50-5, January, 1962.

particular there has been a growing tendency to include field trips and some type of work activity performed by the students. In the Northeastern United States, the work activity has frequently consisted of tree planting. However, the attitudes of students and their possible attitude changes are of utmost importance in the teaching of science, especially conservation of natural resources. An evaluation of attitude change in response to conservation work activities was the subject of the first author's investigation.

Before discussing the details of attitude testing and their results, we should describe the particular activities of the students who were the subject of this study. In the early 1950s the Faculty-Student Association of the State University of New York College of Education at Buffalo purchased an abandoned farm of 435 acres at Franklinville, New York. One of its prime purposes was to provide firsthand experiences in conservation practices. The purchase of the land was an outgrowth of an effort of many years to incorporate a greater degree of conservation education into the State University Colleges of Education. George Laug was appointed conservation manager of the property.

The first step was consultation with conservation technicians. With the assistance of Mr. Edward Whalen, District Forester, the property was registered under the New York State Forest Practice Act. With the very able assistance of Mr. Homer Stennett, Cattaraugus County Soil Conservationist, we received benefits by becoming associated with Cattaraugus County Soil Conservation District. On the advice of Mr. Richard Hyde, District Game Manager, we established the property as a game preserve. Repeated meetings were held with these conservation men and number of interested students. An overall farm plan was developed which could be carried out over a period of many years. In this way successive classes of students could take part in the planning and carrying on of conservation activities for any one year. The comprehensive farm plan included:

1. Provision for eventual reforestation of approximately 120 acres of the property
2. A soil map of the property with the best land usage indicated
3. A series of suggested plantings of shrubs to improve wildlife habitat
4. The suggested location of a number of farm ponds
5. Suggested methods of improving two of the streams on the property in order that they might eventually support fish.

The next task involved incorporating what had been learned through the conservation experts into a meaningful program for our students. The first step was to develop a unit in conservation which could be used in all classes in general biology. This unit had to be general by its very nature but also specific in that it was to be directed to those aspects of conservation which would be observed and carried out on the college property by the students. Actually a great many varied activities have been performed by successive groups of students since 1953. The authors will confine themselves to the total program for the students during the year in which the attitude study was made.

The attitudes of students were measured in the spring of 1958. The final unit plan as used in all biology classes was improved and refined over the original one in 1953. Four instructors participated in the experimental program, consisting of class presentation and the field trip activites. Four instructors cooperated in the control program in which conservation was presented incidentally from the text, without the experimental classroom unit or the field trips. A complete conservation bibliography for use of students and instructors was included in the conservation unit. The following films were made available on campus: 1. Future Forests in the Making. 2. Birth of the Soil. 3. Arteries of Life. 4. Then It Happened. 5. Wildlife in Slow Motion. 6. Trees for Tomorrow.

The field trips of the experimental groups were of two types, a one-day field trip in which students were in the environment from 10:00 a.m. to 3:30 p.m., and the other, a two-day overnight trip in which the students were in the field from 10:00 a.m. of the first day until 3:30 p.m. of the second day. The authors had charge of the two-day trip. Because the single-day trip students were the largest group, 370, the details of this type of field trip will be presented first.

The work activities of the one-day field trip students consisted of tree planting and shrub planting. The instructions for these two activities were spelled out in great detail for the benefit of the cooperating faculty. Failure to do this could result in confusion during the work experience. Confusion in the field is even more fatal than in the classroom. A single sheet explaining these two activities was passed out to all students going to camp.

By agreement of the participating faculty, the non-work activities included: 1. Pond ecology. 2. Observation and discussion of existing forest plantations. 3. Observation and discussion of previously planted hedge rows. 4. Basic field ecology. 5. Wildlife management. 6. Forest ecology.

The two-day overnight conservation experience could be chosen by students as an alternative to the day trip. So far, only the authors have conducted overnight trips to the college camp and usually, as was true in 1958, they are joint affairs involving the cooperation of the authors of this article. As would be expected, the overnight conservation activities were considerably more detailed and included a greater variety of field activities. Each student going on the overnight trip received an extensive manual which included many facets of conservation and ecology. The manual included check lists of common spring flowers, wildlife signs, amphibians and reptiles, birds and mammals. The work activities of the overnight group were: 1. Taking part in landscaping of the camp lodge. 2. Woodlot management including thinning. 3. Tree planting. 4. Shrub planting.

The non-work activities included: 1. Discussion and observation of wildlife signs. 2. An address by Mr. Homer Stennett on land management throughout the country and Cattaraugus County in particular. 3. Discussion and observation of the uses of farm ponds and pond ecology. 4. A night hike for orientation by the stars, night sounds, and night nature study. 5. Bird hike.

To construct a valid and reliable attitude scale was very important in order to accomplish the aims of the study. The scale finally decided upon was the Likert type. The Likert type of scale involves the use of statements of attitudes toward some psychological object. The student indicates his or her degree of agreement or disagreement with the statements. The usual method of constructing the scale is to employ five degrees of response, SA meaning strongly agree, A meaning agree, U meaning undecided, D meaning disagree, and SD meaning strongly disagree. The statements represent favorable and unfavorable attitudes. The student is scored on the basis of 4 points for full agreement with a favorable attitude, 3 points for one step removed from full agreement, 2 points for two steps removed, 1 point for three steps removed and 0 for complete lack of agreement with a favorable attitude. For an unfavorable attitude statement, the scoring is reversed. The student's total score is the sum of the weights of his responses.

Attitude items were collected by placing those heard among people of many walks of life on 3 x 5 cards. Over a period of years the frequency of verbal expression of these attitudes was checked as well as the frequency of expression in the conservation literature. Only the more frequently expressed attitudes were used in the scale. Eventually nearly 300 attitude items were compiled.

However, the criteria for judging an attitude item by Wang, Thurstone, Clave, Likert, Bird, Edwards, and Kilpatrick were used. This type of careful scrutiny narrowed the attitude items down to 84. When the attitude scale seemed to be in workable order, it was submitted to eight well-known persons in conservation education or science education. These men were asked to examine the scale items for the purpose of establishing the validity of each attitude item for inclusion in the final scale. They also proceeded to respond to the scale in the same manner as would the students. If an item was approved by six out of eight experts, it was retained. Regarding any one attitude item, if six out of eight responded in the same way, the item was retained. The refined attitude scale was established by having a reliability coefficient of .94 by using the Pearson product moment "r" and the Spearman-Brown prophecy formula.

Before the first administration of the attitude scale, all participating faculty were brought into a meeting in which the purposes of the research were outlined and the details of administering the scale were explained. Although the faculty knew the keyed responses to the scale, they were instructed to in no way teach to the individual attitude items in the scale. Change in attitude had to be in response to the student's exposure to conservation. The instructions for the administration of the attitude scale were fully standardized. Students were identified only by a number drawn at random from a cigar box. The number was known only by the student, and it was used only in identifying the student in the pre-testing and in the post-testing situations.

The statistical treatment of the data concerned many separate factors such as relating the experimental and the nonexperimental groups, rural, suburban and urban background, boy scout and girl scout activity, and many others. Naturally, all of these cannot be reported here, but selected tables are included.

The first concern was as to whether a significant difference existed between the mean of the pre-test and the mean of the post-test for the entire experimental group and the control group. This involved the use of "t" for correlated means.

The results of this statistical treatment appear in the following combined table.

For the experimental group, the observed "t" turned out to be significant. It appears that there has been a favorable change in the mean of the experimental group taken as a whole from the time of the pre-test to the time-of the post-test

TABLE 1

"t" for Correlated Means of the Entire Experimental Group and Control Group, Pre- and Post-Testing

Experimental Group	N	Mean	$\overline{D}$	Sum of Squares $\Sigma(D - \overline{D})^2$	$S\overline{D}$	t
Pre-Test	427	178.47	11.51	37384	.45	25.58**
Post-Test	427	189.98		**Sig. at 1% level of confidence		
Control Group	N	Mean	$\overline{D}$	Sum of Squares $\Sigma(D - \overline{D})^2$	$S\overline{D}$	t
Pre-Test	287	182.81	3.16	23990	.54	5.85**
Post-Test	287	179.65		**Sig. at 1% level of confidence		

TABLE 2

"t" for Uncorrelated Means of Experimental and Control Groups Compared on the Pre-Test and Post-Testing Situation

Testing Situation	N	Mean	Difference In Means	S^2	t
Pre-Test Exper.	427	178.47	4.34	205.62	3.94**
Pre-Test Con.	287	182.81			
Post-Test Exper.	427	189.98	10.33	228.44	8.98**
Post-Test Con.	287	179.65	**Sig. at 1% level of confidence		

TABLE 3

"t" for Correlated Means of Three Experimental Conditions Pre- and Post-Testing

Experimental Group	N	Mean	D	Sum of Squares $\Sigma (D - D)^2$	t
Overnight					
Pre-Test	39	184.97	17.46	5952	8.73**
Post-Test	39	202.43			
Day Trip					
Pre-Test	370	177.83	11.39	31337	23.73**
Post-Test	370	189.22			
Missed Trips					
Pre-Test	19	177.10	1.47	623	1.06
Post-Test	19	178.57	**Sig. at 1% level of confidence		

with an advance of 11.51 points. For the control group, the observed "t" also turned out to be significant. It will be noted that the mean for the control group has moved significantly, 3.16 points in an unfavorable direction.

The same data was now handled by means of the uncorrelated "t" technique contrasting the experimental with the control group. Obviously, the groups in question were different as different individuals were involved and no matching technique was used.

Both "t" 's are significant at the 1% level of confidence. The mean of the control group was, significantly, 4.34 points high in the pre-testing situation as compared with the experimental group. The "t" observed for the post-test situation is highly significant with an advance of 10.33 points for the experimental group over the control group. This seems all the more important in view of the fact that the control group started out with a significantly higher mean.

Within the experimental group, three possible situations existed. Thirty-nine students experienced the overnight experimental program and 370 students experienced the single-day trip experimental program. Nineteen students were instructed according to the conservation unit outline in the classroom situation but did not go on any of the field trips.

It would have been preferred to have the last group larger, but an administrative factor made this impossible. As a result, the smaller control group was composed of those students who were absent on the day of the trip. The following table contrasts these three groups in the pre- and post-testing situation by the use of the correlated "t."

The "t" 's for the overnight and day-trip groups were significant, indicating that an important change in attitude had occurred for these two groups. The mean attitude score advanced for those students who missed the trips, but not

TABLE 4
Pre- and Post-Testing Means of the Four Experimental Groups According to Instructors

Instructor	N	Pre-Test Mean	Post-Test Mean	Diff In Mean
I	145	179.93	186.70	+6.77
II	114	179.64	193.44	+13.80
III	65	179.95	194.78	+14.83
IV	102	174.36	187.63	+13.27

significantly. Additional statistical treatment showed that the overnight students were already significantly higher in mean in the pre-testing situation than the day-trip group. The day-trip group was not significantly higher than the group which missed the trips.

The next matter of interest in the study was the question of possible effect of individual instructors upon expressed attitudes of students within the experimental program. It could well be that individual instructors, dealing with the same material, could cause a different development of student attitude in accordance with the individual instructor's background and interest. The names of these instructors will be kept anonymous and designated by number. A simple table showing the pre- and post-testing means for these instructors is helpful.

In the pre-testing situation, one instructor (number IV) had students significantly lower in mean than the other groups. No attempt has been made to explain this situation.

The following table pairs the instructors in the post-testing situation, indicating significance of difference in mean between these groups by means of the uncorrelated "t."

It can be seen that a significant difference appears in many of these pairs.

In spite of the differences between instructors, students taking part in the full experimental program showed a significant advance in their "means." It is evident from these data and is supported by others not included here that the total program was effective in favorably changing the attitudes of those students involved. On the basis of this evidence and our experience with the program, we are confidently going ahead with development of new experiments and techniques.

For the coming year a new work activities program is being planned. One of these activities is explained here. This will involve a combination of forest ecology and forest management experiences. This project is still in a formative stage, but a diagram might help to explain the new venture.

The area involves a section in which a young climax type forest is naturally regenerating. Enough plots 46' on a side will be laid out to accommodate all

TABLE 5
"t" for Uncorrelated Means of Four Experimental Groups
in the Post-Testing Situation

Instructor Pairs	N	Mean	Diff In Mean	S^2	t
I	145	186.70	.93	222.22	.48
IV	102	187.63			
IV	102	187.63	5.81	222.23	2.86**
II	114	193.44			
II	114	193.44	1.34	222.23	.57
III	65	194.78			
I	145	186.70	6.74	222.23	3.60**
II	114	193.44			
I	145	186.70	8.08	222.23	3.64**
III	65	194.78			
IV	102	187.63	7.15	222.23	3.03**
III	65	194.781		**Sig. at 1% level of confidence	

sections of General Biology. In each plot assigned, the students will count all trees in the plot. This will include the total number by species and diameter. The students will survey the distribution of herbaceous plants of the forest floor. Some plots as designated would not be thinned at all, while others would receive light and heavy thinning. Light thinning would keep the forest canopy closed. Heavy thinning will allow sunlight to reach the forest floor between the remaining trees.

The principles and practices of forest management will be explained to all students. Working in small groups, they will then select and mark the trees to be removed. However, before the tree is cut the entire group with the instructor would have to agree with the decision of the small group. The thinnings could then be left on the ground or used to establish brush shelters for small game. Accurate records of the entire procedure will be kept so that future groups of students will be able to analyze possible ecological changes.

Control	Thin Light	Thin Heavy
Thin Heavy	Control	Thin Light
Thin Light	Thin Heavy	Control

REPORT OF RESEARCH—A FACTOR ANALYSIS OF ATTITUDES TOWARD THE TERM "OUTDOOR EDUCATION" *

B. RAY HORN

The problem was to determine similarities and differences in attitudes toward the meaning of the term "outdoor education." The examined population comprised the members of the American Association of Health, Physical Education, and Recreation's Council on Outdoor Education and Camping who were in colleges and universities. This was the first study that attempted to clarify the various schools of thought toward the meaning of "outdoor education."

The results were significant. Ninety-seven per cent (114 of a possible 118) of the respondents completed the test instrument. The results indicated that the AAHPER Council was divided into three partially overlapping interest groups, each group having some individual and some shared attitudes toward the meaning of "outdoor education." It is the opinion of this researcher that these groups should be defined, their interests determined, and their individual and shared objectives established.

The research hypothesis was that agreement existed among the members of the AAHPER Council on the meaning of "outdoor education." "Agreement" was operationally defined as at least 70 per cent of the respondents appearing on any one of the attitude factors abstracted by a factor analytic computer program (Q-methodology). Since 70 per cent of the respondents did not appear on any one of the factors, the hypothesis was rejected. Since areas of disagreement appeared, it was within the scope of the inquiry to describe the nature of this disagreement. An analysis and interpretation of the extracted factors and an explanation of the concomitant attitude groups described the areas of this disagreement. The three prominent attitude groups were the following:

I. *"Environment-Oriented Group":* The members of this group were primarily media-oriented; that is, they tended to view the use of the outdoors as a learning medium, as a vehicle of communication. At the same time, however, they did not want to exclude activities related to conservation education. This group coalesced those who were apparently interested in the instructional implications of outdoor education and regarded the outdoors as an educational tool.

*Reprinted with permission from *Journal of Education* 4:15-17, Fall 1969.

II. *"Conservation-Oriented Group":* The members of this group were generally conservation-oriented; that is, they felt that "outdoor education" encompassed those activities that focus upon conservational ends. The group coalesced those who had partial interests in groups I and III, but who clustered into a discernibly different group with predominantly wildlife, natural science, and conservation education interests.

III. *"Outdoor Activity-Oriented Group":* This group was oriented toward the physical location of where an activity is conducted and felt that an interaction with a natural environment was not a necessary condition of "outdoor education." This was the most distinctive group. They were mainly physical-education and recreation-education oriented and were primarily interested in activities conducted in an outdoor setting and education for outdoor recreation.

For clarification, the commonalities and disparities of the three attitude types or interest groups may be demonstrated with the accompanying Venn diagram (See Figure 1). Three overlapping groups or types (I, II, and III) were defined. Diagram area "A" illustrates the commonalities of all three groups whereas areas "B," "C," and "D" indicate attitudes shared by an adjoining set. Each set also had distinctive characteristics, represented by areas "E," "F," and "G."

Diagram area "A" represents the criterion of "outdoors" and all of its varied connotations, such as the use of the outdoors as a vehicle of communication, the use of the outdoors as the content of communication, and the use of the outdoors as a location for something to happen but not intrinsically dependent upon that location for the happening. The three types were almost of equal size,

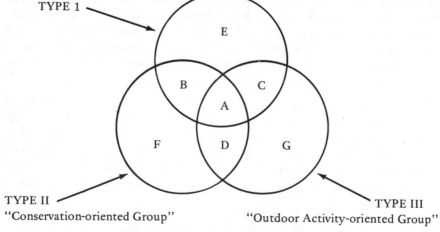

"Environment-oriented Group"
   TYPE 1

TYPE II
"Conservation-oriented Group"

TYPE III
"Outdoor Activity-oriented Group"

FIGURE 1. Three types of attitudes toward the meaning of the term "Outdoor Education"

each comprising about the same number of the respondents. The attitude groups apparently were defined according to their emphasized interests which are implied in the label given to each group.

Lloyd L. Cockrell conducted a study in 1962 that indicated there had been great lack of understanding as to what was meant by the term "outdoor education." [1:11] He demonstrated that there was no standard terminology existing in the area of outdoor education and that such a variety of programs and activities were carried on under the guise of "outdoor education" that the term tended to defy definition. Later, Federally funded outdoor education projects gave the field of outdoor education a new impetus and increased the demand for university trained outdoor educators. This impetus created new literature and a myriad of conferences and workshops designed to communicate the meaning, scope, and implications of outdoor education. It was difficult, however, to communicate with a term containing diverse meanings. Many leaders merely assumed they were using the term in similar ways, thus leaving accurate communication to chance.

The research techniques available to unveil attitude groups are many, such as multivariate analysis, factor analysis, and computer processing. However, educational researchers have remained egregiously ignorant of such advances.

. . . *Researchers in schools of education need to be apprised of the techniques which are available for social research on education.* [3:275]

"Since 1930 approximately 200 studies have been conducted at the master's and doctoral levels. Research dealing with the various aspects of outdoor education is by no means complete." [4:5]

Research . . . has not been abundant in the area of outdoor education. The role of research in outdoor education is to bring substantiation and meaning to theory and to improve the pragmatic application of this theory through experimentation. [4:7]

"No study in the research conducted thus far has undertaken the problem of constructing a theoretical framework for the various aspects of outdoor education. This is a top priority problem." [5:89] The main strength of the design of this study was its close affinity to theory. This study was, by its very nature, theoretical and therefore lent itself readily as a base upon which to build operatively definable areas of investigation. It is important to mature beyond the use of *a priori* evidence in support of outdoor education.

REFERENCES

1. Lloyd L. Cockrell, "A Survey of Outdoor Teacher Education Programs in Higher Education" (unpublished research report, Northern Illinois University, 1962).
2. U. S. Office of Education, *Pacesetters in Innovation*, Descriptions of the First Projects Approved, Title III, Elementary and Secondary Education Act of

1965, Supplementary Centers and Services Program, Office of Education No. OE-23046, February, 1966.

3. Sam D. Sieber, "The Case of the Misconstrued Technique," *Phi Delta Kappan*, Vol. XLIX, No. 5 (January, 1968).

4. Thomas J. Rillo, "Summary of Current Trends and Research in School Camping and Outdoor Education." A Paper presented at the Midwest AAHPER Convention, Cincinnati, Ohio, 1967. (Mimeographed.)

5. Donald R. Hammerman, "Research Implications in Outdoor Education," *Journal of Health, Physical Education, and Recreation*, Vol. XXXV, No. 3 (March, 1964).

CONSERVATION IN SCHOOL CAMPING *

WILLIAM L. HOWENSTINE

I firmly believe that one of the important objectives in the teaching of biology is the development of an understanding of the principles of conservation. I firmly believe that a school camping program offers one of the better means of achieving this conservation education. I also believe that no such value accrues from such a program automatically.

School camping started in the decades of 1930 and 1940, and as it has developed has had a profound effect upon public school education in many parts of the country. For many years organized camps for children have been a familiar part of summer vacation activities. However, the unique aspect of camping as embodied in the modern school camp program is the acceptance of an educational camp experience as part of the school curriculum. *School camping is a resident experience in an outdoor setting, sponsored by a school system during the school year as part of the school curriculum.*

The advocates of school camping have stated many objectives for the program, but from the early days of this movement one of the more important objectives has been that of conservation or resource-use education. This has been reiterated many times by many authorities, including groups within the National Association of Biology Teachers. The *1955 Handbook for Teaching of Conservation and Resource Use* of the National Conservation Committee of the National Association of Biology Teachers gave emphasis to school camping as one of the ways in which the teacher could use the community in conservation education.

Conservation educators have good reasons to support school camping as a

*Reprinted by permission of the National Association of Biology Teachers from *The American Biology Teacher* 24:40-5, January, 1962.

means of conservation education. In my view there are four subject areas of the school curriculum which, by their nature, are especially suited to learning in a school camp. These are citizenship, conservation, natural science, and physical education. It is recognized that citizenship and conservation, as such, are seldom listed as school subjects, but they are among the goals of most schools.

What are the factors which make this environment excellent for education in these areas? First, the twenty-four-hour-a-day living situation presents an opportunity for citizenship education, unmatched by any day-school situation, where the total living activities of a child may come under the guidance of one authority. This same all-day experience provides many opportunities for physical education, in the larger sense of the word, where rest, cleanliness, and proper food are not read about from a book, but are actually within the guiding control of the school teachers. Secondly, the outdoor aspect of camp life contributes another opportunity for physical education, for these outdoor spaces, of necessity, require physical exertion to be utilized. This is meaningful physical activity. Finally, it goes without saying that much of the learning material of natural science and conservation is in the field, and therefore the outdoor laboratory is one of the better places to learn about such material. One only needs to consider the folly of trying to train a forester without ever getting him into the woods or, indeed, of studying any area of ecology without having access to material beyond the classroom, to see the close ties between school camping and the subjects of natural science and conservation. There is no need to labor this point with biology teachers.

And so the involvement of conservation education in the school camping movement has been constantly in evidence, and the support of conservation educators has rightfully added greatly to the rapid development of this educational program. Yet in these early years of the school camping movement there has been very little objective evaluation of the school camp as an agency for conservation education.

In 1954 and 1955 I had the opportunity to engage in a detailed study of the programs of eight school camps in the Michigan-Ohio region. Special attention was given in this study to the status of conservation education in the camps.

One of the major questions was, "What emphasis do the staff members of these camps place upon conservation education as an objective of the program?" I have mentioned the support given to conservation education in camping by professional conservation educators nationally. But what about the rank and file of classroom teachers, college students, and others who serve as school camp staff members?

To determine the answer to this question the staff members in these eight school camps were interviewed and asked to participate in a selection device involving 28 different potential objectives for a school camping program. For purposes of handling the data these objectives were grouped into six categories as follows: conservation and natural science; health, safety, physical education, and recreation; classroom correlation; school subjects; personal values; and social objectives. For example, the four objectives in the "conservation and natural science" grouping were as follows: "to provide functional learning of the principles of conservation; e.g., to teach the wise use of our natural resources through care of them in the camp setting"; "to increase sensitivity to the beauty of nature"; "to teach citizenship in a democratic community; e.g., in determining camp policy, in caring for public property"; "to emphasize relationships in nature; e.g., the effect of an animal upon its habitat, the relationship between geologic forces and present land form."

Eighty-six staff members completed this selection of objectives, and the response of this group was most gratifying for those of us interested in natural science and conservation. The specific objective which dealt with conservation received the second highest rating among the 28 objectives, significantly higher statistically than the ratings for 14 of the 28 objectives. When the constellation of objectives dealing with conservation and natural science is considered as a whole the same high rating is seen. This group of objectives was rated significantly higher than all but one of the other groups; i.e., higher than: health-safety-physical education-recreation; school subjects; classroom correlation; and personal values. Only the social objectives rated anywhere close to the conservation-natural science group. It is interesting that of the two major groups of objectives chosen by these school camp staff members one is a subject matter grouping, and the other is a group of so-called "intangibles" related to group living. This may be of some assurance to school camp people that there is a balance in their programs. Certainly the great majority of the staff members working in these school camps considered teaching about nature, and man's relationships with nature, of primary importance in a school camping program.

A second major question in the study was, "What emphasis did these school camps give to natural science and conservation in their actual programs?"

To secure this information observations were made of a weekly program of each of the camps, and detailed records were made both of the number of minutes devoted to different subject areas of the camp program and of the exact nature of the material covered in each of these subject areas. The subject areas chosen for tabulation were: arithmetic, arts and crafts, campcraft, conservation, health and safety, language arts, music, natural science, physical activities, and social studies. This analysis of the use of time in school camp programs dealt not only with the morning and afternoon activity periods when field trips usually take place but also with the more routine periods of meals, clean-up periods, evening programs, etc. In this way only can an appreciation be gained of the total program of a camp and of the relative role which one activity or subject field plays.

For the conservation educator the results of this time study were as disheartening as the results of the objective study were heartening. The actual amount of conservation education carried on at the eight camps was greatly in contrast with the high rating of conservation education as an objective. Of all the program time in which the activities were directed or guided by staff members, only 3.8% was devoted to conservation education. Of the 10 subject areas already mentioned, conservation ranked seventh in per cent of time devoted to it, outranking only language arts, arithmetic, and health-safety. It ranked significantly lower than physical activity and natural science. The small amount of time spent on conservation education becomes more apparent, perhaps, when one speaks in terms of minutes rather than percentages. The mean number of staff-directed minutes per camp week devoted to conservation education was 72. One hour and 12 minutes of staff-directed activities dealing with conservation in a week would hardly make one think it was a major objective.

Perhaps it should be mentioned here that in this study conservation was strictly separated from natural science in definition. Worthy as natural science and nature appreciation may be in establishing a milieu favorable to conservation, conservation itself does not begin until there is a concern over the management of natural resources. Only that education which had this quality was considered "conservation education."

For natural science, the time study at these eight school camps showed a great emphasis, completely in line, this time, with the importance placed upon objectives in this area by the school camp staff members. The mean per cent for all camps of directed time devoted to natural science was 15.7%, significantly higher than the means for six other subjects; viz., arithmetic, art and crafts, conservation, health and safety, language arts, and social studies. To the extent that knowledge and appreciation of natural science provides a background for conservation learning, conservationists may take pleasure in this ascendancy of natural science.

I would like to enlarge upon this point somewhat. The belief is widely held among conservationists that an understanding of ecology is essential to an understanding of conservation. Intelligent management of natural resources must take into account the many, varied relationships which exist among the forces of nature, including man. Nature education which is ecological in character can have a direct connection with conservation. Nature education which deals only with identification, or other isolated facts, can have only a remote connection, if any at all, with conservation. For instance, while it may be interesting and enjoyable for a person to be able to identify an elm tree or a fox squirrel, there can be little connection with conservation understandings unless the person goes a step further and learns something about such relationships as exist among the elm tree, the elm bark beetle, and the Dutch elm disease, or until one learns something about the food and shelter requirements of a fox squirrel.

The problem resolves to the fact that, in spite of the very high placement of conservation education among the objectives of school camping by the majority of people connected with the field, and in spite of the widespread belief that the school camp offers one of the most valuable opportunities that we have for conservation education, there is a small amount and a low quality of conservation education in many of our school camps. In the study which I have mentioned we have seen that conservation ranks low among the subjects of the school camps in terms of the amount of time devoted to it. In addition, the detailed accounts of material studied in conservation at each of the observed camps showed notable lack of coverage in certain areas. Even at the camp which spent the greatest percentage of time on conservation education, practically no attention was given to forest conservation. In another case there was practically no attention given to either forest or wildlife conservation, and in still another camp, at a site which abounds with opportunities for teaching soil conservation, there was no mention made of it.

But just as disconcerting as the relative lack of conservation education was the poor quality of much of what did exist. This poor quality was evident in three respects:

1. *The tolerance of negative "conservation activities."* Educators say we learn by doing. If camp staff members permit campers to do things of a harmful nature to our natural resources what kind of resource stewardship is then being learned?

Two campers chopped down a live tree in the presence of a staff member; there was no reason to do so other than to have some chopping practice, and there was plenty of dead wood to practice upon. Campers swept the leaves away from a large area adjacent to their cabins in one camp, completely exposing the soil to the force of rain and water runoff. A camp director leading a hike told the forty-nine campers with him, "Everyone get a Jack-in-the-pulpit."

2. *Inconsistency between what staff members tell the campers and what the staff members do.* The first weakness, already mentioned, might be excused on the basis that such staff members simply did not understand relationships in nature and their connection with conservation. The second weakness is more difficult to explain or accept. How can a child be expected to believe what he has been told about conservation if he sees his leader doing almost the very opposite thing? On one trip two staff members led a group of campers past a "No trespassing" sign into a field which was being severely eroded but which juniper trees were invading. One of the leaders led a discussion about the erosion and told the campers that the farmer had received an offer to sell his juniper trees to a nurseryman but that he did not want to sell them. Then, in spite of all these indications that one should treat this farmer's property with great care, these leaders permitted the campers to pull up young juniper trees to take to their homes to plant.

On a wildflower field trip in a metropolitan park, some campers and their leader walked past signs saying, "Do Not Pick the Wildflowers." One camper saw another pick some flowers and said twice, "Hey, you aren't supposed to pick them!" The leader said nothing and led the group on down the trail, picking some flowers, himself, as he went.

A sense of stewardship for our natural resources begins with little things. All of a leader's talk about care of resources means nothing if the camper sees this leader do the very opposite.

3. *The choice of less appropriate methods of teaching conservation.* School camp leaders have accepted the following two principles as part of the very basis of their camping philosophy. First, those things should be done at camp which are suitable thereto but which are difficult or impossible to accomplish in the classroom. Second, effective learning requires a certain amount of direct learning experience.

Acceptance of these beliefs would indicate that in conservation education at school camps a premium should be placed upon projects which include "doing activities"; e.g., building check dams, planting trees, along with discussion. A second choice would be the observation of many things related to conservation which one would not easily find in the ordinary school setting. The last choice would be those things such as reading books, watching motion pictures, and hearing lectures, which can be done just as well, if not better, in the classroom. Yet, in seven weeks of observations, only one work project in conservation was observed; namely, construction of check dams in a gully.

Of the 56 minutes spent on conservation education at one camp only two minutes were spent teaching outdoors. Of the 46 minutes spent on conservation at another camp only four minutes were spent teaching outdoors. Most of the indoor time at both these camps was devoted to the showing of a motion picture dealing primarily with soil and water conservation. Both camps had streams passing through their camp sites—streams having problems of stream bank erosion, spring flooding, pollution. Both camps had bare soil and gullies available for observation or conservation projects. Yet in the two camps combined, the observer noted only one minute of time devoted to teaching about soil or water conservation outdoors.

All of this does not mean that motion pictures, books, and indoor lectures or discussions should have no place in a school camp program. Such teaching aids are valuable supplements to the field work. But there is no justification for teaching conservation indoors at school camp, just as one would do in the classroom at school, while disregarding fine teaching opportunities on the camp' site.

One must not assume that there were no outstanding examples of conservation education observed in these camps. There were, in fact, some very fine teaching activities in conservation or ecology.

A forestry session conducted by a resource person included: growth ring studies on parking lot posts; a game involving study of a large white oak as a wolf tree, a den tree, and a shade tree; digging of soil samples; and a contest in deciding whether certain tagged trees should be cut for lumber or not.

A mammal study field trip, conducted by a university student, involved observations, trapping of meadow mice, and making of plaster casts of animal tracks.

A self-guided nature trail, using an ecological approach, was devised by another leader.

Several fine field trips were conducted at abandoned farms—including one conducted by a classroom teacher, another conducted by a graduate student using maps and compasses.

In a number of cases staff members were noted seizing opportunities to involve conservation in other activities, not so directly concerned with conservation, e.g., cook-outs.

No one could ask for better teaching than what is represented by these examples. But the fact remains that in these school camps, generally, neither the quantity nor the quality of conservation education was what the observer would have expected to find on the basis of the selection of objectives by staff members.

The crux of the problem lies, of course, in the poor training of staff members in this subject field. These camp leaders certainly did not plan to slight conservation; they simply were not prepared to do what they would like to do. Many leaders are confused as to what conservation is and have a vague feeling that when they are teaching identification of trees or when they observe pond life, they are teaching conservation. Of those who know what conservation is about, there are not many who are competent enough in the subject to be able to do an adequate job of teaching. Unfortunately, the reverse side of the coin is true, also. Many of the resource people who know natural science or conservation facts have little knowledge of how to teach; this results in such things as indoor lectures at camp.

The importance of the situation becomes greater when one considers classroom education in our schools. If in school camp, where conservation is one of the major objectives, the status of conservation education is so low, what, then is its position in the classroom where, as an objective, it probably becomes comparatively less important? Many of the same leaders are teaching there as at camp, but there is not the stimulus of the environment which is present at camp.

Hope in the future may lie in the following areas:

1. *Realistic leadership on the part of school camp directors.* There is a growing group of highly dedicated, professional school camp leaders, centering around those who are directing the programs. It is this group which holds the key to the future of school camping. So far, in the development of school camping, these people have had to spend a great portion of their time in public

relations and in organizing new programs. These people realize they have a valuable educational program in school camping. Furthermore, they are essentially in agreement on the importance of conservation education in the school camping plan. However, they have been so involved in the spread of this program that many of them have not appraised it carefully enough. When one is so close to a program it is difficult to see it in perspective, and there have been few objective studies of school camping to help these people in their appraisals.

If we professional school camp staff members can carefully reexamine our objectives, take a realistic look at our programs, and accept justifiable criticism, school camping will have the leadership it needs. If an attitude prevails that there is no poor school camping, that a child only needs to go to camp to reap its benefits, then not only will conservation education be weak, but also a valuable educational program will gradually wither.

2. *Reorganization of the use of resource people.* Very much of the conservation taught at school camps has been dependent upon the use of resource people brought in for this purpose on a short-time basis. For example, a district forester will spend a morning at a school camp to work with students in forestry. I believe that it is time for school camps to reorganize the manner in which these resource people are used.

The use of resource people in direct teaching of children probably has persisted because of attitudes on the part of both school people and nonschool conservationists. The school leaders have used the resource people, partly because this represents a way to teach conservation when one knows little about it himself, but also partly because it represents a way to increase the staff of the school camp. Conservationists have accepted the resource person role because, recognizing that very little conservation is taught in the schools anyway, they see here an opportunity to teach a few more children.

I believe that both groups are defeating their own purpose in the long run. Such a staff organization results in weaknesses in the program—leaders not knowing how to teach, leaders not knowing the nature of the children they are teaching, and activities unrelated to one another. The net effect produces little conservation education, at best, and a camp program which may not stand the test of time. It is the school-employed teacher who must teach conservation, either in the classroom or at camp, and if that person does not know conservation, then he must learn it. It is recognized that there is educational value in occasional use of resource people for specific objectives; however, this is different from the wholesale use of resource people to cover a complete subject area.

I believe that the following specific steps must be pursued: First, the regular camp leader must retain control of the learning situation when a resource person is used. The regular leader must always be present, must not only introduce and close a session with a resource person, but also continually contribute during the session, if necessary, asking questions where needed, restating in understandable language any material which children cannot understand, and seizing control of the situation in cases where obviously the resource person is going in the wrong direction. The regular teacher must remember that he is basically responsible for all the learning during a session with a resource person. The resource person should be what the title says, a "resource," not the director of the learning situation.

Second, a resource person should be careful in accepting a resource role in a school camp. He should be sure that both he and the regular leaders understand the objectives of the particular activity session. He should expect the regular teacher to accompany him on the session for two reasons—because the regular teacher is responsible for the learning process, and because it is an opportunity for the regular teacher to learn the subject matter of conservation.

Third, in cases where a resource person is used, an attempt should be made to have the person spend as long a time as possible at camp, staying through meals, evening programs, free-time periods, etc. The resource person then would have a better chance to know the children and the whole program, and the other staff members would have more opportunity to gain knowledge from the resource person. Finally, in order to accomplish more quickly the needed staff training in this field, school camp leaders and conservationists, alike, must work toward a shift of emphasis from resource people working largely with children to resource people working largely with adult leaders—at adult conferences and training programs.

3. *Greater use of college students in school camps.* A final, practical step which school camping leaders can pursue to improve the status of conservation education in school camps is to achieve greater participation of college students in a training role at camp. Prospective teachers of today are the teachers who will be going to school camp with their own classes in five years. If properly handled, their college experiences at school camps can be invaluable to the school camping movement in the future. College students can be helpful in the camp program, but the experience should be looked upon primarily as an educational experience for them. If this experience can give them a sound approach to conservation education, then school camping in the future will be different from what has been portrayed in this report.

CONCLUSION

I do not believe that what criticism I have made of school camping programs implies exceptional weaknesses on the part of the staff members. I have been concerned about the nature of school camp programs and especially about the status of conservation education. As such, I have reported the situation as observed with the hope that this information might lead to improved practice. It is very likely that if such close scrutiny, as has been given to these eight school camps, were given to similar programs such as those of the classroom or the summer camp, the same disparity between practice and ideal would exist.

There is no question that school camping offers some excellent opportunities for conservation education. However, school camping leaders and conservationists, alike, must realize that we are a long way from making full use of these opportunities. School camp leaders must appraise their programs carefully and work to bring their programs more closely in line with their objectives—or else change their objectives. Conservationists must work hard to train the school camping leaders in the field of conservation. If fuller use is made of the opportunity to teach conservation in school camps, it is very likely that school camping will prove to be a lever having an effect upon the whole school program.

Author Index